Language Acquisition
After Puberty

Language Acquisition After Puberty

Judith R. Strozer

GEORGETOWN UNIVERSITY PRESS / WASHINGTON, D.C.

Georgetown University Press, Washington, D.C.

© 1994 by Georgetown University Press. All rights reserved.

Printed in the United States of America

10 9 8 7 6 5 4 3 2   1994

THIS VOLUME IS PRINTED ON ACID-FREE OFFSET BOOK PAPER

Library of Congress Cataloging-in-Publication Data

Strozer, Judith R.
    Language acquisition after puberty / Judith R. Strozer.
        p. cm. — (Georgetown studies in Romance linguistics)
    Includes bibliographical references and index.
    1. Language acquisition. 2. Child development. 3. Innateness
hypothesis (Linguistics) 4. Principles and parameters (Linguistics)
5. Language and languages—Study and teaching.   I. Title.
II. Series.
P118.S78   1994
418—dc20

ISBN 0-87840-244-6 (cloth)   ISBN 0-87840-245-4 (paper)   94-5106

Contents

Preface   ix

1 **Introduction: Of chimps, children, and grown-ups**   **1**
  1.1 Language as a defining human attribute   3
    1.1.1 Diverse semiotic systems   3
    1.1.2 The uniqueness of human language   8
  1.2 Native language as childhood language   11
  NOTES   15

2 **Nature and nurture: The poverty of the stimulus**   **18**
  2.1 Language and nurture: The contribution of the environment   18
  2.2 Language and human nature: Phenotype from genotype   22
  2.3 Human nature and nature: A deep parallel between ontogenesis and speciation   28
  NOTES   31

3 **Human nature and culture: Concept labeling**   **34**
  3.1 Language and thought: Speechless rational animals   34
  3.2 The conceptual system: A common heritage of apes and humans?   35
  3.3 Increasing vocabularies: Label learning   38
    3.3.1 "A rose by any other name . . .": Saussurean arbitrariness   38
    3.3.2 Numbers and colors versus smells   40
  3.4 Unlabeled and labeled inborn concepts   45
    3.4.1 A parallel with the immune system   46
    3.4.2 Genetically programmed semantic fields   47
  NOTES   51

4 Culture and language: Civilization and its progress   55

4.1 Knowing and doing: Diverging humanities and postmodern humanists   55

4.2 Interpretation and translation: Not just indeterminacy   59

   4.2.1 Semantic connections: Truths of meaning   60

   4.2.2 New words and enriched notions (with an excursus on Newspeak)   64

   4.2.3 Intertranslatability and cultural wealth: Levels of understanding   68

4.3 Semantic roles: Conceptual and linguistic structure at the interface   74

NOTES   78

5 Language explanation: The growth of a child's mind   81

5.1 Some elementary properties of human language   81

   5.1.1 The creative aspect of language use: Descartes's Problem   82

   5.1.2 The recursive property of linguistic knowledge: Humboldt's Problem   85

   5.1.3 The logical problem of knowledge acquisition: Plato's Problem   86

5.2 Chomsky's solution: The development of transformational generative grammar   87

   5.2.1 The first thirty years (1949–79): An updated revival of a classical tradition   90

   5.2.2 The radical departure of 1980: A principles-and-parameters framework   94

NOTES   97

6 Linguistic knowledge: Universals and particulars   100

6.1 Language invariance: Part of the genetic endowment   100

   6.1.1 Phrase structure: Two-level binary branching   100

   6.1.2 Transformations: Structure-dependent operations   114

6.2 Language variation: The newborn's questionnaire   119

   6.2.1 Morphology as paradigmatic grammar   120

   6.2.2 The syntagmatic grammar and its interfaces   125

NOTES   126

7   Language maturation and beyond: A new look at the Critical
    Period Hypothesis   130
    7.1 Language and puberty: A parallel between linguistic maturity and
        sexual maturity   130
    7.2 From Skinner to Chomsky: Lenneberg's Problem   133
    7.3 An embryological solution: Blame the brain   137
        7.3.1 The active language organ: Lifelong innate knowledge   139
        7.3.2 Unsettable switches: Lifelong patchwork   143
    7.4 Other hypotheses   156
    ' NOTES   161

8   Language research and language teaching: A renewed
    promise   172
    8.1 Language theory and methods of instruction   173
    8.2 Scientific grammars and pedagogic grammars   177
    8.3 A range of options for language programs   183
    NOTES   192

9   Overview: New prospects for the study of language   198
    9.1 Baby or beast: Human language and other semiotic systems   198
    9.2 Child or grown-up: Language universals and language
        particulars   203
    9.3 Design or randomness: A new kind of language program   204
    9.4 Conclusion: A modest proposal   211
    NOTES   214

Bibliography   218
Index   267

Preface

We are all aware that major advances of understanding brought about by the modern natural sciences tend to become part of general education, often within the span of a generation. The consequences of this process are not difficult to illustrate. We all know undergraduate students who have a deeper understanding of basic principles of the biochemistry of life than the discoverers of DNA had ten years after their discovery, and a far deeper and more extensive understanding than the greatest geniuses of earlier generations.

It is natural then to wonder why the study of language continues to be an exception to this generalization. It certainly cannot be because our understanding of language continues to be what it was two generations ago. In the course of this century, and particularly since about 1950, the study of language has made enormous strides; with little or no exaggeration we could say that it has advanced more in the last ten or fifteen years than in the previous thirty centuries. Nor can it be because the study of language is less central or less important than other intellectual pursuits, since that would be to have things backwards. After all, language, which is at the core of our very essence, provides the main gateway to most intellectual pursuits, and nothing could be more crucial than that. The explanation for the different treatment of language studies must therefore lie elsewhere.

The main concern of this book is not to search for the roots of the oddity but to make a contribution, even if only a modest one, to overcoming the disparity with other natural sciences by "bridging the gap" in one particular direction, the one the author happens to be most familiar with. It is no secret that these are exciting times for those intrigued by the fundamental questions of language theory. This book focuses on a particular aspect of the main question, namely, what the recent theoretical advances suggest about the acquisition of a language after a stage of biological maturation here identified with the end of childhood or the onset of puberty (roughly), a process which is here assumed to differ in important respects (as many people would agree) from the attainment of one or more languages by the child. The reason for this choice of focus is that this appears to be an important and intriguing subquestion, with proliferating many sided consequences, that it is empirical in nature, and that it is now open to serious investigation (for the first time in the long history of the field, it would appear). In fact, the logical problem of the acquisition of a foreign language is emerging as an important new domain in the research on language, with the potential to also make an (until recently unexpected) contribution to a deeper understanding of human language.

A first step in this direction is to present an overview of current issues in language theory and foreign language research as they relate to the main questions involved. This is what is attempted in chapters 1 through 4 in terms which will hopefully be accessible to the non-specialist. The first chapter lays out the basic questions, the second examines the respective contributions of the brain and the environment, and the third and fourth discuss the meaning and interpretation of words, an attempt to segregate questions in the study of the conceptual system and the vocabulary from questions in the study of language structure, and to open the way to a proper understanding of the nature of "human language" (in the precise sense in which this notion can be understood today).

It is the following four chapters which constitute the heart of the book. Chapter 5 provides the general background for chapter 6, where the outlines of an up-to-date version of language theory are presented within the framework of the principles-and-parameters approach first developed in the 1980s (a radical, perhaps revolutionary, departure from a tradition of over two millenia). Only within this framework is it possible to really come to grips with our topic, and in particular to take a fresh look at the Critical Period Hypothesis, presented in chapter 7 from the vantage point of current understanding. What is at issue is the availability of the mental structure investigated in the studies of Universal Grammar (UG), that is to say, the availability of the innate universal schematism provided by the language faculty (or the language organ, as it is sometimes called), a cognitive structure of the brain of which UG purports to be a theory. It is argued that the first step towards a reasonable alternative to either of the two contradictory theses with respect to UG widely discussed in the 1980s is readily available within the principles-and-parameters framework. The first necessary step is to break the question "UG or not UG?" into two subquestions:

(Q1) Are the invariant principles of UG operative in the process of non-native language acquisition?

(Q2) Can the parameterized principles be fixed once more for a new language after the critical period?

These questions are at the root of chapter 7, which focuses on the implications of the Critical Period Hypothesis, in particular the relation between the existence of invariant principles and the logical problem of adult language acquisition.

In chapter 8 we turn our attention to the implications of our findings, which indicate that a negative answer (the one the evidence appears to suggest) to the question of whether the parameters can be appropriately set by the adult acquirer would seem to carry significant implications for the design and execution of a successful foreign language program. Among the topics discussed in this chapter are the relation between language theory and the choice of a method of instruction, the relation between scientific grammars and pedagogic grammars, and a range of options for language programs. The closing chapter provides an overview of the book and concludes with a "modest proposal."

The exposition strategy was chosen with a skeptical reader in mind who is insufficiently informed about the recent advances in the study of language or unconvinced by the technical results it has to offer. It begins with a presentation of the most basic and most evident facts, which will have to be faced by any serious investigation, independently of the choice of a theoretical perspective. This is largely true of the first five (or at least four) chapters, which are scarcely dependent on the relative truth of the author's view. Not until chapter 6 is a definite language theory (Chomsky's version of generative grammar) adopted. This is one of the reasons the core of the book is expected to be of use even if Chomsky's theory turns out to be less on the right track than it appears to be at the present level of understanding. But although a sustained effort has been made to make the presentation accessible to the initially uninformed reader, it is hoped that the unusual scope of the book (comprising material which, to the best of my knowledge, cannot be found between two covers) and the extensive and up-to-date information it brings together (some of it based on heretofore unpublished or little known writings) will make it helpful to a broad range of potential readers, from the "lay" public to the specialist.

It could be thought that a preferable (or at least alternative) way of organizing the exposition, with some advantages over the one chosen, would have been to place the technical discussion of language at the very beginning and then proceed to questions not strictly linguistic against the background of current understanding. But this might have put off a considerable part of the potential audience the author has in mind. A decisive advantage of the course adopted, it would appear, is that it will presumably make things much easier and accessible for the "lay" (and perhaps even for the not so "lay") reader, who will be able to go through a considerable part of the book without having to confront the (sometimes imposing) technicalities of transformational generative grammar. One would hope that the intrinsic interest of the initial chapters will entice the non-specialist enough to justify the effort that the more technical chapters require. On the other hand, the readers who so choose may decide to skip to chapter 5, or even chapter 6, and then come back to where they left off. From this perspective only after the assimilation of the recent advances in the study of language reaches a "critical mass" now nowhere in sight will the alternative disregarded here begin to appear attractive.

A word about terminology is in order at this point. If the view presented in this book is on the right track, the terms "native language" (NL) and "non-native or foreign language" (NNL or FL) are to be preferred to "mother tongue" (a native language need not be a mother tongue) and to "second language" (L2), respectively. L2 (or L1, L3, . . .) is therefore to be understood in this book (except in the quotes) in their strict sense, preferably with their range of application restricted to native languages (NLs); similarly, FL1, FL2, . . . , are taken to be the corresponding terms for successively acquired non-native languages (NNLs). Again, from the perspective adopted in the book, the term "learning", which is always misleading when applied to the internalization of a NL, can also be misleading when it is applied to the internalization of a NNL, even if the two processes are very different in character, as they may very well be. If both NLs and NNLs are made possible by the innate universal schematism provided by the language organ, both involve "acquisition" in the sense the term has in, e.g., native language acquisition, although only NLs involve solely "acquisition" (more exactly, biological growth). This is not to say that the term "learning" is never applicable to describe what a student of a foreign language does. It may be, for all we know. At any rate, the reader should keep in mind that some of the uses of the terms "acquisition" and "learning" in the subfield of foreign language research as developed in the 1980s differ from the way they are used in the following pages.

Although (or perhaps because) the book was written from a very definite point of view, with an undisguised preference for some writings over many others, the Bibliography at the end of the volume has been allowed to extend over a fairly broad range (showing special favor to recent developments in language theory and to English and Spanish syntax), in particular to include many references to foreign language studies that are partially or thoroughly inconsistent with the assumptions adopted and the conclusions drawn below. Special attention has been given to what appear to be basic references in the intellectual history of the exciting new subfield of foreign language research.

The Bibliography may thus serve as a point of departure for further study and research, in addition to giving a sense of the true dimensions of the field, including some evidence and argument in support of the ideas and theses defended in the following chapters.

It is a deep satisfaction for me to acknowledge here the debts I have incurred during the preparation and writing of this book, which, as is often the case with books, was a complex and time consuming process. I was fortunate to be released from a quarter's teaching which allowed for the completion of the first draft. Flo Ariessohn provided crucial help and day to day encouragement and support during a demanding period, and Paloma Borreguero has invariably been enormously helpful, dedicated and equanimous; without their assistance my life would have been much different. Juana Liceras thoughtfully supplied a wealth of relevant materials, and Julia Herschensohn has more than once made things easier for me, for which I am grateful. I owe special thanks to Karen Zagona for the helpful questions she raised in her comments on an early version of this work, and for her support when it counted most. The final version benefitted in several ways from the perceptive and extensive comments of two anonymous referees, and from the comments and reactions of a number of students and colleagues. I am especially indebted to Héctor Campos for his unfailing encouragement and generosity, particularly with everything having to do with this book. Daniel Otero has greatly contributed to my keeping things in perspective and in other ways. As to the contribution of Carlos Otero, always in a class by itself, this time it breaks all previous records. Without his constant help and advice and without direct and continuous access to his work and files, the book would have not been what it is.

1

Introduction: Of chimps, children, and grown-ups

This is a study on language acquisition, and the very topic requires some preliminary clarification given the current stage of the field. An obvious difference between the study of language and the "hard" sciences is that linguists have not yet reached general agreement even on some of the most fundamental questions. In linguistics some central topics are still controversial.

The controversial nature of many linguistic discussions has been if anything more obvious since the 1940s, when a few linguists (most of them working in the United States) raised considerably the level of rigor and precision of the discipline, and even more so since the 1950s, when the study of language was directly affected by then-recent developments in logic and mathematics, specifically by the emergence of the theory of computation (recursive function theory). One of the consequences of this impact was a considerable increase in the technical difficulty posed by the new type of linguistic research developed at the time (transformational generative grammar). The level of difficulty surged again, even more dramatically, around 1980, this time because of internal developments within the field. This technical difficulty has been increasing at an accelerated rate ever since, especially after 1988.[1] It is getting more and more difficult to follow and keep abreast of research at the cutting edge. As is to be expected, these recent developments have placed some additional barriers in an already divided field.

It is then highly appropriate for someone who is about to address a particularly controversial linguistic topic to begin with some background information. It is a truism that no author can be completely unbiased. We are all biased to some extent and cannot help being biased, however slightly, since we can only look at things from where we are. It has also been generally understood since the midseventeenth century that no one is, or has ever been, in possession of the truth, the whole truth, and nothing but the truth.[2] The best any researcher can do is to attempt to get the most reasonable current answer to a question, that is, the best answer available at the level of understanding of his or her time. Furthermore, this is likely to be the human condition for as long as there is cultural development on the face of the earth.

1

The present author's particular bias has its roots in her education and in her professional work. She was privileged to graduate from the University of California at Los Angeles when it was widely considered to be one of the two top schools in the country for the study of linguistics, particularly Romance linguistics (in fact, a sort of oasis at that time). Her doctoral dissertation addressed what were then, and in a sense continue to be, central questions in the study of Romance syntax. On the other hand, since her graduation she has been directly involved in the language teaching programs of three major universities (UCLA, Yale, and the University of Washington). In the course of this work her interest in studying some central aspects of language research within the framework of the emerging cognitive sciences has if anything increased, and the empirical basis of her work was greatly expanded in the process. She is particularly interested in the nature of **knowledge** of human language in native and nonnative speakers as well as in specific aspects of the **use** of that knowledge in speaking and writing (what is sometimes called linguistic performance, which is to be carefully distinguished from just the knowledge that serves as its basis).

Being directly involved in the operation of a language program, she is well aware that the general problem for any teacher is to circumscribe what is to be taught, what the **subject matter** is, and that in the case of language students (researchers or teachers) the general problem takes this specific form:

What does a person who knows a human language (say, a variety of English) know? What does knowledge of a human language involve?

A helpful preliminary step, in her view, toward an answer that would in principle be of interest to both the language researcher and the language teacher is to begin by carefully considering the following two claims:

Claim #1: *No* nonhuman animal is capable of mastering a human language.

Claim #2: *Any* normal human child has the capacity to become a native speaker of any human language (from Arabic, Berber, Cantonese, Danish, or English, to Spanish, Turkish, Urdu, Vietnamese, Xhosa, Yoruba, or Zulu). What is more, any child can attain any language without explicit instruction, with surprising ease, in a relatively short time.

Since these two claims may not be readily acceptable to the reader, some elaboration is in order.

1.1. Language as a defining human attribute

It is natural to begin with Claim #1. We will first suggest that human language has little in common with other semiotic systems (Subsection 1), and then go on to consider some of its unique properties (Subsection 2) as a sort of preview of subsequent chapters.

1.1.1. Diverse semiotic systems

The long-held traditional belief expressed in Claim #1 may not have been challenged in earnest until the 1950s, when two American behaviorist psychologists moved a baby chimpanzee they named Vickie into their home and tried to teach it to talk.[3] The choice of species was not unreasonable: In recent years evidence has been found that leads us to believe that the chimpanzee is our closest relative in the animal family.[4] In particular, it appears to be the case that the average human protein is more than ninety-nine percent identical in amino acid sequence to its chimpanzee homolog.[5] This and other findings suggest that not only is the chimp our closest relative but the genetic distance between humans and chimps is very small. However, the organismal differences between the two species are vast. A decisive one, which is perhaps a key to others, is implicit in Claim #1: There are no speakers among the chimps. No wonder the attempt to teach Vickie to talk was a total failure. The reason is not hard to find: The vocal tract of a chimp is not suitable for the production of speech sounds.[6]

An early attempt to bypass the vocal tract limitations of the chimp, and one of the most carefully designed, made use of abstract visual symbols for lexical items. The chimp involved in this case was named Lana and had an advantage over other chimps in that the symbolic system devised by the experimenters was accessible to their experimental subject twenty-four hours a day. Lana made considerable progress, but the system taught had little in common with human language, hence the project is of little consequence for our purposes. In fact, it has been suggested that Lana's productions could perhaps be accounted for by a complex stimulus-response sequence, and that even pigeons can be trained to do many of the things that Lana was capable of.[7]

The prospects of any attempt to teach a chimp some human language appeared to improve in the 1960s and early 1970s, when it was finally realized that human languages are not limited to the spoken modality. This is the case of the signed languages of the deaf, in particular American Sign Language (ASL). These languages were later shown to be another realization of human language and just as fully expressive, although communicated in an extraordinary channel, namely **gestural/visual** rather than **spoken/auditory**. Since the 1960s it has been known that sign languages are true languages with all the formal complexity and expressive power of spoken languages. Like spoken languages, sign languages can be mutually unintelligible (a person fluent in the sign language of London will find the sign language of New York, and not just that of Paris, incomprehensible).[8]

As was to be expected, it was not long before psychologists attempted to teach ASL to a chimp.[9] The first and probably the most famous attempt was that of Drs. Beatrice and Allan Gardner, a husband and wife team of psychologists then working at the University of Nevada in Reno who had seen a movie of Vickie and were led to believe that a chimp's ability to gesture could be turned to good advantage. The Gardners tried to teach sign language to a one-year-old chimp they called Washoe, who was still signing (at the University of Washington) many years later, but again the success was less than total.[10]

This is indirectly made clear by the Gardners themselves, who in their 1978 review of attempts not unlike their own argued that virtually all of them (apart from their own) were undermined by a false analogy: It was the researchers who labeled the symbols taught to apes with values derived from human languages and who then mistakenly concluded that the symbol correlated by the human researcher with a term of human language was being used by the chimp with the properties of its human language correlate.

An example may be helpful here. Suppose that a pigeon has been trained to tap four colored buttons in sequence to obtain food, as was in fact claimed the very same year the Gardners' article appeared. Suppose further that the four buttons are labeled, successively *please, give, me, food*. Using the logic of the students of animal communication the Gardners criticized, we could conclude that when a pigeon taps the four buttons in sequence to obtain food it is saying *please give me food*. It is not surprising that this sort of reasoning did not impress the Gardners more than it impresses most other people. What is really surprising is the Gardners' belief that Washoe was an exception to their rule on this score since he was being taught an actual human language, namely ASL. It should be obvious that the claim underlying such a belief begs the question. True, they were teaching Washoe (and later other chimps) signs correlated with symbols of ASL, but the researchers they criticized were also teaching their chimps signs correlated with symbols of a natural language. In each case the correlation is imposed by the researcher. In each case the crucial question is: Are the chimps using symbols with properties of their natural language correlates? The answer appears to be "No."[11]

The radical difference between chimps and human children in the attainment of language is perhaps clearer in the case of another chimp on the roster of language research subjects (this time at Columbia University), no less known than Washoe: "the execrably named Nim Chimpsky."[12] A definite advantage of Nim over Washoe was that Nim was reared in a deaf family, as some deaf children are. But it soon became apparent that there was little in common between whatever was happening in Nim's brain and the internalization of ASL by deaf children. Just as with Washoe, Nim had to be explicitly taught and practically every one of his utterances had to be heavily prompted, while deaf children spontaneously pick up sign language without any explicit instruction, apparently much in the same way that hearing children pick up spoken language. There is no significant analogy between the two processes.

The reader may be aware, as many readers of the popular press are, of beliefs such as the Gardners' that appear to undermine Claim #1.[13] The Washoe and Nim experiments, which are perhaps the most interesting of their kind, suggest that the credibility of such beliefs is not very high, and we will find more reasons to reject them directly. Their factual basis is this: After laborious, intensive, and prolonged training, some chimps have been shown to be capable of reaching a state in which they are able to associate one of a small number of signals with some object, that is, they can get a handle on a small number of signal-meaning pairs. One of the most distinguished students of the chimp's mind, Dr. David Premack, then working at the University of California at Santa Barbara, found that the first chimp he studied (in the 1960s), Sarah, learned to manipulate abstract symbols and could do phenomenal things with plastic.[14] Like most other researchers at the time, Premack first assumed that the plastic things meant the same thing to the chimp as they meant to the researcher, but unlike others he was not long in seeing beyond his initial assumptions. As he put it in 1979:

> As early as 1970, I essentially quit concentrating on the attempt to operationally analyze some aspects of human language, develop training procedures for them and instill them in the ape, because it was clear to me that the accomplishments of which the ape was capable with regard to human-type language were very slight. Matters could have ended there; they didn't because if you look at other aspects of ape intelligence you get suggestions that they are much less trivial than the ape language faculty. For example, the manner in which the ape perceives the social behavior of the "other," even perhaps the social attributions which they make, are reminiscent of those that we humans make. If this is true, then

one isn't eager to let go of the ape just because he's a poor model for human language.

There's another reason why we still want to hang on to him. He may be a decent model for pathological human cases, severely retarded children who do not acquire language in the normal course of events, or global aphasics who lose language through neurological damage. When you train, or retrain these people using procedures like those used with the ape, what you end up with is not, in my experience, normal human language but a system rather like the one the ape acquires. The similarity between the two cases makes the ape an interesting model for the human pathological population.[15]

The relevant question again is: Is the chimp using symbols with properties of their natural language correlates? As before, the answer appears to be "No." For example, a chimp can be trained to distinguish simple sequences such as "red on green" versus "green on red," both in comprehension and production, or to relate a signal (say, a particular token) to some notion of "banana" or some more complex notion of which "banana" is the central element, say, "I'd like a banana." One interpretation of such findings, to which we return in the next chapter, is that the chimp's brain develops a system of concepts not unlike the system of concepts developed by the human brain (see chapter 3). What it certainly does not mean, as we will see, is that "human language" (in the technical sense of chapter 6) or something akin to it develops in the chimp's mind.

Is this not-implausible similarity between chimp and human a sufficient basis to conclude that chimps have been shown to be capable of learning human language? Of course not. For one thing, there is no reason to accept the widely spread belief that the human conceptual system and the human language system are one and the same system (see chapters 3 and 6). For another, even if the chimp's conceptual system is not unlike the human conceptual system (or systems), it appears to be far more rudimentary than the human one. Let us assume for the sake of argument that even the least smart chimps can be made to understand (no small feat) that the signals standing for the words *table* and *chair* refer to the particular objects. Now let us ask: Can they be made to understand the difference between *table* and *desk*? This seems unlikely, but for the sake of the argument suppose that the answer is "Yes." Can they be made to understand the difference between *chair* as a piece of furniture and *chair* as head of a committee? It is more than unlikely. Suppose they understand that *my house* and *my home* may be the same object. Can they also understand that if *my house* used to be in Los

Angeles and is now in Seattle a particular object was moved, while if *my home* used to be in Los Angeles and is now in Seattle no object was moved?

It is doubtful that very many people, no matter how inclined they may be to see the chimp under a strongly anthropomorphic light, would be prepared to answer "Yes" to all of these questions. In any case, if they do, we can go on and on. For example, any human knows that *my brown house* may have a nonbrown interior; that if I am near *my brown house* I am outside my house, not inside (no matter how near I am to the inner face of the exterior walls); and that if I see *my house* when I am inside it I am seeing part of its exterior (perhaps with the help of a mirror). And so on and on.[16] Is it conceivable that a chimp comes to know, even with specific and prolonged instruction (not needed by the child), all these and other things that all humans know about their native language?

The question is of course a rhetorical one. There is not the slightest reason to doubt the traditional assumption that chimps lack the mental makeup required by human language. This is not to say that they cannot think or solve some problems retarded humans are incapable of solving. It is also clear that they are in possession of a system of communication of their own. This semiotic system, however, has virtually nothing in common with human language. For one thing, it consists of a finite (in fact, fairly small) number of discrete and not very structured calls, whereas a human language defines an infinite number of expressions, which as a rule are intricately structured.

The origin of the contemporary confusion on the matter (something apparently new under the sun, since the contrary view was not open to question until very recently) seems to be a loose use of the term "language."[17] What is a language? Is the communication system of bees a language? Is the system of ape calls a language? Is Washoe's signing system a language? Is music a language? Is mathematics a language? These and similar questions are not questions of fact but questions of definition, and as such they pose problems of conceptual analysis rather than problems of empirical science. To answer a question of this nature we must first be told what is to count as a language. If we take language to mean human language, the answer is trivially "No"; if we take language to mean "system of communication" or "symbolic system" or "semiotic system," then all of these systems will be languages. But so will be numerous other systems, for example, a semaphore system or even a style of walking, which "is in some respects a conventional culturally-determined system used to communicate attitude."[18]

Now we may ask: Is there a significant analogy between any of these systems and human language? In particular, is Washoe's system an incipient manifestation of a system with some of the fundamental properties of human

language as the babbling of an infant could possibly be an incipient manifestation of mature human language? Is Washoe exhibiting the first stage of language development as three-year-old children are? These questions appear to
be analogous to questions such as this: Is a child who flutters her arms more
or less in the way a fledgling flutters its wings exhibiting incipient flight
motion? Not many people would be willing to give a positive answer to such
questions.

We conclude then that failure to distinguish between the two terms ("language" and "human language") can easily lead one astray. This will become
even clearer in the next subsection.

1.1.2. The uniqueness of human language

When we ask, What is human language?, as when we ask, What is the
mammalian (or human) visual system? or, What is the insect visual system?,
we are asking questions of fact that belong in principle to the natural sciences
and may be studied along several dimensions of inquiry. A crucial dimension
has to do with the character of the mature state of the system and the structural
principles at work. This is why even a positive answer to the questions raised
about the chimp's command of the aspects of the vocabulary sampled above
would not take us very far toward establishing that the chimp has English the
way you and I have it. The reason is that such a capacity would not go beyond
assigning labels to more or less complex concepts, a process that is at best
analogous to the process of relating English **vocabulary** items (actually, a
tiny and not particularly rich part of the English vocabulary in our illustration)
to some of the simplest concepts of a human language.

A human language, however, is far more than a vocabulary. It is a highly
intricate system, specifically a **generative procedure** that, as far as we know,
is way beyond the chimp's intellectual reach, as the following considerations
strongly suggest.

To begin with, it is easy to show that the same string of words may mean
two very different things for a human (*Mary taught John Spanish* means
something very different from *John taught Mary Spanish*), and we have no
evidence whatsoever that the same is true of a chimp. But there is more to
structure than word order. Perhaps the simplest illustration is a phrase such
as *Spanish language teacher*, where *language* can be grouped in the mind of
the listener with *Spanish* (to form the subphrases *Spanish-language teacher*),
or it can be grouped with *teacher* (to form the subphrases *Spanish language-
teacher*), the consequence of these alternative groupings bearing directly on
the interpretation of the expression: Either the language (with the first grouping)

or the teacher (with the second) may be understood to be Spanish (but, crucially, not both the language **and** the teacher).

More complex examples are not hard to find. For example, to say that *Mary is eager to please* is to say that Mary feels a keen desire to please someone (Mary does the pleasing), while to say that *Mary is easy to please* is to say that anyone will find it easy to please Mary (Mary is not the one who pleases but the pleased one). In other words, the first expression is akin to *Mary is eager to please someone*, while the second is akin to *it is easy for someone to please Mary*, both of these expressions being closer than the other two to their hidden, nonsuperficial structures (in human language, what we see or hear is often remote from what we get). It is the intricate system involved in these computations (the essence of human language) that makes it possible for a speaker (any speaker) to recover and "piece together" two very different nonsuperficial structures from superficially alike surface structures and to assign each underlying structure its proper meaning. Is it conceivable that the greatest communicators among the chimps are able to grasp the sharp difference any human speaker is able to perceive between the two analogous expressions at the beginning of this paragraph?

Perhaps even more to the point: To say that *after she sang, Mary delighted everyone* may or may not be to say that Mary sang, but to say that *she sang after Mary delighted everyone* is most definitely not to say that Mary sang, a difference readily apparent to any fluent speaker of English but perhaps not to an otherwise intelligent and thoughtful chimp. Still, grammatical structures can be even less transparent (for nonhumans). Thus, *the two girls expected to see them* may not be interpreted to mean that what was seen was the girls, while in *the boys wonder who the two girls expected to see them* (the two girls expected someone to see them, and the boys wonder who that person was), containing the very same string of words of the previous expression, what was seen may very well be the girls (although it does not have to be).

If the reader still harbors some doubts, the following alternative route may help to resolve them. To say that *Mary and John defend each other* is to say that *Mary defends John* AND *John defends Mary*, while to say that *Mary and John defend themselves* may be to say that *Mary defends herself* AND *John defends himself* or to say that *Mary defends herself and Mary defends John* AND *John defends himself and John defends Mary*. It is hard to imagine that the smartest among the chimps, much less every chimp (as in the case of humans), can get a handle on these or similar mental computations. If there is still any doubt in the mind of the reader, we can easily raise the line a few notches. First we try to find out whether a chimp can be made to understand that in *Mary expects to defend herself*, Mary is the person defended. If the answer is "No," the game is of course over. If the answer is not clear-cut enough, we go up a few more notches to test something like *Mary wonders who Mary expects to defend herself*, with a string of words identical to the previous example. Is there any chance that the chimp under study, like any English speaker, comes to the conclusion that in this case the person defended is neither the Mary who expects nor the Mary who wonders? Again, if the answer is "No," as presumably it is, we have no reason to believe that the chimp is in possession of the computational system of human language as we know it.

Given these considerations, which could be easily extended with even more complex examples, it does not seem unreasonable to conclude that Claim #1 is indeed credible under the assumption that human language is far more than a long list of vocabulary items (far longer than the chimp can handle). It is in any case the claim put forth by the most careful students of the chimp mind. Thus, after four decades of research, David Premack, the author of *Intelligence in Ape and Man* (1976) and many other studies on the same general subject and a coauthor of *The Mind of an Ape* (1983), states: "The sentence is the most abstract representation of which humans are capable and, as such, is far beyond the capacity of the chimpanzee."[19] The great logician and philosopher Bertrand Russell put it more forcefully when he said that he would be prepared to accept that apes could speak when someone presented for his consideration a specimen that could fathom the meaning of a sentence such as "My father was poor but honest."

Consider now Claim #2, which is far less controversial. By the time he is three years old a child on the way to knowing English natively is already able to correct a foreigner unerringly over a fairly wide range, by the time he is five he can speak and understand English over an enormous (astronomical, in fact) range with native facility, and by the time he is ten or so he has a complete knowledge of the language system (although he of course may continue to enrich his vocabulary for the rest of his life—see chapter 3). Furthermore, direct instruction must be dispensed with. Anyone who has attempted to correct a three-year-old knows perfectly well that it cannot be done. Older relatives or friends may perhaps lend a helping hand with particular items of the vocabulary but not much else. As everyone knows, young children are notoriously resistant to syntactic correction. A good illustration, often repeated, is provided by a child who said *Nobody don't like me* and was urged time after time to say *Nobody likes me*. Each time the child dutifully tried to repeat the model expression (or so it seemed), but repeated instead his own expression. Finally, after many repetitions he seemed to have gotten a hold of the difference and triumphantly said instead, relishing his accomplishment: *Ah! Nobody don't likes me.*[20] Is there anything apelike in this?

But observations of this type are actually unnecessary to conclude that children attain their native language without the benefit of instruction. It is clear that the child's ability to use language, like the ability of the adult, stems from a system of principles, specifically a generative procedure (see chapter 6), and most adults do not have the foggiest idea of what these principles are. Like children, they know the principles unconsciously (no amount of introspection or hypnosis can make a speaker aware of these principles). This being the case, it would be impossible for them to impart the unconscious knowledge involved to the child, who would not be able to understand an explicit explanation at the required level of abstraction in any event. Worse still, it is immediately obvious that in the early stages of language development the principles the child is putting to use are not identical to the principles of the adult (as the last example illustrates), so the adult does not know the child's principles even unconsciously.

All this suggests that attaining a language is not something that the child does, but rather something that happens to the child who is in the right place at the right time, as we will see in chapter 2.

1.2. Native language as childhood language

We turn now to the third and final claim, which is by far the most controversial of the three. It is also the central claim of this book, its main thesis in fact, so it is only fair to refer to it as such. Let us call it the "Never after Puberty" thesis:

Claim #3 (the "Never after Puberty" thesis):
All and only (normal) children can attain language natively.

This thesis is to be understood in the sense that all and only normal children can be bona fide native speakers of a human language. There seems to be something having to do with language development that goes on around puberty (roughly). Only before puberty (give or take a few years) is it possible for a human to attain language natively, if this book is on the right track. The boundary tentatively set as decisive—the time of puberty—is of course just a rough first approximation. There is still much to be learned, as will become clear as we proceed.

A minimal definition of human language is that it is a system that relates a meaning to a signal over an unbounded range of meanings and signals.

Such a system can be realized in a variety of ways. As we have seen, in American Sign Language (ASL), the signals are manifested as gestures of various kinds, used among others by people in which hearing is absent even from birth. (There are schools where most of the students and teachers come from deaf families and can nevertheless attain language, though in a different mode.) On the other hand, in spoken language (speech) the signals are sounds, an approximate transcription of which is sometimes committed to writing. It is by now fairly clear that the system of signals in a broad sense (including both its elements and their arrangement in ever larger units, from word parts and words—or their signable equivalents—to sentences and discourses) is the most obvious difference between any two languages (and, in some precise sense, perhaps the only difference, a topic to which we return in chapter 6). If so, attaining a new spoken or signed language involves at the very least (possibly at most, under the proper interpretation) coming to possess a new system of signals (in the case of spoken language, a new sound system in the broad sense), something of special interest for the language teacher.

At this point we can ask: Are there any detectable differences between the way the system of signals (possibly a sound system) of a particular language is used by a speaker who has been part of a linguistic community since childhood and the way it is used by a speaker who was first exposed to the language for a sustained period of time and under certain conditions only after puberty? The answer is obviously "Yes" in the case of a speaker who has a more or less marked "foreign accent," something not unusual among postpuberty speakers of a tongue other than their mother tongue. This hardly needs demonstration.

Suppose it is argued, as it sometimes has, that a foreign accent, even a marked one, is perfectly compatible with being a native speaker in a nonsuperficial sense. After all, speakers with very different, even mutually unintelligible, accents can be native speakers of what appears to be, and to some extent may be, one and the same language. Still, this does not seem to be the case with foreign speakers. Is there any hard evidence bearing on the matter? Simple honesty would force us to recognize before going any further that the evidence available at this stage of our knowledge (or ignorance) is mostly at the anecdotal level, based on everyday experience and on intuitions about what happens with language teaching, and is generally less solid than would be desirable. The bulk of the work is still to be done. Nevertheless, it is a reasonable hypothesis that the language experience is very different when the would-be speakers have not reached puberty and when they are past puberty, roughly. Anyone who has had any relevant information knows that there seems to be something right about this belief. Children just seem to develop language differently than adults do. The faculty or faculties involved do not appear to be functioning in the same way before and after puberty, as we will see shortly.

This is not to say that anybody has ever been able to nail down the hypothesis experimentally (in spite of the fact that intricate and extensive studies have been carried out on occasion). It seems nevertheless natural and reasonable to assume that this is simply because the study of the main topics of this book is still in its infancy. The basis of this conclusion is that the available evidence, weak as it may be, is extremely suggestive. It is well known, for example, that immigrant children usually acquire the indigenous language rapidly and completely from their peers, without the benefit of drills or any other form of instruction, in a very short period of time, while their parents just as usually fail to match the achievement of their offspring, even after working at it with no lack of determination for fifty years or more. In fact, the consequences of this contingency are being dramatically illustrated in many parts of the United States right now, where many parents have to rely heavily on their children (sometimes on very small children) as interpreters when they go, for example, to the doctor or to a government office, a reversal that is giving rise to hitherto unknown interpersonal relationship problems that are beginning to attract the attention of a diverse group of specialists.

A very important thing to note is that *any* child who is part of a linguistic community comes to be in possession of at least one language at a tender age and that, as already mentioned, by the time the child reaches puberty his or her linguistic maturation has reached a steady state that does not differ in any essential way, as far as we know, from that of any other child of roughly the same age in the community (in sharp contrast with the well-known dissimilarities among adult language learners). There are also no significant differences between children in this respect, short of pathology. (This close similarity in the knowledge of the language system is of course perfectly compatible with a great diversity in the skill of using it, as will become clear later.)

On the other hand, no one to my knowledge has ever claimed that *any* adult can become a native speaker of any language. It is generally recognized that, although children are all capable of becoming native speakers of at least one language, not every adult who attempts to master a foreign language is capable of matching the child's feat; furthermore, some foreign languages offer greater difficulties than others to the speaker of a particular language (for example, Spanish is less difficult than Japanese for speakers of English), while all languages are equally easy for a child. The most that has been claimed is that *some* adults (usually a tiny proportion of those that give it a try) are—or at least appear to be—a match for the child, there being very striking differences between adults in this respect, while all children are equally native. Notice incidentally that, true or false, the claim that some adults can develop an admirable mastery of a language (whatever this means) should not be confused with a different, and no doubt plausible, one, namely, the claim that some of the speakers of a language acquired after puberty (with or without heavy accents) are sometimes able to express themselves better than unquestionably native speakers. This is a claim about the output (what is said) and as such is compatible with quite different assumptions about the systems involved. Very different systems may generate the same sort of ouput, and even perfect output would not entail native knowledge of the language.

The claim that some adults become native speakers of a language other than their first language is not completely incompatible with a slightly weaker form of the "Never after Puberty" (NAP) thesis, namely, one that allows for cases out of the ordinary (presumably few and far between). But although the existence of rare exceptions among adult language learners is not open to question, the existence of exceptions to the NAP thesis is yet to be established. To begin with, specific individuals cited as a sort of existence proof of exceptions to the NAP thesis, who undeniably are highly plausible candidates for adult speakers at the highest level of achievement, have little doubt themselves that they process their postpuberty language and their native language or languages in very different ways.[21]

In any case, it is easy to put the alternative speculations to the test. There are several types of experiments that could yield decisive results. One is that, in contrast with computer "languages" such as BASIC, in which the slightest deviation from the prescriptions of the system may result in total incomprehension, for a native speaker human speech can withstand "all kinds of distortions, noise, chopping out of its upper frequency range (as in telephones), and general abuse."[22] As native speakers we can listen to people with food in their mouths or with bad head colds, even after they have had several drinks of Scotch, and still the message gets through. Furthermore, the native speaker can generally understand an impressive variety of dialectal and even foreign accents, or highly distorted synthesized speech, possibly in a background that includes jackhammers or the Rolling Stones.

Is this equally true of the most fluent nonnative speakers? The little we know about it suggests that the answer is "No," and the tentative character of this answer can easily be removed by experiments carried out at any level of rigor the experimenter chooses. Under the NAP thesis, the expectation is that differences in comprehension between prepuberty and postpuberty speakers should be detectable, if not striking, under nonordinary conditions (a considerable level of noise and/or assorted distortions). A variant of this experiment, perhaps even more telling than the one just outlined, would be to explore the differences in comprehension between native and nonnative speakers when exposed to an unfamiliar dialect that is as far removed from the standard language as possible. The prediction again is that the native speakers will fare noticeably better, and the limited evidence available strongly suggests this to be the case.

The main points in this section may be summarized as follows. In contrast with the child, the adolescents or adults striving to develop competence in a language usually avail themselves of instruction (including corrections and other negative evidence). In spite of these "advantages," few, if any, attain the language natively. This crucial difference, manifested in imperfect intuitions, foreign accents, and other limitations alien to the native speaker, can be tested in various ways.

The present study takes all the available evidence, such as it is, seriously and assumes that it can, and no doubt will, be confirmed to everybody's satisfaction in the future, perhaps in the not-distant future. Under this assumption, it is natural to focus on the central question, which is the explanation of the NAP thesis. The answer to this question, and what we learn in the process of seeking it, has implications for language theory and language research as well as for language teaching, in particular for the design and implementation of teaching programs. There is then a corollary to the NAP thesis: A foreign language program needs to be carefully designed. The randomness of first language acquisition is not a good model for language teaching.

In the investigation of this topic, as in the investigation of other topics, it is only natural to begin at the beginning, that is, by considering what is really at issue. In the present case the first and fundamental step in this direction is the nature and origin of knowledge of language, and the distinct contributions of the individual and the environment to mental development. This is the topic of the next chapter.

NOTES TO CHAPTER 1

1. For extensive discussion of the line of development sketched in this paragraph, see Otero (ed.) 1994, vol. 1 (in particular the introduction) and Otero (forthcoming).

2. On the assumptions of "constructive skepticism," see Popkin 1979:48,140; cf. Chomsky 1980:15–16, 142.

3. They were Drs. Keith and Virginia Hayes, the first husband and wife team of contemporary psychologists to study the communication abilities of chimps. There were of course earlier attempts to teach apes human language, going back to at

least the time of La Mettrie's *L'homme-machine* (1747). For a recent overview, see Lieberman 1984, chapter 10.

4. See the introduction to Chomsky 1989, note 69. There was at least one attempt to teach signs to a gorilla, who was named Koko. However, little evidence was offered in support of the claims about Koko's abilities (to make reference to past events and emotions and to create new words, as in "water bird" for "swan"), which are hard to believe (see Patterson 1979).

5. See Otero 1991, note 2, in particular the quotes from King and Wilson 1975, and Diamond 1992, chapter 1, for a more general discussion. Cf. Lieberman 1991.

6. It is precisely because mammals other than humans lack the ability to imitate speech sounds that the comparative ethologist W. H. Thorpe expected birds (many of which have this ability to a remarkable extent) to be "the group which ought to have been able to evolve language in the true sense, and not the mammals," an implausible hypothesis for rather obvious reasons. See Chomsky 1968, chapter 3, for a critique of Thorpe's suggestion.

7. See Rumbaugh & Rumbaugh 1977 for a description of the experiment.

8. See Fischer 1994 and references therein. The by-now extensive body of research on ASL includes Fischer 1974, Jones & Quigley 1979, Klima *et al.* 1979, Padden 1983, Newport 1984, Lillo-Martin 1985, 1986, 1990, Padden 1988, Mayberry & Fischer 1989, Fischer & Siple (eds.) 1990, Lucas (ed.) 1990, Siple & Fischer (eds.) 1991, Perlmutter 1992. For a general introduction to "the cultural life of Deaf people" by two deaf authors who have both "participated in a new generation of research on signed languages" (with two chapters about how this research "has influenced the way Deaf people think and talk about their language"), see Padden & Humphries 1988 (for reviews of signed language structure, see the references on p. 8, including Klima *et al.* 1979 and Padden 1983; cf. p. 58); see also Plann (in preparation).

9. "One instinctual rather than physical problem in using sign language with chimpanzees is that making eye contact is seen as threatening behavior in chimpanzee 'culture', yet eye gaze is crucial to the grammar of ASL." (Fischer 1994, n. 7.)

10. See Gardner & Gardner 1969, Gardner et al. 1989, and Chomsky 1979 (and now Fischer 1994) for a detailed critique.

11. See Chomsky 1979 for a fuller and extremely illuminating discussion of these questions. It should perhaps be added that the then-available films of Washoe show a lot more extraneous hand movement than was glossed by Beatrice Gardner in the film, according to Petitto & Seidenberg 1979, who also point out that a large proportion of the "signs" occurred in the wild. See also Seidenberg & Petitto 1979, 1981.

12. The quote is from Fisher 1994. See also Terrace 1979.

13. For more serious sources, see Linden 1976, Seidenberg & Pettito 1979, and Ristau & Robbins 1982.

14. See Premack 1976. Significantly, Premack was unable to replicate his success with Sarah with subsequent chimpanzees, which suggests that Sarah was out of the ordinary (extraordinarily intelligent). This is reminiscent of earlier findings by Koehler which will be referred to in chapter 3.

15. *The Sciences*, November 1979, p. 7. Cf. Chomsky 1980, p. 57.

16. For a broader sample, see Chomsky 1992a, from which some of these remarks have been culled.

17. The fad may be abating. As Premack writes in his "future history of the animal language controversy" (1986:32), "one must recall that there was a period during which extraordinary claims for apes were commonplace (not that they have disappeared entirely)." To which he adds: "No one was more responsible for these claims than the Gardners. The impression left by their work is that the language of the signing ape and that of the signing child could only be differentiated through close analysis. Indeed, in one study they found the ape superior to the child (Gardner and Gardner 1974 [read 1975])."

18. The quote is from Chomsky 1979 (p. 32), from where these and the immediately following remarks are abstracted. See also Limber 1977.

19. Quoted in Restak 1988:230.

20. See McNeill 1966, 1970. Cf. McNeill 1987, Goodluck 1991, and Atkinson 1992.

21. It could be argued that the difference in processing is consistent with a native knowledge of the language, but this seems rather implausible, particularly in view of some of the specifics of the reports, for example the need to monitor properties of some of the structures used to avoid certain types of errors.

22. Kaye 1989, p. 157, a passage from which I draw in the remarks that follow.

2

Nature and nurture:
The poverty of the stimulus

The examples used in chapter 1 as a basis for Claim #1 raise an interesting question, which has been debated for centuries (and not always fruitfully). What is the origin of what we know? Where is our knowledge coming from? There are essentially three possibilities: It may be coming from the outside (as in the case of the telephone numbers we have committed to memory), from the inside (as our blood type does), or some of each. Which is the right answer in the case of knowledge of language?

2.1. Language and nurture: The contribution of the environment

A good point to begin is this simple observation: English (more accurately, a particular variety of English) is one of the thousands of different languages spoken by humans. Therefore, it must be the environment that determines whether we are native speakers of (a variety of) English and/or Arabic, Berber, Cantonese, Danish, Eskimo, . . . Spanish, Turkish, Urdu, Vietnamese, Xhosa, Yoruba, or Zulu. Note that we need to go no further to be able to discard one of the three possibilities listed above: Our knowledge cannot all be due to nature. If it were, we would all speak exactly the same language. This much is clear. What we need to explore next is the kind of role the environment plays.

For concreteness, consider some of the differences between two of the most widely spoken languages: English and Spanish. In neither language is a word like *bnid* possible, although it is possible in Arabic. On the other hand, *Spaniard* and *spaniel* are possible and actual words in English but are impossible in Spanish, while *strid* is still impossible in Spanish but possible and nonexistent in English, as any native speaker knows. There is no string of sounds in Spanish that remotely resembles *house* or *home*, to take two of the words we discussed briefly in chapter 1; in fact, the first sound in those strings often poses insurmountable difficulties for many Spanish speakers, while it is familiar to others.

If we now consider *brown house*, we notice immediately that the two substrings sound alike. Specifically, they are in the formal relation of **assonance**, while, for example, *house* and *mouse* are in the formal relation of **rhyme**, two relations in linguistic expressions definable in terms of their sound sequences. Facts such as these may open all kinds of vistas for an English poet that are unavailable to a Spanish poet. (It is only by sheer chance that the two words in *casa castaña*, one of the Spanish translations of *brown house*, are also in the formal relation of assonance, in sharp contrast with *casa* and *ratón*, the Spanish equivalents of *house* and *mouse*.) There is also a sharp contrast in the number of syllables, *casa* by itself having as many syllables as *brown house* and *castaña* adding three more. On the other hand, rhyme will never lead the English poet to associate *luck* and *death*, while it may lead the Spanish poet to associate their equivalents *suerte* and *muerte*, as in *la suerte o la muerte* "luck or death." We return to the topic in chapter 4.

When we consider the strings of sounds as words (a very important notion, as we will see, still not fully understood), we quickly discover that in Spanish there is no word that translates *home* when I refer to Los Angeles, the United States, planet Earth, our galaxy, or the universe as *my home*. In other words, the knowledge that *house* is distinguished from *home* (in particular, the knowledge that in English I return to my home after work, while in Spanish, as in Hebrew, I return "to the house"—or "to house," depending on the variety of Spanish) has to involve some "nurture."

If we move on to other items of the vocabulary, we continue to find striking differences. For example, the words *sixteen, seventeen, eighteen,* and *nineteen* are equivalent to the Spanish words *diez y seis, diez y siete, diez y ocho,* and *diez y nueve,* respectively, but in English there is no "oneteen" or "twoteen" and in Spanish there is no "diez y uno," "diez y dos," "diez y tres," "diez y cuatro" or "diez y cinco." The terms *time, weather, tense,* may each be translated into Spanish as *tiempo,* and *one* may be translated as *uno*; on the other hand, *one time* is not equivalent to "uno tiempo" but rather to *una vez,* and *ten times ten* may be rendered into Spanish either as *diez veces diez* or *diez (multiplicado) por diez,* which are all ways of saying *one hundred* (*cien* in Spanish). No Spanish speaker will ever say "uno tiempo" or "diez tiempos diez." In English, *losing the train* is one thing and *missing the train* is something else, but both are rendered into Spanish as *perder el tren.*

On the other hand, *to leave* is often equivalent to Spanish *dejar* (as in *to leave in the dark* or *to leave alone*) but it sometimes is equivalent to Spanish *irse* (as in *leave early*), and *to be* is sometimes equivalent to Spanish *ser* (as in *he is cold=es frío*), sometimes to Spanish *estar* (as in *he is here=está aquí*), and occasionaly to *tener* (as in *he is cold=tiene frío* and *he is right=tiene razón*) or to *hacer* (as in *it is cold=hace frío*) or to *quedarse* (as in *he was speechless=se quedó sin palabras*) or to *deber* (as in *he is to do it immediately=debe hacerlo inmediatamente*).

People may *get up on the wrong side of the bed* and even *kick the bucket* in English; in Spanish they "get up with the left foot" and "stretch out the leg" instead (*leg* being in this case not *pierna*, 'human leg', but *pata*, 'foot or leg of an animal or an object', as in *a cuatro patas*, 'on all fours' or in *metieron la pata* 'they put their foot into it'). Spanish speakers never *spill the beans* or *let the cat out of the bag* (although they are certainly just as capable of revealing a secret unintentionally as anyone else) or *make both ends meet* (instead, they "live with what they earn"). Nor do they do something *off and on, now and then,* or *from time to time*; only "from time in when." In English one may *be head over heels in love* or *through and through*, while in Spanish one may "be in love until the marrows" (down to the marrow), which is *estar*—not *ser* for *be*, notice— *enamorado hasta los tuétanos* (a word, the last one, that we will meet again in a quite different context in the next chapter).

Evidently, all these things and many others have to be learned by the speakers of English or the speakers of Spanish (overlapping sets, as we know) in the course of their lives, so the type of knowledge involved in this and similar instances has to come in part from the environment (in part because even in these instances the environment does not tell them that the sounds they build their words with are all taken from the universal "sound alphabet" of human language).

So far we have not gone beyond what is sometimes called Saussurean arbitrariness (after the much admired Swiss linguist Ferdinand de Saussure), that is, the pairing up of meanings and sound representations in arbitrary ways. But, though a not easily surmountable barrier for a grown-up trying to learn a new language, the class of differences just illustrated is the more trivial part of language variation. Things get more interesting when we move on to differences in the grammatical elements, a highly privileged part of the vocabulary. For example, for referring to more than one house we use the word *houses* if we speak English and *casas* if we speak Spanish, the final *s* being part of a grammatical element in both words, so here we find more similarity between English and Spanish than when we compare *house* and *casa*. There is more to it than meets the eye, however. One crucial difference is that in English people use *the* in both *the house* and *the houses*, while in Spanish the equivalent of *the* appears in different garb in *la casa* and *las casas*, with *la* changing to *las* as *casa* changes to *casas*, and in *el ratón, los ratones* (*the mouse/mice*), where *el* and *los* are less obviously related. Even more interestingly, in Spanish the equivalent of *brown* may be either *castaño* or *castaña*. The equivalent of *brown house* is *casa castaña*, as already mentioned, but that of *brown mouse* is *ratón castaño*, not "*ratón castaña*," the reason being that in Spanish the two words of each pair must agree in gender overtly, a sharp difference from English with considerable consequences. Another important systematic difference between the two languages is the order of the words: In English, the noun (*house, mouse*) appears last, while in Spanish the noun (*casa, ratón*) appears first. These and other differences of the same nature must also be due to the environment.

Moving on to a lexical category of even more complexity, consider verbs such as *give* or *donate*, which are very close in meaning, *donating* being a special kind of *giving* found at relatively advanced cultural levels (presumably, every language has the equivalent of *give*, but the equivalent of *donate* requires the previous development of relevant institutions).[1] The *ing* ending shared by the last two forms is again a good example of a grammatical element. It corresponds to at least two Spanish endings (*ndo*, as in *teniendo eso en cuenta* for *keeping that in mind*, or *r*, as in *perder el tren* for either *missing the train* or *losing the train*, as above), and there is no easy recipe for choosing between them.[2] Other differences between the two languages are not less obvious. We can say either *Mary and I gave a collection of books to the library* or *Mary and John gave a collection of books to the library*, with *gave* in both cases, while in Spanish we would have to say *dimos* in the first case and *dieron* in the second. On the other hand, if we substitute *collections* for *a collection*, *dábamos* and *daban* respectively might be better equivalents of *gave*. Observe that the endings (*mos, n*) are as before. This is because the ending of every Spanish verb form that goes with the Spanish equivalent of *Mary and I* or *we* is necessarily *mos*, and the ending of every Spanish verb form that goes with the Spanish equivalent of *Mary and John* or *they* is necessarily *n*, two examples of another difference between English and Spanish with far-reaching consequences.

A different type of dissimilarity is that in English it is also possible to say *Mary and John gave the library a collection of books*, an expression that cannot be translated word for word into Spanish.[3] Interestingly, in this respect the Spanish verb *dar*, "give," is more like the English verb *donate* (which cannot be substituted for *give* in the last expression) than like its English equivalent. A perhaps not unrelated difference may be exemplified by the contrast between *John gave it to him* and its Spanish equivalent, *Juan se lo dio*, which word for word would translate into English as "John him it gave," a word order typical of languages such as Latin or Japanese (a similarity far from accidental). Another major difference between English and Spanish, closely related to the difference between *gave* and its various Spanish counterparts, is that in Spanish it is possible to simply say, at the appropriate moment, *se lo dio* (actually pronounced as a single word, as if it were written *selodió*, by every native speaker). Again, the knowledge underlying these differences has to come, at least in part, from the environment. This is hardly open to doubt.

We could go on, and we will in the following chapters, but this brief sample is perhaps enough at this point to suggest that not only is there no way to leave nurture out, but the environment has a definite role to play in any attempt to account for knowledge of language. It is true that understanding this much does not require too great an intellectual effort. What does require unusual effort is to go beyond the obvious. This is because resisting the lures of common sense is never easy for a creature who thrives on commonsense understanding, as we do. Our perception of the sunrise is a good example: We see the sun rising no matter how hard we try to remind ourselves that there is plenty of evidence showing that the rising is only apparent and that what is actually happening is that the "spaceship" on which we are travelling nonstop is turning. No wonder it took so many centuries to begin to overcome our geocentric prejudices. Still, to begin to overcome our prejudices about language has been even harder. That is why it took humankind much longer to begin to put together the language puzzle than to put the earth in its place. The first significant glimmerings of deep understanding came as late as the midseventeenth century (with the Port-Royal grammar and logic), and only with the rise of generative grammar in the midtwentieth century, no less than three hundred years later, have we begun to understand why it is that the deep elements and principles of language cannot possibly come from outside us.

2.2. Language and human nature: Phenotype from genotype

Common sense tells us that language is learned the way other things are learned (nonsense rhyming pairs or the nicknames or phone numbers of our best friends, for example), and to some extent it appears to be true, as we have just seen. But since this is the same common sense that continues to tell us that the sun is revolving around the earth centuries after the Copernican revolution, perhaps a fuller understanding of the nature of language calls for a measure of **uncommon sense**, which is often much harder to come by. The following considerations may be of help.

Let us begin with some aspects of simple words deliberately left out in the preceding section. As was fleetingly mentioned in chapter 1, any human knows that a *brown house* may have a nonbrown interior; that if I am near *my brown house*, I am outside my house, not inside (no matter how near I am to the inner face of the exterior walls); and that if I see *my house* when I am inside it I am seeing part of its exterior (perhaps with the help of a mirror). Exactly the same is true of *casa castaña* and *mi casa (castaña)* for a Spanish speaker. This is no sheer coincidence. It appears to be a fact that a brown house has a brown exterior, not interior, in every human language, a universal property that is apparently also true of other **container words** such as *cabin, palace, castle, tower, city hall, church, lean-to, igloo, box, ship*, . . . (Spanish *cabaña, palacio, castillo, torre, ayuntamiento, iglesia, cobertizo, iglu, caja, nave*, . . .), including recent inventions such as *airplane* (Spanish *aeroplano* or *avión*). To paint any of these objects brown is to give it a brown exterior no matter what the language is. Suppose that a large, sturdy tentlike structure made of poles covered with felt, skins, or often canvas is called *yurt* in Russian and *ger* in Mongolian. We can immediately predict that to paint a *yurt* or a *ger* brown is to give it a brown exterior and that people or things near the *yurt* or the *ger* are outside of it.

To see that there is a problem here one might have to begin by gaining a measure of psychic distance—the sort of psychic distance needed to overcome the effects of familiarity with everyday phenomena, which we tend to take for granted as necessary or somehow natural. It has often been noted, particularly by philosophers and literary theorists, that familiarity tends to breed the sort of attitude that makes it difficult for us to perceive the obvious. An often-cited case is that of people living at the seashore, who grow so accustomed to the murmur of the waves that they virtually never hear it. Another case is the famous apple falling from the tree. How many people are capable of being as puzzled by its fall as Newton was? How many can see that to simply assume that its natural place is on the ground will not do if what we are trying to understand is the principle (gravitation) that explains the falling of anything, not just the falling of an apple?

What is the root of the universal properties of container words? The idea that it is due to "nurture" can be readily discarded. The reason is that the objects out there have all kinds of properties, not just the ones they have universally across languages (which of course are also true properties of the objects under consideration but far from the only ones). The question is: Why precisely those properties, across languages and cultures, and not other true properties? It is easy to imagine a language, spoken by a differently constituted extraterrestrial creature, in which the word *house* is associated with a very different collection of properties (for example, the property that if two objects are equidistant to the exterior wall of the house, one outside and the other inside, both are near the house if one is). If so, since willful agreement among speakers of one language, even less of all languages, is out of the question, the only alternative we are left with is that the knowledge is not coming from the environment.

Further exploration provides additional supporting evidence. Consider again our earlier example *Mary gave a collection of books to the library*, irrelevantly shortened for ease of exposition. When we hear this expression we understand that there is a giver (more generally, a human agent), *Mary*; something given (more generally, a "theme," to use a technical term for lack of a more familiar one), *a collection of books*; and a recipient, *the library*. Exactly the same is true of Spanish *dar* (or of *donar*, the equivalent of *donate*). Suppose we make the expression part of a more complex expression, as in *John persuaded Mary to give a collection of books to the library*. If the statement is true, we know without further information that John caused Mary to decide to give a collection of books to the library and that at some point Mary intended to give a collection of books to the library. Again, exactly the same is true of the equivalent Spanish expression. If so, excluding the possibility of a conspiracy among all English and Spanish speakers without exception, we are forced to conclude that this type of knowledge is not coming from the environment.

When we move beyond lexical structure, we find stronger reasons to draw the same conclusion. Consider first a familiar saying: *All that glitters is not gold*. Is the statement true or false? It depends on the interpretation. On one reading it is equivalent to *not all that glitters is gold*, which as an assertion is unquestionably true. On another reading it is equivalent to *anything that glitters is not gold*, which is false because gold glitters. Again, the same is true of its Spanish counterpart, *todo lo que reluce no es oro* (with parallel word order) or, as some speakers may prefer, *no es oro todo lo que reluce*. Hence, there must be something inside us from which the parallel facts derive.

The most complex expressions considered in chapter 1, say, *Mary wonders who Mary expects to defend herself*, provide even more persuasive evidence about our inner richness. Suppose we agree that a chimp cannot compute at least this and similar expressions. The question now is: How come some humans (namely, those who know English) can? In other words, how is it possible that speakers of English know instantly, when they first come across this expression, most likely for the first time in their lives, that the person doing the defending is not Mary, even though Mary is the one doing the defending in the partially identical expression *Mary expects to defend herself*? Even more to the point in this context: How come speakers of English as a foreign language who are incapable of mastering things as simple as the use of *ed* forms such as *remembered* (they may say "Did you remembered that" or "I've just remember that,") do not have the slightest difficulty in understanding either example the right way?

Since such pairs are virtually never found in everyday speech as exemplifications of the contrast—and apparently no one was conscious of the striking difference in interpretation between the partially identical expressions until a few years ago—we can be sure that the knowledge the English speakers have about the two expressions is not something learned, even less taught. What then is the source of their knowledge? How is it possible that all speakers come to agree on those two very different interpretations (no dialectal differences here)?

As in the case of the falling apple, to say that this is the way things are is no answer at all. The question is: Why are humans capable of doing it when chimps are not? It cannot be the result of learning because even the very few who could do the teaching now were not familiar with the contrast until very recently, and speakers of English have been able to understand this class of expressions for a very long time.

The point becomes clearer when we understand what it is exactly that the speaker has to know to interpret each expression in the right way. Since in the case under consideration this requires a fairly technical discussion, as we will have occasion to see later, let us take a different type of example that can be explained in simpler terms. Not much reflection is needed to come to the realization that an expression such as *John kept the car in the garage* is open to two very different interpretations (but crucially not both simultaneously), namely,

(1) the garage is the place where John kept the car, or
(2) the car in the garage is the one John kept

(maybe he sold the other one).[4] How do we know? How does every speaker of English know? Interestingly, a word for word translation into Spanish has only one interpretation (the first). Why are Spanish speakers limited to one? Even more intriguing: When we ask *in which garage did John keep the car?*, a way of turning that expression into a question, the expression is no longer open to two interpretations, only to one; and the surviving interpretation happens to be the interpretation of its Spanish equivalent, namely the one corresponding to (1) above. Why is it that English speakers and Spanish speakers unerringly converge on the one interpretation when they are not even aware of what they are doing? Can we suppose that the individual experience of each English speaker is close enough to the individual experience of each Spanish speaker, and that they all learned how to interpret those expressions in the course of their diverse individual lives?

There are two problems with this guess. One is that a not very resourceful English speaker can come up with one interpretation more than the brightest Spanish speaker. The other problem is far more serious: The information required to understand whether one of the expressions at issue is open to only one or to one of two interpretations cannot be found in the linguistic environment even by a legion of linguists working together for a whole lifetime, no matter how intensely they work at it. It is then no more likely that it is discovered by a single individual on his or her own in the span of just a few years. The reason could not be simpler: It is not in the environment.

The evidence provided by unusual, including very extreme, cases should be mentioned here. We may begin with the case of blind children, who attain linguistic "milestones" for both syntax and words—even those words that have to do with visual experience—at the same age as the sighted.[5] Even more strikingly, deaf-blind adults, including one who was both profoundly deaf and blind from birth, have been able to develop extensive language abilities (comparing favorably in many areas with hearing individuals) through the medium of touch by using a vibrotactile method of speech perception (the Tadoma method of speech-reading) used in training deaf and deaf-blind individuals for both receiving and producing speech, and there are apparently reasons to believe that their limited language exposure had only a minor effect on their eventual language achievement.[6] Consider now sign language. It is well known that, other choices being closed to them, deaf individuals often develop sign languages, and very quickly. What is even more striking is that deaf children with zero linguistic input have nevertheless been able to spontaneously develop a sign system remarkably like human language (one three-year-old is reported to have produced "sentences" up to thirteen signs in length, a feat not matched by any chimp). In other words, even individuals who essentially have no externally available linguistic input are able to develop human language, which means that whatever language they do produce is virtually a product of their innate capacity for language.[7]

Let us turn now to the questions left unanswered. Here is the key to the puzzle, worked out only a generation ago. As every culturally nondeprived schoolboy or schoolgirl knows, words like *car* and *garage* belong to the category Noun (N for short). A phrase built on an N is called, naturally enough, a Noun Phrase (NP for short). Together with the little but extremely important word *the*, the N *garage* forms the phrase *the garage*. As a first approximation we can take this phrase to be an NP. It is easy to see that *the car* is a phrase of the same type, hence also an NP. Now comes the crucial question: In the expression *John kept the car in the garage*, is the string of words *the car in the garage* a phrase? If we take it to be a phrase, more or less equivalent to *the car that is in the garage*, it is a phrase of the same type as the other two (hence also an NP), in which case the sense of the whole expression is more or less identical to the sense of *John kept the car that is in the garage*, that is, sense (2), page 25. If, on the other hand, *the car* and *in the garage* do not form a phrase, as in *this is the garage where John kept the car*, where *in* is not even present, the meaning is that of (1), not (2).

It should be fairly obvious by now that the crucial information about whether in the string *John kept the car in the garage* the last five words form a phrase cannot be found in the environment. The pronunciation is usually the same whether or not the five words form a phrase. Furthermore, the environment contains no NPs. The NPs and other abstract entities of mental linguistic representations have to be supplied by the speaker or the listener (or reader). All the environment provides is sounds or signals (handwritten or "handsigned").

But even if the NPs were supplied by the environment we would not be much better off. We would still have to discover the principle underlying the puzzle. Here is a sort of password for it: It is not possible to ask a question about an NP that is part of another NP (in particular, about the NP *the garage* when it is part of the NP *the car in the garage*). It follows that if a question is asked about *the garage* in the string *John kept the car in the garage*, both the speaker and the listener instantly take it for granted (without of course being aware of it) that *the garage* cannot be part of a larger NP. This means that the other interpretation, which is possible only when *the car in the garage* is an NP (making *John kept the car in the garage* virtually equivalent to *John kept the car that is in the garage*) is automatically excluded. The impossibility of interpretation (2) when we ask a question about *the garage* is therefore explained.

What then is the source of the knowledge that leads every speaker of English (no dialectal variation here either) to understand these and many other expressions the way they do? Well, if the source cannot possibly be found in the environment, we are left with essentially two options: (1) It is all miraculous, due perhaps to divine intervention, or (2) it is genetic (part of the genetic endowment of the individual). Since the first option will instantly be discarded by most (both those who take miracles seriously and those who do not, since neither group takes miracles to occur myriads of times every day), we have only one way out: The answer is to be sought in the genetic endowment. Since the brain is the seat of what defines a human being both as a member of the species and as an individual (a person's identity, of which a first language is an essential part, cannot survive a brain transplant the way it survives a heart or liver transplant), the answer is to be sought specifically in the human brain; more precisely, in whatever it is that distinguishes the human brain from the chimp's brain.

We are, in other words, appealing to the workings of evolution. This is only natural: Newborns have precious little time to develop anything from scratch, be it a capacity for seeing or hearing or a capacity for talking, but they do not need much time to inherit a genetic endowment from their ancestors. It is then reasonable to assume that the language faculty is part of an individual's genetic constitution, that is, of his or her genotype (to put it in the terms of the biologist), and that the phenotype of the mature individual (which may include English and/or Spanish or some other language) is the outcome of the interaction of the genotype with experience. In other words, the inborn language (part of the genotype) is mapped into one or more particular languages (part of the phenotype) in the course of the individual's experience. The question now is: How could the individual's human ancestors have first developed their traits?

2.3. Human nature and nature: A deep parallel between ontogenesis and speciation

It is not unreasonable to assume that the physical basis for language has been shaped in some respects by natural selection, but it is certainly no less true that natural selection cannot explain fundamental aspects of the emergence of the physical basis for the language capacity. The first thing to note is that in the case of the emergence of language in the species (the phylogenesis of language), just as in the case of the development of language in an individual child, the question of nature versus nurture continues to be the first and fundamental one: Is the new organism a product of its environment or is it the outcome of natural processes? Is the emergence of human beings (and perhaps equivalently the emergence of the capacity for language) the haphazard result of enviromental vicissitudes or is it essentially the outcome of physical law?

The problem then is analogous to the one raised in the preceding section, and is open to the same kind of argumentation.[8] The main point to be made is the same: The environment is just too poor and unorganized to provide what is needed. It is not the environment (in particular nutrition, which is certainly necessary) that turns a particular embryo into a butterfly or an elephant, into a chimp or a human. We argued above that if there is nothing in the environment that can supply the structure that accounts in part for the fact that only one interpretation is available for *in which garage did John keep the car?*, our only viable option is to assume that this structure derives in part from language principles of human nature that are "wired in" (part of the brain's "hardware"). Analogously, if there is nothing in the environment that can supply the structure of that part of the human brain that encodes the language principles, our only viable option is to assume that the brain structure in question derives from principles of nature (Spinoza's "Natura sive Deus").

It is easy to see that one crucial difference between the (phylogenetic) development of the species and the (ontogenetic) development of the individual is the length of time involved. If the "Never after Puberty" thesis of chapter 1 is essentially correct, in the case of language the ontogenetic development reaches a mature, steady state in less than ten years (as a first, but perhaps essentially correct, approximation). On the other hand, the development of the human species, though perhaps fairly rapid in evolutionary terms, appears to have reached a steady state only after millions of years of evolution.[9] If so, our emergent species had a far longer span of time to develop human structures than the child has. It makes sense then to shift the burden of development from the child to the species.

From this perspective, the emergence of what we may call the language faculty in traditional terms, or the cognitive structure for language in more recent terms, is not unlike the emergence of the heart or some other physical organ, only more rare in the long course of biological evolution (there are no animals with a language faculty but without a heart, while the reverse is not true). From the perspective of current understanding, the capacity for human language appears to be a by-product of the relative increase in the size and complexity of the brain in the course of the evolution of the species, from living organisms that were neither plants nor animals to the earliest type of fish, from fish to mammal, from mammal to a chimplike creature (possibly with a conceptual capacity quite similar to ours, as we will see in chapter 3, but without language), and from our chimplike ancestors of more than five million years ago to the creatures who first discovered fire 100,000 years ago and to Cro-Magnon humans, who lived some 30,000 years ago and were presumably biologically identical to us. A particularly puzzling thing from this perspective, which in fact poses a problem for the evolutionary biologist, is the variety of languages. If language is genetically programmed at birth, why do we all not speak the same language? (It is true that in a way we do, a topic we take up in chapter 6.)

We may in other words think of the language faculty as a sort of "mental organ" (as Chomsky has been suggesting since the 1970s), or an organ of the mind/brain, that is, a physical organ with mental properties (not necessarily all in one place, as the circulatory system, for example, is not all in one place). In fact, every cognitive faculty may be thought of as a "mental organ." A proposal along these lines can be traced back to about 1800, when it was first made by the Viennese anatomist Franz Joseph Gall, a contemporary of Mozart and Goya. Gall was the first to propose separate mental functions for distinct anatomical parts of the brain and to put his specific proposals to the test.[10] The most relevant in this context is his association of language with the frontal lobe of the brain, a suggestion that turned out to be at least partially true (some of his other suggestions did not fare as well).

It was not until the early 1860s that the French physician Pierre Broca showed to the satisfaction of leading contemporary students of the brain that the area of the left frontal lobe known today as **Broca's area** is specialized for language. His evidence came from patients who could comprehend speech but could not produce it. About ten years later (1874), the German physician Carl Wernicke, studying patients with language disorders differing sharply from those described by Broca (they could not understand speech, but they could produce a type of generally meaningless or incoherent speech with undiminished fluency), discovered that their disturbance correlated with damage to the first convolution of the left temporal lobe (the relevant area, known today as **Wernicke's area**, turned out to be somewhat larger).

Almost a century after the identification of Broca's area, two neurologists working in Montreal succeeded in obtaining considerable information about the diversity of function of different parts of the brain by stimulating specific parts of the cortex with a weak electrical current in the process of treating patients for epilepsy (a disorder characterized by abnormal electrical discharges in the brain).[11] Using this technique on a variety of patients, they were able to map the entire cortex, publishing their findings in 1959. In general, their findings are consistent with those of Broca and Wernicke, except that they discovered that Wernicke's area is larger than originally thought, extending to parts of the left parietal lobe. Interestingly, the two major areas are part of the left hemisphere (now we know that for all right-handers and most left-handers, covering perhaps no less than ninety-eight percent of the population, language is represented in the left hemisphere). They also identified a third major language area of the brain, the **supplementary motor cortex**, also part of the frontal lobe, and ranked the three areas according to the degree of language disfunction that damage to each area could be expected to cause (in descending order of importance, they go from Wernicke's area to the supplementary motor cortex).[12]

One of the most interesting findings to come out of the study of the representation of language in the brain is that the left and right hemispheres are each specialized to carry out separate but complementary functions. This was the result of the availability of two new kinds of evidence beginning in the 1960s: evidence from so-called "dichotic listening" (the feeding of two auditory signals simultaneously through headphones to the right and left ears) and from split-brain patients, which have provided some of the best probes so far on some cognitive aspects of the brain. Since these studies were initiated only in the early 1960s, it is a fair guess that the subfield of brain research concerned with the physical underpinnings of language is still in its infancy.[13] What is important to keep in mind when considering the question of localization of language function is that even if it were to turn out that there are no specific areas of the brain in which language function is localized (which at the moment does not appear to be the most plausible hypothesis), there are surely specific mechanisms involved in the representation of language knowledge and the capacity to use this knowledge, that are perhaps discoverable. In fact, one might argue that "localization is interesting only insofar as it leads to the discovery of specific mechanisms and their organization."[14]

Summing up, to say that the answer to the fundamental question raised in this chapter is to be found in the human brain is of course a way of taking sides in the controversy between the advocates of nature and the advocates of nurture. We are definitely betting on nature. But there are plenty of reasons that favor this option, some of which we are already familiar with. We will find some additional ones in the next two chapters.

NOTES TO CHAPTER 2

1. For an enlightening discussion, and evidence from "exotic" languages, see Dixon 1970.

2. See Plann 1984a.

3. In contrast this is the only one of the two alternatives that is admissible in Tzotzil (a Mayan language) or in ASL (see Padden & Humphries 1988, p. 8). Cf. Strozer 1976, p. 555, note 24.

4. The example is discussed in Chomsky 1989, pp. 103ff. For the difference with Spanish discussed below, see Gunnarson 1993, where it is suggested that directive prepositions may assign an external q-role in Germanic but not in Romance languages.

5. It is well known that before a certain age (roughly, until they are two and a half or somewhat older) children use color words as if to dress up the expression

without regard for their meaning, and then, almost all of a sudden, they begin to use them in their general senses (*red* for red color, *green* for green color, and so on). Interestingly, blind children do exactly the same up to a point—the point at which sighted children begin to apply them accurately to what they see. See Landau & Gleitman 1985. (We return to the topic in the next chapter, section 3.3.2.)

6. For a report on the three adults using the Tadoma method, see Carol Chomsky 1986.

7. On the children with zero input, see Feldman, Goldin-Meadow, & Gleitman 1977, and also Goldin-Meadow, & Feldman 1977 and Goldin-Meadow 1982. Even limited morphological elaboration has been found in children with no external language model. See Goldin-Meadow & Mylander 1990, 1991.

8. For more extensive discussion than is possible here and for some basic references, see Otero 1990a. Cf. Diamond 1992, chapter 2 (to cite only one of the most recent discussions of the topic), where it is suggested that the only "plausible answer" to "why have apes not gone on to develop much more complex natural languages of their own?" is "the anatomical basis for spoken complex language," "the structure of the larynx, tongue, and associated muscles that give us fine control over spoken sounds" (pp. 54, 55). There is little question that this anatomical basis is necessary for *speaking* (a creature incapable of pronouncing the basic vowels *a, i, u*, cannot possibly speak—see Miller 1981, chapter 4), but it is difficult to see the relation between the anatomical basis for speech and, for example, the underlying properties of *John kept the car in the garage* discussed above, which are not required by an efficient system of communication (indeed, they impede communication). It is easy to lose track of the fact that human language is rooted in the human brain, not in the mouth, as the users of sign language testify. This is not to deny that the emergence of the anatomical basis for speech in the course of evolution raises nontrivial questions for the biologist.

9. On the basis of differences in anatomical traits suggested by the sparse and patchy fossil record, paleontologists had surmised that African apes and humans diverged some 20 million to 25 million years ago. Recent analyses of the "molecular trees" led biologists to conclude that the branching off of the chimp lineage from our own lineage may have taken place as late as 5 million to 10 million years ago (*Scientific American*, March 1988, p. 18). Molecular biologists have also speculated that today's human being descends from a single woman who lived in Africa only 200,000 years ago (*Scientific American*, April 1992, pp. 66ff.), that is, 100,000 years before the discovery of fire (92,000-year-old fossils of modern-type *Homo Sapiens* were discovered in Israel in 1988); cf. Diamond 1992, chapter 2. But even 200,000 years is 20,000 times longer than 10 years.

10. Perhaps a measure of his originality was that he was thrown out of Vienna by decree of Emperor Francis I in 1802 and excommunicated by Pius VII in 1817, with his books placed on the Roman Catholic Index. His work began to be appreciated only a century later. See Marshall 1980.

11. It is only now that electrical stimulation is being replaced by "optical imaging," a new technique, pioneered at the University of Washington, that may increase the accuracy and decrease some of the chance involved in electrical stimulation. For a recent report, see *Nature*, August 1992.

12. See Penfield & Roberts 1959, an important early overview of the brain mechanisms subserving knowledge and use of language and a fascinating account of three decades of research on brain stimulation at the Montreal Neurological Institute, where the whole brain was first mapped out (by using direct electrical stimulation of the cortex at the time of surgery). Cf. Lenneberg 1960b.

13. On clinical evidence for brain asymmetries, including evidence derived from the study of individuals who had undergone split-brain surgery, see Springer & Deutch 1989 (on dichotic listening, the technique pioneered by Doreen Kimura, pp. 79–86 and *passim*). Both approaches provided much evidence in support of the claim of so-called cerebral dominance, in particular left-hemisphere dominance for language for most of the population (language is commonly assumed to be represented in the left hemisphere of the brain for all but about two or three percent of the population, a percentage made up of left-handers). Of special interest in this context is Bogen 1975 (the author, a pioneer in bisected brain studies, is a surgeon in Los Angeles, where the field originated).

14. Chomsky 1980a, p. 49.

3

Human nature and culture: Concept labeling

In the opening section of this book we have seen that the results of the most enlightening work on chimps have shown that in the area of human language the similarities between us and our closest nonhuman relatives are slight, as had been traditionally assumed down to our own time. More specifically, "recent work substantiates the familiar view that even the most elementary properties of human language (say, the use of recursive embedding to generate a discrete infinity of sentences) are beyond the capacities of apes."[1] This is to say that the lack of homology between human language and ape symbol systems entails a separate course of evolution, not "discontinuities" in evolution. For evidence of continuity, understood as a common course of evolution to the shared ancestor of chimp and human, we must turn elsewhere.

3.1. Language and thought: Speechless rational animals

In fact, the very work that has substantiated the traditional view about the uniqueness of human language has also brought out striking similarities in other domains. For one thing, we have new evidence that chimps, which should of course be included in the class of thinking creatures, are capable of drawing fairly intricate inferences (some of which exceed the capacities of some subnormal humans). There are in other words "rational animals," though in a limited sense of the term, as we are about to see.

This should come as no surprise to people who reject the common but groundless identification of language and thought (an entrenched traditional idea). To begin with, an essential aspect of thinking is the ability to categorize, that is, to judge whether a particular thing is or is not an instance of a particular category, and animals with much smaller brains than a chimp (or a cat or a rat) are able to categorize; otherwise they would not be capable of performing the discrimination tasks they routinely perform. Thus, in order to reliably press a lever when presented with, say, a square (instead of a circle), an animal must make a judgment about the categorization of the newly presented stimulus.[2] It should also be obvious that to excel along some dimension (as pigeons excel in finding their way home or squirrels in moving around barriers) an animal has to be able to carry out fairly sophisticated thinking.[3]

As for the chimp, David Premack's work has shown that it not only can learn to distinguish simple sequences such as "red on green" versus "green on red," both in comprehension and production (as already mentioned), but it also can "use sequences of wordlike items to describe simple acts such as 'Mary cut apple' and 'Mary wash apple', and interestingly some animals describe their own acts better than they do those of others." What is more important, and more to the point in the context of this chapter, is that "the abstractness of the ape's concepts, its ability to transfer words taught with limited exemplars to indefinitely many other exemplars, is like that of human concepts and unlike that of other species." Apes and humans are in fact "the only species which so far have been taught to make [symbolic] same/different judgements . . . if the test is given a paper [and] pencil format," which "tells us that man and ape are alike in some basic perceptual respects, for both the ape and man can do what the monkey cannot: 'read' a question on one line, and find its answer on a different line." Furthermore, like a human, a chimp "can recognize and judge the relation between an item and an arbitrary representation of an item."[4] And given a pair of objects such as a dry towel and a wet towel, or an entire apple and an apple cut into pieces, a chimp appears to understand that water made the towel wet and an apple can be cut with a knife. Perhaps even more impressive than this understanding of causation is that the chimp is capable of attributing intentions to others.[5]

Considerations such as these suggest both that chimps have much in common with humans and that there is more to what we informally call language than meets the eye. Could it be that what is usually called language results from the interaction of more than one cognitive system (more than one "mental organ")? If the answer is "Yes," it would be very misleading to assume, as is often done, that language is a simple and unitary phenomenon. This is our next topic.

3.2. The conceptual system: A common heritage of apes and humans?

In the first two chapters we came across a number of expressions that exemplify typical language computations. Representative instances are the computations that lead us to understand that in *Mary is eager to please* Mary does the pleasing, while in *Mary is easy to please*, which is superficially parallel in structure, Mary is the pleased one; that in *after she sang, Mary delighted everyone*, with *she* preceding *Mary*, Mary may or may not be the one doing the singing, while in *after Mary sang, she delighted everyone*, with *Mary* preceding *she*, as antecedents of pronouns usually do, Mary cannot be doing the delighting; or that in *the boys wonder who the two girls expected to see them* the last word may stand for the two girls, while this is out of the question in *the two girls expected to see them*, which is identical to the last part of the longer string. Computations such as these appear to involve a system of representations and principles (the main component of the language faculty) that is at the very core of language. It is these principles (what is sometimes called "knowledge of language" in a precise sense—see chapters 5 and 6) that form syntactic constructions and phonetic or semantic patterns of varied sorts, thus providing the rich expressive power of language.

However, this computational system is not the only component of what we call language in everyday talk (speaking or writing and comprehension). If present understanding is not far off the mark, what we informally call language is not a unitary phenomenon, but must be resolved into at least two separate though interacting components. The computational system (in a technical sense, still to be made precise—see chapter 6) is just one such component. A second component involves "the principles that enter into categorization, naming and other cognitive functions," and it is no doubt involved in "many aspects of perception, thought and expression beyond language." Part of this component is the system of object-reference and also such relations as "agent," "instrument," and the like, referred to in chapter 1 (we return to the topic at the end of chapter 4). For want of a better term, Chomsky calls this second cognitive structure a "conceptual system" (or systems). That the two components interact is rather obvious: We can speak about what we think (as we can speak about what we see). Nevertheless, the conceptual system appears to be quite distinct from the language system. It may be, in a sense, more "primitive," in that it is not exclusively human but shared with other species, promoting the erroneous belief that their rudimentary symbolic behavior, perhaps evidence of evolutionary "continuity," that is, of a single course of development as far as conceptualization (or perceptual categorization) goes, "is homologous with human language in some non-trivial sense, a highly unlikely eventuality that receives no support from the actual study of humans and other organisms."[6] It may also have a central role in all sorts of mental acts and processes in which language plays no significant part.

In fact, this conceptual faculty might have an entirely different physical basis from the language faculty, the latter being the result of a different evolutionary history (what is sometimes misleadingly called discontinuity, as if it implied that the chimp's immediate ancestors are not our ancestors).

There is good reason to believe that language had its own evolutionary history, that it developed in the human species "millions of years after the separation from other primates," and that it "was undoubtedly a major factor in human biological success." In particular, it is reasonable to assume that "whatever intellectual capacities evolved in humans in the last million years or so presumably have little to do with any other animal." If so, "there's no reason to believe that whatever faculties apes use to solve language-like problems have any connection with the faculties humans use in human language."[7] This is even more plausible if, as seems likely, language essentially developed within the last half million years, perhaps within the last quarter million years (our early ancestors moved beyond the chimp world in their use and control of fire only some 100,000 years ago, it appears, and the earliest artistic works we know of are five times more recent).

Since the higher apes, in particular the chimps, apparently lack the capacity to develop even the rudiments of the computational structure of human language, and on the other hand appear to share with humans some other capacity, we might speculate that they "may command parts of the conceptual structure" and thus are "capable of elementary forms of symbolic function or symbolic communication." Indirect support for this conclusion is provided by the fact that humans with severe language deficit ("global aphasics"), including cases involving perhaps the literal destruction of the language faculty, can acquire systems similar to those that have been taught to chimps. It is "as if, to put it very loosely, apes were in this regard like humans without the language faculty."[8] In other words, it seems that it is possible for the conceptual system to be intact and functioning even though the computational and representational aspects of the language system in a precise sense are impaired or even destroyed. If so, there is some reason to believe that a divorce between the language system, strictly speaking, and the conceptual systems "may be observed to a degree in certain pathological contexts, though here one must be cautious, as nature's experiments are not well designed for the purposes of inquiry."[9]

These speculations appear to depart sharply from the traditional belief that reason is a distinctly human possession and that the use of language is evidence of possession of reason, as in Descartes's *Gedankenexperiments,* or that *ratio* (reason) is reduced to *oratio* (linguistic expression), as in Schopenhauer's philosophy. Nevertheless, "while the two views are different, they are extensionally similar, insofar as *ratio* devoid of the projective mechanisms of the computational system of human language is severely impaired, almost mute."[10] In other words, the coupling of the conceptual system and the language system make available a range of thoughts (and expressions) that is incomparably richer than the range made available by just the conceptual system, the only one the chimp has. This is why the range of the chimp, or for that matter the range of a representative case of global aphasic, is so much poorer than that of a nonimpaired human.

Another case in point is that of a child, known in the professional literature as "Genie," who was deprived of language experience until after puberty, and under the assumptions of chapter 1 is expected not to develop language in the normal way. This prediction may surprise those familiar with the fact that "Genie" showed a degree of apparent language development after she was rescued from the conditions of deprivation (including isolation) in which she had lived until age 13, and that she went on to attain a considerable degree of comprehension. However, as Chomsky has pointed out, "there is some reason to believe that her knowledge of language does not involve the normal computational system of language, but rather may involve the use of a conceptual system," which we are assuming is quite distinct from "human language" strictly speaking, and older and more "primitive" in evolutionary terms.[11] Another thing to keep in mind is that "Genie"'s subsequent development was due in part to therapy and training, while normal children do not need either in order to develop both a conceptual system and a language system in the early years, which they develop spontaneously.

If the conceptual system is not to be identified with the language system, as the foregoing considerations suggest, it is natural to raise the question of the relationship between the two. We may ask, in other words, where the interface between the two systems is to be found. A good place to begin looking is vocabulary development, as we will see in the next section.

3.3. Increasing vocabularies: Label learning

To clear the way we must first consider the relation between concepts and their names, since a vocabulary item (a word, in one sense) may be seen as a pair: a meaning and the string of sounds that labels it. What is the nature of this relationship?

3.3.1. "A rose by any other name . . . ": Saussurean arbitrariness

We are all familiar with the Shakespearean remark: "A rose by any other name would smell as sweet." The current label for this idea, which can be traced back to Aristotle, is also well known and often used or misused: Saussurean arbitrariness. It is plain that there is no particular reason for the choice of a specific label such as, say, the English word-form *house* or its

Spanish or French counterpart (*casa*, *maison*), which are associated with a relatively uncomplicated concept (though far more complex than it appears to be at first blush, as suggested above and in chapter 1): any other label within a very large class of labels (the class that falls within the sound pattern of the language) would do just as well. In particular, what we call a *house* could be called a "bouse," a "couse," a "douse," and so on, or a "louse" or a "mouse" (and vice versa), though not "rouse" with the initial sound of Italian or Spanish *Roma*, which is not allowed by the English sound pattern.

In this respect appearances can be deceiving. Thus, the word spelled *banana* does not sound the same in English and Spanish, for example. In Spanish the vowel spelled *a* always sounds very much like the vowel in English *cot* (for most American speakers), never like the vowel in *cat* (as the second *a* in English *banana*) or like the *a* in *abut* (as the first and third vowels of English *banana* sound). This is in fact a notorious source of trouble for speakers of languages with lax vowels such as those of *abut* when they try to learn Spanish, since *a* is by far the most frequent Spanish sound, as Spanish writers are well aware (one of the most gifted of them, the Nicaraguan poet Ruben Darío, once wrote a short story as if there were no other vowels in the language, a feat that even Darío would not have been able to perform with any other vowel). It is just not easy for a speaker to use labels that do not conform to their pronunciation. For example, it takes some care for a speaker of American English to pronounce, say, Spanish *hombre* ("man") close enough to rule out the possibility of being understood as saying *hambre* ("hunger"), a very different thing for a native. In a word: English *banana* and Spanish *banana* are quite different labels, the apparent similarity not withstanding, and so are English *rodeo* and Spanish *rodeo* and many such pairs.

But this aside, the labels a language attaches to the concepts the community makes use of are quite arbitrary. For example "tako" means one thing in Mexican Spanish (where it is spelled *taco*) and another thing in Japanese; on the other hand, what the Japanese call *tako* is called *octopus* in English. The differences between languages on this score go well beyond this. We already encountered some illustrations in chapter 1. The reader may remember that *weather*, *time*, and *tense* are all rendered *tiempo* in Spanish. Other examples are not hard to find. Here are a couple, chosen virtually at random: *customs* may be Spanish *costumbres* or *aduanas*, but English distinguishes between a *monkey* and an *ape*, while Spanish does not contrast *mono* and *simio* in a similar way, and French has only one term (*singe*), which again goes to show that languages are lexically nonisomorphic. These idiosyncracies are not without consequences: Spanish speakers cannot *ape* anyone; all they can do is *remedar*. This does not mean that they can *parrot*, even though they have a word for parrot (*loro*, *cotorra*); they can only *repetir* or *imitar como loro*, which is not striking for its concision. On the other hand, English speakers can *gossip* or *gabble*, but they do not consider that *cotorrear* (as their Spanish interlocutors do), nor do they associate a *chatterbox* with a *cotorra* (not hard to do if you speak Spanish).

One more example may be helpful. How does one say *to touch*, *to knock*, *to play* (*the cello*, say), *to sound* (*the trumpets*), *to hit* (*bottom*), *to ring or toll* (*the bells*), *to handle* (as in *do not handle the merchandise*), *to call* (as in *this ship doesn't call at San Francisco*) in Spanish? The answer is easy: *tocar*. However, Saussurean arbitrariness does not end there. Thus, *to touch up* translates as *retocar* in Spanish (not as *"tocar arriba"*), *to play reveille* as *tocar diana*, *to sound the alarm* as *tocar a rebato*, *to sound the call to arms* as *tocar la generala*, *to hit home* as *tocar a uno de cerca*, and *to toll the death knell* as *tocar a muerto*. There is more: *tocárselas* means *to beat it*, *me toca a mí* means *it is my turn*, but *me toca a mí darle la noticia* is the Spanish way of saying *it falls on me to give him the news*, while *ahora toca pagar* is equivalent to *now it is time to pay*, and *les tocaron tres* to *they got three* (or to *they play three for them* or again *three touched them*, depending on what the speaker "has in mind"—in a literal sense).

A question that immediately arises in this context is this: Do humans label every concept they have, or at least commonplace ones? The answer, which may come as something of a surprise, is "No." An examination of some illuminating classes of concepts will prove quite rewarding in this respect.

3.3.2. Numbers and colors versus smells

One of the conclusions of recent studies that is generally taken to be true is that there are no primitive languages. This would follow from the fact (if it is indeed a fact, as is widely assumed) that the computational core of language is genetically programmed, and the program has presumably not changed since the first human speakers appeared on the face of the earth no less than thirty-five thousand years ago (see below). But although there are no primitive languages, there are primitive vocabularies, since vocabulary development is closely associated with cultural development (and not just with biological evolution, as the computational system is), in particular with the advances of science and technology. A perhaps not-unrelated difference between the computational system of language and the noncomputational part of the vocabulary (not all of which is noncomputational) is that the former reaches a mature, steady state by the time of puberty and is no longer open to change, while biology does not prevent the vocabulary from increasing throughout the lifetime of an individual speaker. Furthermore, people can enrich their vocabulary in other ways, as we will see, the reason being that words and their meanings are not impervious to cultural development as the computational system is.

A ready way to find a primitive vocabulary is to look at the numerals (the terms for the number concepts). It is well known that there are languages that lack conventionalized numerals (Walbiri, spoken in Australia, is a case in point). However, when the speakers of these languages are exposed to a culture that makes use of numerals (e.g., a culture with a market economy), they quickly learn to count. This appears to be an indication that they have the concepts of the numbers (a class of concepts beyond even the chimp's reach) still unlabeled.[12]

Another family of concepts, or "semantic field," that is of particular interest in this context, and perhaps even more enlightening because it is at least partially shared by humans and chimps, is that of color terms, which until recently were often assumed (even by philosophers as distinguished as Bertrand Russell) to be particularly simple and learned in isolation by conditioning, ostension, or association. Now it appears that nothing could be further from the truth than Russell's assumption, since "even those afflicted by congenital color blindness know that certain ranges of hue (chroma) band together and are different from other ranges, independent of their brightness and saturation."[13]

It so happens that color vision, which has developed independently in species of fish, birds, and mammals (as G. Walls made clear half a century ago), has been one of the most intensely studied sensory processes, in part perhaps because of its profound aesthetic value. We have also learned a great deal about color terms in the last twenty years or so. Extremely interesting anthropological investigations have shown that color terms have interesting systematic properties and are actually picked up as part of a system of color expressions at a certain stage of maturation (including language development). Thus, as mentioned in chapter 2, before they are two and a half or so, children, sighted or blind, use color words at random, as if to dress up their expressions; then, virtually overnight, sighted children are able to use them all appropriately, moving ahead of blind children, who lack empirical grounding for them (a deficiency that they partially overcome later).[14]

A systematic property of color terms is that humans (like other primates) have to break up the color spectrum in certain ways, although it could of course be broken up in all sorts of different ways by differently endowed creatures, and the relevant chromatic categories are universal. Neurophysiological and psychological research has shown that color perception is organized around three opponent processes, mediated by three independent neural mechanisms, about which a great deal is already known (in sharp contrast with the little that is known about the neural mechanisms underlying language), in particular about the transduction and low-level neural processing of spectral information.[15] One proposal that is particularly suggestive in this context is that the elements of the three perceptual oppositions are the six psychological primary colors, as follows:

> black versus white
> red versus green
> yellow versus blue

In English color terminology the oppositions defined by the three neural mechanisms, from which our color concepts directly spring, are reflected in the fact that although we have color mixtures like blue-green or purple (the latter a mixture about midway between red and blue in hue), there are no such color terms as "whitish-black," "greenish-red," or "bluish-yellow."

Another systematic property of color terms is that they impose structure on the choices, so there is a natural progression of possible color terms. Anthropologists have found that there is a pattern in the colors that are named. It appears that all languages have at least two basic color terms, but some do not have distinct names for all six psychological primary colors. When they do not, we can make some predictions about the color terms a language has, as follows: If a language has only two (as does the language of the Dani, a Stone Age people of New Guinea), the two terms will divide the colors into what we might call dark-cool and light-warm (*mola* and *mili*, respectively, for the Dani). If a language has three basic color terms, they will be the terms for black, white, and red. Languages that have four basic color terms will also have a term for either yellow or green, while languages with five basic color terms will have both. Finally, languages that have six basic color terms will have a term for every one of the six psychological primary colors. Beyond blue, the next basic color term added appears to be brown. Then others may follow (gray, pink, orange, purple).

The progression in the development of basic color terms can therefore be reduced to the following implicational statement:

> black and white < red < green or yellow < blue
> < brown < gray, pink, orange, purple

That is, if a language has a term to the right of a particular instance of <, it will have all the terms to the left of <. What this means is that if people who speak a language L are shown a large color chart and asked to point to the best instances of colors to which the basic color terms in L refer to, they will point to colors that are very close to what English speakers would choose as the best instances of black, white, red, and so on.

Nothing said so far of course implies that people who speak languages with six basic color terms or less are color-blind or organically inferior in any way. They are not.[16] If necessary, they can identify colors for which they have no basic term by using descriptive phrases (e.g., "this is the color of blood") or by using the names of familiar objects having that color, as we sometimes do (the origin of color terms such as "orange," "indigo," and "purple"). The deficiency is not in their visual system or in their conceptual system but in their vocabulary perhaps because, as in the case of numbers without names, the colors without names do not stand out enough in their culture at a particular stage for such a naming convention to develop.

Assuming that if this process is true of human languages today, it was probably true in the past as well, and that basic terms, once introduced, are never dropped from the vocabulary of a language, there would appear to be a fixed sequence of developmental stages through which all natural vocabularies pass as their basic color terms increase, which is a result quite unexpected under the assumptions of behaviorist psychology (including behaviorist linguistics).

What is particularly important to keep in mind here is that vocabulary development does not require organic evolution. If it is true, as is generally assumed, that for at least the last thirty-five thousand years (since the time our Cro-Magnon ancestors roamed around) humans have been gifted with the biological endowment required to attain a modern language (i.e., no further biological evolution was necessary to bring the human brain to its present-day capacity), it is reasonable to assume that Cro-Magnon people already had the concepts for all the psychologically primary colors. (This is the weakest thesis. As suggested above, other primates might also have some of these concepts.) It follows that the children of any living human group have the capacity to become native speakers of any language and to master the everyday vocabulary of any language. In contrast, cultural development, made possible by the biological gifts of humans and humans only (in particular by the coupling of the conceptual system and the language system), can be very different at different stages of civilization, since this development results from the interaction of nature and successive (and sometimes progressive) layers of nurtured understanding accumulated in the course of history.

Another systematic property of human chromatic concepts is subcategorization. Thus, magenta, scarlet, and vermilion are types of red, indigo and turquoise are types of blue, emerald is a type of green, and so on.

Of particular interest in the context of this chapter is that we find an interesting and quite enlightening contrast between colors and smells.[17] It should be obvious that the discriminative capability of some olfactory systems is remarkable. For example, a dog can be taught rapidly to recognize the distinctive odor of a single person. Our olfactory neurosensory cells cannot match those of the dog, but still humans can distinguish between scores, if not thousands, of odoriferous chemicals. Students of wine insist that they can distinguish more than 100 different components of taste in a wine, and to identify a considerable number of wines they do not need to taste them: the fragrance (bouquet) suffices. Moreover, the human olfactory system is extremely sensitive: We can detect the presence of as few as 100 million molecules of an odorant in a room, which is enough to bring back a stream of remembrances of things past even if we are far less gifted than Marcel Proust. This celebrated sort of association is not too surprising: an object "may be remembered in more than one way—as a visual image, as a set of words and their related sounds, or even as a touch or a smell."[18]

All this can only mean that we have every one of the corresponding conceptual categories. Yet, in spite of all this capability of our conceptual system, when it comes to discriminating smells, there is no smell taxonomy comparable to our color taxonomy, even though it has been proposed that there are at least seven primary odors, as there are six psychologically primary colors. The very names of the primary odors proposed shows that we are not dealing with commonsense notions: "camphoraceous," "ethereal," "pungent," "putrid," "musk," "floral," and "peppermint." Furthermore, there is no counterpart to indigo or vermilion in this system. The sharp contrast with color terms may perhaps be related to the fact that smell (like taste) is a phylogenetically primitive sense, since the olfactory system is unique among the sensory systems in that its central connections first project to phylogenetically older portions of the cerebral cortex (paleocortex) before relaying to the neocortex via the thalamus.[19] Whatever the explanation, the fact remains that the language faculty does not readily assign names to smell concepts, and perhaps other concepts as well, which again can only come as a surprise to behaviorists (including naive laypeople unable to go beyond their commonsense understanding).

If we nevertheless are able to speak of a "camphoraceous odor," as we speak of "middle C" in music or "quantum of light" in physics, it might be because the conceptual faculty and the language faculty are not the only faculties of the mind/brain. We appear to have a lot more up there: a musical faculty, a science-forming faculty, a number faculty, and no doubt several more. Failure to keep this family of considerations well in mind can only lead to misunderstandings about the true nature of human language.

3.4. Unlabeled and labeled inborn concepts

The considerations of the preceding section suggest that we have more concepts than concept names, and that the names and terms we have are not learned just haphazardly. It is now time to ask, How do we learn the underlying concepts—or do we? Instead of jumping to conclusions, it may be helpful to ask questions such as the following: Does a kitten learn that it will fall over a cliff if it walks past the edge? Does an infant learn to visually track an object moving along a straight line (or a parabola) even as it passes behind a screen, anticipating its emergence at a particular point? More to the point: Does an infant learn the concepts *1*, *3*, *7* (labeled *one*, *three*, *seven* in English, *uno*, *tres*, *siete* in Spanish, *un*, *trois*, *sept* in French, and so on) or, wonder of wonders (out of reach for every other animal) that after *7* there is another number, and then another, and then another *ad infinitum*? Does anyone learn the meaning of, say, *person*, which raises many questions the philosophers have yet to settle? Does anyone learn that the meaning of the verb *persuade* includes CAUSE TO DECIDE and INTEND? (We return to the topics of the last two questions.)

Surprising as it may seem, there are good reasons to believe that in all these cases the answer is "No." As in the cases considered in chapter 2, the environmental stimulus plays no relevant role. The reason is that the kitten knows that it will fall, the infant that the object will emerge at a particular point, and the language speaker that the meaning of, say, *persuade* includes CAUSE TO DECIDE and INTEND, even without relevant experience. The knowledge involved in all three cases is untaught, unlearned, and not grounded in experience. It is simply furnished by the biological endowment of the organism. Could it be otherwise, given "the poverty of the stimulus"? Hardly. "The rate of vocabulary acquisition is so high at certain stages of life, and the precision and delicacy of the concepts acquired so remarkable, that it seems necessary to conclude that in some manner the conceptual system with which lexical items are connected is already substantially in place."[20]

There is also some experimental evidence bearing on the matter. For example, "the emergence of the earliest numerical abilities does not depend upon the developments of language or complex actions, or upon cultural experience with number," a study of six- to eight-month-old infants concludes, and children as young as seventeen months know that proper names, which identify particular individuals, can be applied to personlike objects (e.g., dolls) but not to inanimate objects such as boxes, although they do not themselves produce linguistic expressions that differentiate proper nouns from common nouns until several months later. Moreover, young children have a concept PERSON, "with the same extension as the adult's," which "plays a central role in even the four-year-old's ontology," and onto which they map the nouns *person* and *people*.[21]

Of course this is not to say that what we might call adventitious aspects of our knowledge (e.g., knowing the word *house* rather than the word *casa* and other idiosyncracies) are not grounded in experience, or that these aspects of our knowledge are not important. Our concern at the moment is just the essential aspects, those that are part of what might be called the human essence. It should perhaps be added here that the fact that our inborn capacities for understanding are rich but meticulously designed is a reason for joy, as has been repeatedly pointed out, since "were it not for these initial constraints, our mature minds would be only a pale reflection of accidental contingency" and we would be "unlike one another, isolated in a meaningless world."[22]

All this may sound far-fetched but if it does, it is simply because some cultural advances of the seventeenth century (unlike the demise of geocentrism) are yet to be assimilated and made part of the mainstream. Meanwhile, those who find it difficult to persuade themselves that there is no other reasonable explanation (short of miraculous intervention of a guardian angel, time after time, until the whole array of concepts is in place) may try to figure out how we manage to derive other human capacities (for example, the capacity to dream) from the environmental stimulus. Or they may try to take a fresh look at the whole thing after reading the next section. At least one thing is clear: We should not hurry to adopt a view just because it is standard. It is certainly not impossible, perhaps not even implausible, that "the notion 'learning' may go the way of the rising and setting of the sun," in which case the term *learning* will turn out to be "analogous to such terms as *witch*, commonly applied at one time but always misapplied."[23]

3.4.1. A parallel with the immune system

Consider now a totally different system, which might shed some light on the issue. What was the early view on the causes of our immunity (our ability to resist a particular disease) and our immune responses to an antigen (by forming antibodies capable of reacting with it and rendering it harmless)? Common sense suggests, and for many years immunologists believed, that formation of antibodies is a sort of "learning process" in which the antigens play an "instructive role." The reason behind this conclusion is that the number of antigens is immense and includes even artificially synthesized substances that did not exist in the world until recently, so no other account seemed conceivable. The idea that our stock of antibodies is actually inborn would not have occurred to any scientist of any standing, at least as a first try.

However, the common sense assumption was eventually and successfully challenged, and many contemporary immunologists consider it to be false. What at first appeared to be an absurd alternative is now given a fighting chance, particularly since one of the most celebrated students of the process, Niels Kaj Jerne, won the Nobel Prize a few years ago for defending an "uncommon sense" conception. As Jerne put it in his Nobel Prize acceptance lecture, "The generative grammar of the immune system," published in *Science* in 1985, an animal "cannot be stimulated to make specific antibodies, unless it has already made antibodies of this specificity before the antigen arrives." In other words, if Jerne is right, as he is generally believed to be, antibody formation is not an instructive process, as common sense would lead us to think, but rather a selective one in which the antigen plays a selective and amplifying role.[24] "Looking back into the history of biology," he had written a few years earlier, "it appears that wherever a phenomenon resembles learning, an instructive theory was first proposed to account for the underlying mechanisms," and "in every case, this was later replaced by a selective theory." He also speculates that some processes of the central nervous system, which for him is analogous to the immune system in relevant respects, might also be selective rather than instructive, so that "perhaps learning is not learning either" in this case (as the sunset is not really the setting of the sun).

Jerne's alternatives are not of course exhaustive, as Chomsky has pointed out. "One can, for example, imagine processes that combine elements of selection and instruction in his sense," hence do not fall within either category, in particular a process in which the mind forms hypotheses according to some principle and "selects among them with reference to evidence and, presumably, other factors."[25]

It is then not in the least unreasonable to suppose that a process of essentially this sort is true of the maturation of our concepts. After all, the number of antibodies we are capable of producing may not be infinite, but the number of concepts we are able to generate is, and our lifetime is far too short for us to learn an astronomical number of things from scratch, let alone an infinite number (the case of human concepts).

3.4.2. Genetically programmed semantic fields

What is in a human concept? As we saw in chapter 1, even a fairly simple word such as *house* has a number of intricate and, crucially, universal properties (shared by all humans) that are not obvious, and in fact may be difficult to discover (some of the most elementary ones were not discovered until the 1990s). For example, it is not immediately obvious that my house is brown just in case its exterior is brown (while my house is not a wooden house if just its exterior is made of wood), or that something was physically moved if my house used to be in Los Angeles and is now in Seattle (while if my home used to be in Los Angeles and is now in Seattle, nothing had to be moved). The same could be said of other nouns such as *person*, on which there is a large philosophical literature, already alluded to, raising innumerable questions, some of them quite exotic (if I am decoded here and recoded in London, am I still the same person?).

If we move on from nouns to verbs such as *kill* or *persuade* things get even more intricate. To know the verb *kill* is to know that it takes one complement, which stands for the recipient of the action (patient), and a subject, which stands for the doer of the action (agent), as in *Mary killed the fly*; to know the verb *persuade* is to know that it takes two complements, one of which is the target of the action (technically, "goal") and the other one a proposition, and that the subject is an agent, as in *Mary persuaded John that he should go to college* or *Mary persuaded John to go to college* or *Mary persuaded John of the importance of going to college*, where the target of the action is *John* and what follows in each case is the proposition (a finite verbal phrase, and infinitival verbal phrase, and a nominal phrase that permits a propositional interpretation, respectively). Furthermore, to understand those expressions is, among other things, to be able to infer some truths of meaning (as opposed to truths of fact), as we will see in the next chapter.

It is easy to see that some words are more basic or elementary than others. The contrast between *give* and *donate* we encountered in chapter 2 is a case in point. But although *give* is more basic than *donate* (a special kind of giving), it is not as basic as *go*. We can paraphrase *give* by saying that the thing given (the technical term for its grammatical role is "theme", as already mentioned) "goes" from the subject to the recipient of the theme (the recipient's role is "goal"), while we cannot paraphrase *go* in terms of *give*. In fact, few verbs are more basic than *go*, as English makes abundantly clear: *enter* is roughly equivalent to *go in*, *exit* is roughly equivalent to *go out*, *continue* is roughly equivalent to *go on*, *accompany* is roughly equivalent to *go with*, *leave* (in one sense) is roughly equivalent to *go away*, and so on and on (*return=go back*, *ascend=go up*, *descend=go down*, *interpose=go between*, *explode=go off*, *traverse=go through*, *sink=go under*, *cross=go across*, *undertake=go about*, *follow=go after*, etc.) In this respect English is a bit unusual in that it does not play with its cards under the table, as Spanish (with no equivalents for the right-hand member of each pair) does.

These and other considerations suggest that the concept the verb of motion *go* labels, which we may refer to as *GO*, is a very basic one. Further investigation has led some students of conceptual structure to the conclusion that *GO* is in fact at the core of one of three important classes of verbs of spatial position (another basic family of concepts or semantic fields), the other two classes being those of *STAY* and *BE* (in the sense of Spanish *estar*, a crucial proviso, which is not very surprising since these two notions involve location).[26] If this is on the right track, we can speak of GO verbs (e.g., *run* in *the dog ran from the house to the church*, where *run* may be roughly paraphrased as *went running*), STAY verbs (e.g., *remain* in *Mother Theresa remained in India*), and BE verbs (e.g., *lie* in *the book lay on the table*).

It is important to note that some of the major conceptual categories involved in these and other expressions are EVENT, STATE, THING, PLACE, and PATH, and that all three classes of sentences (one with a motional verb, the other two with locational verbs) involve an object with a certain property (theme): it does or does not change location (it moves or it stays in place in a particular location). In the first example, this object (*the dog*) travels along a path (further differentiated into an initial point or "source" and a final point or "goal" in the first example), while in the other two examples it (*Mother Theresa, the book*) is in a particular location. Thus GO verbs differ from the other two classes in that they fall under the category of EVENT (things that happen), while STAY and BE verbs fall under the category of STATE. In turn, GO verbs and STAY verbs have an important property in common (not shared by BE verbs): They can occur after the phrase *what happened was*, as in *what happened was that the eagle flew over the cloud* (*fly* being another instance of a GO verb) or *what happened was that the book remained on the shelf*, but not "what happened was that the book lay on the table."

If we now move from the semantic field of spatial position to the semantic field of possession, we discover that the basic notions are still the same. Thus in *Mary gave a collection of books to the library*, an example discussed in chapter 2, the books "go" from giver to givee, while in *the library kept the books* the books "stay" in the library and in *the books belong to the library* the books are ("be" of possession) in the library.

Let us take now another semantic field, what might be called adscription. The basic notions are again the same. For example, in *the metal turned red*, *turn* labels another instance of the concept GO (the metal "goes" from nonred to red), while in *the metal stayed red* we obviously have an instance of "stay" and in *the metal was rusted*, an instance of "be." However, this time what we may call the field modifier is not positional (as in the first set of examples) or possessional (as in the second) but something else, the claim being about a property of the theme, rather than where the theme is or whose it is.[27]

We see then that conceptual structures include basic semantic functions such as [GO (X,P)], [STAY (X,L)], and [BE (X,L)], where X is the theme (the object being moved or located), P is some path along which the theme moves, and L is a location.

Similar cross-field generalizations can be discovered in the notions of causality.[28] Note that *to rust*, as in *the dew will rust the swords*, includes the notion "CAUSE to form rust," as *to kill* includes the notion "CAUSE to die" (or "make dead," for a five-year-old) and *persuade* the notion "CAUSE to intend," a topic to which we will return in the next chapter. Interestingly, it turns out that "the conception of physical force and causation, as well as that of resistance or acquiescence of one object to force applied by another object, finds parallels in such domains as social coercion and resistance and in logical and moral necessity." Apparently even "the most abstract of these domains, that of logical relations, . . . has formal parallels to a very concrete semantic field having to do with pushing objects around in space," a result that "makes a good deal of sense in the context of a theory of meaning as conceptualization."[29]

Just as the domain of spatial concepts is pervaded by notions such as physical object, motion, location, and force, other domains may be expected to reveal a similar underpinning of basic concepts, for example, the domain of social cognition, perhaps a subspecialization of the level of conceptual structure (as voice recognition is specialized within the auditory system and face recognition within the visual system—in fact, the latter is known to be localized in a particular area of the brain with its own developmental course).[30] And just as the fundamental units of spatial cognition are physical objects in space, those of social cognition are persons in social interaction, the notion of a *person* being the fundamental unit of social cognition. It is easy to see that what makes a person a *companion*, a *fellow worker,* or a *boss* is quite different from what makes something a *bird* or a *tree* or *gold*. Even simple words like *request* imply basic elementary notions that serve as abstract components on which a particular culture builds, in this case the notion labeled by *equality*, in contrast with the word *order*, which has been taken to imply inequality.[31] Furthermore, social cognition, like spatial cognition and in sharp contrast with language, is far from exclusively human, since it is also found among other animals, especially among mammals, and not only among primates. This of course does not mean that nonhuman animals are in possession of human concepts such as *modality*, even less that they can correlate deontic notions such as *permission* and *obligation* with logical notions such as *possibility* and *necessity*, respectively.

We have to leave the topic here. Admittedly, the preceding discussion does little more than scratch the surface, but hopefully it will contribute to clarifying some basic ideas (there is still much confusion on these fundamental matters) and to preparing the ground for further discussion in the next chapter. Even this sketch should be enough to make it clear that it is reasonable to distinguish between certain aspects of speaking and understanding—or writing and reading, respectively—and other aspects. It should now be clear that what might be called computational aspects of phrases are a unique and perhaps defining possession of the human brain, while the so-called conceptual aspects of words appear to be shared by humans and chimps over a broad range. If these two strikingly different aspects are not properly understood, there seems to be little chance to understand the nature of human language (in the precise sense of chapter 6). The attempt at clarification initiated here will be continued in the next chapter, which takes up other controversial questions on the meaning and interpretation of words and expressions.

NOTES TO CHAPTER 3

1. Chomsky 1980, p. 261. See also Chomsky 1979 and Limber 1977.

2. "Surveying some recent experimental work, Monod remarks that animals are capable of classifying objects and relations according to abstract categories, specifically geometric categories such as 'triangle' and 'circle'; to some extent experimental work has even identified the neural basis for such work." (Chomsky 1971, p. 13).

3. The following unreferenced quote, which has recently come to my attention, is very much to the point here: "Isn't it remarkable how much we can learn about **animal awareness** when we live with animals and share our home with them? If more dog and cat owners were to observe their **animal companions** more closely, they would realize animals aren't dumb—but we are if we believe they don't have emotions and the power to reason." Dr. Michael W. Fox, Director, Center for Respect of Life and the Environment, Humane Society of the United States, Washington, D.C.

4. David Premack in *The Sciences*, November 1979, p. 8.

5. All this was true at least of Sarah. As mentioned in chapter 1, note 12, Premack was unable to replicate his success with Sarah with subsequent chimpanzees. Similarly, Koehler (see below) found enormous individual differences among the chimpanzees in the colony he studied on Tenerife (Canary Islands). This, however, does not invalidate the point being made.

6. The quotes are from Chomsky 1978. Chomsky goes on to say that "some other systems, for example those involved in perceptual categorization, one would expect to be homologous in part to systems of other primates." In particular, he continues,

There seems little reason to suppose that the capacity to think, to judge, etc.—perhaps even to attribute mental states, if one accepts David Premack's (Premack

& Woodruff 1978) interpretation of some of his interesting recent work—are uniquely human attributes. "Reason" in the traditional sense need not be an undifferentiated, let alone universal instrument. Rather it can be decomposed into various systems and capacities, each with their specific form, scope and limits. Recall the discussion in chapter 1.

7. Chomsky in *The Sciences*, November 1979, p. 8.

8. The three partial quotes in this paragraph are from Chomsky 1980, p. 57; for some studies of global aphasics, see note 15 on his page 265; for a general introduction, see Caplan 1987. Recall the discussion in chapter 1, in particular the quote from Premack.

9. Chomsky 1978. See now Damasio & Damasio 1992 for other evidence. They claim that lesions "in the anterior and middle regions of both temporal lobes impair the brain's conceptual system," while "injuries to the left hemisphere in the vicinity of the sylvian fissure, in contrast, interfere with the proper formation of words and sentences" regardless of sensory channel (i.e., including sign-language aphasia), and that "between the brain's concept-processing systems and those that generate words and sentences, . . . causing appropriately correlated word-forms and syntactic structures to be generated," lie "mediation systems" that "not only select the correct words to express a particular concept, but also direct the generation of sentence structures that express relations among concepts." These mediation systems "are confined to specific regions. . . . Indeed, the neural structures that mediate between concepts and word-forms appear to be graded from back to front along the occipotemporal axis of the brain. Mediation of many general concepts seems to occur at the rear, in the most posterior left temporal regions; mediation for the most specific concepts takes place at the front, near the left temporal lobe." (p. 92, 91, 93, 94)

10. Chomsky 1980, p. 58. As he had written one year earlier, "linked to the human language faculty, the ability to reason, judge, and think becomes an instrument of marvelous range and power; decoupled from the human language faculty with its mechanisms of recursive generation, it is highly restricted, virtually mute" (Chomsky 1979).

11. Chomsky 1980, p. 57. Cf. Curtiss 1977 and her subsequent publications.

12. "The very essence of the number system is the concept of adding one indefinitely," so "one should not be misled by the fact that some birds, for example, can be taught to pick n elements from an array for a small n—about up to seven." (Chomsky 1980:38).

13. Damasio & Damasio 1992:90. They go on to say that the cortical regions that "participate in color processing [see below] fabricate what we know as the experience of color." See also Zeki 1992, where it is emphasized that the brain cannot "merely analyze the images presented by the retina; it must actively construct a visual world," that is, "fabricate" or "invent" the world that we see.

14. As we have seen in chapter 2 (see in particular note 3), blind children attain linguistic "milestones" for both syntax and words (even those words that have to do with visual experience) at the same age as the sighted. See Landau & Gleitman 1985.

15. See Kandel & Schwartz, eds., 1985, and for a more recent and far more technical discussion, Rubin & Richards 1987.

16. Damasio & Damasio 1992, who claim that "the temporal segment of the left lingual gyrus supports mediation between color concepts and color names" (p. 94); refer to the classic work of Brent Berlin and Eleanor H. Rosch, which showed in the late 1960s that "color concepts are fairly universal and develop whether or not a given culture actually has names to denote them" (p. 90).

17. The point, further elaborated here, is made in different contexts (literary theory and theoretical and applied semantics, respectively) in Otero 1980a and Otero 1987a.

18. Crick & Koch 1992, p. 154.

19. See Kandel & Schwartz, eds., 1985, in particular pp. 409 and 423. Damasio and Damasio "believe the brain processes language by means of three interacting sets of structures," the first being "a large collection of neural systems in both the right and the left cerebral hemispheres [that] represents nonlanguage interactions between the body and its environment, as mediated by varied sensory and motor systems" (1992:89).

20. Chomsky 1980, p. 139. Cf. Carey 1985, 1988.

21. On "numerical abstraction by infants," see Starkey, Spelke, and Gelman 1990, from which the first quote is taken; on knowledge of proper names, Katz, Baker, and Macnamara 1974; on knowledge of PERSON, Carey 1985:183. Carey concludes also (p. 194) that, "contrary to Piaget's claims, . . . infants seem to appreciate mechanical causality." Even if there is revision and restructuring of conceptual schemes, "care must be taken to separate out the various factors that enter into the course of development, including, quite possibly, genetically-determined maturation that yields effects perceived only in late stages of cognitive growth" (Chomsky 1988a).

22. The quote is from Chomsky 1978. See Chomsky 1976 for further discussion.

23. Chomsky 1980:139, 138. We return to the topic in the next chapter.

24. Another example Jerne cites is the well-known case of a factory wall covered with brown moths, later found to be covered with white moths after it is painted white, for which Darwinian theory offers a selective account (moths of lighter color were already present before the new signal arrived). "In this case," Jerne points out, "the signal that entered into the system, i.e., the color change, was not even received by the moths, but by the birds" that fed on them.

As we can see, Jerne distinguishes between instructive and selective theories in biology. In the first type of theory a signal from the outside imparts its character to the system that receives it, while in the second type the system changes when some already present character is identified and amplified by the intruding stimulus.

25. See Chomsky 1980:136–9, 1988a, and for more extensive discussion, Piattelli-Palmarini 1986, 1988.

26. The reference is to research best represented by the work of Ray Jackendoff, which I follow closely in this paragraph and the next. For a lucid summary of some of these ideas in more technical terms, see Jakendoff 1987, in particular 8.5, and for extended discussion, Jackendoff 1990, "one of the few works . . . that do for lexical semantics what is more frequently done for syntax—develop an adequate formalism for the description of semantic phenomena and refine it to increase explanatory power" (Ravin 1992, a review of the more recent book from a perspective somewhat different from the one adopted in this book). It has been claimed that "aspects of neural representation bear a strong resemblance to the primitives of conceptual structure proposed by Ray Jackendoff of Brandeis University and the cognitive schemas hypothesized by George P. Lakoff of the University of California at Berkeley, both working from purely linguistic grounds" (Damasio & Damasio 1992:91).

27. For Jackendoff, *loc. cit.*, the third field modifier is "identificational," but this does not seem the most appropriate term, as the Spanish counterparts of his examples (in contrast with sentences with *ser*, which translates some uses of *be*) make clear.

28. They are "developed in splendid detail" (Jackendoff 1987:157) in Talmy 1985.

29. Jackendoff 1987, p. 157.

30. There is some evidence (Sacks 1985) that individuals suffering brain damage in the area of the brain involved in face recognition do not necessarily lose general-purpose spatial cognition even when they are incapable of recognizing faces (even their own). On the questions of localization and development, see Carey 1979, Carey & Diamond 1980.

31. See Jackendoff 1991. Cf. Chomsky 1976 and Otero 1984, III.4, in particular pp. 182–83 (including note 168).

4

Semantic primitives > separates language from thought (handwritten annotation)

Culture and language:
Civilization and its progress

The main purpose of chapter 3 was to try to show that it is reasonable to distinguish between certain aspects of speaking and understanding—or writing and reading, respectively—and other aspects. Following a long and not insignificant tradition, it was argued there that what we called the computational aspects of phrases are a unique and perhaps defining possession of the human brain, while the so-called conceptual aspects of words appear to be shared by humans and chimps over a broad range.

Our next step is to try to see that much of what we think of as the semantics of natural "language" is more properly understood in terms of the structure of the conceptual system, which, if the hypothesized split is a real one, is not strictly speaking part of human language, though of course it interacts with the language faculty when we speak (or write) or understand what we read (or are told). In the process it will hopefully become clear that many of the confusions often found in discussions of language and literature, including some by widely admired practitioners, often result from rather gross misunderstanding, hence they should not be very difficult to overcome even for beginners, once the questions are considered from the proper perspective. The chapter closes with some remarks on the nature of the interface between the conceptual systems and the language system.

4.1. Knowing and doing: Diverging humanities and postmodern humanists

The first pitfall to be avoided has to do with a conceptual distinction that was already clear for Aristotle but is often lost track of even today, surprising as it may seem[1]—surprising because it involves little difficulty. Consider first a simple example: One can know the multiplication table perfectly well and still make mistakes when one tries to carry out a simple computation, say, 987×789, let alone a less simple one, say, $9898989898 \times 9988998899$. Perfect knowledge of the rules does not guarantee flawless computations. It would then be wrong to say that a person who cannot multiply without making mistakes does not know the rules of multiplication perfectly well or that the result of a particular computation shows that it is allowed by the multiplication rules. If the result can be shown to be wrong, the reasonable thing to conclude is that the rules were not properly put to use, which does not mean that the person who obtained the flawed result does not know the rules of multiplication. The fact that a person is in possession of some knowledge, to put it in Aristotelian terms, does not entail that he or she can always make perfect use of it, or that he or she can use it as effectively as any other person who has exactly the same knowledge. It is no secret that "two individuals may have the same overall intelligence but have varying patterns of ability," that people have different strengths. For example, "some are especially good with words, others at using objects—for instance, at constructing or fixing things."[2] In fact, exactly the same knowledge can be put to better or worse use by a particular person on different occasions. We all have days in which we are less lucid than usual.

Linguistic computations are not unlike arithmetical ones in this respect. No one is too surprised by a run-of-the-mill slip of the tongue, even though some may be amusing or perhaps revealing (the "Freudian" ones). Nor do we have to go to the comics page to find something like "herrible" for *horrible* (with a push from *terrible*), "they soil the till" for *they till the soil*, "bridge of the neck" for *bridge of the nose*, and so on. We all make slips of one sort or another, going sometimes well beyond the ground covered by this tiny sample. That is why some linguists, following in the footsteps of Aristotle, are careful to distinguish between the system of linguistic *knowledge* (somewhat misleadingly referred to as *competence*, a cognitive construct not to be lightly identified with Saussure's *langue*, rooted in social convention) and the actual use of this knowledge (*linguistic performance*, corresponding to Saussure's *parole*). Another word for perfomance is "art" in a traditional sense, as when "grammar" is defined as the art of speaking or is referred to as a "liberal art," that is, one of the humanities. When the creative use of knowledge produces works of aesthetic value we move from mere "art" in the old sense to "fine art." The central idea behind both performance and art in the relevant sense is the idea of execution (occasionally involving unusual powers of imagination, as in the fine arts), not just knowledge.

The distinction between knowledge and use of knowledge (performance) is as simple and elementary as it is crucial. If kept firmly in mind, it alone can spare us from fatal mistakes, some of which are unfortunately common not only among laypeople but also among professional students of language in a variety of fields ranging from literary study to philosophy and "artificial intelligence."

In this respect, the influence, still pervasive, of the much-admired Austrian philosopher Ludwig Wittgenstein (1889–1951), who pointed the way in attempting to overcome many common errors, has not helped. Among Wittgensteinians it is still not uncommon to identify knowledge of a language with ability to use the language.[3] To see how questionable this lack of discrimination is, consider the case of Jones, a monolingual speaker of English temporarily deprived of the use of English by a stroke. Suppose that Jones completely loses the ability to use the language (he cannot say a word and he cannot understand a thing) for a considerable period of time and that during this period he has no linguistic experience whatsoever. Suppose further that eventually the effects of the stroke begin to recede and are successfully overcome, and he ends up recovering his ability to speak English. The question now is: Did Jones have knowledge of English during the period he was under the effects of the stroke and could not speak a word or understand a thing? It is hardly in doubt that the answer has to be "Yes," otherwise we are faced with a mystery: How come he came out speaking English, not Spanish, even though he had no linguistic experience whatsoever during the intervening period? (A monolingual Spanish speaker would presumably come out speaking Spanish, not English.)

It is for reasons such as these that it is necessary to distinguish sharply between knowledge of language and use of language (it is possible to have knowledge of a language and lack the ability to use it). It is also extremely important. Failure to make the distinction preempts the possibility of making sense of even the most elementary facts about language and its use (including, of course, literary use, a literary work being the outcome of a very special kind of language use).

More generally, the distinction between a system of knowledge and the use of that knowledge system throws light on other distinctions. For example, it is a key to the split between the sciences and the humanities and its future, a split that was already going strong at the time of Galileo, the first scientist in the modern sense. From the vantage point of the distinction between knowledge and use of knowledge, the different humanities can be divided into those that are concerned with systems of knowledge (cognitive structures), which can be approached as potential natural sciences (specifically, cognitive sciences, the most advanced of which appears to be linguistics), and those that are concerned with the use those systems are put to (the "applications" of those systems).

The future of the humanities concerned with systems of knowledge is of course linked to the future of the cognitive sciences, which have already claimed some of the territory of the humanities and may still claim more of it (including parts of literary theory, at least in principle, as they include music theory, in particular the generative grammar of tonal music).[4] On the other hand, it would appear that the humanities understood as "applied" disciplines—that is, as disciplines that study the use of systems of knowledge, in particular language use and its products (for example, the criticism and analysis of literary masterpieces, among other products of linguistic performance)—are much less easy to take over. Since the use of language, like performance in general, involves the human will, specifically freedom of choice in the use of language, it becomes plain that there is no chance that the "applied" humanities will fall under the range of the sciences until we leap (if we ever do) from today's cognitive sciences to what might be called the "volitive sciences" of the future, which for Descartes were definitely beyond the reach of the human mind, and for Chomsky may very well be. One of the immediate consequences of this conjecture, of course, hits close to home: If it turns out that, as Descartes surmised, we do not have brains enough to understand what today can only be described as mysteries of the human will, "literature will forever give far deeper insight into what is sometimes called 'the full human person' than any mode of scientific inquiry can hope to do" (as Chomsky writes in *Rules and Representations*), a perhaps not discomforting thought for some of us. An observation of the "curious character" and celebrated Nobel Prize-winning physicist Richard Feynman, who described himself as always having been "very one-sided about science," may help to complete the picture. He had an artist friend who claimed that, as an artist, he could see "how beautiful a flower is," but Feynman, as a scientist, took it "all apart" and the flower became "dull." Feynman's reply was that the beauty that an artist sees in a flower is available to other people, including him (even if he was not as refined aesthetically as his friend was), but at the same time he could see much more in the flower than his friend could see, since for a scientist like Feynman, who could "imagine the cells inside, which also have a beauty," "there's beauty not just at the dimension of one centimeter; there's also beauty at a smaller dimension." There are also "all kinds of interesting questions that come from a knowledge of science, which only adds to the excitement and mystery and awe of a flower." "It only adds," he concluded; "I don't understand how it subtracts" (1988:11). We return to the topic in chapter 9.

But even if this conjecture turns out to be wrong, we can be sure that the scope of the human mind, like the scope of any other cognitive structure, is not unlimited. It follows that each of the systems of knowledge the human mind is capable of constructing is also limited—which is not to say that there are finite limits on human progress (the set of prime numbers is infinite but does not contain any nonprime). If so, as mathematics and the sciences press on toward the limits of cognitive capacity, we may find "various forms of intellectual play, and significant differentiation among individuals who vary little within the domain of cognitive capacity," but may vary greatly in their performance, in particular in their creative achievements (in the way they put their capacity to use). This suggests a new approach to the "crisis of modernism" or "postmodernism" (which is sure to come, if it is not already here), but the topic would take us too far afield.[5]

From the perspective of this section, the topics that follow might appear in a new light, as seems desirable, and we will hopefully succeed in avoiding the worst snares.

4.2. Interpretation and translation: Not just indeterminacy

Let us begin with the indeterminacy of meaning, one of the most persistent themes of the 1980s. As everyone would agree, one's interpretation of an utterance or a text depends on all sorts of things supplied by history (including the current cultural environment, of which the interpreter is of course a part). The reason is that it seems doubtful that one can separate semantic representation from beliefs or knowledge about the world, as Wittgenstein, Quine, and Chomsky (and Leibniz before them) emphasize. For example, to interpret *they shall not pass* one needs to know who those are who are hiding behind *they*, to interpret *it is in our interest* one needs to know who is behind *we*, to interpret *those who cannot remember the Third Reich are condemned to repeat it* one needs to have the relevant information about the Third Reich, to interpret *tilting at windmills is easier than taking the bull by the horns* one needs to have the relevant information about Spanish culture, among other things, and to interpret *life is but a walking shadow, a poor player . . .* one has to know far more than a six-year-old. The list could go on and on, inexhaustibly.

Less generally, an expression such as *yesterday was a disaster*, for example, does not say anything about lecturing or about playing tennis or about the days of the week—in its literal interpretation. But suppose that my friend says that to me when we come across each other in the hall, and I know that she lectures on Monday, Wednesday, and Friday and plays tennis on Tuesday and Thursday. Although the words say only what they say, if I hear the expression on Friday, I understand that my friend is trying to tell me that her tennis game on Thursday was nothing to rave about; on the other hand, if she tells me exactly the same thing on Tuesday, I understand that her lecture on Monday was not too inspiring.

All this is obvious enough. What is less obvious is why this long-known and not very startling idea came to occupy center stage during the Reagan years. This, however, is not our topic here. The purpose of this section is a more modest one. It is just to try to throw some light on a few questions hidden behind the well-known assumption and on some related misconceptions that often lead to untold confusion.

4.2.1. Semantic connections: Truths of meaning

The most obvious antecedent of the so-called thesis of indeterminacy of interpretation (translation or paraphrase) in the recent philosophical literature is no doubt W. V. Quine's "almost infamous doctrine of the *indeterminacy of translation.*"[6] Some would say it could not have a more reputable antecedent. Twenty years ago Quine was described as "the most distinguished living systematic philosopher," and there is no denying that he has made many important contributions to the study of logic and philosophy, some of which have considerably influenced the study of language, notably, the development of generative grammar.[7]

Other Quinian doctrines may or may not be less close to being infamous, but they are certainly far more controversial. Among other things, Quine has "urged" that "there is no place in science for ideas", that "there is no place in the theory of knowledge for knowledge," and that "there is no place in the theory of meaning for meanings, commonly so called." Like "John Dewey and in later years Ludwig Wittgenstein," Quine "[stresses] that there is no more to the meaning of an expression than the overt use that we make of that expression." In his view,

> Uncritical semantics is the myth of the museum in which the exhibits are meanings and the words are labels. To switch languages is to change labels. . . . Semantics is vitiated by a pernicious mentalism as long as we regard a man's semantics as somehow determinate in his mind beyond what might be implicit in his dispositions to overt behavior.[8]

Furthermore, for Quine "conceptualization to any significant extent is inseparable from language" and "language is a social art."[9]

It is plain that this view is inconsistent with the view outlined in the preceding chapter. There are several reasons for this discrepancy. One stems from Quine's failure to distinguish language as knowledge from the art of putting our knowledge of language to use (for example, in communication), in particular from the "social art" that he takes language to be. Another is a consequence of his failure to separate the language system from the conceptual system. A third derives from his position on the question of nature or nurture.[10]

As is well known, Quine is an avowed empiricist, albeit an "enlightened" one. The reason he thinks of his doctrine as differing substantially from what he calls the "old" one is his rejection of "two dogmas of empiricism," the title of one of his papers, which has had a considerable impact. One of these "dogmas," he believes, is "a belief in some fundamental cleavage between truths which are *analytic*, or grounded in meanings independently of matters of fact, and truths that are *synthetic*, or grounded on fact," as he writes in the opening of his celebrated paper. It is to this "dogma," the so-called analytic-synthetic distinction, that we now turn.

As Quine points out in his much-hailed paper (reprinted in his 1953 book *From a Logical Point of View*), the analytic-synthetic distinction that he rejects, usually associated with Kant, can be traced back to Leibniz's truths-of-reason/truth-of-facts dichotomy. Quine is not satisfied with any of the earlier dichotomies, but he extracts from them what he takes to be an intuitive criterion of analyticity: "a statement is analytic when it is true by virtue of meanings and independently of fact." A statement that was often assumed to meet this criterion is this:

(1) No unmarried man is married.

Quine argues that statements of this general form are in general logical truths, a logical truth being "a statement which is true and remains true under all the reinterpretations of the logical particles, . . . if we suppose a prior inventory of *logical* particles, comprising 'no', 'un-', 'not', 'if', 'then', 'and', etc." In others words, (1) is equivalent to "No nonmarried man is married," "A nonmarried man is not married," and "A man who is not married is not married," which are tautological. The theory of logical truth is then sufficient to explain the analyticity of this class of statements.

Another type of statement that also meets Quine's criterion of analyticity is (2):

(2) No bachelor is married.

He argues that statements of this general form can be turned into logical truths by substituting synonyms for synonyms. In the case of (2), the substitution of "unmarried man" for "bachelor" yields (1). But we are not exactly back where we started, because we have had to lean on a notion of synonymy, which for Quine "is no less in need of clarification than analyticity itself."

This may all be right, but it does not seem to go very far. There appears to be more to language than meets Quine's eye and the eye of those persuaded by his attack on the analytic-synthetic distinction. Consider, for example, an expression such as *the man who is a bachelor is a bachelor*. This is a truth of meaning (an analytic truth). One does not have to check the facts in order to conclude that it is true that the man who is a bachelor is a bachelor, in contrast with, say, *the man who is a bachelor is tall*. When we move from relative constructions to causative construction we again find truths of meaning, as in *the man who is a bachelor made his son copy the letter by hand*. If his son did not copy the letter by hand, then the man did not make his son copy it. Other constructions that induce cases of the analytic-synthetic distinction, as a matter of empirical fact, are those involving referential dependence, for example *Mary expects to defend herself*, discussed in chapter 1. Thus, "Mary expects to defend herself, so Mary expects to defend Mary" is a truth of meaning (with the three occurrences of Mary taken to be coreferential), while "Mary wonders who Mary expects to defend herself, so Mary wonders who Mary expects to defend Mary" is not a truth of meaning (under the same interpretation).

If we now turn from constructions with the syntactic-semantic properties illustrated above to concepts with an inherent relational structure such as some of the examples of the preceding chapter (which we promised to reconsider later in a new light), we obtain similar results. We may begin with *Mary killed the fly*. It is clear that there is a qualitative distinction between "Mary killed the fly, so the fly is dead" and "Mary killed the fly, so Mary is dead." If it is true that Mary killed the fly, it has to be true that the fly is dead, otherwise Mary didn't kill the fly. However, to ascertain whether Mary is or is not dead, one needs to check the facts. We conclude then that the first expression in quotes states a truth of meaning (an analytic truth), while in the second expression (a non-sequitur as a whole) "Mary is dead" states a truth of fact only if it is the case that Mary is dead, something we have to find out.

Similarly with the expresion *Mary persuaded John to go to college*. To persuade John to go to college is to cause him to decide or intend to do it; if he never decides or intends to do it, we have not succeeded in persuading him. Therefore, "If Mary persuaded John to go to college, John decided or intended to go to college" is again a truth of meaning (an analytical truth).

Given the existence of cases such as those just reviewed, we can only conclude that there is a rather clear distinction between truths of meaning and truths of fact. If so, the contention that one can make no principled distinction between questions of fact and questions of meaning (often taken to be one of the central conclusions of modern philosophy), which is supposed to have been established by work of Quine and others, appears to be rather dubious. It is just an artifact of the artificially narrow class of examples considered and the limited or nonexistent relational structure of the concepts involved in the examples chosen by Quine and others.

The question of analyticity is, however, just a special case. The more general question at issue is whether or not there are connections of meaning among words. Here again there appears to be something of a split between philosophers and linguists. Quine and other philosophers of his persuasion assume (again without engaging in sustained empirical investigation of language structure) that the answer is "No." In contrast, the linguists who study lexical semantics typically assume that the answer is "Yes" and proceed to offer empirical evidence in support of their assumption. As an illustration, consider the words *follow* and *chase* (*seguir* and *perseguir*—cf. *persecute*—respectively, in Spanish). There is an obvious systematic relation between the corresponding underlying concepts, which in Spanish happens to be reflected morphologically. (The etymological sense of the prefix *per* of *per-seguir* or, e.g., *per-durable*, is 'through(out), thoroughly'; cf. *perforate*, *permeate*, *persuade*, . . .). Like *persuade*, *chase* clearly involves a reference to human intention. If I say *Mary chased John*, I am not just saying that Mary followed John, but that Mary followed John with the intent of staying on his path, perhaps to catch him.

Facts of this nature, incidentally, lend themselves to various uses. Since to be persuaded John must decide or intend to go to college by his own volition, not under duress, if we say that the police persuaded John to confess by torture, we are using the term ironically.

So we see that the same notions (CAUSE, INTEND) turn up again and again (*to close the door* or *cerrar la puerta* in Spanish or *fermer la porte* in French, and so on, is to cause the door to be closed, *to break the glass* is to cause the glass to be broken, *to divide into classes* is to cause to be separated into classes, *to blacken the wall* is to cause the wall to become black, *to melt the ice* is to cause the ice to become water, *to raise the rent* is to cause the rent to rise, *a splitting headache* is one that causes a piercing sensation, etc.[11] Since these facts are known essentially without evidence and since the same notions are found to underlie other languages, they must be unlearned, as argued in chapter 3. It must be that "the child approaches language with an intuitive understanding of concepts involving intending, causation, goal of action, event, and so on, and places the words that are heard in a nexus that is permitted by the principles of universal grammar, which provide the framework for thought and language, and are common to human languages as systems that enter into various aspects of human life."[12]

But even if it were to turn out that this conclusion leaves something to be desired, it seems to make far more sense, at least at the present stage of our understanding, than the seemingly groundless suggestion that lexical semantics is not determinate in the human mind "beyond what might be implicit in [one's] dispositions to overt behavior" for the simple reason that "there is no place in the theory of meaning for meanings" (in the view of the philosopher, quite at odds here with the view of the linguist). Furthermore, since the child or adult who knows the word *persuade*, say, knows that its meaning includes at the very least CAUSE TO DECIDE and INTEND, we must conclude, at least for the time being, that not all aspects of meaning are indeterminate, as some philosophers and literary critics would have us believe. We return to the topic in the last section.

The philosophers and literary critics are, however, right when they claim that universal semantics does not provide an exact representation of the full meaning of each word and the meaning of expressions in which the words appear. The main reason for being skeptical about a claim to the contrary is that a careful examination of concepts shows that they involve beliefs about the world and about lawful behavior of objects (as Wittgenstein and Quine, among others, have emphasized). As Chomsky put it, following, as already mentioned, in the footsteps of Wittgenstein and Quine (and Leibniz before them), "much of what is often regarded as central to the study of meaning cannot be dissociated from systems of belief in any natural way."[13] In this sense meaning is indeed indeterminate, even if (crucially) aspects of it are not, as we have just seen.

4.2.2. New words and enriched notions (with an excursus on Newspeak)

It is a well-known fact that at peak periods of language development, children are picking up many words a day, perhaps a dozen or more.[14] This means that they are picking up words on very few exposures, even just one. There may be revision and restructuring of the integrated "conceptual scheme" (a component of the initial state of the language faculty that is fleshed out in specific ways in the course of language maturation, one aspect of cognitive development), but "care must be taken to separate out the various factors that enter into the course of development, including, quite possibly, genetically-determined maturation that yields effects perceived only in late stages of cognitive growth."[15] The fact that few exposures are needed seems in turn to indicate that the concepts are already available, with much or all of their intricacy and structure predetermined, and that the child's task is to assign labels to concepts (as suggested in chapter 3), contrary to what is usually assumed (in particular by Quine, as discussed in the preceding section).

The alternative views are not very persuasive. Practitioners of descriptive semantics report that it is a very difficult matter to describe the meaning of a word, which typically has great intricacy and involves the most remarkable assumptions (as we have seen in our discussion of *house* in chapters 1 and 3). This appears to be true even in the case of very simple concepts, such as what counts as a nameable thing. Spatiotemporal continuity is no doubt a possible factor, according to Bertrand Russell, "as are certain figure-ground and other gestalt properties, or the function of an object in a space of human action." For example, "if some physical arrangement of objects is created by an artist as an example of a particular art form," say, a Calder mobile (a scattered entity that need not meet the condition of spatial continuity), it is a nameable "thing," while a collection of leaves on a tree or the single object consisting of an animal's four legs are not nameable things (there is no word that designates either in any language, as far as we know). It is then reasonable to assume that there are universal formal constraints that severely limit the class of possible words, since certain combinations of elementary semantic predicates do not seem to be lexicalizable in any natural language.

How does a child attain knowledge of these and many other things he knows about words? Something to keep in mind is that it is extremely difficult to define even the simplest words, as already mentioned. The dictionaries give just mere hints, which would be of little use for someone who has not already attained highly articulated knowledge of language and the world. Even the strenuous attempts to define ordinary concepts such as GAME or PROMISE by distinguished philosophers have been only partially successful.

Another important thing to remember is that there is no way of accounting for the uniformity and specificity with which a child or an adult will understand what a word means or denotes under the assumption that it is learned by ostensive definition or by some other type of experience, something that "will become quite obvious to anyone who attempts, say, to program a computer to do likewise," Chomsky notes. The fact is that under normal conditions a child attains knowledge of a word by limited exposure to its use—on very few exposures, even just one, as suggested at the beginning of this section—and that "brief and personal and limited contact with the world" (to echo a memorable passage from Russell's *Human Knowledge*) suffices for the child to determine what the word means. This is all the more remarkable because when we try to analyze any specific instance, say, such readily attainable words as *die*, *try*, *expect*, *compare*—or even common nouns—"we find that rather rich assumptions about the world of fact and the interconnections of concepts come into play in placing the item properly in the system of language." No doubt experience is necessary to activate the inborn system of concepts and also to account for "such differences as exist among individuals and across languages in the systems of concepts employed," but the complexity and specificity of what the child comes to know "as compared with the poverty of experience leads one to suspect that it is at best misleading to claim that words that I understand derive their meaning from my experience."[16]

Since even the meaning of most common words is very complicated (it is extremely difficult to define a word like "table" or "book," and even more so a word like "climb") and we know that every child figures out the meaning of a word with only a very small number of presentations of the sound, we are driven to conclude that human nature gives us the concepts for free.[17] All we have to learn is "the label that goes with the preexisting concept." As Chomsky puts it,

> It is as if the child, prior to any experience, has a long list of concepts . . . , and then the child is looking at the world to figure out which sound goes with the concept. . . .
>
> However surprising the conclusion may be that nature has provided us with an innate stock of concepts, and that the child's task is to discover their labels, the empirical facts appear to leave open few other possibilities. Other possibilities (say, in terms of "generalized learning mechanisms") have yet to be coherently formulated, and if some day they are, it may well be that the apparent issue will dissolve.

As he remarks, "That is probably true for most concepts that have words for them in language. . . . It surely appears to be the case for the terms of ordinary discourse," and "The same is often true of technical terms of science and mathematics."[18]

It is of particular interest in the context of this book that the process of picking up words is open ended, in contrast with the maturation of the computational system, which reaches a steady state around the time of puberty, a state presumably immune to further change. The vocabulary of a speaker is most unsteady. Those in possession of knowledge of at least one computational system can go on picking up labels for concepts to the end of their lives. It is always possible to pick up one more label. Moreover, the choice of labels open to them is not as fully determined by the biological endowment as the choice of the computational system is. The latter choice is of course not independent of historical factors (the form of the language spoken in the community at a particular time is the only one available to the child), but it can be only trivially influenced by cultural factors. In contrast, the choice of the vocabulary is dramatically influenced by the particular stage of cultural development available to the speaker. It was not so long ago that people started *parenting*, *wordprocessing*, or doing *brain mapping*, let alone *optical imaging* (an event still rare outside the campus of the University of Washington). And less than three thousand years ago no language had a label for *alphabet* or *book* or *science*, three hundred years ago no language had a label for *mechanics* or *molecule*, and thirty years ago not very many languages had a label for *machismo, sexism, sexploitation, bullet train, electronic computer, molecular biology,* or *generative grammar*. It is a fair guess that some of these labels are not yet part of the vocabulary of many languages.

The inborn concepts themselves are open to cultural development—or cultural reversion, as the case may be. A change in moral consciousness, like the realization that slavery is an intolerable affront to human dignity, which "is not merely a change but an advance, an advance toward understanding of our own nature and the moral and ethical principles that derive from it," leads to "a better understanding of who and what we are in our inner nature, and who and what we should be in our actual lives."[19] This improvement in our understanding extends to the sense we make of many words, particularly those involving culturally evolving concepts (*slavery, wage slavery, fellow human, fellow worker, freedom, freedom fighter, equality, solidarity,* and so on). A case particularly to the point in this context is the notion of *freedom of speech*, which was very poorly understood, it appears, until about the year 1800, and it is often not properly understood even today, a sign of cultural underdevelopment in most countries and of cultural regression in others.[20]

The assumptions underlying the principles of Newspeak that George Orwell outlines at the end of *1984* are interesting from this perspective. He refers, for example, to crimes and errors that would be beyond the power of a person growing up with Newspeak to commit "simply because they were nameless and therefore unimaginable." As we have seen, it is not the label *red* that gives normal human beings the idea of RED. Similarly, the labels *homeless* or *mass murder*, and so on, are not responsible for our ideas of "homelessness" or "mass murder." Nor are the concepts available to us picked out of the air and legislated. If we hear someone say, "When *I* use a word, it means just what I choose it to mean—neither more nor less," we immediately think of Humpty Dumpty. But as a distinguished annotator of *Alice* (Martin Gardner) has pointed out, Humpty Dumpty, like many logical empiricists after him, "takes the point of view known in the Middle Ages as nominalism," that is, "the view that universal terms do not refer to objective existences but are nothing more than *flatus vocis.*" Only on Humptydumptian assumptions could *slavery* and *solidarity* be assigned exactly the same meaning (or two different arbitrary meanings) or could *war* be taken to mean "peace", *freedom* to mean "slavery", and *ignorance* to mean "strength."[21]

There is little reason to doubt that language can be used as a loaded weapon (to use Dwight Bolinger's metaphor), as many practitioners of textual criticism have made abundantly clear, but it is the mushiness of our understanding that deserves to be blamed, not our concepts and their labels—a fortunate thing for us, otherwise translation (among other things) would be entirely out of the question.

4.2.3. Intertranslatability and cultural wealth:
Levels of understanding

As we saw in chapter 3, to the extent that anything is understood about lexical items and their nature, it seems that they are based on conceptual structures and that these (inborn) structures are of a specific and closely integrated type. Among the pervasive elements of lexical structure we find concepts of a locational nature, including goal and source of action, object moved, etc., and also notions like causation, intention, and so on.

But even if it is true that there is a core of determinate inborn concepts and semantic connections among words across languages and, more generally, that "languages are to a significant extent cast in the same mold," as will be argued in the next chapter, there is little reason to suppose that there is "any point by point correspondence between particular languages" or that "reasonable procedures of translation are in general possible," where by "reasonable procedure" it is meant one that does not involve extralinguistic (encyclopedic) information.[22] Such information is needed because, as we have seen, some aspects of the meanings of words are indeterminate and depend on all sorts of information about traditions and experiences transmitted from people to people and from generation to generation. A full and perfect translation of a rich text is therefore never assured. What we have instead are degrees of translatability, and this is interest relative. In other words, being translatable is like being "almost home" or being "near home," expressions that depend on the relevant and current conditions of nearness: For someone living in Los Angeles, Seattle is near (in comparison with New Haven) and not near (in comparison with Santa Monica).

The question, "Is this text translatable?" then, only has answers relative to some specific human concerns. Relative to certain kinds of human concerns a sentence in, say, English may or may not be translatable into another language. It may have different associations, it may be embedded in a different array of interests, understanding, and so on. The question, "Is this text translatable?" is really no more answerable than a typical "too-many-variable" question such as, "What course will this feather follow in its fall?" In other words, when we talk about translatability, we are talking about cultural wealth at a level that goes far beyond anything we can say with a certain degree of precision about language. If we lose sight of this elementary observation we are in for a lot of confusion, easy to bypass with just a little care.

It is not hard to see that the degree of translatability between two languages will increase as the degree of similarity between the corresponding two cultures or two subcultures increases (for example, the word *donate*, a by-product of particular institutional provisions, will be readily translatable only if the other language has a similar term, hence similar associated institutions). The cultural dissimilarity may be along universal or particular lines, that is, because of differences in the level of civilization or because of idiosyncratic differences.[23] In this context we may refer to both as differences in cultural wealth. A good example is the jazz subculture, both in its superficial and underlying aspects, which is without parallel. The challenge facing the programs that attempt to teach culture through language is to teach something deeper than the most superficial aspects, which often lead to unwarranted or misleading generalizations, to ideological preconceptions, or to stereotypic perceptions. Professional translators are well aware that many of the choices they make when they translate are based, though not always consciously, on the depth of their understanding of the two cultures involved, and that, all things being equal, the more thoroughly acquainted they are with both cultures, the better the translation is likely to be.[24]

However, no degree of acquaintance with the culture behind Salinger's *The Catcher in the Rye*, for example, will make the novel more translatable if there is no counterpart to its slang in the target language. A simpler but perhaps adequate illustration can be provided by a single sentence, say, *America's business is business*, which is too culture-bound to be fully translatable into any language. The first difficulty stems from the use of "America" as a designation of a single country and what this use implies. But let us focus on another one, the multiple senses of *business*. The expression *this is serious business* would have to be translated as something like *this is a serious matter* or *this is no joke* in Spanish, for example, which would not be very helpful when it comes to what is idiosyncratic about *America's business is business* (or about *there is no business like show business* and the like). In fact, meanings are often heavily culturally-dependent even among speakers of one and the same "language" (where by "language" what is really meant is a set of languages that are close enough for many purposes, say, Mexican Spanish and Castilian). For example, the meaning of *tortilla* or *taco* or *maria-chis* in Mexican varieties of Spanish is beyond the reach of many speakers of other varieties of Spanish (which from the Mexican point of view are sometimes seen as "culturally deprived"). Unsurprisingly, some bilingual speakers of English and Spanish feel more comfortable using one of the two languages for a particular general topic (say, English to discuss a football game, Spanish to discuss a soccer game or bullfighting).

A belief system embedded in a culture may also make all the difference in the interpretation of an expression. For example, an expression involving the equation DEATH IS SLEEP may be open to a metaphorical interpretation in a culture in which the equation does not state (literally) a belief, but not in a culture in which people believe that the soul quite literally departs from the body during sleep, being restored upon awakening, and, conversely, that death is a form of sleep, differentiated only by its length and quality, as was the case in many ancient cultures, including the Hebrew culture (this is why "resurrection in the earliest Judaic and Christian sources was quite naturally viewed as awakening from sleep"). Furthermore, the interpretation of the corresponding expression in a culture without such a belief may be tainted by "cultural contact," as is possibly the case with authors as different and remote from each other as Aristophanes and Shakespeare (cf. the latter's "Death's second self [i.e., sleep] that seals up all in rest"). The same problem is raised by DEATH IS DEPARTURE, the reason being that "many cultures view death literally as the soul (or person) passing on to its next existence." Thus, the very same equation that may constitute a fairly conventional meta-phor for one culture may fail to qualify for metaphorical interpretation in other cultures.[25]

The degree of translatability may also be reduced by many-to-one map-pings (e.g. *humid*, *damp*, *moist*, *wet*, and *clammy* all translate into Spanish as *húmedo*, though not in, say, *the clammy atmosphere of the court*, since *húmedo* does not suggest "lacking normal human worth" to a Spanish speaker). It may also be reduced by the lack of isomorphy we referred to in the preceding chapter, something that did not escape Saussure's attention. To illustrate with one of his examples: French *mouton* or Spanish *carnero* are close in meaning to English *sheep*, but far from equivalent to it, since English does not use *sheep* to refer to the flesh of a mature sheep used for food; it uses the Romance borrowing *mutton*. This is more general. It "has often been repeated, especially since Sir Walter Scott made it popular in *Ivanhoe*, that while the names of several animals in their lifetime are English (*ox*, *cow*, *calf*, *sheep*, *swine*, *boar*, *deer*), they appear on the table with French names (*beef*, *veal*, *mutton*, *pork, bacon, brawn, venison*)," which, incidentally, only goes to show that the French masters of England were "the rich, the powerful and the refined classes."[26]

This duplication of the vocabulary (Germanic and Romance), which T. S. Eliot, for example, saw as a great advantage of the English writer, may serve to illustrate the difficulties of translation in a different way. How likely is it that the Shakespearian *sightless view*, for example, may be fully translatable into the next language rather than turned into "view without view" or something of the sort, a very different thing?

The very way a language physically wraps its expressions can pose serious barriers to the translator. Compare *freeze*, for example, which is just a single syllable with four sounds, with *congelamiento*, where the same concept soaks up no less than five syllables and thirteen sound segments. It is no secret that this is not just a quirk, but a regular difference between English and Spanish, which quickly adds up: *bottle up* (2 syllables, 5 segments): *reprimir temporalmente* (8 syllables, 21 segments); *closely linked* (3 syllables, 11 segments): *estrechamente vinculado* (9 syllables, 22 segments). Can a bilingual speaker convey exactly the same thing when he or she uses the English expression as when he or she uses the Spanish expression?

The question may be easier to answer after looking at some well-known lines of verse.[27] Consider the beginning of the famous Shakespearean sonnet that suggested the title *A la recherche du temp perdu* to Marcel Proust:

When to the sessions of sweet silent thought
I summon up remembrance of things past . . .

The expression *sweet silent thought* apparently made an impression on a Spanish poet who was much influenced by English poetry, Miguel de Unamuno, who used the idea in the last line of one of his sonnets (he happened to believe that the only justification for some sonnets was their last line). But what in Shakespeare's sonnet was less than half a line (four syllables to be exact) is a whole line (eleven syllables) in Unamuno's:

el dulce silencioso pensamiento.

Again this is typical (English sonnets are difficult to accommodate in Spanish even using fourteen-syllable lines, as some translators have tried to do). And the implications are too obvious to deserve further elaboration.

Less obvious perhaps is the fact that the very form a language allows its labels to have (or lack) has considerable implications. To see this one may begin by translating the expression *wear and tear vs. use it or lose it*, which is part of the title of a recent article on the brain, into a language other than English. A more interesting example is provided by some famous lines from Leopardi:

> Fratelli, a un tempo stesso, amore e morte
> Ingenerò la sorte.

("Fate generated the two brothers, love and death, at the same time.") Here Leopardi puts the rhyming pair *morte/sorte* "death/fate" to a very different use than it is put in the often-repeated Spanish expression we mentioned in chapter 1, *la suerte o la muerte*, which is usually applied to the bullfighter. Obviously, *luck/fate or death* is not exactly equivalent to either of the Romance expressions. It is also worth noting that the difference in levels of cultural development may influence the interpretation in unexpected ways, since after modern biology came to the conclusion that sex and death are the two most important "inventions" of evolution, Leopardi's insight may have additional meaning for some non-"culturally deprived" readers.

Rhyme can also pose insurmountable difficulties for the translator in more subtle ways, as can be seen very clearly in the final couplet of Shakespeare's sonnet:

> But if the while I think on thee, dear friend,
> All losses are restor'd, and sorrows end.

Here we can consider only one feature of these remarkable lines (in which only three words are more than one syllable long, but only by one syllable, presumably not an accident): The shape of the last label, *end*, with which the sonnet comes effectively to an end. The idea that the sounds appear to emphasize is that the very thought brings all the misery to a sudden, brusque end, an idea that is reinforced by the last sound of *end*, phonetically a "stop" (the air coming out of the mouth is instantly arrested at precisely the point in which both the sorrow and the sonnet come to an abrupt end). A Spanish translator, for example, no matter how gifted, will have no chance of transferring this effect, for the simple reason that the phonological form vowel-nasal-stop is not a possible form in the language (cf., for example, *yendo,* 'going').

As teachers of composition or translation are well aware, "an individual can expand his facility or the subtlety of his comprehension of the devices of language through his own creative activities or immersion in the cultural wealth of his society," perhaps to the point of being able to take advantage of the enrichment of the resources of language brought about by great thinkers or writers (among which Shakespeare has few rivals), without any change in the language system itself.[28] Likewise, a diligent translator can expand and refine his comprehension of the devices of two or more languages and their interrelations. However, no degree of competence will make it possible for the translator to break down the barriers of a language, in particular the "sound barrier." There is nothing, for example, that a translator can do to change the fact that the English "keyboard" of sound segments is about one third larger than the Spanish one.

From the point of view of a human being as such (i.e., *qua* human being), and in particular for a student of a language as a foreign language, the differences exemplified above are all important. The reason is that the diversity among languages, which is readily detectable, is striking, while their uniformity is hidden and elusive and often not within the reach of unaided common sense. As we will see in the next chapter, a first step toward a deeper understanding is to distinguish between language as a real thing (the cognitive system in the mind of the speaker) on the one hand, and the utterances that it makes possible, which are the ones that make life difficult for the conscientious student or translator, on the other. But, as we have seen, knowledge of the language is possible without utterances (spoken or signed). What there cannot be are utterances without prior cognition (parroting is something else). Furthermore, cognition is mostly universal, while utterances can only be parochial. The priority then is clear. It is simply like driving in a one-way alley—with the possibility of driving up one's alley.

The same is true of culture. The diversity of cultural manifestations, for the most part directly observable, is also most striking, while their uniformity is less easy to grasp, particularly for the uninitiated. And yet the superficially diverse cultures are but variations on a theme (as languages are), built on networks of concepts such as kinship, group membership, social (in)equality, and a whole family of concepts related to causation (perhaps an instance of "force-dynamics") such as letting, helping, resisting, overcoming, and hindering (including the English words *make/let/have/help*, *permit/forbid/require*, and so on). Again, it is clear that also in the realm of culture cognition takes precedence over performance, which is always local, while most of the knowledge underlying it is likely to be no less universal than the knowledge underlying linguistic performance.

It is to this deep knowledge of language that we turn in the next chapter. The next section may serve as a bridge.

4.3. Semantic roles: Conceptual and linguistic structure at the interface

For centuries now, studies of language have agreed that the two major lexical categories are noun and verb. Every language appears to have nouns and verbs (e.g., English *woman* or *gift*, and *write* or *give*, respectively). The two are similar in some respects but very different in others. This difference may even be reflected in the supporting neural hardware. There appears to be recently discovered neurological evidence that nouns are supported by one region of the brain and verbs by a different region. Rough correlations between brain lesions and linguistic deficits appear to suggest that damage in the left temporal region is associated with trouble with nouns, with some interesting gradation from back to front (for example, mediation between concepts of unique persons and their names appears to be supported by a subregion in the anterior temporal lobe), while damage in a specific area of the left frontal cortex causes more trouble with verb retrieval than with noun retrieval.

Interestingly, there is a class of patients with temporal damage that have no difficulty producing constructions with verbs (properly inflected for tense and person), but with pronouns or jacks-of-all-trades like *thing* or *stuff* substituting for less general nouns. Nevertheless their structures are properly constructed and, significantly, the pronunciation and prosody of the individual words and the entire expression are unexceptionable too. Also interesting is that the damage that disturbs the retrieval of verbs disturbs the structure of the expressions the patients produce, which may suggest that verbs and related inflectional elements "constitute the core of grammatical structure."[29] There is nothing surprising about this. After all, the "head" of the "longest" phrase is always a verb (e.g., *denied* in *they denied something*). This is not to deny that nouns are also lexical heads (as adjectives are), or that they are second only to verbs in importance.

This emerging picture may or may not be on the right track, but it brings to mind so-called thematic theory, the topic of this section. As will be seen in chapter 6, a current and fairly widespread view holds that grammatical theory is modular, that is, it is made up of several interacting subsystems or modules. One of these modules is thematic theory, which may be seen as providing the point of contact between the conceptual system and the language system in a strict sense. It is called "thematic" because "theme" is the name of one of the "roles" involved, namely, the thematic role associated with the object in motion or being located (e.g., *the door* and *Mary* in *the door opened* and *Mary is upstairs*, respectively), thematic roles being nothing but particular structural positions in configurations of conceptual structure. As a first approximation we may say that thematic structure is "the part of conceptual structure that is 'visible' to the syntax" and that "only limited aspects of conceptual structure interact with syntax" (e.g., the plural/nonplural distinction but not the black/red distinction), keeping in mind that "the fundamental point, from which all else proceeds, is that thematic roles are part of the level of conceptual structure, not part of syntax."[30]

Every content-bearing major phrasal constituent of a sentence—sentence (as in the last two examples), noun phrase (as in *the door, many large doors*, or *Mary*), adjective phrase (as in *very clever* or *rather dark*), prepositional phrase (as in *near the door* or *right behind the desk*, where the heads are *near* and *behind*)—corresponds to a conceptual constituent in some major conceptual category, while words in general need not correspond to complete conceptual constituents (they correspond to constituents with open positions). For instance, a noun phrase can express almost any conceptual category, a sentence can express an event or a state, and so on. Other major conceptual categories (the "parts of speech" of the innate conceptual system), in addition to event and state, are "thing," "place," "action," "path," "property," and "amount." The inferential possibilities we examined in the preceding section grow directly out of the syntactic structure in which the thematic roles are embedded when these roles are regarded as structural relations in conceptual structure. For example, the causative-noncausative pairs we examined, and others such as *Mary lifted John* and *John rose*, are all instances of a schema of the form "X causes event to occur, event occurs" (roughly).

We have already mentioned some of the concepts involved, for instance "goal" (the object to which motion proceeds), another thematic role of a locational nature that can be readily illustrated: in *Mary entered the room*, *Mary* is again the theme in the structure, and *the room* is the (spatial) goal; on the other hand, in *Mary received the letter*, *Mary* is the (possessional) goal and *the letter* is the theme. (It is worth noting that the spatial goal is to the right of the theme, while the possessional goal is to the left of the theme.) Other examples of goal are the adjective *green* in *the light changed from red to green* and (roughly) "unspecified subject *shut up*" in *Mary talked John into shutting up*.

Another thematic role of a locational nature is "source" (the object from which motion proceeds), for example, *Mary* in *Mary promised to go*. (As made clear earlier, the motion and location involved may be highly abstract in some cases.) In other words, such expressions as *the door, Mary* (or *she*), and so on, referred to as arguments, are assigned thematic roles (also called theta-roles or θ-roles), that is, they are assigned to the status of terms in a thematic relation.[31] Differences in locational structure underlie, for example, the fact that there is no word-for-word Spanish translation for an expression such as *the bottle floated to the cave* (Spanish speakers can only say "the bottle moved-in to the cave floating," that is, *la botella entró a la cueva flotando*) or *Mary danced into John's hands* (a paraphrase such as *Mary went into John's hands (by) dancing* is essentially the only way to render the shorter expression into Spanish).

It has been claimed that locational notions such as theme, goal, source, and so on (the names are just convenient mnemonics for some particularly prominent structural positions with conceptual content, many others being still unnamed) are not primitives of semantic theory but relational notions defined structurally over conceptual structure, similar in status to syntactic relations such as subject and object in some grammatical theories. A more recent claim is that the locational theta-roles belong to one of two tiers, what we may call the location tier, and that in structures thematically more complex than the ones just analyzed there may also be an action tier, dealing with actor-patient relations (which involve a different subclass of theta-roles).[32] The term "actor" denotes the doer of the action and the term "patient" the "affected entity," as in traditional descriptions. Here are some examples, informally annotated:

	Mary hit John	
Location tier	Theme	Goal
Action tier	Actor	Patient

	Mary threw the ball	
Location tier	Source	Theme
Action tier	Actor	Patient

This approach makes it possible to dissect the traditional notion of agent into a number of independent senses. One sense, that of (nonvolitional) extrinsic instigator of action, is an element of the location tier associated with CAUSE (e.g., *the wind* in *the wind rolled the ball down the hill*). Another sense is "volitional actor," as in one interpretation of *Mary rolled down the hill*, a type of example that has been much discussed since it was uncovered twenty years ago. In the relevant interpretation Mary is performing the action willfully, that is, she is not an extrinsic instigator but a willful agent. This is the preferred reading when a verb is open to a volitional or nonvolitional interpretation, as *roll* is, and the only reading when the verb is preceded by *deliberately*. In general, when an animate entity has the actor role, volitionality becomes an issue and any animate thematic actor is subject to this kind of ambiguity unless the verb "selects for" (requires) a volitional actor (e.g. *buy*, *look*). In another possible interpretation of the example, Mary is not a willful agent but rather an undergoer of the action.

The notion "cause" also appears to be decomposable, depending on whether the outcome is undetermined or determined (either successfully or unsuccessfully). For example, in expressions involving *pressure, resist*, or *impede*, the outcome is undetermined (but it can be settled by adding *successfully* or *unsuccessfully*); in expressions involving *force* (or *prevent, manage*, or *succeed*), or *fail*, the outcome is determined (unsuccessfully in the case of *fail* and successfully in the other cases). There is a test that shows that in such structures a "reactor" (e.g., a resister) is actually a kind of actor: We can say *what Mary did was resist (successfully)*. An expression such as *Mary gave John the book* is also an example of successful causation in the locational tier (Mary causes the book to change possession), while in the action tier the thematic goal is construed as beneficiary, as in other verbs of transfer of possession (Mary benefits John); by contrast, in *Mary gave the book to John*, the theme (*the book*) is a sort of quasi-patient in the action tier.[33]

Another dimension of causation involves the temporal relation between the thematic instigator of the action (the cause) and the effect. For example, in *Mary dragged the car down the road*, Mary's dragging is temporally coextensive with the motion of the car; by contrast, in *Mary threw the ball into the field*, Mary's throwing only initiates the ball's motion.

It is of particular interest that an analysis along these lines is applicable to verbs that introduce new semantic fields of causation such as the verbs of logical relation, which are all stative, like *stay* (rather than eventive, like *run*). The relevant intuition is that "verbs of logical relation express an abstract form of force-dynamic interaction, not too distantly related to verbs that express pushing things around in space." Thus, *imply* or *entail* include CAUSE, *preclude* or *rule out* include CAUSE NOT, and *permit* or *be consistent with* include LET. Furthermore, *support* and *reinforce* emerge clearly as members of the same family as *imply* and *entail* under this approach, which goes some distance toward explaining why they play such a prominent role in argumentation.[34]

This is not the place to try to go beyond this small but hopefully representative sample, which might be enough for our purposes. A point to be made is that the association between assigned theta-roles and appropriate syntactic positions is to a large extent predictable by the "thematic hierarchy," which is roughly as follows: the thematic actor occupies the highest position in the structure (the subject position) in English and other languages; if there is no actor, the patient or the beneficiary occupies the highest position, otherwise it is occupied by the theme (the leftmost theta-role of all event and state verbs other than cause verbs); finally, goal, source, and location are the last to occupy the highest position. To the extent that the association between thematic role and appropriate syntactic position is predictable, it need not (hence must not under current assumptions) be stated in the entries of particular words in the lexicon. A general principle requires that every major syntactic constituent is uniquely linked to a conceptual constituent that holds the dominant thematic role in a bound complex of one or more theta-roles (the highest in the thematic hierarchy being the dominant one), and every constituent that is required to be linked is in fact linked.[35]

In summary, there are some elements of the conceptual system (the thematic relations) that appear to be shared by the language faculty in its initial state and are perhaps fleshed out in the course of language maturation (one aspect of cognitive development). This means that there are universal semantic properties that are available for semantic representation, possibly in the sense in which phonological features are available for phonological representation. But, as we have seen, it does not mean that the principles of language in a strict sense literally map formal structure into representations of meaning, as some students of language, particularly philosophers, have advocated.

It is now time to consider what is meant by "language system" in a strict sense. This is the topic of the following two chapters.

NOTES TO CHAPTER 4

1. The reference is to Aristotle's first or second grade of actuality of form (*De anima*, Book II, Chapter i). See Chomsky 1966, p. 28.

2. Kimura 1992, p. 119. Recall (chapter 2, note 11) that Doreen Kimura pioneered in the 1960s the technique called dichotic listening.

3. See Chomsky 1988, pp. 9f. See also Otero (ed.) 1994, vol. 2, in particular the introduction and reference therein.

4. See Otero 1991, especially pp. 34 and 54. See also Jackendoff 1987, chapter 2, and references therein, for a theory of tonal music, and Kiparsky and Youmans 1989 and references therein, in particular Piera 1980, for insightful work on the theory of verse.

5. See Chomsky 1975:124–25, from which the quote is taken, and Otero 1984:84f; for illustration, Otero 1980a, 1981b.

6. Gibson 1982, p. 65. Where "the language being translated into (say) English is completely without preexisting aids to translation—as a Martian language would presumably be," Quine speaks of "radical translation."

7. For the reference to the quote, due to Professor Stuart Hampshire, see Gibson 1982, p. xvii. For background and discussion, see Otero (ed.) 1994, vol. 2, in particular the introduction.

8. Quoted in Gibson 1982, p. 64. The preceding three quotes are from Quine 1987, pp. 131, 130.

9. Gibson, p. 29 and (quoting Quine) 31. Under these assumptions, "the various theories comprising our overall theory of the world could be taken as systems of sentences." Language is then at the heart of Quine's philosophy, which is characterized in this "expository essay" as "a systematic attempt to answer . . . what he takes to be the central question of epistemology, namely, 'How do we acquire our theory of the world?'" this question being "one of giving an account of the relation between observation and our theoretical *talk*" (Gibson 1982, pp. xviii, 29).

10. This is no small matter. As Gibson shrewdly observes (p. xx), "Quine's commitment to behaviorism may very well prove to be his Achilles' heel; for if . . . behaviorism (in Quine's sense of the term) is abandoned, say, in favor of some form of mentalism, then an overwhelming majority of Quine's cardinal doctrines and theses would be left without any obvious firm support and, therefore, cast into doubt."

11. Actually, "the idea of causation is now seen as just one notion within a related set," within a "force dynamics" framework that can be extended to social reference (a familiar example is *peer pressure*), as already mentioned in chapter 3. See Talmy 1985 and, for a detailed analysis of some crucial Spanish constructions from an earlier, but closely related, perspective, Strozer 1976, pp. 391–538.

12. The quote is from Chomsky 1988a, a very illuminating discussion of the topic of this subsection (in a much broader context) from which some of the ideas just presented were drawn; see also Chomsky 1992a. For further discussion of Quine's views, see Chomsky 1972, in particular the last paper, written in April 1968 (see also the paper cited on p. 72, note 6), 1975, pp. 179–204, and 1980, pp. 12–16, *passim*.

13. Introduction (written in 1973) to the published version of Chomsky 1955, p. 23.

14. See chapter 3, note 19, and associated quote.

15. Chomsky 1988a. On the question of revision and restructuring, see Carey 1985.

16. Chomsky 1971, pp. 14–17, 1975, p. 203. The second example of unnameable "thing" (the single object consisting of an animal's four legs) is from Chomsky 1965, pp. 29–30.

17. On the difficulties of defining a word, see, e.g., Jackendoff 1987, 8.2, and references therein.

18. Chomsky 1988:191, 1988a. For further discussion, see Chomsky 1992a.

19. See Chomsky 1988, p. 152, and related discussion.

20. See Otero 1990b and references therein (in particular the studies by Leonard W. Levy and Harry Kalven, Jr.) for extensive discussion. Cf. now Hentoff 1992, Smolla 1992.

21. See Otero 1987a for further discussion.

22. Chomsky 1965, p. 30 and p. 201, n. 17, with reference to a 1960 article by Bar-Hillel on the status of automatic translation.

23. It seems clear, even if there is no general agreement on it, that along a particular dimension one culture may be more advanced than another—for example, the Phoenician culture, which opened the way to the alphabet, or Indian culture after the discovery of zero—with respect to cultures without writing or the decimal system. It is also easy to be misled on this score. Cf. Pearce 1953, Steele 1985, and for further discussion within a broader context Otero 1984, 1987a, 1987b, 1988b, 1990b, 1991.

24. For the view of a professional translator, see Vázquez-Ayora 1977, pp. 387–88; cf. Frawley, ed., 1984 (in particular the paper by Bly), Biguenet, John & Schulte, eds. 1989, Bell 1991, Baker 1992, Child 1992, Hervey, Sándor & Higgins 1992. On the teaching of culture, see Seelye 1974, Omaggio 1986 (chapter 9), Damen 1987, Kramsch 1989, and Section III in Kramsch & McConnell-Ginet (eds.) 1992.

25. For further discussion of metaphorical interpretation from a cognitive point of view (with reference to the thematic relations we take up in the next section), see Jackendoff & Aaron 1991 and references therein.

26. The quotes are from chapter 5 of Jespersen's "great little book of 1905" (as Randolph Quirk remarks in the Foreword to the 1982 reprint).

27. In what follows I draw closely from Otero 1972, chapter 4, and Otero 1982, where these questions are discussed further.

28. See Chomsky 1980, p. 234, where the idea that "the resources of a language can be enriched by a great thinker or writer, without any change in the grammar" is attributed to Wilhelm von Humboldt.

29. Damasio and Damasio 1992, p. 94–95. The briefness of the report makes it difficult to extract the information that appears to be relevant in this context, increasing its tentativeness.

30. Jackendoff 1990, pp. 48, 49, 46. In what follows I draw freely from this book of Jackendoff's (which builds on much earlier work by him and others), a large-scale study of conceptual structure and its lexical and syntactic expression in English and no doubt a major contribution to the field. Cf. Ravin 1992.

31. See Chomsky 1981, 2.2.2. On the possible relevance of sign language in identifying some of the elements involved and distinguishing their roles, see Chomsky 1986a, IV note 27 and references therein.

32. Jackendoff uses the term "thematic tier" instead of "location tier," which seems more appropriate in itself and also does not compete with the more general sense of "thematic."

33. Still to be explained is the fact that, as far as we know, there is no verb, or language, that allows only the *gave John* construction, while there are verbs (e.g., *donate*, as already mentioned), and languages (e.g., Spanish), that allow only the *gave . . . to* construction. Cf. Jackendoff 1990, p. 300.

34. See Jackendoff 1990, p. 131–42. As Jackendoff points out, his approach also throws light on the fact that the concepts of logical relation appear relatively late in child development, an observation that led Piaget to the conclusion that they are abstractions of concepts involved in our understanding of the physical world (a point that resonates with the type of analysis just sketched and perhaps should not be lightly dismissed). If this line of thought is on the right track, the relation of logical concepts to at least one family of concepts runs in the opposite direction of what is usually assumed, since they derive from them and are therefore less basic, a conclusion that would elevate the conceptualization of the physical world to a more prominent status than the logical vocabulary, again contrary to standard assumptions.

35. Jackendoff 1990, pp. 278–79. This is Jackendoff's counterpart of the so-called θ-Criterion. It appears to be consistent with at least the spirit of Chomsky's formulation of the θ-Criterion. Cf. Chomsky 1981, p. 139, note 14.

5

Language explanation:
The growth of a child's mind

In this chapter we will be mainly concerned with the two main shifts in the recent study of language and in particular with the general answers to two of the three major questions linguists have to face, together with their historical antecedents, a matter of some importance only recently brought to the fore. We will pay special attention to some ideas that are now much better understood than they were half a century ago, since they appear to shed considerable light on the central question of this book, to be taken up in chapter 8. We leave for the next chapter the presentation of some specific features of the current version of the theory, including some of the radically new ideas developed since about 1980.

5.1. Some elementary properties of human language

A field of inquiry, no matter what it is, is established by the questions that are posed, and asking the right questions is usually the hardest part of the task. How does one determine that some of the questions that have been asked are right (or closer to being right than others)? One way, perhaps the most reliable way, is to see whether they have succeeded, at least partially, in opening up a program of inquiry that leads to insights into problems that are worth understanding.

Often the right questions are disarmingly simple. They are no more than invitations to become surprised about perfectly ordinary things, the sort of thing that is usually taken for granted because of the dulling effect of familiarity, one difficulty especially hard to overcome in the psychological sciences, as discussed in chapter 2. It requires a certain intellectual effort to see how everyday phenomena can pose serious problems or call for intricate explanatory theories, a hard alternative to just taking them for granted. Like people living at the seashore who grow so accustomed to the murmur of the ocean that they never hear it, we scarcely hear the words we utter, let alone wonder at the astonishing properties of their combinations.

But as many people know who have heard the story we already referred to of the apple falling from the tree, it is simple questions that are behind the scientific revolution of the 17th century (something really new under the sun), which eventually set off the modern natural sciences. Only people who are not satisfied with commonsensical explanations and are willing to find the falling of the apple (as well as the properties of the motion) surprising and puzzling have a chance to lift a little (ever so slightly) the veil of mystery of the world by eventually finding the way to naturalistic scientific inquiry in the modern sense and beginning the search for the hidden realities that lie behind the misleading (and for the scientist largely irrelevant) flux of phenomena. It is this search for hidden realities that is the essence of the so-called Galilean style of the natural sciences. The scientific study of human language is no exception, as the brief and rapid course of development of transformational generative grammar strikingly shows.

In searching for the right questions we may begin by considering two problems that are often identified (wrongly, as will hopefully become clear in what follows), particularly by contemporary philosophers: The problem of accounting for the creative ability of language users ("Descartes's Problem," in Chomsky's view) and the problem of accounting for the tacit knowledge that a particular speaker has of his or her native language ("Humboldt's Problem," as Chomsky sees it). We will then go on to consider the problem of accounting for the acquisition of tacit knowledge (what Chomsky calls "Plato's Problem"), in particular the acquisition of linguistic knowledge, the key to our quest.

5.1.1. The creative aspect of language use: Descartes's Problem

Every developed reader or professional student of literariness (a property sometimes attained by linguistic expression) is well aware that the likes of Plato, Cervantes, Shakespeare, Rousseau, or Goethe are capable of truly exceptional creative power. How can a human being conceive of and be able to give form to a masterpiece such as *Don Quixote*? The Spanish "natural philosopher" Juan Huarte, who may have unwittingly provided Cervantes with the germ of the idea behind his masterpiece, suggested in his widely read *Examen de ingenios* (1575) that there is a special kind of "wit" "by means of which some, without art or study, speak such subtle and surprising things, yet true, that were never before seen, heard, or writ, no, nor ever so much as thought of." If this is essentially correct, a literary giant is capable of exercising his creative imagination and using language in ways not within the reach of ordinary humans (ways that appear to go beyond normal intelligence). Does the true creativity of the genius (to use the term much in vogue with the Romantics a couple of centuries later) involve "a mixture of madness," as Huarte and others before and after him have suspected? Could it be that it even requires the sort of inspiration that only the "muses" can provide? These are all very difficult questions, which fortunately do not have to be answered here. Suffice it to say that the last and possibly crucial one would be easier to answer if we knew more about the nature of the "muses."

More relevant, for our purposes, is the case of the truly active minds of ordinary humans (Huarte's second kind of "wit"), which Huarte was careful to distinguish from the sprinkling of "docile wits" (yet another, and very different, kind of intelligence), who are deprived, by birth or accident, of any creative capacity. (It is important to note that in this discussion creativity provides a criterion for "wits" that will reappear in Descartes half a century later.) Huarte agrees with Cicero that all the "honor and nobility" of a normal human being "consists in his being favoured with, and having an~eloquent tongue." "In this alone," he suggested, a human "distinguishes himself from the brutes, and approaches near to God, as being the greatest glory which is possible to be obtained in Nature."[1] Huarte may have never suspected that he was to be in very good company in the years to come. For Descartes and his followers the essential difference between humans and other animals is also exhibited most clearly by human language, in particular by the human ability to form new phrases that express new thoughts and that are appropriate to new situations. These important observations, later forgotten for over a century (with unhelpful consequences for the study of language), deserve some attention, and this seems to be the right place to expand on them.

Although Descartes does not say much about language in his writings, certain observations about the nature of language, which for him are crucial, play a significant role in the formulation of his theory of human nature. In his view, humans are fundamentally different from everything else in the physical world in that they have a species-specific capacity, a unique type of intellectual organization that manifests itself in what Chomsky refers to as "the creative aspect of ordinary language use," which for Descartes is the only sign that an organism is human. Thus, "language is available for the free expression of thought or for appropriate response in any new context and is undetermined by any fixed association of utterances to external stimuli or physiological states (identifiable in any noncircular fashion)." In other words, the normal use of language (as human thought and action more generally) has these three important properties:

(i) it is innovative and potentially infinite in scope.
(ii) it is free from stimulus control.
(iii) it is appropriate to the situation.

Language use is innovative in the sense that much of what we say is entirely novel, not a repetition of anything that we have heard before (one does not merely repeat what one has heard, clichés aside), and it is unbounded in scope in the sense that it has no particular limits; in other words, there is an infinity of things that humans can say. This is obviously a truism, particularly from our vantage point, but the observation is nevertheless an important one and was in fact often overlooked and not infrequently denied at the time Chomsky appeared on the scene. To appreciate its importance one has only to consider that it was a virtually universal claim of behaviorist psychologists for many years that "a person's knowledge of language is representable as a stored set of patterns, overlearned through constant repetition and detailed training, with innovation being at most a matter of 'analogy'."[2] The fact is, however, that the number of expressions any native speaker can understand is astronomical—orders of magnitude greater than the number of seconds in a lifetime.[3]

In addition to being potentially infinite in its variety, language use is free from the control of external stimuli or internal states (this is important for the Cartesians because in their view even animal behavior can vary over an indefinite range). As Chomsky wrote a quarter of a century ago, "it is because of this freedom from stimulus control that language can serve as an instrument of thought and self-expression, as it does not only for the exceptionally gifted and talented, but also, in fact, for every normal human."

Still, the decisive property for the Cartesians is the third one, the fact that the everyday use of language is coherent and "appropriate to the situation," an entirely different matter because the properties of being potentially infinite and being free from control from external stimuli do not exceed the bounds of automata. Ordinary speech, though not determined by the situation, is not random. As Chomsky notes, "we can distinguish normal use of language from the ravings of a maniac or the output of a computer with a random element." Everyday speech is appropriate to the situation but apparently not caused by the situation, a crucial if obscure difference. Furthermore, it evokes thoughts that correspond to those of the listener and that the listener might have expressed in similar ways.

As the Cartesians recognized, these elementary and relatively uncontroversial observations about human language (and, more generally, human behavior), are manifestations of the property of free will, which is phenomenologically obvious, as apparent to us as anything we know, but a mystery for the scientist, at least for the present. Chomsky's assessment of a quarter of a century ago has lost none of its validity: "Honesty forces us to admit that we are as far today as Descartes was three centuries ago from understanding just what enables a human to speak in a way that is innovative, free from stimulus control, and also appropriate and coherent."[4] However, there is no need to wait until the problem is understood in depth to draw some relevant conclusions. One of them is that the creativity of language use has to have a basis in the linguistic knowledge of the speaker, our next topic.

5.1.2. The recursive property of linguistic knowledge: Humboldt's Problem

The most elementary property of the linguistic knowledge of a native speaker (say, John Smith's variety of colloquial English) is that it is a system that "makes infinite use of finite means," as the great linguist Wilhelm von Humboldt put it over a century and a half ago. He conceived of a language not as a set of constructed objects (utterances), but as an inexhaustible process of generation. The infinity of expressions such a process makes possible is easy to illustrate:

(1) Jon thinks that Jean ate two/three/four/. . . raisins.
    Sue believes that Jon thinks that Jean ate . . . raisins.
    Ben knows that Sue believes that. . . .
    Jill said that Ben knows that Sue believes that. . . .
    Sy doesn't know that Jill said that Ben knows that Sue. . . .
    Al doesn't believe that Sy doesn't know that Jill said. . . .
    Tim knows that Al doesn't believe that Sy doesn't know. . . .
    It is a fact that Tim knows that Al doesn't believe. . . .
    Some suspect that it is a fact that Tim knows. . . .

and on and on *ad infinitum*. Here the sentence "Jean ate *x* raisins," where *x* may be replaced by any number (out of an infinity of them), becomes part of the sentence "Jon thinks that . . . ," and the resulting complex expression becomes part of the sentence "Sue believes that . . .," and so on and on. These operations are all "recursive" (they can be repeated indefinitely). In fact, every operation that makes a type of phrase part of a phrase of the same type (a sentence part of a sentence, a noun phrase part of a noun phrase, etc.) is a recursive operation. A perhaps more familiar illustration goes something like this:

(2) This is the house that Jack built.
    This is the table that sits in the house that Jack built.
    This is the cheese that fell off the table that sits. . . .
    This is the mouse that ate the cheese that fell off. . . .
    This is the cat that chased the mouse that ate. . . .
    This is the dog that ran after the cat that chased. . . .

Here a noun phrase, "the house that Jack built" (which itself is closely related to the sentence "Jack built a house"), becomes part of the noun phrase "the table that sits in . . . ," which in turn becomes part of the noun phrase "the cheese that fell off . . . ," and so on and on.[5]

However, the fact that the phenomenon is easy to illustrate does not mean that it is easy to define explicitly. This is what Chomsky refers to as "Humboldt's Problem," which before the late 1930s neither Humboldt nor anyone else would have been able to address. In his day means were lacking to express clearly his insight that human language is a system that makes infinite use of finite means, so the notion lapsed and was forgotten for a long period. The technical tools required to carry out a program of research along the lines his insight suggested were not available until certain advances were made in the foundations of mathematics, in particular the development of the theory of computation, also known as recursive function theory. It was this theory that opened the way to a solution by making available the technical means needed to formulate the fundamental questions, which could at last be squarely faced. For this and other reasons progress had been limited for many centuries, so even the most elementary question the study of language raises was not addressed until about 1950.[6] We return to the topic later in this chapter, when we consider Chomsky's solutions.

5.1.3. The logical problem of knowledge acquisition: Plato's Problem

Another elementary property of linguistic knowledge is that speakers come to know things they have never learned. Actually, this is a property of human knowledge more generally, as we saw in chapter 2. The relevant question then is: How do humans know so much, when they have so little evidence (often no evidence at all)? The first on record as having asked this question in a classical form (it is one of the main questions of his universally admired dialogues) is the Greek philosopher Plato, which is why Chomsky refers to it as "Plato's Problem." The illustration given in *The Meno* (the first recorded psychological experiment—at least the first recorded "thought experiment") is the demonstration by Socrates that an untutored slave boy had knowledge of the principles of geometry (through a series of questions, the boy is led to the discovery of theorems of geometry). How was the boy able to discover truths of geometry without being provided any information?

Plato even had an answer. His answer was that the boy knew those truths by reminiscence (because he remembered them from another existence, basically). We might ask what other form the right answer could have taken twenty-four centuries ago. From our vantage point it certainly seems a lot better than the answers that have been given over the last couple of centuries (the answer of the associationists, for example). Two thousand years later, Leibniz ("one of the supreme intellects of all time," in the opinion of Bertrand Russell) found Plato's answer to be essentially right; it just had to be, as he put it, "purged of the error of reminiscence." But even in Leibniz's time it was not possible to say what one gets when Plato's answer is purged of the error of reminiscence. Today a high-school student can immediately see it: What one gets is the idea that our knowledge of geometry (language, vision, and so on) is determined genetically as part of our biological endowment, of the structure of our brain, which is just built that way. It is all in the genes. So the reason we know all these things is exactly the same reason why we become such complex organisms with so little input. Since we do not get the structure of our legs or arms or liver or heart from the food we eat or from any other contribution of the environment, it makes sense to think that the brain (in particular the part of the brain that serves as the material basis for our knowledge of geometry or language or vision) is no different. The challenge after Plato (as after Leibniz two thousand years later) was to give substantive content to this generality.

5.2. Chomsky's solution: The development of transformational generative grammar

Let us begin by summing up the previous section. A normal child is born with a certain genetic endowment, develops native knowledge of at least one language within its first few years, and soon becomes an ordinary language user. These three stages give rise to three classical problems, which in Chomsky's reformulation are as follows:

P1. Plato's Problem:
What makes it possible for a system of knowledge to arise in the brain? How is knowledge of language acquired?

P2. Humboldt's Problem:

What is the system of linguistic knowledge in the brain of a particular native speaker? What constitutes knowledge of language?

P3. Descartes's Problem:

How is this knowledge put to use in speech (or in secondary systems such as writing)?[7]

As is generally known by now, the first scientist to offer substantive answers to the first two of these classical problems was Noam Chomsky. As for the third, undoubtedly the hardest of the three, no one so far has been able to even formulate it insightfully, let alone solve it. The reason is that it involves the question of free will, about which we continue to have not much of a clue (even if we put aside the special case of the true creativity of the gifted few who are capable of writing a masterpiece or producing some other work of genius). No one knows what makes some people more articulate or eloquent than others, for example. About this we are as much in the dark as the ancient Greeks were, or so it seems (Descartes was sure we do not have enough brains to understand it in depth, and Chomsky suspects he may be right), a clear indication that the assimilation of this problem with Humboldt's Problem, which is amenable to inquiry, is not warranted.[8]

The tentative **answers** to the questions raised by the first two problems that Chomsky suggested from the very beginning, and which still appear to be essentially correct, are the following:

P1. How is knowledge of language acquired?
By making use of an innate faculty for language (a sort of language organ, genetically determined).

P2. What constitutes knowledge of language?
A mental generative procedure (a mental language).

From the perspective of the new technical understanding provided by the theory of computation in the 1930s, adopted and adapted by Chomsky, it is clear that a system with the elementary property expressed in Humboldt's insight (from the viewpoint of the linguist, a grammar of a language) can be seen as a recursive function that generates the expressions of the language, as Chomsky showed in the early 1950s. The solution to Humboldt's Problem then is to attempt to construct a generative (explicit) grammar for each known language, a difficult and demanding task.

However, the next task is even more difficult. It is to explain why the facts are the way they are. This problem of explanation, which is the oldest and the crucial one for the scientist (the one that defines the field), is the problem raised by the poverty of the stimulus (recall the discussion in chapter 2). Plato's Problem arises in a striking way in the study of language. The modern variant sketched in chapter 2 is that "certain aspects of our knowledge and understanding are innate, part of our biological endowment, genetically determined, on a par with the elements of our common nature that cause us to grow arms and legs rather than wings."[9] This conclusion is crucial for the proper understanding of Problem 2—and also for the proper understanding of the central question of this book, which we will be discussing in chapter 8.

From the perspective of the answer to Plato's Problem (in its modern variant), the human brain may be seen as a complex (modular) system with various interacting subsystems, one of which we may call the language faculty, in traditional terms. This subsystem, which appears to be unique in essentials to the human species and common to members of the species, when presented with data, undergoes a process of maturation and comes to determine an individual variety of a particular language (the Spanish, English, etc., of a specific person). This mental system in turn determines a wide range of potential phenomena, including phenomena that go far beyond the data presented.

To put it a little more precisely: The language faculty is essentially a function that takes experience as input (a relatively small and far from optimal amount of experience, in the case of the infant) and generates a specific cognitive structure (a language L) as "output" (in quotes because it is internal to the brain). The linguist's theory of this specific "output" is called a grammar of the language L. The linguist's theory of the initial state of the language faculty or language organ (sometimes called the language acquisition device, or LAD for short) is often called, in traditional terms, universal grammar (UG), even though the research program of contemporary generative grammar differs in conception from its clearest historical antecedents (ancient, medieval, or modern). We may think of UG as the theory of the sum total of all the immutable principles (of syntax, sound, and meaning) that heredity builds into the language organ. Put differently, UG is the linguist's theory of the inherited genetic endowment that makes it possible for us to come to master human languages.[10]

The model of language maturation underlying these remarks can be schematically represented as follows:

child's data → LAD → language L → structured expressions

A specification of LAD would provide a specific answer to the fundamental question (Plato's Problem in the domain of language), and a specification of a particular language L, say English (we can take the variety of English in the head of an individual speaker as a first approximation) would provide the answer to Problem 2, a derived question. A successful inquiry into the LAD would lead to the discovery of the schema that underlies every human language (given that a child, under the appropriate conditions, can become a native speaker of any human language). This then is Chomsky's solution to Plato's Problem in the domain of language (one of the cognitive structures of the human brain). To the extent that we can construct a universal grammar (a theory of the innate schema supplied by the language faculty) we have succeeded in solving Plato's Problem.

Universal grammar is an account of the initial state of the language faculty (the mental organ for language) before any experience, and the grammar of a particular language (say, John Smith's variety of colloquial English) is an account of the language mental organ after it has been presented with data of experience. Crucially, UG must be activated in the early years of the child's life, and the maturation of the language organ reaches a steady state quite early in the life of the individual (roughly before the onset of puberty—we return to the topic in chapter 8). After this steady state is attained, the system of language in the mind of the speaker does not change, which of course does not mean that it is no longer possible for the speaker to come to know more words or idioms (as discussed in chapter 3, vocabulary enrichment continues to be possible throughout one's life). What becomes steady is language as a computational system, not to be confused with a list of vocabulary items (a particular computational system can interface with different vocabularies, as the consideration of slang, for example, or British and American vocabulary choices makes immediately clear).

Since the generative research program was initiated over forty years ago, the questions raised by language and the human mind have been studied very productively and there has really been substantial progress. Two main phases can be distinguished in its development, as we will see in the next two subsections.

5.2.1. The first thirty years (1949–79): An updated revival of a classical tradition

When we conceive of a particular language as a recursive function that generates a set or collection of expressions, we regard the language **in intension**. An alternative conception, which was being adopted by many students of language when Chomsky appeared on the scene (and still is, particularly by literary critics or by the heirs of "ordinary language philosophy") regards language **in extension**, that is, as just a collection of expressions, without regard to how the collection is specified or identified. For example, a representative view, contrasting sharply with Humboldt's view of a century and a half earlier, was that a language is the totality of expressions that can be produced, in principle, in some speech community (understood to be homogeneous).[11]

A simple example will clarify the crucial difference between the two diametrically opposed conceptions. Consider the set of even numbers, $\{0,2,4,6,8, \ldots \}$, where the ". . ." passes on to the reader the responsibility of specifying the set. The reader may fulfill his responsibility by following one of several instructions, for example, Instruction 1 or Instruction 2:

I1. Begin with zero, add two, add two again, etc.

I2. Select a number and multiply it by two.

Each instruction, I1 or I2, might be considered a **generative grammar** that generates the members of the set. The two grammars (or functions) specify the same set, that is, the set of even numbers. Considered **in extension** they are the same, since they generate the same set; considered **in intension** they are very different, since they generate the set in very different ways.

From this perspective it is easy to see that in the case of the language of a particular speaker, say, John Smith's variety of colloquial English, the open-ended collection of expressions can be generated by very different generative grammars. A scientist who studies human language in intension differs from a mathematician who studies the properties of a particular collection of expressions in that the former inquires about the nature of the system that is hypothesized to be neurologically represented in the speaker's brain (Smith's mental language, one of the cognitive structures in Smith's head, hence part of the real world), whereas the mathematician may be satisfied with any grammar that generates the collection of expressions at issue and has the right properties for the task at hand.

Since a mental language is a recursive system, it can be characterized as a generative procedure. The potential infinity of the set of expressions generated by the mental language follows from the fact that there is no "longest" expression. Given any expression, it is always possible to make it longer (as the illustrations given above suggest). There is little reason to doubt that the number of expressions in one's native language that one would immediately understand with no difficulty or feeling of strangeness is astronomical. The fact that a speaker may run out of breath (or out of life) on his or her way to never-reachable infinity is obviously irrelevant. What is crucial is that a native speaker is in principle able to understand or produce any one of an infinite number of expressions, even though no amount of time is enough to use an infinity of them.

This potentially infinite capacity is precisely what makes possible the linguistic creativity every normal human possesses and exercises all the time (in other words, the potentially infinite capacity is a necessary condition for creativity). But the recursivity underlying the potentially infinite capacity is only a prerequisite for our linguistic creativity (it is not a sufficient condition), and one should be careful not to identify the two (creativity and recursivity).[12] Since creativity involves free will and choice, and normal humans (in sharp contrast to automata) are able to choose expressions that are appropriate to the situation, as discussed above, it is clear that there is more to creativity than mere recursivity.

Recursivity is sufficient, however, to draw a very important conclusion, which is already irreconcilable with the approach to the investigation of human nature Chomsky and the students of his generation were taught. Since most expressions heard or spoken by a particular individual in the course of a day or a lifetime are new and have never been used, exactly as they are, before and since there is an infinite variety of them, there is no way of filing them (as in a filing cabinet) in a single human brain, given that the human brain is not only finite, but rather small (three pounds or less). The only plausible alternative is to assume that what the native speaker has in his or her brain is a generative procedure, that is, **knowledge of a language**, the language that the speaker knows. This mental language (generative procedure) specifies an unbounded set of expressions, among them the vast subset (yet relatively small next to an infinite set) that the speaker actually uses over the years. The linguist's generative grammar is just a theory of the speaker's mental language.

It hardly needs to be emphasized that the emergence of generative grammar in the contemporary sense (as it has developed since about 1950) represented a significant shift of focus in the approach to the investigation of human nature. The approach of the "behavioral sciences," in vogue at the time, focused on the study of behavior or the products of behavior, in our case speech (a set of expressions) or "verbal behavior," as the behaviorist psychologists preferred to call it. Generative grammar chose instead to focus attention on the states of the mind/brain that enter into behavior (the system of rules or principles defining the expressions, as in the even numbers example), behavior just providing the evidence for the inquiry into the mental states. The central concern from this point of view then is not the use of language but the knowledge of language that underlies its use, in particular the nature and origins of such knowledge. It is under this approach that the three basic questions that arise are the ones we considered above.

As repeatedly mentioned, the first proposals as to the form that answers to these questions might take were advanced in the early 1950s, serving as the basis for a general research program that has since been developing along a family of paths (and applying, sharpening, and enriching the original proposals in the process). This program was one of the strands that led to the development of the cognitive sciences in the contemporary sense, sharing with other cognitive approaches the belief that certain aspects of the mind/brain can be usefully construed on the model of computational systems of rules or principles that form and modify mental representations and that are put to use in action and interpretation, in particular in speech, reading, or writing.

A natural question with respect to computational systems is what are called economy considerations (least-effort type of considerations, generally speaking), which have to be made very precise because a great deal depends on what they are. Economy considerations were present from the beginning of generative grammar some forty-three years ago, although in the beginning they entered into the subject in a way quite different from the current approach. The basic assumption then was that the way universal grammar specifies a set of languages is by determining a format for rules systems. This format included two very different types of rules, phrase-structure rules and transformational rules, integrated in a particular way (see the next chapter), and with "traffic rules" connecting the transformations.

Explanatory adequacy (that is, the transition from the primary linguistic data available to the child to a particular generative procedure, say, the child's English) was achieved by finding a rule system consistent with the data and applying an evaluation metric showing that the rule system selected is the most highly valued. This is the framework for inquiry into what the child does who becomes a native speaker of a variety of a particular language. The child has some data, unconsciously knows what the right rule systems are, has an evaluation metric to compare alternative rule systems consistent with the data, and selects the most economical instantiation of the rule system given the data (here is where the economy considerations fitted in at the time). The system that is selected is the language, and the linguist's theory of this language is the grammar (we may ignore purely terminological changes).[13]

This approach, initiated in the late 1940s and fully developed by the mid-1950s, which has a rather traditional flavor (and was quite at odds with the kind of structural linguistics dominant at the time), did not essentially change for the next thirty years.[14] However, in the course of its development the class of possible rule systems was reduced to the point where the rules gave way to general principles and to a much deeper understanding of the solution to Plato's Problem in the domain of language (the problem that defines the field, as we know). After 1980, when the new ideas crystallized, there are no traditional constructions (interrogative, relative, passive, causative, etc.) and there are virtually no rules (hence no rule systems). The constructions and the rules were shown to be just taxonomic epiphenomena. This is a way of saying that the whole of the traditional approach to language of the last couple of thousand years suddenly became obsolete, as we will see in the next subsection.

5.2.2. The radical departure of 1980:
A principles-and-parameters framework

Early work in present-day generative grammar was, to a considerable extent, work in traditional grammar of great sophistication (made possible by then-recent developments in mathematics). This is not to deny that from the very beginning generative grammar developed a general framework and conceptual structure without parallel in the tradition (something new in the history of the discipline) or that it went a long way in the direction of filling in the huge gaps that still remained even in the most comprehensive traditional grammars because of their lack of attention to the massive initial contribution of the language organ (the richest traditional grammars barely go beyond an array of examples and hints). Nevertheless, although the framework was new and quite different from anything known at the time, the rule systems proposed were, in essentials, of the traditional type.

In contrast, the conceptual framework of the 1980s and 1990s is quite new and sharply different from anything that preceded it. The differences stand out when we consider two properties that descriptive statements about language might have or lack. Every grammatical statement may or may not be language-invariant (a necessary choice), and some statements may or may not be construction-invariant:

Typology of grammatical statements
(i) Language-invariant or not language-invariant
(ii) Construction-invariant or not construction-invariant

The statements of both traditional grammar and early generative grammar are neither language-invariant nor construction-invariant (they are typically language-particular and construction-particular), while the statements of post-

1980 generative grammar are often language-invariant and always construction-invariant (illustrations will be provided in the next chapter). In fact, the notion of construction in the traditional sense (interrogative, relative, passive, causative, etc.) no longer plays a role in grammar (which is not to say it may not be a useful notion for descriptive taxonomy, on a par with "terrestrial animal" in zoology).

If there are no constructions (that is, if the constructions are nothing but taxonomic epiphenomena), there cannot be rules for the constructions, which is not very surprising when we remember that the original rules of generative grammar (phrase structural or transformational) were adaptations of the rules of traditional grammar to a new framework. If there are no rules, there cannot be an evaluation metric to choose among rule systems. There is no longer any evaluation metric because there are no alternatives. A basic assumption nowadays is that the initial state of the language organ is so constrained that there is only one general procedure consistent with the primary linguistic data, namely, the one that results when the choices left open by human nature are fixed by the primary data. If that is the case, the new type of theory is a much superior type of theory and, if on the right track, it represents enormous progress since it comes much closer to dealing with the basic problem of explanatory adequacy. To begin with, it eliminates the economy considerations in the old form: The choice of the language is just fixed (there is only one possible outcome).

What then is the new explanation for the growth of knowledge of language in the brain of the child and how does it differ from the earlier ones? The main problem to be addressed has always been that the differences between languages must be determinable from a very small amount of data because that is all that children have at their disposal. The child's feat is possible in principle if, for starters, languages have approximately the same kind of phrase structure system at some abstract level, a property that is not easy to reconcile with the systems of rules proposed in early generative grammar (see the next chapter). There is then no conceivable way a child could develop some of the rules proposed before roughly 1980 on the basis of the small amount of data available in childhood. It is for this reason, among others, that the earlier theory was in need of radical revision.

The problem facing the linguist is not unlike the one faced by the embryologist, where a slight shift in the gene mechanisms regulating growth may be all that separates a fertilized egg from developing into a butterfly rather than a whale. In other words, the problem of accounting for language growth is conceptually similar to the so-called gene-control problem, except for an irrelevant difference: In the case of language growth, part of the information needed for development comes in the form of interaction with early experience, including linguistic expressions (sounds or signs). When we stop to think and overcome our natural inclination to disembody language from its physical basis we can see that the language organ, like the rest of the brain, develops or grows, like any other body organ, from an initial state to a steady state, part of which is a mature representation of the language that the child speaks. There is more to growth and maturation than size or number of cells.

An even closer analogy to language growth (recall the discussion in chapter 2) is provided by a type of growth that occurs in human beings after birth: The onset of puberty. No one would take very seriously the hypothesis that children undergo puberty because they see other people undergoing it and imitate them, perhaps out of a desire to be like them. We all assume that the course of puberty, which part of the way at least runs in parallel with the course of language development, is genetically determined.

The question then is: What is genetically determined in language and how are we to account for what happens to the child that develops native mastery of a particular language? The answer is not exactly immediately obvious. In fact, no one had a really plausible answer before 1979, remarkable as this might seem when we consider that Newtonian physics was developed over three hundred years ago and that the fundamentals of elementary mathematics, masterfully presented by Euclid in "the most renowned mathematical work in history," were fully understood well over two thousand years before Newton.[15] But although not immediately obvious, the answer is not hard to understand, once it is discovered. Actually, part of it was understood long before Newtonian physics, namely, the part that says that all languages are built on the same schema (are cast to the same mold) and therefore have fundamental properties in common. These are the language-invariant properties linguists try to capture in their language-invariant statements (referred to above).

The remaining problem was to account for the fact that humans speak not one but thousands of different languages, and these languages appear to be very diverse (although not as diverse as butterflies and whales), at least on the surface. How come children throughout the world do not have to give any thought to the process by which their universal schema is brought in line with the specific form the schema takes in the minds of the speakers they interact with? The answer that is widely accepted today is that the universal schema provided by the genetic endowment comes with a number of open choices or parameters of variation, perhaps two-valued, and what the child has to do is to set the parameters to the value that is consistent with the primary linguistic data. As Chomsky has suggested, we may think of the language organ "as a complex and intricate network of some sort associated with a switch box consisting of an array of switches that can be in one of two positions" (in fact, a number of switch boxes, since there are people who speak more than one language natively), where the fixed network is the system of invariant principles of the universal schema and "the switches are the parameters to be fixed by experience." For the system to function, the switches have to be set one way or another. "When they are set in one of the permissible ways, then the system functions in accordance to its nature," but differently depending on whether they are set for, say, a variety of California English or a variety of California Spanish. The meager data available to the child exposed to the language "must suffice to set the switches one way or another."[16] When these switches are set, the child has native command of the particular variety of the language internalized in the process and knows the facts of the language (that a particular expression is ambiguous, that it can have this or that meaning, and so on). To get a particular language, the child's brain just makes sure each switch is set to the right value (either plus or minus); equivalently, the child just goes through the complete list of parametric values provided by mother nature and "checks off" the appropriate values (in a figurative way of speaking), so a variety of English is some set of parameter settings and a variety of Spanish is a different set of parameter settings. And that is it. It is just like answering a questionnaire.

It is easy to see that this is "a very radical departure from the tradition of study of language over the past several thousand years."[17] The new principles-and-parameters approach to language theory presents a radically new way of understanding both the nature and the growth of a first language, making possible a deeper study than was possible heretofore of a central cognitive structure. We expand on this in the next chapter, where some concrete examples are offered as first approximations (the study of parametric variation is still in its infancy). It also places the problem of adult language acquisition in an entirely new light, as should become clear in chapter 7.

NOTES TO CHAPTER 5

1. See Chomsky 1966, especially note 9, from which the quotes are taken (the next one below is from page 5), except that the orthography has been standardized. Chomsky is quoting from Bellamy's (1698) rendition of the first (1575) edition of Huarte's book (later revised to conform to the dictates of the Inquisition), which was widely translated and circulated. As Chomsky notes, Huarte understands the Spanish word *ingenio* 'wit', which he relates to *gigno, genero, ingenero*, to have the meaning 'engender,' 'generate', and he speaks of "two generative powers" in humans, "one common with the beasts and plants, and the other participating of spiritual substances, God and the angels," a profound insight when it is reinterpreted in modern terms, as it is by Chomsky.

2. The quote is from Chomsky (1968:10–11; 1972a:12), also the source of the next quote in the text. Leonard Bloomfield, perhaps the most influential linguist of his generation, recognized in his 1933 book that there is no hope of accounting for language use on the basis of repetition or listing, since "the possibilities of combination are practically infinite," but he had nothing further to say about the problem beyond the remark that when speakers utter forms that they have not heard, they do it "on the analogy of similar forms" that they have heard previously. Fifteen year later, Charles Hockett, one of his most influential students (who, as Chomsky noted, is unusual among modern linguists "in that he has at least noticed that a problem exists"), accepted the view that when people speak they are either "mimicking or analogizing" and went on to say that "when we hear a fairly long and involved utterance which is evidently not a direct quotation, we can be reasonably certain that analogy is at work." Similar remarks can be found earlier in Paul, Saussure, Jespersen, and many others. As Chomsky pointed out in the 1950s, "to attribute the creative aspect of language use to 'analogy' or 'grammatical patterns' is to use these terms in a completely metaphorical way, with no clear sense and with no relation to the technical usage of linguistic theory" (1966:nn. 21, 22).

3. Numbers can perhaps reinforce the implications of the property of unboundedness. Since "a simple English sentence can easily run to a length of twenty words, . . . elementary arithmetic tells us that there must be at least 10^{20} such sentences that a person who knows English must know how to deal with," so it would take 10^{13} years "to utter all the admissible twenty-word sentences of English." This means that the probability that a speaker of English might have heard any particular twenty-word expression before is neglible. See Miller 1967, p. 80.

4. Chomsky 1972, pp. 12–13.

5. For further discussion of this topic, see Jackendoff 1993, chapter 1.

6. For further discussion, see Otero 1991 and Otero (ed.) 1994, in particular vols. 1 and 2.

7. These are the traditional questions listed in Chomsky 1988, p. 3, slightly adapted. They have appeared, in trivially different guises, in many other publications by Chomsky (some since 1955). A fourth question, a relatively new one, still on the horizon, is the following:

> What are the physical mechanisms that serve as the material basis for the system of knowledge and for the use of this knowledge?

This is one of the central questions of the neurosciences, of which little is known, so caution is necessary in making any direct claims. What is generally assumed is that the representation and use of language involve specific neural structures, even if their nature is not well understood. For a readable overview, see Parker 1986, chapter 9; for further discussion and references, Otero (ed.) 1994, vol. 4.

8. Descartes's Problem can be divided into two aspects: The production problem (the one the text refers to) and the perception problem (having to do with how we interpret what we hear—or read, a secondary matter in this context). The subquestion raised by the perception problem is not as obscure as that raised by the production

problem and is in fact under investigation. The answer often given to this subquestion is that perception of a language involves a parser, this parser presumably including the appropriate generative procedure (since the parsing of a monolingual speaker of English differs radically from that of a monolingual speaker of Basque or Japanese). See, in particular, the publications of Robert C. Berwick and his associates listed in the references. Cf. Horgan 1991, Horning 1991.

9. Chomsky 1988, p. 4.

10. There is a lot of linguistic evidence to support the idea of a genetically programmed language organ in the brain. But, as discussed in chapter 2 (particularly in section 2.3), even in advance of detailed linguistic research, we should expect heredity to play a major role in language because there is really no other way to account for the fact that children develop native mastery of a language. After all, no chimp can match the child's feat. No one doubts that the fact that humans develop arms and birds wings is due to heredity, the reason being that nothing in the fetal environments of the human or bird embryo can account for the differences between birds and humans. Exactly the same kinds of genetic arguments hold for language growth (part of the physical development of the brain) as hold for embryological development. See below.

11. See Chomsky 1986a, p. 16. This assumption "enters in one or another form, explicitly or tacitly," in other approaches, including those that "understand language to be a social product in accordance with the Saussurean concept of 'langue'."

12. As even professional linguists (including some sometimes referred to as mathematical linguists) do. Cf. Chomsky 1972, p. viii.

13. For many years Chomsky continued the traditional practice of referring to a set of expressions as the "language," and to the generative procedure as the "grammar," a terminological decision that resulted in some confusion.

14. See Chomsky 1951, 1955, 1957, 1965, 1972b, 1977. See also Culicover 1976 and Baker 1978 for an exceptionally successful exposition of the theory toward the end of its first phase, both from the intellectual and the pedagogical point of view.

15. See Otero 1991, especially the last section.

16. Chomsky 1988, pp. 62–63. The image of the switch box only partially "wired up" was actually suggested by a colleague of Chomsky's, the philosopher James Higginbotham (Chomsky 1986a:146).

17. The quote is from Chomsky 1989, p. 501. The first major exposition of the theory, Chomsky 1981, has been further elaborated and revised in many other publications. Among the most important are Chomsky 1986a,b, 1988b, 1992b. See also references therein and, for more recent related proposals, Kayne 1993a, 1993b (and Zwart 1992a, 1992b, 1993, Koster 1993b, Wu 1993a, 1993b, 1994) and Sportiche 1992, 1993a, 1993b.

6

Linguistic knowledge:
Universals and particulars

It is obviously not possible to give a full exposition of the current state of our understanding of human language in the space of this chapter, but just the flavor of it suffices in this context. As mentioned in the preface, the study of language has made enormous strides in the course of this century, particularly since about 1950. With little or no exaggeration we could say that it has advanced more in the last ten or fifteen years (certainly in the last forty years) than in the previous thirty centuries.

For the purposes of this book it is perhaps enough to give a sampling of a framework of ideas that serves as a guide to grammatical research for a community of linguists that has constituted an important strand within the larger community of students of language since the emergence of generative grammar at about 1950. We will consider some specific features of the current version of the theory, paying special attention to radically new ideas developed since about 1980. Hopefully, even a brief overview, though a pale image of present-day understanding, may serve as a necessary background for the next chapter (the heart of the book) and will contribute to making the more concrete discussion of chapter 8 more accessible.[1]

6.1. Language invariance: Part of the genetic endowment

There are of course invariant elements outside the syntax of a human language, but the syntactic ones are of particular interest for us. Syntactic invariance may be essentially of two types, which will be examined separately in the following two subsections.

6.1.1. Phrase structure: Two-level binary branching

Suppose that we want to construct a theory of grammar from scratch and, to avoid duplication of effort, we decide that a prudent first step is to look at the twenty-five-century history of the study of language from our vantage point and try to find some traditional insight that can serve as the initial basis for our theory. Where would we start looking?

If we are trying to select the most basic subfield of grammatical study, a good point to begin is the study of the so-called parts of speech, since these basic elements provide the building blocks that are a prerequisite for any theory construction in the domain of language. It is obviously not possible to construct a theory without basic (sometimes called primitive) elements because the rules or principles of any theory (in particular, any theory of language) will of necessity have to refer to some basic elements. For example, to be able to say that at one level of analysis an expression such as *birds fly* is made up of a noun and a verb we have to be able to refer to noun and verb.

Perhaps the most evident observation about human language is that the words that make up the complex expressions belong to different classes, and since antiquity it has been known that the two most important classes are Noun (which we may abbreviate N, for perspicuity) and Verb (V for short), as in *birds fly, dogs bark, teachers teach, preachers preach*, and so on, expressions that at one level of analysis are of the form N–V, meaning a noun followed by a verb. Every language has nouns and verbs. Some languages also have Adjectives (which we may abbreviate A), as in *big birds, old dogs, teachable teachers*, and so on, which at one level are of the form A–N, that is, an adjective followed by a noun. Nouns, verbs, and adjectives are of course the three large classes of words, which are open classes in the sense that there is not a fixed number of them in the language (tomorrow there can be one more noun, or one more verb, or one more adjective).

In contrast, the number of items in each of the other classes is essentially fixed. To begin with, there is a very limited number of "adpositions" (P for short), which in some languages come **before** their complement, the reason they are called prepositions. English examples are *after lunch, by coincidence, from California, in Seattle*, and so on, which at one level are of the form P–N. In other languages a P comes **after** its complement (we return to the topic in the next section) and they are referred to as "postpositions," the resulting phrase being of the form N–P (compare *hereafter, thereafter, hereby, thereby, whereby, therefrom, wherefrom, therein, wherein, whereof, whereon, whereupon, whereto, wherewith*, and so on, or Spanish *conmigo* 'with me', where "migo" derives from Latin *mecum* 'me with').

The simplest framework for grammatical description is what we might call a word-class grammar. A grammar of this type consists of two parts: a collection of words listed by class, and a collection of formulas for the expressions that result from stringing words together. Here is a minuscule illustration of the model as applied to English:

(i) Word classes

N	V	A	P
birds	fly	big	from
dogs	bark	old	by
teachers	teach	small	in
preachers	preach	young	to
lunch	play	curious	after
coincidence			
California			
Seattle			

(ii) Formulas

F1: N–V
F2: A–N–V
F3: A–N–V–P–N
F4: A–N–V–P–N–P–N

And here is a representative sample of the expressions generated by the formulas of this minute grammar when each symbol is replaced by a word of the appropriate class:

By F1: Birds fly. Dogs bark. Teachers teach.
        Preachers preach. Preachers teach. Preachers bark.
        Preachers fly. Teachers preach. Birds teach. . . .
By F2: Big birds fly. Old dogs bark. Small teachers teach.
        Young teachers preach. Young birds bark. . . .
By F3: Old birds fly from California. Old dogs bark in
        Seattle. Young preachers teach to dogs. . . .
By F4: Small birds fly from California to Seattle.
        Old teachers bark from dogs to preachers. . . .

We can bypass the question of whether some of these expressions are or are not English, but one thing we cannot overlook is that there are many English expressions that this type of grammar does not generate. At first glance, it may appear that this fundamental inadequacy may be overcome by adding more formulas and more words (including words from other classes, say determiners, conjunctions, and so on). But if we stop to think, we will soon realize that no word-class grammar can generate all the possible expressions of English. Put in terms of chapter 5, it is obvious that a word-class grammar offers no solution for Humboldt's Problem: Since there is no "longest" expression of English, no formula of the type illustrated in (ii), no matter how long, will ever be long enough.[2]

This, however, is not the only inadequacy of this extremely rudimentary type of framework for grammatical description, which, surprising as it might seem, was one of the competitors early generative grammar had to contend with (in fact, it carried the day in many language classes well into the 1960s).[3] Word-class grammar fails to capture a basic property of language that had been known to traditional grammar for centuries: Complex linguistic expressions are not just sequences of words, but rather sequences of **groups of words**, traditionally called phrases, of which the all-encompassing one is sometimes referred to as "Sentence" (S for short). We would do well not to give up this crucial discovery of traditional grammarians, since the willingness to give it up would be nothing less than a cultural regression.

As has been known for many centuries, it is not just a coincidence that some sequences of particular word classes appear again and again. Even the miniscule sample of the extremely rudimentary grammar we are considering provides an example: in its longest formula the sequence P–N appears twice. Expressions such as *after lunch*, *by coincidence*, and *from California* are all examples of P–N sequences that are actually phrases, in this case formed by what we may call a head (*after*, *by*, *from*) and its complement. Since the head here is a Preposition, the phrase is called a Prepositional Phrase (PP for short). A PP may of course be part of a larger phrase, as in *go to California*, which at one level may be analyzed as V–PP, where the PP is the complement and the V is the head of the phrase, hence its name of Verb Phrase (abbreviated VP). We just give perspicuous expression to the traditional idea that a verb phrase consists of a verb followed by a complement when we represent the expression in an upside-down tree diagram (with the "root" at the top) such as in diagram 6.1.

In early generative grammar it was assumed that a tree diagram such as this was just a reflection of a rule such as the following

$$VP \rightarrow V\text{--}PP$$

which may be paraphrased "a VP consists of a V immediately followed by a PP," taking the arrow to mean "consists of," "is made up of," or some such expression. This type of rule is called a "phrase-structure rule," and a grammar made up of rules of this type is called a "phrase-structure grammar."[4]

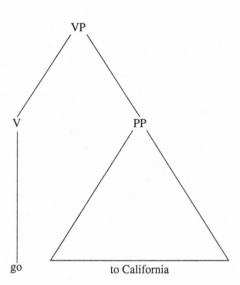

Diagram 6.1

Many such rules were proposed, a proliferation that was one of the shortcomings of early generative grammar, as was eventually discovered. The reason was that they allowed a great deal of arbitrariness. One example of the late 1970s is given in diagram 6.2 (NP is short for Noun Phrase, D for determiner) where the lower S could be the highest node of the structure of any sentence (*the young girl knows math, the earth is flat, it was good while it lasted*, and so on). A measure of the rapid advances of the 1980s and early 1990s is that little in this tree diagram is taken to be correct today. Perhaps the most obviously arbitrary assumption in it is that the sequence *that S* is an NP. Why should that be? Presumably because it can be replaced by, for example, *that lie* (which is of the form *that N*), preserving acceptability, or because one could say something like *[that the earth is flat] was believed for centuries* (where the brackets demarcate an instantiation of *that S*).

The assumption that *that S* is an NP even though neither *that* nor *S* is an N is not excluded by a language theory that does not take a phrase to be a "projection" of a "head" (in the sense that a VP can only be a projection of a V, as in tree diagram 6.1, an NP can only be a projection of an N, a PP a projection of a P, an AP a projection of an A, and so on); in other words, the phrasal category (NP, VP, . . .) has the features of its head (in a technical sense we will consider directly), hence the name of NP for the phrase headed by N, and so on. This conception of a phrase, however, first propounded in 1967, was slow in gaining general acceptance among generative grammarians. In fact, the pivotal function of the head of a projection is only now beginning to be understood in some depth.

Diagram 6.2

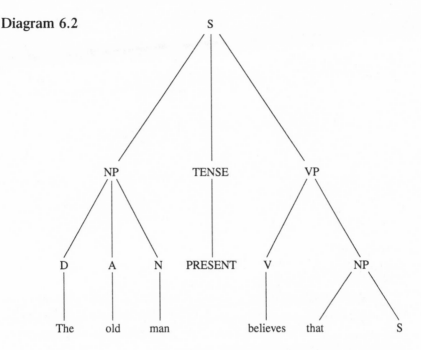

Despite the slow start, since 1967 and in particular since the early 1980s there has been substantial progress in the study of the theory of phrase structure, now one of the better understood subtheories or submodules of the theory of language. It is also, in a way, the most basic, since without the well-defined structures this subtheory generates there is nothing for the other submodules of the grammar to operate on. An understanding of this theory then is a prerequisite for understanding anything about syntax, and in turn an understanding of syntax is crucial for understanding anything about language (and about language acquisition after puberty). Since this subtheory or submodule of the theory of grammar is the most fundamental one, its most fundamental elements will necessarily be some of the most fundamental elements of the entire system of grammar. So if what we know in this area is a good first approximation to the truth, we can be sure we have discovered something that is fundamental for the whole system, hence something of very great value. A serious student of language cannot possibly ignore it.

That phrases have a hierarchical structure is an idea that, in a somewhat obscure and unsophisticated form, has been around for centuries. The best traditional grammarians (from our vantage point) had a basic grasp of it and struggled to get to understand it better. Early generative grammar reformulated it with a precision unknown until then, but not until recently has it become

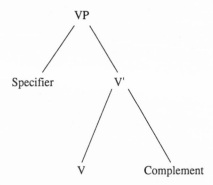

Diagram 6.3

clear that the basic phrase structure schematism for English-type languages is exemplified by the VP structure in diagram 6.3, to be compared with the one we considered above (as a first approximation) for *go to California*.

One important difference to notice is that there are two levels, of which the lowest corresponds to the subphrase V–complement, where complement is just the name of a position (sister of V), specifier is just the name of a position (sister of V'), and each of the two positions may be occupied by a phrase of any type (PP, as in *go to California*, the sequence *that*-S, as in *believes that the earth is flat*, and so on); the names are also applied to the phrases that occupy those positions, so subjects are specifiers because they are in a specifier position and objects are complements because they are in a complement position.[5]

We can represent the underlying schematism in more general terms by replacing the variable V (ranging over verbs only) by the more general variable X (ranging over all possible heads: V, N, A, P, . . .). If we also take VP to actually be V″, that is, level two of the hierarchical structure, the resulting tree diagram is as shown in diagram 6.4.

Since this is the fundamental schematism, we can refer to the submodule it is part of as X-bar theory, as is now common. It is important to note that, in contrast with the diagram for S illustrated above, this phrase structure schematism does not allow for anything beyond binary branching, meaning that a node cannot have more than one sister (compare the substructure for *the old man* or the also ternary branching of the higher S itself).[6] This already suggests that the two basic configurational relations are X–complement and X–specifier, an indication of the pivotal role of the head (X) referred to above, hence of the central importance of this subtheory or module of the grammatical system. The bottom line is that phrase-structure theory has been reduced to

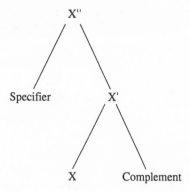

Diagram 6.4

where X={V, N, A, P, . . . }

X-bar theory, which is an extremely simple theory and until recently appeared to be quite well motivated.

However, the notation VP or NP, or even V″ or N″, which makes things easier for our conscious mind, is somewhat misleading, and AP or PP even more so. The reason is that A and P are not really among the basic (primitive) terms of current language theory, and the elements V and N are actually more abstract than the notation we have been using suggests. Again, the basic insight can be traced back to traditional grammar, which assumed not only that V and N are two of the lexical categories, but also that they are sort of archicategories. This is made particularly obvious by some traditional terms such as the Spanish expressions for noun (*nombre substantivo*, that is, "substantival noun") and for adjective (*nombre adjetivo*, "adjectival noun"), which implies that there are two kinds of noun (*Nombre*) and that the two share a property that we might call Nounness. This suggests that N is actually a property or distinctive feature that either adjectives or "substantives" may have, an idea that may be expressed by saying that the two nominal categories N and A share the feature specification [+N], that is, are positively specified with respect to the feature [N]. It is immediately obvious that nouns and adjectives have some things in common, for example inflection for number (singular, nonsingular) and gender in many languages.

Now recall that both adjectives and verbs may be predicates (*round* is a predicate in *the earth is round*, *spins* in *the earth spins*), and that sometimes it is notoriously difficult to decide whether a particular word is an instantiation of an adjective or of a verb, for example in *the door was closed* (compare *the door was open* with *the door was opened*, where both *open* and *opened* are translated into Spanish as *abierta*). Could it be that the two share a property we may call verbness, and that [V] is no less a distinctive feature than [N]? Many linguists believe there are reasons to conclude that this is exactly the case, and that both verbs and adjectives are positively specified with respect to this feature, that is, each has the feature specification [+V].

The obvious thing to do at this point is to bring the traditional notions within the logic of distinctive feature theory, making use of a notation that allows us to express the traditional ideas in a sharper and more perspicuous way. We may begin by asking whether the category adjective, which is traditionally assumed to have the property of nounness, also has the property of verbness (compare *abierta* with *open* and *opened*). It is a fact that some languages do not really have adjectives, and in those languages the words that do the work of our adjectives are verbs. It seems plausible then that adjectives have both properties, nounness and verbness, as many contemporary linguists assume. In distinctive feature notation this assumption may be expressed by saying that the feature specification for adjectives includes the two feature specifications [+V, +N]. This in turn suggests that the submatrix of feature specifications for verbs is [+V, −N], given that verbs and nouns are poles apart in the system of lexical categories. The next step is rather obvious: Since in at least a fundamental dimension a noun appears to be the very opposite of a verb, it makes sense to assume that the submatrices for nouns and verbs have opposite values with respect to [V] and [N], that is, if a verb is [+V, −N], a noun is [−V, +N].

At this point we should perhaps sum up our conclusions in a chart to be able to see them all at a glance, in part because there is no better way of discovering an interesting gap in the system we have developed so far:

Lexical categories

(1) V	(verbs)	[+V, −N]
(2) N	(nouns)	[−V, +N]
(3) A	(adjectives)	[+V, +N]
(4)	?	[−V, −N]

We can now see why the categories that make things easier for our conscious mind, in particular A, do not tell us very much about the ones presumably used by our unconscious mind (if our theory so far is on the right track), which are the ones between brackets, so we should keep in mind that the nodes in our VP tree diagram above would have to be replaced by feature complexes including [+V, −N]. There is a big difference between the formal syntactic feature [V], which can be specified as + or −, yielding [+/−V], and our informal abbreviation V, which can be now formally represented as

[+V, −N]. The implicit claim is that the formal features are mentally represented in the language organ, although we have no conscious knowledge of their representation, while the informal abbreviations V, N, and A are not part of the language organ at all, but simply a crutch for our conscious understanding and reasoning.

This is of some interest: We find the conscious manipulation of the abbreviations easier than the conscious manipulations of the formal features, even though the language organ manipulates only the formal features, and it does so with complete ease. The formal features are part of the **unconscious knowledge** coded in the language organ of the speaker, while the abbreviations are artifacts contrived to make easier our conscious understanding and reasoning, which involves other parts or faculties of the mind, in particular what we might call the rational faculty.

Another thing to note is that, thanks to the advantages of our notation over the traditional terminology, we are led to a category with negative values for both features, namely [−V, −N]. What could be a natural instantiation of this fourth category? Traditional grammar does not really help very much here, since it offers a proliferation of choices: prepositions (or postpositions, as the case may be in a particular language), particles, adverbs, conjunctions, interjections, and so on. Some would think that a natural choice at this point would be preposition, that is P, but since the status of P is somewhat problematic and we do not need to choose right away, we might as well leave the question open. Notice also that now we have a technical way to refer to both substantival nouns and adjectival nouns: they are both [+N]. We may say, for example, that [+N] elements are inflected for both number and gender.

So far we have covered only part of the picture. A fairly recent important discovery that has received a good deal of attention in recent years is that lexical heads (V, N, A, . . .) are only one of two types of heads, the other type being the functional heads, as they are usually called. Consider again the sequence *that S,* as in *that birds fly* in *that birds fly would surprise no one*. What kind of category is this *that*, usually referred to as complementizer and abbreviated C (the counterpart to Spanish, Portuguese, or French *que*, Italian *che*, German *dass*, and so on), which is very different from the *that* related to *those*? Could it actually be the head of its phrase? This is exactly what some students of language concluded in the early 1980s. If so, X={V, N, A, P, C . . . }, and the X-bar schematism leads us to posit the structure shown in diagram 6.5 where C is *that* and complement=S, that is, in our example complement=*birds fly*. Now, if complements are X-bar phrases, and every X-bar phrase has to have a head, the obvious next question is: What is the head of S?

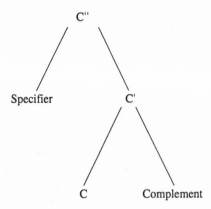

Diagram 6.5

A hint comes from expressions of the form *birds will fly, birds can fly*, and so on, where the modals *will* and *can* are good candidates for head of S. Another hint comes from the fact that *will fly* is translated by a single word with an inflection or inflectional ending for future in some languages, including Spanish, Portuguese, and Italian. So the first step in what now seems the right direction was to assume that what may be called "Inflection" (I for short) plays a role in the syntax (after all, the subject and the verbal inflection have to agree), and a second step was to assume that I is the head of its phrase (S), that is, the head of IP or I″. When we replace complement by I″ in the previous tree diagram and develop I″ in accordance with the X-bar schematism, the resulting tree diagram is as shown in diagram 6.6.

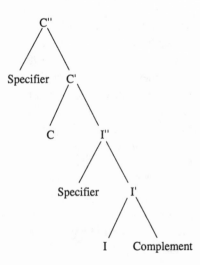

Diagram 6.6

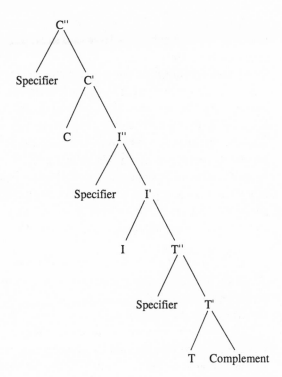

Diagram 6.7

By now it is plain that there is more to our unconscious knowledge of language than meets the eye. But we still have a long way to go. An obvious question to ask at this point is: What could be a suitable complement for I if we take I to cover only person-number agreement, for example, the abstract specification (that is, non-first person, non-second person, non-singular) realized as *n* in Spanish *interpretan* 'they interpret', related to *interpretar*, "to interpret"? It might help to compare *interpreta-n* with *interpreta-ba-n*, where *-ba-* is the overt realization of imperfect preterit, which is obviously an abstract tense specification. If we now recall that in some languages tense specifications are realized as independent words (compare *will* in *birds will fly*, which, however, does not show overt agreement, a particular property of English), it will come as no surprise that in recent years it has been proposed that Tense (T for short) is the head of its phrase.[7] We may tentatively assume, as some linguists do, that this phrase, TP or T″, is the complement of IP, which allows us to extend the previous tree diagram as in diagram 6.7.

Now suppose we assume that complement is to be replaced by the X-bar structure for VP given above, and that the complement of VP is some nominal substructure. The resulting tree diagram would still be far from representing a complete verbal (clausal) structure. For one thing, it would not provide a basis for representing the agreement between a past participle and an (underlying) direct object, a well-known phenomenon that may be illustrated with a Romance example such as French *Paul les a repeintes* (as against *repeint*) 'Paul has repainted them', where *les* and *repeintes* agree, or Spanish *las sillas fueron repintadas* 'the chairs were repainted', related to 'someone repainted the chairs'. This and other considerations led some linguists in the late 1980s to the conclusion that there are in fact two "agreement phrases," here referred to as IP phrases, in a "verbal" (clause) structure, one immediately below CP (the one represented in the last two diagrams) and one immediately above VP. Diagram 6.8 is a tree diagram with all the substructures mentioned so far ("spec" is an abbreviation for specifier; ZP is any phrase, a complement in this particular tree).

This could be the X-bar structure for a CP such as *that the teacher believes this claim* (if we take ZP to be a nominal such as *this claim*) or for a CP such as *that the teacher believes that there are students who are skeptical about the claims that are put forth by teachers whose professional training doesn't include basic knowledge needed to answer the queries that the most thoughtful students come up with when they stumble upon intriguing questions that . . . ,* and on and on (if we take ZP to be a CP and we want to illustrate the recursive property of our mental generative procedure).

Does this tree diagram come close to representing the structural complexity of a "verbal" (clausal) structure? In the chapter after next we will find some reasons to doubt it. In any case, we still have not said anything about "nominal" structures. It has been argued that, in an important sense, V is the head of the largest structure we have considered so far, namely CP (or C''), not just the head of VP (or V''). Since there appears to be a deep parallelism between VP and NP, it is reasonable to suspect that there is an extended "nominal" structure not unlike the extended "verbal" structure we have been considering, with similar "agreement phrases" (after all, nouns and articles "agree" overtly in many languages), although without the counterpart to a tense phrase, an exclusive property of clauses. But these intriguing questions are beyond the scope of this book. Another inciting topic we have to bypass is the crucial interrelation between functional and lexical categories.[8] What we have seen in this subsection, however, will hopefully be enough to give the flavor of current research on the topic (in the process suggesting that the days of commonsense language theory, though far less remote than the days of Aristotelian physics, are now over) and to make the more concrete discussion in chapter 7 considerably more accessible.[9]

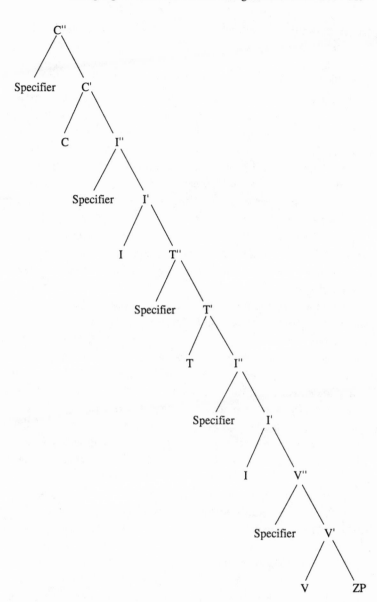

Diagram 6.8

We turn now to a very different type of grammatical principle that operates on X-bar structures.

6.1.2. Transformations: Structure-dependent operations

One of the things that recent research on language makes clear is that what you hear or see is remote from what goes on in your language organ. Paraphrasing the often-heard disclaimer, we may say that any similarity between the actual string of words in a clause (the surface linear structure) and the underlying mental structure is sheer coincidence. This is of course quite an exaggeration, but to some extent it points in the right direction because it tells us to expect to find many differences between the surface appearance and the underlying mental reality.

Consider a very simple example such as *the teacher appears to believe a false claim*. Does *the teacher* really go with *appears*? Obviously not. Just think of *it appears that the teacher believes a false claim*, which is closer to the underlying mental structure. A way of relating the two instantiations is to say that in the first one the phrase *the teacher* moved from the position immediately to the left of *to believe* to its surface position, which will give something along the lines of *appears the teacher to believe a false claim*, obviously not English (at this point we do not have to ask why). Since we understand the first sentence of this paragraph to mean roughly the same thing as the second sentence (the one beginning with *it*), in our interpretation of either expression the teacher is the one doing the believing (in grammatical terms, *the teacher* is the subject of the verb *believe*), so it must be that in some way *the teacher* never completely leaves its original place (next to the verb *believe*) in our minds. As a first approximation we may suppose (or hypothesize, to use the more technical term) that a phrase that is moved by a grammatical transformation (the name of the mental operation—a movement, specifically "raising," operation in this case) leaves a trace of some sort behind, "t" for short. We then have

(1) *The teacher appears* t *to believe a false claim.*

We next ask whether *appears* is where it seems to be. The last tree diagram in the preceding section could be taken to mean that the answer is "No," and this would be the correct answer for a language such as Spanish or Italian, but it does not seem to be the correct answer for English (although in English also, presumably, the verb will eventually end up in the same type of position of our mental tree diagram as the Spanish verb, another topic beyond the scope of this book). The point is that there is more to the question than meets the eye, because if *appears* is under the V position in our tree diagram and *the teacher* is under the spec of the higher IP, as is usually assumed, several nodes intervene between *teacher* and *appears*, while in (1) they are next to each other.

More surprising still: The difference between the surface position of the English verb with respect to the surface position of the Spanish verb seems to have a parallel in the "nominal" system in that the Spanish translation of *false claim* is *afirmación falsa*, where the noun *afirmación* seems to have moved past the adjective *falsa*. Again this is beyond the scope of this book. It is just a hint about the vast expanse we cannot cover here.

One topic we cannot fail to say something about is the ubiquity of transformational operations, of which we have just seen two instances (if we count the movement of *afirmación* in the Spanish nominal phrase *afirmación falsa*). A slightly more complex example such as *the teacher appears to believe the claim that the students seem to think that the serious study of language is taken to offer many bonuses* may suffice for our purposes. It is not difficult to see that here the phrase *the teacher* has moved from immediately before *to believe* and the phrase *the students* has moved from immediately before *to think*. And it is not very difficult to see that the phrase *the serious study of language* has also moved from the position it has in *many take the serious study of language to offer many bonuses*, of which . . . *is taken* . . . is just the passive counterpart (this being one of the constructions studied in both traditional grammar and early generative grammar—recall the discussion in chapter 5). Now it is clear that in all three cases we have instances of the application of one and the same mental operation, namely movement of a nominal phrase (we are not calling it noun phrase or NP for a reason) to a higher Spec position, what is still sometimes called raising.

This is only the tip of the transformational iceberg, but it is all we have room for here. The main point is that the effects of this principle of "action at a distance," which has nothing to do with the one that struck Newton as "occult" but is no less real (if current results can be trusted), are pervasive in language structure.[10] One can ignore this only at his or her own peril, as many linguists of the generation after Ferdinand de Saussure's eventually discovered. A structural approach that limits itself to the surface structure leaves out most of the picture, which is why the "methods of structural linguistics" with which Chomsky began as a student did not go beyond the segmentation of the surface form or "spell-out" of an expression (the string of words that realize its abstract structure) and the classification of segmented units (a sort of taxonomy, all told). Pre-Chomskyan structural linguistics did little to overcome these limitations, which were in fact held to be necessary limitations.[11] As astonishing as it might seem in retrospect, the attempt to study the transformational principles that relate the surface form to the form hidden below the surface was taken at the time, and in some quarters also later, to indicate lack of respect for the "real language" (meaning the expression as it appears to the ear or the eye) and lack of concern for "linguistic fact" (that is, the physically identifiable subparts of actual utterances and their superficially marked formal relations).

But it is immediately obvious that in an expression such as *the teacher appears to believe this claim*, to go back to our example, nothing in the spell-out relates *teacher* and *believe*, which is one of the relations that play a fundamental role in the interpretation of the expression. This is because in general it is not the structure of the spelled-out expression that defines the interpretation. Rather, the interpretation is defined by what we may call the "Logical Form" (LF), related but not identical to the "logical form" of the logician (for one thing, the linguist's "LF" has empirical properties, not usually found in the logician's "LF," which are often difficult to discover and test). From this perspective we may say that a grammatical transformation is an operation that relates the abstract LF structure to a representation of the sound of the expression, what is called "Phonetic Form" (PF), LF and PF representations presumably being constituted of elements that belong to what is usually called universal phonetics and what might be called "universal logic" (perhaps part of "universal semantics"), respectively. In essence, this is the concept of grammatical structure that is being developed and elaborated today. It should be added that PF and LF are the two interface levels, that is, the levels that provide the instructions for the two types of performance system: the articulatory-perceptual and conceptual-intentional systems, respectively. The first makes it possible for us to speak and understand what we hear spoken or what we read, the second to dress our thoughts in linguistic garb.

A striking property of transformational operations is that they are not structure-independent, that is, they do not apply to a sentence independently of any structure, merely by virtue of the physical forms that constitute it (which would make for a mathematically much simpler system), as pre-Chomskyan structuralism would lead us to expect. Quite the contrary, a grammatical transformation is a structure-dependent operation, and the structure that is relevant for the transformation to apply is not physically marked in any way in the linguistic signal. Rather, the relevant structure, which is imposed by some mental operation as we hear or read the sentence, happens to be quite abstract.

As a concrete illustration, consider the transformation associated with question formation. A way of turning the simple statement *the teacher is interested in the subject she specialized in* into the question *is the teacher interested in the subject she specialized in?* is to find the first occurrence of the word *is* and move it to the front. Nothing could be simpler than that. However, the actual mental operation involved is rather different (and far more complicated), as can immediately be seen if we add *who is serious* after *the teacher* so that the statement reads *the teacher who is serious is interested in . . . .* We cannot now turn the statement into a question by saying *is the teacher who serious is interested in . . . ,* which is gibberish. Rather, we have to inspect the structure (unconsciously, of course) in order to identify the whole phrase that functions as a subject of the main verb (that is, the phrase *the teacher who is serious*) and move the occurrence of *is* that agrees with it to the front, which yields *is the teacher who is serious interested in the subject she specialized in?*[12]

A question we may ask at this point is: Why are grammatical operations structure-dependent (rather than structure-independent)? It could be argued— and indeed it was argued by Chomsky many years ago—that the principles of transformational grammar that provide an explanation for the structure-dependent property of the question formation rule themselves have a functional explanation, in that they can be shown to be appropriate to a certain form of organization of memory. But this is another topic beyond the scope of this book.

Other properties of transformations should at least be mentioned. An important one that has come to be much better understood in the last couple of years is that they always are raising (rather than lowering) operations. In other words, constituents can only move up the tree (not down). This is of course closely related to the hierarchical structure provided by X-bar theory. For concreteness, compare the following two alternative expressions:

(i) The teachers are all interested in their subject.
(ii) All the teachers are interested in their subject.

One thing that is obvious is that *all* and *the teachers* go together (they are understood as part of the same phrase). In (i), however, they are apart, and in other sentences they can be separated by many words. To account for the underlying relation, it was argued by some linguists and assumed by many more for many years that there is a transformation that moves *all* down the tree to the left of *interested* in (i) and similar structures. It was only in 1987 that it became clear that *all* is actually left behind (in the place in which it originates in underlying structure) when *the teachers* moves up the tree from a position between *all* and *interested*.[13]

Another important property of grammatical transformations is that they are "structure preserving." Structure preservation is understood nowadays a bit differently than when it was first proposed in 1970, but in a way this is just a refinement.[14] In present-day X-bar theory terms, we may say that a level two phrase, for example, can only move to an XP (X″) position, and a level zero phrase can only move to an X position. Furthermore, only an XP position that does not receive a thematic role (agent, patient, goal, instrument, and so on—see chapter 4) can be the target of movement. The two (or more) positions occupied by a particular abstract phrase during the "derivation" of the structure (comprising all the steps that lead from the underlying structure to the surface form) are said to be part of a "chain," and such chains serve as the elements of the logical form (LF). There are basically four types of chains, roughly those corresponding to words, arguments (subjects, objects, etc.), modifiers, and operator-variable structures (e.g., the one underlying *What do you say?*).

Grammatical transformations share with X-bar principles the property that their application is never required. It is, in other words, an option offered by the system. Take, for example, *the teacher appears to believe this claim*, which we considered a moment ago. As we have seen, it is widely assumed that at some point its underlying structure is, roughly, *appears the teacher to believe this claim*. What if *the teacher* remains in its underlying position, one of the options available? The answer is that the resulting structure is illegitimate because a basic requirement, case (to use the traditional term), cannot be satisfied. The reason is that *to believe* cannot "assign" case to *the teacher*, and neither can *appears* (compare *John believes him to have made the claim*, where *him* (which may be replaced by, say, *the teacher*) is assigned case by *believes*). Thus, in this class of structures the transformational movement is due to the requirements of a particular subtheory or module of the grammar, namely, case theory. It is the interaction between this subtheory and other principles of grammar that is behind the movement.

In other structures, the movement may be due to some other type of interaction among the principles of grammar. Again, the topic is beyond the scope of this book. Suffice it to mention that a very important subtheory or module (binding theory), which deals with the relationship between a pronoun (or, more generally, any "bindable" element) and its antecedent, as *they* and *the teachers* in *the teachers stated that they believe this claim* (on the reading in which *they* is referentially dependent on *the teachers*), relies very heavily on the hierarchical structure defined by X-bar theory. Roughly, the pronoun has to be lower in the tree than its antecedent. Compare *they stated that the teachers believe this claim*, where *they* cannot be referentially dependent on *the teachers*, with the previous example. It might be thought that precedence of the antecedent is enough, but this is obviously wrong, as the following example, where *they* may be referentially dependent on *the teachers*, shows: *After they became familiar with the appropriate research, the teachers believed the claim*. What is more, the "local" binding relationship has been extended to the chains created by transformation under the assumption that the element moved leaves behind a "trace," as exemplified above, and that it becomes the (immediate or remote) antecedent of its trace (or copy).[15]

Once the different subtheories or modules (case theory, binding, and so on) are properly developed, the construction-particular transformations of early generative grammar are no longer necessary. All that is needed is the general principle "Move anything anywhere" or "Move a category anywhere." This is the principle sometimes referred as "Move α" (or, even more generally, "Affect α," that is "Do anything to anything"), the basic principle of "bounding theory," another module of the universal theory of language.[16] Other principles of universal grammar such as those of X-bar theory, case theory, binding theory, and so on, will ensure that only the right category moves to the right position (or is erased).

In some ways, the theory sketched in this section is very different from the earlier ones, although it is also a very natural development of the earliest proposal, as formulated in the mid-1950s. A crucial way in which it differs from the earlier theories (up to 1980) is that it provides a true explanation for the logical problem of language "acquisition" (that is, biological growth), as we will see directly.

We have barely scratched the surface of some important invariant principles of grammar and have simply left others unmentioned, but it will have to do for the moment. The next section takes up the parametrized principles.

6.2. Language variation: The newborn's questionnaire

Students of universal grammar are well aware that not all principles of grammar are invariant. If they were, there would be only one language even in surface terms. But this is obviously not the case: Monolingual speakers of English cannot understand what is said by a speaker of some other language (Spanish, Basque, Berber, Korean, Chinese, Vietnamese—or, for that matter, some remote variety of what we informally call "English"). This diversity, which for the biologist might come as a surprise, requires explanation.

6.2.1. Morphology as paradigmatic grammar

As pointed out in chapter 5, when we seek a true explanation for the growth of knowledge of language in the brain of the child, the main problem to be addressed is, and has always been, that the differences between languages must be determinable from a very small amount of data, because that is all that children have at their disposal. To repeat: The child's feat is possible in principle if, for starters, languages have approximately the same kind of phrase structure systems at some abstract level, a property that is not easy to reconcile with the systems of rules proposed in early generative grammar but can easily be accommodated in a framework including the theory of phrase structure (X-bar theory) outlined in the previous section (or a better theory), and the same kind of transformational operations.

But since languages are not entirely identical, this cannot be the whole story. We still have to account for the striking diversity. After all, English differs from Spanish or Basque (no matter which variety we pick of each). Is there now (that is, after 1980) a plausible general explanation for the astonishing fact that under the proper conditions a child can develop knowledge of any language on the basis of the small amount of data available in childhood?

Many linguists would unhesitantly answer "Yes." It seems that for the first time in the long history of the study of language (no less than twenty-some centuries) we have come to understand at least the logic of the growth of language in the child's mind.

This logic appears to be disarmingly simple. Let us begin by considering a difference that until 1993 was taken to be an underlying one: word order, or more precisely constituent order. Compare the following two sets of examples:

(1)

    (i) read [the book] (VP)
       with [the book] (PP)
    (ii) [the book] read (VP)
       [the book] with (PP)

In terms of the X-bar theory sketched above, *the book* is the complement in each case; *read* and *with* are the heads (V and P, respectively). The difference between (i) and (ii) is that in the X′ subphrase (V′ or P′) X precedes the complement in (i), while X follows the complement in (ii). If these are the only possible values of this purported parametric choice (to use a technical term), we may say that a language of the first type is head first or [+head first], whereas a language of the second type (Basque, for example) is head last or [−head first]. If a language is of the first type, we expect that when the head of the X′ subphrase is a noun (N) such as *fact* or an adjective (A) such as *happy*, it will also precede its complement, as in

(i′) fact [that the book came out]
      happy [that the book came out]

and that in a language of the second type the head N (or A) will follow its complement. In fact, we expect every head (C, I, T, . . .) to immediately precede its complement in a [+head first] language and to immediately follow its complement in a [−head first] language. If this is on the right track, there are two types of languages in terms of head-complement relative position. English is a typical [+head first] language; Japanese is a typical [−head first] language. It is to be noted that with this and a few other options fixed, the effects of the phrase structure rules of the early generative grammars are essentially given; they do not have to be learned and do not constitute an independent part of our knowledge, which is why there is no need for the proliferation of phrase structure rules typical of those grammars, and we may even dispense with the notion of phrase structure rule so prominent in early generative grammars.

It is important to note that a parameter is assumed to have the property that it can be determined by a very small amount of data, which is all that children have, as already pointed out. The leading idea is that a few simple examples such as those in (i) would be enough for the child to determine (unconsciously, of course) that the language he or she hears is a [+head first] language. What is more, this determination would immediately lead to another one, the position of a head such as *have* in, for example,

(iii) have [read [the book]]

since this head also would have to precede in a language of the first type and follow in a language of the second type, as Basque or Japanese, or for that matter an earlier stage of English or a remote stage of Spanish, say Latin or early Romance. Compare Spanish *ha de leer el libro* 'has to read the book' with *[lo leer] ha* (literally, "it to read has," in the sense of "has to read it"), now spelled *lo leerá* 'will read it', a vestige from a remote stage of the language indicating that some time in the past a verbal head, in this case the ancestor of *leer*, followed its complement (*lo* in our example) and that the higher verbal head *ha* followed its complement, here *[lo leer]*.

The choice of head-first or not head-first could then be a parameter in terms of which languages can vary. It would also be a very basic one, with multiple effects. In this sense, a parametric choice is reminiscent of the choice in a computer-program menu or a restaurant menu, particularly the choices in menus with some internal structure. For example, it is like choosing between fish or meat and then being committed to choosing white wine with the fish or red wine with the meat, except that in the case of language the choice has already been made for the child by the ancestors of the people speaking the language of the community. What the child unconsciously "chooses" is to align the mental "switches" of his or her language organ with those of the speakers who unwittingly provide the primary linguistic data children make use of. However, although the switch settings may vary, the configurations attainable are otherwise largely invariant.

The question is: Is the contrast in (1) really due to a parametric difference? If a radically new proposal, half a year old at the time of writing, is essentially correct, the answer is "No." There are reasons to believe that, contrary to what has been assumed for years, spec-head-complement order, associated with English and other languages usually assumed to differ in underlying order from Basque, Japanese, Dutch, and other languages, is in fact universal. This of course does not mean that the problem the head direction parameter addressed is no longer a problem. It is still necessary to explain the word order differences between, say, English and Dutch. Even if the contrast (head first in English, head last in Dutch) is not the surface manifestation of a difference in underlying order, it still has to result from the interaction of one or more parametric differences. It would appear that important steps in this direction have already been taken, one not insignificant bonus being that under the new analysis Dutch (one of the best studied head-last languages) is less puzzling than it used to be in at least one important respect: There is no longer a need to assume that CP complements are "extraposed" to the right (clearly a stopgap solution that is not allowed under current assumptions).[17] Even more recently (fall 1993) it has been argued that if we construct a kind of bare phrase structure that is really motivated (a phrase structure that is derivable from the most trivial and uncontroversial facts about PF and LF interface conditions), a number of interesting conclusions, including universal underlying order, (mostly) follow trivially.

The differences due to constituent order are among the most obvious and the easiest to illustrate (hence the choice of first example). Matters are far more subtle when we turn to less obvious differences (for example, the contrast between Romance and English discussed in the next chapter), and even mere exemplification would require a more elaborate technical apparatus. But it is possible to give at least the flavor of what appears to be a true parameter, recently figured out, of very noticeable and well-known effects. The two resulting types of languages in this case are what we may call nominative (or nominative-accusative) languages and absolutive (or ergative-absolutive) languages. The basic contrast may be brought out by means of a simple pair of examples together with an oversimplified schematism of their respective structures:

(2)

    (i) The child broke the glass. $(NP_1 \ V \ NP_2)$
    (ii) The glass broke. $(NP_2 \ V)$

It is obvious that the relation between NP_2 and V—*the glass* and *broke*, respectively, in this case—is the same in both (i) and (ii). Superficially, however, *the glass* is an object in the first example and a subject in the second. In absolutive-type languages, *the glass* bears absolutive case both when it is an object, as in the counterparts to (i), and when it is a subject, as in the counterparts to (ii), while in nominative-type languages it bears accusative case when it is an object, as in (i), and nominative case when it is a subject, as in (ii). This puzzling difference (both NP_2s carry absolutive case, NP_1 and NP_2 of (ii) both carry nominative case), which led many linguists astray over the years, appears to reduce to a very simple parametric choice. There are apparently two grammatical cases available, which we may refer to as subjective and objective. When only one of them is needed, as in (ii), there are two options available: Either objective case is inert and subjective is active (the nominative choice) or objective case is active and subjective case, referred to as ergative, is inert (the absolutive case). This, which once understood seems trivial, is apparently all there is to it.[18]

There are of course several other parametric choices that languages make, as will be seen in chapter 8, but the small sample in this subsection may be enough to get the idea across. If this principles-and-parameters approach is on the right track, the language organ allows only a number of values for each parametric choice, perhaps no more than two (say, + and −, as suggested above). A language pedigree, that is, a linguistic system evolving across the centuries (say, pre-English to proto-English to Old English to Middle English to Modern English), can change its mind, as it were, on one or more parametric choices in the course of its history (for example, Old English was not head first, as Modern English is, and the same can be said of a remote ancestor of Spanish and Modern Spanish, as illustrated above). Each time there is a shift in the value of a parameter, all sorts of superficial things change almost at once in clusters, something that was very puzzling before the new approach just sketched was put forth. Now it seems that the divergence in a certain cluster of properties flows from one choice (one parameter). The study of such cluster changes falls within the domain of historical linguistics.[19]

If a language is essentially a small set of parametric choices, what happens to the child that becomes a native speaker of a particular language, a process that until recently was seen as "language learning" by practically everyone, may actually be likened to the child filling out a questionnaire with a limited number of binary choices: Does the head precede the complement (or, perhaps more accurately, does the nominal complement move to the left of the head)? Is the subjective case active? Is agreement strong? and so on and so forth. All the child has to do is to "inspect" the primary linguistic data and answer each question "Yes" or "No," that is, set each of its mental switches in the Yes or No position. This of course is not to be taken literally, but it appears to be closer to the real thing than saying that the knowledge of language of a native speaker is due to "conditioning," "association," practice in exercising skills, and so on. There is little doubt that the child develops such knowledge on the basis of a very rich biological endowment that determines, quite precisely, the kinds of systems that can develop in language growth, and the idea of a questionnaire of parametric choices appears to point in the right direction.

The nominative/absolutive parameter clearly shows that morphological properties (in particular, case endings) play a significant role in setting parameters that have widespread syntactic effects. In other words, there is a close correspondence between morphological properties and parametric values. Thus, the syntactic structures of a language are essentially a reflection of its morphological properties, which play a role in the triggering of specific parametric values. If a parameter is set one way, the result is one set of consequences, while if it is set another way, the result is another set of consequences. One such set of consequences differentiates French from Spanish, or French and English from Spanish, French, Catalan, and other Romance languages that allow silent grammatical subjects, a topic to which we return in the next chapter.

Oversimplifying, we may say that from the point of view of the linguist a language system is made up of two subgrammars, one syntagmatic, the other paradigmatic, to use the terms of one of the three celebrated Saussurean dichotomies, albeit in a very different sense (a Chomskyan sense).[20] Both subgrammars are computational systems, although very different in character. The syntagmatic grammar, which is universal except for the idiosyncracies of the spell-out, defines the syntactic structures and their phonetic and logical interpretations. Paradigmatic grammars, in contrast, are the repository of language variation (the peculiarities of a language have traditionally been related to its words), which appears to be limited to nonsubstantive parts of the vocabulary except for Saussurean arbitrariness (the association of concepts with sequences of sounds—more precisely, phonological structures—discussed in chapter 3) and general properties of heads.

Another name for paradigmatic grammar is of course morphology, taking the term in a very broad sense. In this broad sense, a morphology defines the words of the language and their structures and thereby determines the character or "genius" of a language.[21] It cannot therefore be neglected in the study of language development in the child—or in the study of the attempts of the adult to replicate the child's feat, a topic that will be taken up again in the next chapter.

6.2.2. The syntagmatic grammar and its interfaces

A language is obviously "embedded in performance systems that enable its expressions to be used for articulating, interpreting, referring, inquiring, reflecting, and other actions."[22] We can think of an abstract grammatical structure as a complex of instructions for these performance systems that provide information relevant to their functioning.

Since the performance systems are of two general types, articulatory-perceptual and conceptual-intentional, and a linguistic expression contains instructions for each of these systems, there must be at least two interface levels that provide the instructions for the articulatory-perceptual and conceptual-intentional systems, respectively. It is then reasonable to think that each language determines a set of pairs of formal representations drawn from these two levels, which in the framework adopted here are taken to be the levels of Phonetic Form (PF) and Logical Form (LF), the formal representations of sound and meaning (insofar as these are determined by the language itself) referred to above. Thus, the derivation of a particular linguistic expression involves two computations: One that generates the pair of interface representations and one that supplies the words to be inserted (each word with all its associated feature specifications in addition to its spelling out) after a number of purely syntactic operations are completed. The level of word insertion, which now comes long after the initial representation and is taken to be open to parametric variation (an important innovation, it would seem), can be seen as an internal interface:[23] the interface between the syntagmatic and the paradigmatic subgrammars.

It is always too early to be sure that a general outlook is on the right track, and the outlook adopted here is of course no exception (if anything, it is more open to question because it is still in its infancy). If it is not too far off, its assumptions are rather attractive. The "minimalist program" for language theory they make possible is a very important and seemingly very promising development of the 1990s. A further assumption of this program is that the conditions on representations—those of case theory, binding theory, theta theory, and other modules of language theory—, which may simply be modes of interpretation by performance systems, hold only at the interface and are motivated by properties of the interface. The linguistic expressions of the language are the optimal realizations of the interface conditions, where "optimality" is determined by the universal economy conditions the language system meets. The intuitive meaning of these "least effort" conditions is that representations and derivations must be as economical as possible, which has the effect of eliminating superfluous symbols in representations (an element can appear in a representation only if it is properly "licensed") and superfluous steps in derivations (only the "shortest move" is available, and only as a "last resort"), thus minimizing their length.[24]

It is conditions of this nature, properly formulated, that would make it possible to move toward the minimalist design of a theory of language that takes a linguistic expression to be nothing other than a formal object that satisfies the interface conditions in the optimal way and perhaps even to go on to show that the basic principles of language are formulated in terms of notions drawn from the domain of (virtual) conceptual necessity. Here we reach the research frontier of the early 1990s.

It is now time for us to turn to the question raised in the opening paragraphs of the book and direct our attention to the so-called critical period hypothesis and its implications for adult language acquisition. This is the topic of the next chapter, which is very much part of the heart of the book.

NOTES TO CHAPTER 6

1. A more thorough introduction can be found in Freidin 1992, which can serve as a basis for further reading (including Haegeman 1991, Cowper 1992, and references therein).

2. For a more detailed discussion than can be given here, see Baker 1978, chapter 2.

3. To quote from the opening paragraph of a paper by Robert B. Lees written in December 1959: "Nearly all contemporary treatments of grammar, especially of English grammar . . . , and especially if they make some overtly expressed claim to incorporate the results of modern linguistic science, have taken over as one of their primary exhibits of modernity a curiously mistaken notion of linguistic rigor . . .

clearly modelled on grammatical descriptions which have been offered as paradigms by linguistic scientists themselves," the "mode of description" being "the substitution-in frames technique." See also Lees 1962 (and Lees 1960, 1965).

4. Actually, a context-free phrase-structure grammar in this case, to be distinguished from a context-sensitive phrase-structure grammar. The distinction, however, may be ignored, particularly in this context, because interest in the latter type declined sharply after the mid 1970s.

Phrase-structure rules were originally developed (with the help of a particular version of recursive function theory due to Emil Post) as a way of expressing the ideas found in the so-called immediate constituent analysis of pre-Chomskyan syntactic studies (mainly in the United States), abstracting away from irrelevant differences among them. See Chomsky 1955, chapter 7 (or 1957, chapter 4, for a summary). For an introductory discussion in retrospect, see Kimball 1973, chapter 1.

5. It seems fair to say that at the present state of our undertanding the notion of complement is somewhat clearer than the notion of specifier, although it is clear that specifier positions are typically subject positions (cf. Jonas and Bobaljik 1993) and, when unfilled, provide landing sites for moved phrases (Sportiche 1993b). For two recent and quite different attempts at clarification, see Kayne 1993b, Sportiche 1993b. Recently (class lectures, fall 1993) Chomsky has been trying to derive phrase structure theory from purely "minimalist" assumptions (see Chomsky 1992b) in order to overcome some of the problems raised (in his view) by the main proposal in Kayne 1993b, which he thinks are overcome when most of the "conventional baggage of X-bar theory" (including lexical projection, any projection where there is no branching, and all node labels apart from the lexical items themselves) is eliminated. Some of the new ideas are reminiscent of a proposal made by Peter Muyskens in 1983.

6. This insight is originally due to Richard Kayne. See chapter 7 of his 1984 book, first published as an independent paper in 1981.

7. This proposal was first made by Jean-Yves Pollock in a paper originally written in 1987 that appeared two years later (one of the most influential papers in the recent history of linguistics), and it was elaborated and extended in Chomsky 1988b (see also Chomsky 1992b).

8. For example, it has been repeatedly suggested that lexical categories and their projections characteristically occur within functional projections, as complements to functional heads, and that only lexical heads take a variety of complements, functional heads being severely restricted in this respect, possibly to a single type of complement.

9. On the topic of the complexity of nominal phrases, see Carstens 1991 for Ki-swahili and English, Valois 1991 for French and English, Parodi 1993 for Spanish and English, and, in particular, Koopman 1993a for several Celtic (Welsh, Irish) and Germanic (English, mainland Scandinavian) languages, with some reference to Romance (French, Spanish); on the deep parallel, Grimshaw 1991.

10. It should be kept in mind that for Chomsky the need for transformations stems from the plain descriptive fact that things appear in places where they are not interpreted; that is, they appear in one place and they are interpreted somewhere else. A different question is the possible empirical difference between Chomsky's derivational approach to transformations (with movement as part of the derivation) and a representational approach (with no need to actually move elements of a representation of an underlying structure), which may be a meaningful choice, contrary to what one may suppose (in other words, it may not be analogous to asking whether 4 is 2 squared or 2 is the square root of 4, as it seems to be at first glance).

11. It is interesting to notice that the Port-Royal grammar (1660), which is apparently the first to develop the notion of phrase structure in any fairly clear way, "also states quite clearly the inadequacy of phrase-structure description for the representation of syntactic structure" and that "it hints at a form of transformational grammar in many respects akin to that which is being actively studied today." However, "the idea that a sentence can be regarded simply as a sequence of words or word categories, with no further structure, is frequently expressed" by many authors after 1660. See Chomsky 1966, p. 42 and note 76.

12. For further discussion see Crain & Nakayama 1987, where Chomsky's proposal of the early 1950s is subjected to an empirical test.

13. See Sportiche 1988, an important breakthrough of the late 1980s. Similarly, it is argued in Chomsky 1992b that there is no rule of "Affix Hopping" (a rule that moves an affix down the tree and attaches it to a verb stem, as proposed since the very beginnings of transformational grammar). Other apparent exceptions (other proposed lowering rules) will presumably be found wanting under closer analysis (except perhaps for some PF operations, in Chomsky's view).

14. See Emonds 1976, a revision of his 1970 MIT doctoral dissertation.

15. See Reinhart & Reuland 1993, Koster 1993a, and references therein (in particular Zribi-Hertz 1989). On acquisition of anaphora, see Chien & Wexler 1990, Grimshaw & Rosen 1990, Sigurjónsdóttir 1992 and Sigurjónsdóttir & Hyams 1992.

16. A basic principle preferable to "Affect α" appears to be "Form Chain" (Chomsky 1992b), a topic that is beyond the scope of this book (but see the last subsection of this chapter, in particular note 24).

17. For the new proposal, see Kayne 1993b (see also 1993a, b and 1994); for the new analysis of Dutch, see Zwart 1992a, b and 1993, and Koster 1993b. The more recent proposal about phrase structure referred to in the next sentence in the text is due to Chomsky (class lectures, fall 1993).

If the underlying order is V–CP there is no need to "extrapose" the CP, since it always appears to the right of the V. On the other hand, a nominal complement generated in the CP position must move to the spec of the IP immediately above the VP so that the "case features" are checked, hence the surface order NP–V (or DP–V, where DP stands for determiner phrase, an "extended" nominal phrase). This leads to the striking conclusion that there is no V-raising in Dutch (cf. Koopman 1993b), as had been assumed since 1975.

18. For the technical details, see Chomsky 1992b, where the suggestion was first made.

19. For a study of the history of English from this perspective, see Lightfoot 1991 (the "loss of object-verb order" is taken up in chapter 3). Cf. Watanabe 1993, Weerman 1993.

20. Actually, Saussure's terms were "syntagms" and "associations." The other two dichotomies are *langue* vs. *parole* (superseded by "competence," in the sense of knowledge of language, and linguistic "performance" or use of language), synchrony vs. diachrony. See Otero 1983, 1991b. Cf. Perlmutter 1988, Hale & Keyser 1993, Halle & Marantz 1993, Harris 1993, and note 21 below.

21. "While the intuition underlying proposals to restrict variation to elements of morphology is clear enough, it would be no trivial matter to make it explicit, given general problems in selecting among equivalent constructional systems," according to Chomsky, who believes that "an effort to address this problem in any general way would seem premature" (1992b).

What seems to be clear is that words are drawn from the paradigmatic grammar fully inflected and with all their feature specifications and that in general these word complexes must raise by LF in order to check (or cancel out) the feature specifications of the associated syntactic elements. Cf. Otero 1991b, Chomsky 1992, Sportiche 1993b (in particular, 6.3.2). It is this proposal that makes it possible to dispense with lowering rules (such as so-called affix hopping—see note 13) in the syntax, surely a desirable result.

22. The quote is from Chomsky 1992b.

23. The hypothesis that word insertion takes place later in the derivation than was generally assumed in generative grammar until the early 1990s, which is "particularly interesting for those languages where inflectional morphology has considerable effect on the internal structure of words," goes back to 1974. See Chomsky 1979 (first recorded in January 1976), p. 174; see also Chomsky & Lasnik 1977, which leaves open the possibility of a theory in which "only abstract features are generated in the base (which is now limited to the categorial component [now the X-bar module]) in positions to be filled by lexical items" (n. 18). Cf. Otero 1983, 1991b; Piera 1983; Bonet 1991; Anderson 1992, p. 90f.

24. As Chomsky (1992b) points out, "there appears to be a conflict between two natural notions of economy: shortest move vs. fewest steps in a derivation. If a derivation keeps to shortest moves, it will have more steps; if it reduces the number of steps, it will have longer moves." But the apparent paradox is resolved, he goes on to say, "if we take the basic transformational operation to be not Move-alpha but Form-Chain," an operation that applies to a structure to form a new structure in a single step.

7

Language maturation and beyond: A new look at the Critical Period Hypothesis

The basic fact to be addressed in the investigation of language maturation is that all normal children are totally successful at acquiring the language or languages of their communities, while most adults who try do not succeed in developing a native mastery of a single foreign language. This sharp disparity along various lines, which at first may strike us as paradoxical (the greatest success is achieved by the least developed organisms, which are in fact less capable at most things than adult organisms), calls for explanation. A hypothesis with considerable explanatory power is the so-called Critical Period Hypothesis, the topic of this chapter.

7.1. Language and puberty: A parallel between linguistic maturity and sexual maturity

The reason why the sharp disparity between the unexceptional success of normal children and the general lack of success of adults may strike some of us as paradoxical at first may have something to do with our common sense, which tends to show markedly behavioristic preferences and inclinations, in particular when it comes to what is called learning.[1] It is easy to see that every child is a wonderfully unique and special individual, different in many ways from every other child living, even from his or her own identical twin (which in a sense is all true) and that at least some of the differences are environmental. But it is no less true that, in a deeper sense, every child is like every other child, and that they all go through the same highly predictable stages, a central topic in the work of Jean Piaget and his associates.[2] It is also easy to see, even without trying very hard, that children develop in a highly patterned way. In fact, students of human development can tell a parent with some confidence what the developmental stages will be for normal boys or girls. Many parents are familiar with titles such as *Your one-year-old, Your two-year-old, Your three-year-old,* . . . or *Your ten-to-fourteen-year old,* or with sweeping characterizations such as *Your four-year-old: Wild and wonderful, Your five-year-old: Calm and serene, Your six-year-old: Loving and defiant, Your seven-year-old: Life in a minor key. . . .*

Naturally enough, a particular child can be somewhat "ahead of schedule," while one of his or her peers (or even close friends) is more or less "behind schedule," but no child reaches the cooing stage in less than two months (or the babbling stage in less than four, or the one-word stage in less than ten, or the two-word stage in less than 18), no child uses color terms properly before the age of two, no child has his or her native language essentially in place before the age of four, no child undergoes puberty before the age of six, to mention just a few well-known "milestones." In fact, most children hit it right on the nose, as it were. The path is not unlike a travel plan. We may go down the predetermined road faster or slower than other travelers, but we are still going down the same road and through the same check points, which is what maps are for.

At the present stage of our knowledge, the researcher's "map" of the childhood path is still rather sketchy and uninformative, but it already provides the beginning of an orientation, in particular that part of it—the maturation of language—that is of crucial importance in a book like this.

Piaget, who was trained in biology (he never obtained a degree in psychology), tentatively mapped the childhood path into four phases or stages. The first goes from birth to about two years and one of its defining features appears to be "out of sight, out of mind." In the second stage, roughly from two to seven years, children are no longer "infants" (Lat. *in-fantem* 'without speech'), but although before age three they already look for a toy that rolled out of sight and at five they are quite sophisticated and tireless talkers and even emerging readers (language is already essentially in place), before seven their math still lags behind and they still appear to be incapable of seeing things from someone else's point of view (not that they will always find it easy as adults). In the third stage, roughly from seven to twelve years, "the age of reason," numbers and logic are no longer arcane, the good is no longer what is permitted, and the point of view of others begins to be appreciated.[3] Finally, in the fourth stage, which starts after the age of twelve or so, abstract reasoning (even about "might have beens"), including the possibility of investigating all aspects of a problem systematically (for some even the possibility of true creation in the formal and empirical sciences or in the arts), is well within reach.

Let us suppose that there is something to the stages, as far as it goes (and it can be readily granted that it does not go very far).[4] The fundamental question now is: Where do the stages come from, particularly (in this context) the stage that sees the emergence and explosive development of language? It is easy to recognize Plato's Problem behind the question and, if the discussion in chapters 2 and 5 is not completely off target, there is only one possible answer, and it is easy to point to it (or in its direction): The stage that brings about the maturation of language comes from inside the organism, more specifically from the genotype, the only thing all human children have in common. At this point, as in chapter 5, it is extremely helpful to think of the maturation of language as the maturation of one particular organ of the body (specifically of that part of the body we call the mind/brain), the language organ, which develops and matures like any other organ of the body, that is, like a system of related physical structures (the visual system, for example). As we will see directly, if we think of language maturation as the maturation of a physical organ, we will not be prone to make some of the mistakes most typically made in discussions of our topic.

It may be helpful at this point to reflect briefly on a typical reaction people sometimes have when they are told that the principles of human language are innate (genetically determined). Some think of it as a kind of explanation of last resort, which just goes to show that "we have not yet been able to figure out how we can extract the principles involved from experience."

This kind of reaction, which is not uncommon, is illuminating. Indeed, it is characteristic enough to constitute an interesting fact about our intellectual culture, which goes back hundreds of years. This is because people who react this way in the case of that subtype of physical processes we call mental processes, of which language maturation is a particularly important one, have a very different reaction to, say, a hypothesis about sexual maturation. When they are told that biologists assume that puberty is genetically programmed (although of course affected by nutritional level, climate, and other environmental factors, just as language is affected by environmental factors), no one finds the hypothesis to be an explanation of last resort. Suppose now that they were to be told that, although we have not figured it out yet, puberty is really the result of environmental influences, including, for example, peer pressure (in other words, young people undergo puberty because they see their friends going through it and they want to be like everyone else). Chances are that the very same people who cannot suspend their disbelief in the case of language would laugh when their commonsense belief is extended to sexual maturation (even though very little is known about the biological factors involved in puberty, while we have already learned a great deal about language in the last forty-some years). The underlying dichotomy appears to be: If the maturation takes place below the neck (in the metaphorical sense of being "nonmental"), it must be coming from inside; on the other hand, if the maturation takes place above the neck (that is, in the mind/brain), it must be the result of experience. Is this not an odd conclusion?

An explanation that has been suggested for this new dualism (which differs from the old mind/body dualism in being unargued and far more pernicious) is that it is the product of an irrational attitude. Why this irrational attitude? One thing to notice is that it has something in common with traditional dualism, which is not surprising. As humans, it is very natural for us to think of people as having a mind and a body that are separate. If so, traditional mind/body dualism was very commonsensical. It is for this reason that we think of someone as being the same person if his or her body undergoes all sorts of changes (a heart transplant, for example), but we would think of him or her as a different person if his or her brain were recoded and came to have somebody else's memories and language and so on. Unsurprisingly, this strong drive of common sense is very difficult to overcome, just as it is very difficult to look at the sun and tell oneself that it is not setting, that what is actually happening is that the earth is turning. We simply cannot get out of our skins: There is no way for us to look up and stop seeing what we see as the sun setting—even for professional astronomers living centuries after the collapse of geocentrism.

Like geocentrism, traditional two-substance (metaphysical) dualism collapsed for scientific reasons. But that does not mean that we can get out of our skins. We still look at people the same way. It is very hard not to see them as minds inside bodies. What has replaced traditional dualism is a kind of epistemological dualism that comes out more or less like this: On the structures that we see as physical we are willing to proceed in accordance with the sciences and, if they lead us to conclude that something is genetically programmed, we accept it; by contrast, on the structures that we see as mental (and perhaps as if they were not just as physical as other physical structures), we develop an irrational attitude. Irrationality seems to be the only explanation for the strange phenomenon, which has been around for hundreds of years. We just seem to be in the domain of trying to account for irrational human beliefs. Because the fact is that the same kind of evidence (in fact even better evidence) that is taken seriously in the case of puberty is summarily dismissed in the case of mental physical development, that is, development of the mind/brain.[5]

7.2. From Skinner to Chomsky: Lenneberg's Problem

Interestingly, an explanation for the sharp disparity between acquisition of language in childhood and later in life was not an issue when behaviorism and "structuralism" (that is, surface structuralism) were the order of the day in psychology and linguistics. Most psychologists of the early 1950s held, with B. F. Skinner (1904–92), that language "learning," the basis for "verbal behavior" (more generally, "learning" of any kind) is a question of drive and reinforcement contingencies, while others held that it is a question of talent.[6] A typical answer to the first central question of chapter 5 would have been something like this: Knowledge of language is acquired by such mechanisms as conditioning, association, practice in exercising skills, and so on, and a typical answer to the second question would have been something like this: A language is a certain system of habits and skills; to know a language is to have mastered these skills.

The fatal flaw of this conception of language is that normal use of language is not an exercise of any "habit" or "skill." As we have seen, use of language typically is creative, in the sense that it constantly involves the production and interpretation of new expressions (new in the experience of the language user or even in the history of a language). Thus readers of these sentences may not have seen any of them before, or anything vaguely resembling them, yet they have no difficulty recognizing them as sentences of their language and interpreting them, and they do this in the same way as other speakers of similar varieties of English. Moreover, there is nothing exotic about this; it is the norm. On the other hand, if these sentences were modified in some arbitrary way, they would be gibberish.

Views such as those of the early 1950s are inconsistent with more recent experimental work.[7] More than twenty years ago, some of this work was taken to suggest that "there is a primitive, neurologically given analytic system which may degenerate if not stimulated at an appropriate critical period, but which otherwise provides a specific interpretation of experience, varying with the organism to some extent. . . . These modern discoveries thus give support, in a new sense, to Descartes and Kant, contrary to the radical empiricism that has dominated science for two centuries, throwing suspicion on any hypothesis that postulates the 'innateness' of forms of knowledge," as the distinguished French biologist Jacques Monod noted. It was already clear at the time that the cognitive systems of animals mature "according to a genetically determined program," and there was no longer reason to doubt that the same was also true of (in Monod's words) "the fundamental categories of human knowledge, and perhaps also other aspects of human behavior, less fundamental, but of great significance for the individual and society." In Chomsky's view, "this may be true of man's apparently unique linguistic faculties, and of his abilities of imaginative thought, as manifested in language, in visual imagery, in plans of action, or in true artistic or scientific creation."[8]

Interest in behaviorist approaches had already begun to drop off rapidly with the emergence of generative grammar in the mid-1950s and the revival of a notion of localization (traceable to the pioneering ideas of Franz-Joseph Gall) and the related idea of "cerebral dominance," which converged with the notion of a "Language Acquisition Device" (LAD), the core of what we are now calling the language organ.[9] The convergence was soon to be exploited by Eric Lenneberg (1921–75), who was well aware of the fact that all normal children are totally successful at acquiring the language or languages of their communities, while most adults who try do not succeed in developing a native mastery of a single foreign language. As Lenneberg put it, "automatic acquisition from mere exposure to a given language seems to disappear after this age [childhood] and foreign languages have to be taught and learned through a conscious and labored effort"; in particular, "foreign accents cannot be overcome easily after puberty."[10] He also understood that this simple and universally known fact must be explained. We may refer to this problem of explanation as "Lenneberg's Problem," in reference to the scientist who first formulated it in essentially the right way.[11]

Lenneberg set himself the task of studying language as "an aspect of [human] biological nature, to be studied in the same manner as, for instance, [human] anatomy" and in his "major study of language and biology (1967), now recognized as a classic in the field," applied the biological concept of a "critical period" to the study of language and argued forcefully for a critical period in language acquisition.[12] According to this Critical Period Hypothesis (CPH), some specific growth can only take place in the maturing organism during a particular time span (roughly before the onset of puberty). As Lenneberg put it in a concise summary of his book,

> All the evidence suggests that the capacities for speech production and related aspects of language acquisition develop according to built-in biological schedules. They appear when the time is ripe and not until then, when a state of what I have called "resonance" exists. . . .
>
> Language development thus runs a definite course on a definite schedule; a critical period extends from about age two to age 12, [the period during which the brain goes through its last stages of physical maturation,] the beginning and the end of resonance.[13]

The crucial point is the remark about "a definite course on a definite schedule," and for the course to begin "a certain degree of maturation of the brain is a prerequisite," as he writes elsewhere. It is important to note in this connection that, details about boundaries aside, once it is assumed that language development "is due to yet unknown species-specific capacities" (which is hardly open to doubt), the CPH is the null hypothesis. There is nothing very radical or striking about it. It is another way of saying that the human brain is part of the biological world. What would be surprising is for someone to expect that something in the human brain is not part of the biological world. It would not be unreasonable in principle to try to show that the critical period does not extend from about age two to age twelve but rather from two to six, or whatever.[14] But it would not make much sense to argue that the essentials of human embryology are completely different from the essentials of nonhuman embryology.

Two dimensions of the CPH are of particular interest from our vantage point. One may be dubbed "the use it or lose it hypothesis" or "the exercise hypothesis": During an early period of their life, humans have a capacity for mastering languages; if the capacity is not exercised during this period, it is inevitably lost. A clear endorsement of this dimension of the CPH is given by Chomsky in his Managua lectures. He begins by offering what he takes to be a parallel case as illustration: There is a certain age at which a pigeon has to fly, but if it is kept in a box beyond that age (beyond "maybe two weeks or so") and then is let out of the box, it will never be able to fly.[15] Chomsky goes on to say that "it is very probable that language is something like that . . . Something must happen to the brain about the time of puberty."[16] A study approximating a direct test of this dimension of the CPH, and perhaps "the best documented test of Lenneberg's original claim," is that of a Los Angeles woman referred to as "Genie" in the literature, deprived of language experience (the victim of severe abuse and almost total isolation from the age of about twenty months to 13.7 years), who was not able to learn even the rudiments of the "computational system" of a first language after puberty.[17]

The second dimension of the CPH may be called "the maturational completion hypothesis": During an early period of their life, and only during this period, humans have a capacity for mastering languages natively, the brain being modified in specific ways during these formative years under the influence of mere language exposure; this capacity cannot be exercised after the period is over (as, for example, people are not expected to grow taller after their teens). This of course is not to deny that, as Lenneberg was quick to point out, "a person can learn to communicate in a foreign language at the age of forty" (and no doubt later).[18] As Chomsky has written, "We say that a child of five and a foreign adult are on their way towards acquiring English, but we have no way to designate whatever it is that they 'have'," and there is a crucial difference between the two cases: "the child, in the normal course of events, will come to 'have' English . . . , though the foreigner probably will not."[19] The claim seems to be that there is something special about a child that makes it perfectly natural not only for a first language, but also for a second or a third or an nth one, to "grow" (Chomsky's term) in its brain. This special capacity of the child is not available after a certain (early) maturational stage. All of these considerations point to the same conclusion: The crucial factor that makes the native command of a language possible "is to be found in an as yet difficult-to-specify aspect of brain physiology."[20]

Lenneberg's hypothesis has triggered much controversy, even disparagement, in the intervening years, in spite of the fact that "it is in accord with results from other behavioral domains in which critical periods have been hypothesized," but it is important to keep in mind that no one appears to have come up with a plausible alternative to a critical period for language acquisition extending from infancy to some prepubescent stage.[21] In fact, the evidence accumulated in the last twenty years, including evidence from the study of acquisition of American Sign Language and from the study of nonnative language acquisition, provides considerable support for it, as we will see.[22] The results now available suggest that "entirely nonmaturational explanations for the age effects would be difficult to support."[23]

7.3. An embryological solution: Blame the brain

An explanation for the sharp disparity between acquisition of language in childhood and later in life is available in terms of the language theory sketched in the preceding chapter. A principles-and-parameters framework immediately suggests a plausible specific reinterpretation of the CPH, which, properly understood, is not at odds with the possibility that some aspects of the language organ remain active after puberty.[24] It comes then as no surprise that there has recently been much debate over whether the LAD (Language Acquisition Device) is available in nonnative language acquisition—a most welcome development, since it might contribute to a better understanding of what is at issue and it might lead to a deeper understanding of the nature and growth of language by opening a new window on the study of unconscious linguistic knowledge and on the process of acquisition.

A convenient point of departure for the study of the crucial question (the role of the language organ in language acquisition after maturation) is provided by two extreme and contradictory positions: The thesis that Universal Grammar (UG)—more precisely, the language organ UG purports to be a theory of—plays no role in adult language acquisition (we may refer to this thesis as T0) and its antithesis, namely, the thesis that UG is no less available to adults than to children (a thesis we may refer to as T1).[25] The version of T1 selected for discussion here crucially distinguishes between two alternatives:[26]

(i) L1 [first language] and L2 [second language] acquisition are alike, with UG mediating both in identical fashion, and
(ii) the interlanguages of L2 learners fall within the range of grammars permitted by UG, but UG does not operate in identical fashion in L1 and L2 acquisition.

The latter is the alternative argued for in the version of T1 under consideration here. In the words of its defenders, "adults may initially assume the wrong parameter settings for the L2, either because of misleading properties of the L2 input or because they transfer settings from the L1," so that "there will be intermediate stages in L2 acquisition when the adult learner shows evidence of having set only some of these parameters appropriately."[27]

In what follows, it is suggested that neither of the two extreme positions has been established. There is strong evidence against the claim that UG plays no role in language acquisition after puberty (LAP), but the counterclaim (T1) appears to be implausible. What seems to be at issue is not so much whether the language organ is involved in nonnative language acquisition (it seems reasonable to assume that it is, since there is a prima facie case for the assumption, as we will see), but rather the nature and extent of this involvement.

A main purpose of the present book is to suggest that a reasonable alternative to the contradictory theses under consideration is readily available within the principles-and-parameters framework. The first step is to break the question "UG or not UG?" into two subquestions:

(Q1) Are the invariant principles of UG operative in the process of non-native language acquisition?
(Q2) Can the values of the parameterized principles be fixed once more for a new language after the critical period?

Another purpose of this book is to suggest that a negative answer to the question of whether the parameters can be appropriately set by the adult acquirer would appear to carry significant implications for the design and execution of a successful foreign language program.

Let us begin by considering Q1.

7.3.1. The active language organ: Lifelong innate knowledge

The fact that adult acquirers are rarely, if ever, fully successful in their attempts to develop a native-like mastery of a foreign language is of course perfectly consistent with the idea that there is a "logical problem of non-native language acquisition."[28] Although the knowledge internalized by advanced adult acquirers reflects their experience in some manner, they appear to know things about the foreign language beyond their experience. It is natural to see here a case of "Plato's problem" and one might wonder to what extent it overlaps with the case of Plato's Problem presented by first language growth. It is reasonable to assume there is some overlap. Like first language growth, adult language acquisition poses in a sharp and clear form "the problem of 'poverty of stimulus,' of accounting for the richness, complexity and specificity of shared knowledge given the limitations of the data available," in Chomsky's words. A great many cases have been given over the years to illustrate this fundamental problem. Perhaps the most familiar one is the structure dependence of rules, "the fact that without instruction or direct evidence, children unerringly use computationally complex structure-dependent rules rather than computationally simple rules that involve only the predicate 'leftmost' in a linear sequence of words," to quote Chomsky again.[29] It appears that we can substitute "adult acquirers" for "children" in the quote (minus the initial remark) without changing its truth value. Thus, no speaker of Spanish capable of constructing minimally appropriate mental representations experiences much difficulty with the fact that the question corresponding to (1) is (2b), not (2a):

(1) El estudiante que es reflexivo es estudioso.
   'The student who is thoughtful is studious.'
(2) a. ¿Es el estudiante que reflexivo es estudioso?
      'Is the student who thoughtful is studious?'
   b. ¿Es el estudiante que es reflexivo estudioso?
      'Is the student who is thoughtful studious?'

Another case is provided by the binding theory, as illustrated in the following two examples:

(3) I wonder who [the men expected to see them]
(4) [the men expected to see them]

As Chomsky points out, both (3) and (4) include the clause given in brackets, but only in (3) may the pronoun be referentially dependent on the antecedent *the men*. Numerous facts of this sort, he goes on to say,

> are known without relevant experience to differentiate the cases. Such facts pose a serious problem that was not recognized in earlier work: How does every child know, unerringly, to interpret the clause differently in the two cases? And why does no pedagogic grammar have to draw the reader's attention to such facts (which were, in fact, noticed only quite recently . . .)?

Significantly, the same is essentially true of a foreign speaker of English who has attained a certain level of proficiency in the language.

Both principles—structure dependence and binding—are exemplified in the following sentences (needless to say, in the first example the person who jumped may be Juan, while in the second example the person who jumped cannot be Juan):

(5) Cuando saltó, Juan sonrió.
     'When he jumped, John smiled.'

(6) Saltó cuando Juan sonrió.
     'He jumped when John smiled.'

Or in the following sentences, which are structurally very different:

(7) a. El estudiante que escribió el ensayo lo distribuyó.
       'The student who wrote the essay distributed it.'
    b. El estudiante que lo escribió distribuyó el ensayo
       'The student who wrote it distributed the essay.'

Again, a foreign speaker of Spanish with a certain level of proficiency in the language does not find it especially difficult to see that *lo* may refer to (may be referentially dependent on) *el ensayo* in both (a) and (b).[30]

A more subtle point can be made with the following examples:

(8) John ate an apple.
(9) John ate.
(10) John is too stubborn to talk to Bill.
(11) John is too stubborn to talk to.

If we were to interpret (10)–(11) on the analogy of (8)–(9), it should be that (11) means that John is so stubborn that he (John) will not talk to some arbitrary person. But, as Chomsky notes, the meaning is in fact quite different, namely, that John is so stubborn that some arbitrary person will not talk to him (John). Again, he goes on to say, this is known without training or relevant evidence; what is more, children do not make errors about the interpretation of such sentences as (10)–(11), "and if they did, the errors would largely be uncorrectable."[31]

Here is a final illustration, of a very different type:

(12) Todos los recibos no están pagados.

In a moment's thought, every native speaker of Spanish realizes that the expression is open to two very different interpretations (it might have to be pointed out to them, but that does not change anything). It can mean roughly 'Not all the receipts are paid' or 'No receipt is paid' (not a trivial difference for someone who has been taken to court for having failed to pay on time). Chances are no student of Spanish who reaches a certain level of proficiency would have to actually learn that the expression is ambiguous (although the ambiguity may not be noticed at first blush), as no advanced student of English would probably have to be taught that *All that glitters is not gold* is open to two interpretations (one of which is obviously false, because gold glitters).

What is crucially important for our purposes is that, at least to a considerable extent, the same is true of the fluent nonnative speaker, a fact that can be readily explained by assuming that the invariant principles of language (which failed to mature in Genie's brain, it appears) continue to play a role beyond the critical period for all normal humans. Furthermore, the properties of (10) and (11) reappear in their Spanish translation, as we would expect, but with an additional twist, to which we return in the next subsection.

The conclusion that nonnative language acquisition is in some important respect not unlike first language acquisition does not lack antecedents in the area of foreign language acquisition research.[32] The evidence adduced in support of a claim of this nature comes from the similarities observed in the process of learning a foreign language by native speakers of very different languages—contrary to what the assumptions of the "contrastive analysis" approach, which postulated the effect of interference and tried to relate specific difficulties to particular features of the student's native language, would lead us to believe.[33] A counterclaim of the critics of contrastive analysis was that the acquisition of at least some elements of a particular target language by speakers of a number of diverse languages proceeds in the same order regardless of the specific properties of those elements in the native language of the acquirer and the degree to which they differ from their counterparts in the target language.[34] In addition, it was observed that there is sometimes great similarity among the errors made by speakers of very different languages in the process of studying a particular target language (say, English, the most intensely researched case). This similarity, and the specific types of error patterns, suggest that some errors are not entirely due to specific differences between the native language of the acquirer and the target language, contrary to what the "contrastive analysis" approach predicts.[35]

More recent studies within the new framework have attempted to show that adult acquirers are sensitive to the effects of principles such as subjacency, directionality, and proper government (among others), in ways that cannot be explained in terms of simple inductive learning strategies from surface data or in terms of explicit teaching.[36]

In evaluating this type of work, we must be careful not to be misled by irrelevant factors. Consider the following two Spanish sentences, which differ only in the presence or absence of *el*, the masculine singular form of the definite article:

(13) (a) Lamento haber perdido la clase.
     'I regret having missed the class.'
    (b) Lamento el haber perdido la clase.
     'I regret (the) having missed the class.'

Some speakers of Spanish take the two forms as alternative expressions of something like the meaning conveyed by the English gloss, and some linguists are no more able to find any essential difference between them.[37] However, many of the native speakers who share this belief would readily find the second of the following questions less acceptable than the first:

(14) (a) ¿Qué lamentas haber perdido?
     'What do you regret having missed?'
    (b) ¿Qué lamentas el haber perdido?
     'What do you regret (the) having missed?'

Are adult acquirers of Spanish capable of this type of deeply rooted discrimination at some point in their development? Suppose a preliminary exploration suggests that the answer is negative at a particular level of proficiency. The result may still be perfectly consistent with the thesis that the invariant aspects of subjacency are accessible to language users after the critical period. The judgment failure may simply show that the acquirers are not or not yet capable of assigning examples such as (b) the underlying structure assigned to them by native speakers. Presumably, if they were, their reaction would be analogous to the reaction elicited by some other violation of the complex noun phrase island constraint (e.g., by the unacceptable *¿Qué lamentas el hecho de haber perdido?* 'What do you regret the fact of having missed?'). In other words, invariant principles are expected to yield the right results only when applied to the mental representation of an appropriate structural description of the sentence at issue (in our case, a structure that presumably includes a silent noun analogous to *hecho*). Adults must be able to approximate underlying structures enough for the operation of universal principles.[38]

Summing up this section, we might say that the thesis that at least some invariant principles of the universal schematism provided by the language organ remain active after the critical period appears to be a highly plausible one. There is no obvious better alternative to explain facts such as those briefly reviewed above. Recent work suggests that the thesis is true, although we may still be far from confirming or disconfirming it (or confirming that it is true to some extent). It seems a fair guess that stronger evidence is obtainable and perhaps will soon be available. If so, we will have little reason to doubt that the language organ is not unlike the acorn in George Bernard Shaw's telling contrast:

> Think of the fierce energy concentrated in an acorn! You bury it in the ground, and it explodes into a great oak. Bury a sheep, and nothing happens but decay.[39]

7.3.2. Unsettable switches: Lifelong patchwork

As in the study of first language growth (as discussed in chapter 5), in the study of foreign language acquisition the crucial question is what it is that is acquired (knowledge or competence), which is rarely addressed in LAP (language acquisition after puberty) research.[40]

A typical case of sharp disparity between children and adults, and in recent years an often-experienced situation, referred to in chapter 1, is that of immigrant children, who usually acquire the indigenous language easily, rapidly, and thoroughly, while their parents, who are not necessarily less intelligent or resourceful than their offspring, generally do not (some speak the new language haltingly or not at all, some still speak self-consciously and with distinct traces of their native languages even after long residence).[41]

Could this be entirely accidental? Chances are that it is not. Because of a variety of evidence such as the immigrant evidence, which is significant if anecdotal, some would claim that no adult is likely to be totally successful as a foreign-language acquirer, the existence of exceptional individuals notwithstanding.[42] Recall the remarks by Chomsky quoted in the previous section (to the effect that the child, "in the normal course of events," will come to "have" a native language, "though the foreigner probably will not"). It is, in any case, uncontroversial that presently available tools reveal no relevant differences in degree of success in the acquisition of a native language among children, whereas the differences between any two postpubescent acquirers can be considerable, even vast.

It is natural then to ask how persuasive are the various claims that developing a new (additional) set of parameter values for a foreign language (sometimes referred to as "parameter resetting") is not out of the reach of any adult. It is true that the claim is not usually made in these terms, but it appears to be understood this way. At any rate, as a necessary step toward establishing the claim that "parameter resetting" (that is, setting the parameters for a new language) is not affected by the age of the individual, as implied in several papers, it would have to be shown that all the parametric values of at least one foreign language have been properly fixed by a number of ordinary human beings, that is, individuals not especially gifted as foreign language acquirers.

The first thing that one should keep in mind in evaluating such claims is that even if it were to be shown that the output of an adult acquirer is indistinguishable from the output of native speakers, it would not follow that the parameters of the foreign language have been appropriately set in the mind/brain of the adult acquirer, let alone fixed exactly the way they are fixed in the mind/brain of a native speaker. For one thing, radically different grammars can generate identical outputs, as is well known. It follows that correctness of output is not a sufficient basis to conclude that the parameters of the language under consideration have been set in the mind/brain of the adult acquirer in a native-like fashion. The most that can be claimed is that the output of the adult acquirer is consistent with such a conclusion. To go beyond this, the study must be carried out in far more indirect and subtle ways than have been used so far. A description of properties of some output and a description of a system of unconscious knowledge not unlike the system of a native speaker are very different things.

A second, no less obvious point is suggested by the fundamental difference between the generative procedure of a native speaker of a particular language L and a successful translation skill of an individual from a particular language L' to L. It is important to keep in mind that although such a skill (equivalently, a machine translation program) could be developed in principle, it would not necessarily provide insight into our understanding of the native speakers' knowledge or of their use of their knowledge. Recall the discussion in chapter 4.

With these preliminary observations in mind, consider a basic systematic difference between languages such as English or French and so-called null subject (or pro-drop) languages such as Spanish or Italian. As is well known, *arrived yesterday (John)* is inadmissible in English, while its counterpart *llegó ayer (Juan)* is common in Spanish. From a "contrastive analysis" point of view it would be natural to hypothesize the "overuse of pronominal subjects" by Anglophone students of Spanish, as was in fact done in the first contrastive grammar of Spanish for English students.[43] This prediction, however, does not seem to be correct. Since, on the other hand, Hispanophone students of English tend to underuse pronominal subjects, we may be tempted to conclude that we have "very indirect support for the hypothesis that acquisition to omit the subjects is easier than acquisition to put them in obligatorily" (something still to be established), but is it reasonable to go on to say that the difference between the two languages "does not pose a sufficiently serious problem for the English speaker learning Spanish to warrant comment" or that "resetting [read: setting] the pro-drop parameter from English and French to Spanish is not difficult with respect to null subjects"?[44]

Some skepticism seems to be in order. Consider again examples (10) and (11), repeated here for convenience:

(10) John is too stubborn to talk to Bill.
(11) John is too stubborn to talk to.

As mentioned above, the properties of these examples we considered reappear in their Spanish translation, as we would expect, but with an additional twist. The Spanish string can have either the sense of (10) or the sense of (11):

(15) Juan es demasiado terco para hablar con él.
    'John is too stuborn to talk to (him).'

Similarly, when the finite subjunctive form *hable* is substituted for the infinitive *hablar* as in (15),

(16) Juan es demasiado terco para que hable con él.
    John is too stubborn for that talk (SUBJ.) with him.

the sentence can translate as either (a) or (b):

(17) a. John is too stuborn for him to talk to him.

    b. John is too stuborn to talk to him.

but

(18) Juan es demasiado terco para que él hable con él.

    John is too stubborn for that he talk (SUBJ.) with him.

with an overt subject pronoun in the subjunctive clause, only has the sense of (a). Now we can ask whether the contrast between (16) and (18) "warrants comment," and the answer seems to be that the question has not even been raised. It would also be interesting to know whether nonnative speakers of Spanish such as those in the studies we are considering have native mastery of expressions with overt and silent subject pronouns.[45] The following two examples show the contrast between an obligatory silent pronoun (a) and an optional silent pronoun (b) (italics indicate identity of intended coreference):

(19) a. Cuando *pro*/*él* trabaja, *Juan* no bebe.

    'When he works, Juan doesn't drink.'

    b. Cuando el director insiste en que *pro*/*él* trabaje, *Juan* no bebe.

    'When the director insists that he work, John doesn't drink.'

The contrast is perhaps even clearer in the following two minidiscourses, which exemplify an interesting and not immediately obvious parallelism between the two languages (capitals indicate contrastive emphasis):

(20) a. ¿Quién cree Juan que ganará el premio?

    'Who does John think will win the award?'

    b. *Juan* cree que **pro/él* ganará el premio.

    'John thinks *he/HE will win the award.'

(21) a. ¿Qué cree Juan que obtendrá en el concurso?

    'What does John think he will get in the competition?'

    b. *Juan* cree que *pro*/*él* ganará el premio.

    'John thinks he/*HE will win the award.'

Again, correctness of output, hard to attain as it might be, is by itself no guarantee of unconscious knowledge of the language analogous to the knowledge of the native speaker.

In an earlier study, it is observed that "verb-subject inversion and *that-t* effects did not have the same status as null subjects in the respective interlanguages" and that "this is not evidence against the possible relationship among the three properties," a reasonable conclusion.[46] If the three properties follow from one and the same parameter, the absence of one of them from the output may be reason enough to conclude that the value of the parameter has not been fixed. The close interrelationship of these or other properties would in any case offer a better chance to determine whether nonnative language acquirers succeed in fixing the value of the relevant parameter. In the case under consideration other properties have been proposed (in addition to missing subjects, free inversion of subject and apparent violations of the so-called *that-t* filter), including empty resumptive pronouns in embedded clauses, long *wh*-movement of subject, and so-called "Clitic Climbing."[47]

It has been argued that the reason why there is no French analogue (c) to the Spanish example (a) or the Italian example (b) is the same reason why there is no Modern French analogue of *llueve/piove,* 'rains':

(22) (a) Juan los quiere ver. ('J them-wants to-see')
    (b) Gianni li vuole vedere. (same)
    (c) * Jean les veut voir.

Linguists are not in agreement about the underlying structure of this class of sentences. It has recently been argued, on the basis of data from Catalan, that their underlying configuration, in relevant respects, is essentially as shown in diagram 7.1.[48]

Now consider Spanish ambiguous strings such as the following:

(23) El niño lo puede beber.
    'It is possible that the child drinks it.'
    'The child is able to drink it.'

In the analysis under consideration the finite form of the modal verb *poder* is generated under T and *beber* under V2 (in which case the VP1 subtree is not part of the configuration) in the underlying structure associated with the first sense (possibility), while in the underlying structure associated with the second sense (ability) only the tense specification is generated under T, the infinitival form of *poder* being generated under V2 and later adjoined to T, and *beber* is generated under V1. If this proposal, or a proposal of a similar nature, turns out to be on the right track, then it is easy to see that to establish that the pro-drop parameter has been set at the Spanish value by the

(24)

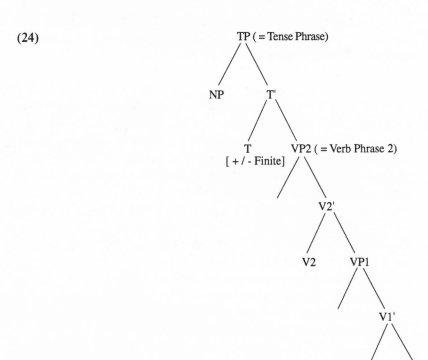

Diagram 7.1

postpubescent language acquirer will be no simple matter. Still, we are far from having exhausted the complexities of this aspect of Spanish. In particular, nothing has been said so far about the generation of the subject and related problems.[49]

The nature of these and other facts suggests the need for more indirect and subtle ways of gaining reliable information. In the case of the family of phenomena under consideration, the output is complex enough to make it possible to test the ability of the adult acquirers to derive facts that they might not be consciously aware of, including the following:

(25) (a) La caja que contiene el paquete es redonda.
  'The box that contains the package is round.'
  'The box that the package contains is round.'
  (La caja que el paquete contiene es redonda.)

  (b) ¿Qué caja contiene el paquete?
  'Which box contains the package?'
  'Which box does the package contain?'
  (* ¿Qué caja el paquete contiene?)

(c) ¿Qué caja dices *(que) contiene el paquete?
'Which box do you say contains the package?'
'Which box do you say the package contains?'
(¿Qué caja dices que el paquete contiene?)

There are several things to be noticed in this paradigm. The most widely known is that *que* cannot be left out in (c), in contrast with the English glosses. Less generally observed is that each of the Spanish examples is open to one of two interpretations (those of the two English glosses). On the other hand, the question within parentheses at the end in each subgroup lacks the meaning of the first gloss (as is to be expected), except that the one corresponding to (b) is not grammatical in Spanish. (In the last examples, *el paquete* is no ordinary subject, but this can be overlooked in this context.) Nonnative speakers of Spanish who have properly set the pro-drop parameter at the Spanish value should at least be able to detect the ambiguity in each of the examples in (25) or comparable (including more complex) examples, and to provide appropriate interpretations. This should also be true of a broad range of other cases. For example, for a native speaker it is easy to determine that the second of the following sentences is no less grammatical than the first:

(26) (a) Creo que los estudiantes están contentos.
'I believe that the students are happy.'
(b) Los estudiantes creo que están contentos.
'The students I believe that they are happy.'

Many other types of tests can of course be devised to delve deeper, but this brief sample is perhaps sufficient to give an idea of what is at issue. There are of course many other possibilities that have not been tried, each of which could provide crucial evidence as to whether the parameter has been properly set at the Spanish value by an adult speaker. It should also be kept in mind that evidence against the possibility of "resetting" (setting) in the case of a single parameter not transparently reflected in the output may be enough to cast serious doubts about "resetting" in general for the adult acquirer(s) involved. One would not expect to find that a speaker failed to fix one of the parameters of his/her native language but succeeded in fixing all the others.

As an illustration, consider a precisely defined parametric option in light of recent discussion of a major systematic difference between English and Romance intensely investigated in recent years.[50] If this work is on the right track, the relevant structure of a sentence, technically a CP (as discussed in

Diagram 7.2

(27)

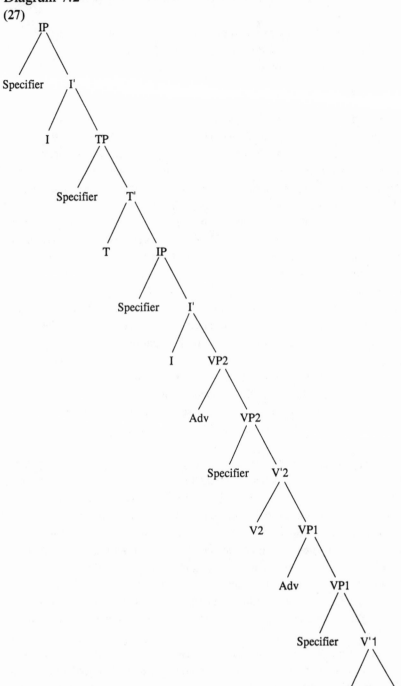

150

chapter 6), in English or French may be represented as in diagram 7.2 (the CP node dominating the highest IP is left out, as is the negation phrase, and nodes for adverbial modifiers are added).

The part of the proposal that is relevant to the point to be made is that the adverbial modifier, Adv(erb), is generated in the same underlying positions in English and French and presumably in Spanish and other languages as well (different classes of adverbs are generated in different positions). In the analysis under consideration the disparity in the surface positions of adverbs in English and French is claimed to be due to a difference in the movement of the verb: Every French verb moves past the adverb to its left in the purely syntactic part of the derivation, leaving behind a trace **t**, and adjoins to the finite tense node [T, +Fin], thus explaining the contrast in outputs, as in

(28) a. John often kisses Mary.
   b. Jean *embrasse* souvent **t** Marie

where *embrasse* has moved from the position immediately after *souvent*. In English, on the other hand, only auxiliary verbs adjoin to T in the purely syntactic part of the derivation, which explains the structural parallelism in

(29) a. John *has* often **t** kissed Mary.
   b. Jean *a* souvent **t** embrassé Marie.

The basis for this contrast between English and French is argued to be the value (+ or −) of a parameter P: French finite tense is strong (i.e., [+P]), while English finite tense is weak (i.e., [−P]), and weak T elements block the transmission of the thematic properties of a main verb to its trace, while a strong T element does not. Therefore only nonthematic verbs will move toward T in English in the overt syntax.

We can now ask whether the output of highly accomplished Anglophone speakers of French who rarely or never make a mistake when using examples such as (28b) and others involving the same parameter provides evidence that their unconscious knowledge of French derives from having fixed P at value [+], and the opposite for highly accomplished Francophone speakers of English.[51] It is immediately obvious that more than mere strict correctness of the output is required to make a positive answer plausible. After all, strict correctness of output (no easy matter in this case if the language acquirer is to go beyond the above examples to encompass the full range of facts) can be obtained resorting to very different strategies.[52]

Anglophone speakers of Spanish have to deal with additional differences, since Spanish lines up with French when there is no auxiliary, as in

(28) c. Juan besa a menudo a María.
Juan kisses often María.
'Juan often kisses María.'

but differs from both French and English (cf. 29) in not favoring the French/English word order and in allowing linear orders not allowed in English or French in examples such as the following:[53]

(30) a. ?* Juan ha a menudo besado a María.
'Juan has often kissed María'.
b. Juan ha besado a menudo a María.
'Juan has kissed often María.'
c. Juan a menudo ha besado a María.
'Juan often has kissed María.'
d. Juan ha besado a María a menudo.
'Juan has kissed María often.'
e. A menudo Juan ha besado a María.
'Often Juan has kissed María.'

It is a fair assumption that the choice among these options is a principled one for native speakers. Can the same be said about those that most successfully learned Spanish as adults, even in their teens?

Consider now the no less revealing difference between Spanish and English that the following example illustrates:

(31) Mara dijo (que) cuántas charlas planeaban los estudiantes.
Mara said (*that) how many talks the students were planning.

Only in Spanish is the element within parenthesis admissible (hence the * before *that*). However, the choice between using *que* in such structures is not free for a native speaker. The reason is that the presence of *que* changes not only the form but also the meaning of the expression. The Spanish structure with *que* is parallel in meaning to *Mara asked how many talks the students were planning* (which could be paraphrased as *Mara asked: How many talks are/were the students planning?*), while the structure without *que* is parallel in meaning to *Mara knew how many talks the students were planning*. In other words, the structure with *que* is an instance of an indirect question.[54]

Again, it would be interesting to determine whether the most proficient speakers of Spanish as a foreign language internalize the grammatical principles underlying the two types of structures under consideration the way native speakers do.

Suppose that a team of enterprising researchers offers what they take to be evidence for a positive answer. To be really persuasive, their demonstration would have to include an answer to a nontrivial question the structure with *que* raises, and that is that the interrogative element (*cuántas*, 'how many') appears to the right of *que*, not to its left, as the most developed tree diagram in chapter 6 would lead us to expect.[55] Things get even more intriguing when we bring in a related contrast between Spanish and English:

(32) ¿Cuántas lenguas todavía estudia Mara?
How many languages still studies Mara?
'How many languages does Mara still study?

The difference to attend to is the position of *todavía*, which appears immediately after the interrogative phrase. This is unexpected (compare the English gloss, or "How many languages still does Mara study?" if you prefer).[56] A perhaps not unrelated difference between Spanish and English is the following:

(33) (a) El aspirante que obtuvo (más) puntos
(b) El aspirante que *(más) puntos obtuvo

If we choose to take *más* (a choice signaled by the parentheses), both expressions mean roughly the same, although their conditions of use are quite different. They may both be translated as 'The candidate who got the highest number of points.' However, *más* may be left out only in (a); if it is left out in (b), the expression is unacceptable, as the star before the first parentheses indicates (that is, the parentheses of option are not admissible because in (b) *más* must be present). Consider now the following paradigm:

(34) (a) No sabemós quiénes ir.
(b) No sabemos quién de nosotros ir.
'We do not know who (of us) should go.'
(c) * Yo no sé quiénes ir.
(d) * Yo no sé quién ir.
'I do not know who should go.'

A peculiarity of Modern Spanish (not found in earlier stages of the language) is that it has two counterparts to *who*: *quién* (singular) and *quiénes* (plural). Either is admissible after a plural verb form such as *sabemos* 'we know', but neither is admissible after the corresponding singular form *sé*, 'I know'.

We could go on and on. Hopefully this is enough to suggest that there is much that is not very well understood in the grammar of Spanish (more precisely, that the structure given in chapter 6 for the "extended verbal projection" perhaps leaves something to be desired), or at least to conclude that the chances are rather slim of succeeding in demonstrating that a speaker of Spanish as a foreign language has "reset" (set) a parameter that we are still unable to formulate adequately (and this may include even the so-called head first parameter of chapter 6, as we know).[57]

One more point should perhaps be made before closing this section. A careful consideration of the pronominal structures included in the foregoing examples, which of course could be even more complex if the examples could have been chosen differently, would quickly increase the complexity of the clausal structures. This is because "extended" noun phrases, rarely investigated from the viewpoint of foreign language acquisition, raise many questions, some of which would take many professionals by surprise. It is not possible to really go into the topic here, but perhaps a few remarks will be enough to give at least the flavor.

Recent research suggests that an "extended" noun phrase, referred to as a Determiner Phrase (DP) in the literature, is not unlike a clause (CP), although it does appear to be a little less complex than the clause (for example, there is no counterpart to a Tense Phrase [TP] in a DP). One important proposal assumes that the basic structure of a DP is as shown in diagram 7.3. Here D is analogous to C, IP is assumed to be related to the presence of a DP internal subject, that is, a genitive DP (as in *John's offer of a bike to his son*), and it is only present when a genitive DP needs to be "licensed." Suppose we consider just pronouns, a class of elements no speaker of a foreign language can do without, as an illustration. What is the distribution of pronominal elements crosslinguistically? It has been argued that pronominal DPs include a NumP (which ends up in Spec of DP, in an agreement relation with D) and that pronouns occupy different positions in a structure such as (35), depending on structural properties of the language: a clitic pronoun such as French *le(s)* (or Spanish *lo(s)*), 'him/it(them)' is generated under D (together with a silent nominal element under Num in an associated phrase) and stays put (while the silent element moves to the Spec that is in a Spec-Head relation with the D dominating *le(s)*, that is, the Spec of the DP); a pronoun such as English *them* is generated under N, then the whole NP moves to the Spec of NumP,

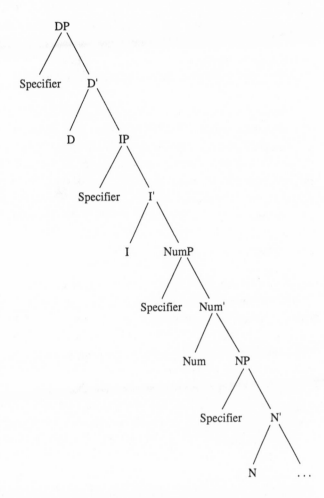

Diagram 7.3

and possibly the whole NumP moves to the Spec of DP in the overt syntax, while a pronoun such as *us* is generated under N (as nonpronominal nouns are), but then the whole NP moves to Spec of NumP and on to Spec of DP, leaving NumP behind (perhaps a way of accounting for the contrast **them two/us two*); a pronoun such as Norwegian *han* 'him' is also generated under N, and perhaps the N moves to Num, and the whole NumP moves to Spec of DP, as in English; in Welsh independent pronouns such as *mi* 'me' are generated under NumP, auxiliary pronouns such as *fi* 'I' under D, and reduplicated/conjunctive pronouns occupy the NumP and the D positions (both positions being filled in this case). And so on.[58]

This proposal may or may not be on the right track, but what matters for our purposes is that, in any case, there is little doubt that we are dealing with fairly complex structures.[59] A reasonable conclusion then is that experimental work attempting to show that adults are capable of setting the parameters responsible for the differences between, say, English and Spanish DPs, would have to attain a very high level of sophistication (well beyond current levels perhaps).

Summing up this section we may say that the thesis that adults are capable of setting the parameters in the process of foreign language acquisition has not been demonstrated (and no one has ever claimed that a particular individual has succeeded in setting all the parameters in the process of acquiring a foreign language, as would eventually be necessary to establish the thesis).[60] Furthermore, it does not appear to be plausible. The failure of ultimate attainment characteristic of many, perhaps most (if not all) adults, and in particular the fact that so-called interlanguage grammars often fossilize in a state that bears little resemblance to the ultimate target language, suggests that a form of the Critical Period Hypothesis (CPH) that places the burden of explanation on the unavailability of parameter fixing after a certain stage of maturation (certainly after puberty) appears to be quite plausible in light of the evidence now available.[61] Even in the best cases, nonnative performance is likely to involve a great deal of conscious or half conscious patchwork on the part of the speaker, who, for all we know, is using strategies and auxiliary routes that the native speaker does not have to resort to. Needless to say, this conclusion, which is even more tentative than other empirical conclusions (given the level of current understanding), does not commit us to positing "general learning strategies."[62] Obviously, the mind has capacities beyond the language faculty, as Chomsky has often emphasized, and "language-like systems might be acquired through the exercise of other faculties of mind, though we should expect to find empirical differences in the manner of acquisition and use in this case."[63] Hopefully, the search for those differences will be very much part of future investigations.

7.4. Other hypotheses

Surprising as it may seem, the CPH is perhaps the minority view among foreign language acquisition researchers, but this is not the place to review the range of positions on record or the range of logical possibilities. It seems advisable, however, to say at least a few words about some stands that might serve as cardinal points, thus helping to prevent misunderstanding.

Let us begin by considering the two families of facts that call for explanation:

(1) Speakers of a foreign language know many things about the language that they have not learned (the ones reviewed in the first part of the previous section among them).

(2) Most normal adults who try do not succeed in developing a native mastery of a single foreign language, no matter how hard they try or for how long, even with the help of instruction, while any normal child can come to speak a number of languages natively without need of instruction or even conscious effort (becoming a native speaker is not something the child does, but something that happens to the child).[64]

These facts suggest that we can safely disregard two extreme positions, referred to as (i) and (ii) below: If we are willing to exclude extranatural intervention, (1) above compels us to assume that the knowledge of language the environment could not possibly have provided (that is, the knowledge available without relevant experience) is coming from within the individual speaker (more precisely, that it is a contribution of the speaker's mind/brain, specifically, of the "language organ" or Language Acquisition Device, LAD for short). This assumption is inconsistent with the first of the following two hypotheses; on the other hand, (2) compels us to reject the second:[65]

(i) The LAD is totally unavailable after the critical period
The mental language organ plays no part in the acquisition of a foreign language. (Other organs of the mind are entirely responsible for it.)
(ii) The LAD is fully available after the critical period
The mental language organ is of no less use in the acquisition of a foreign language than in the growth of a first language.

Another hypothesis that can be quickly dismissed is the following variant of (i):

(iii) The LAD is available via the native language(s) after the critical period
Nothing in the mental language organ is available after puberty except the knowledge derived from the native language(s).

This variant of hypothesis (i) is not a true alternative because under the assumptions of the previous section language "growth" is essentially physical development of the language organ, not unlike the development of other organs of the body, so either the LAD develops, partially or fully, or it does not (in the case of "Genie" presumably it did not develop, at least not sufficiently). If the LAD has undergone full development, the process is presumably just as irreversible as the growth of one's arms or legs. An analogy may help to clarify the point: If a child does not develop normal legs, s/he will not be able to walk; if a child develops normal legs, s/he will be able to use them not only for walking, but also (perhaps later in life) for swimming or whatever. Is it reasonable to say that the child's swimming is "mediated via" her walking?

As Chomsky has noted, "There are empirical consequences to [the] assumptions" that at least some of the invariant principles "remain active in adult acquisition, while parameter-changing raises difficulties," since "they entail that at the steady state attained in language acquisition," the invariant principles of language are "wired-in," and "remain distinct from language-particular properties," hence distinct from "the acquired elements of language, which bear a greater cost." On another occasion (a few months later) he put it this way:

It seems that invariant principles of language count as "less costly" than those that reflect particular parametric choices. Intuitively, it is as if the invariant principles are "wired in" and therefore less costly than language-specific properties. If this is correct, then in the steady state of mature knowledge of language, there must still be a differentiation between invariant principles of the biological endowment and language-specific principles.[66]

There is a variant of hypothesis (iii), which postulates that the parameter settings of the native language(s) "are used, at least initially, as an interim theory about" the target language, and that parameter "resetting" (setting) to the values of the target language continues to be possible after the critical period, on the basis of input from the target language. Since knowledge of a native language is unconscious knowledge, not accessible to introspection, the interim theory part of this hypothesis may be understood as a particular proposal about the nature of the initial phase in the acquisition of a foreign language. This proposal appears to imply that the foreign-language acquirer essentially begins by attempting to speak her language with foreign words (that is, engages in a sort of wholesale syntactic transfer).[67] If so, the acquisition of the target grammar has yet to begin. As for the "parameter resetting" part of the hypothesis, no persuasive evidence or argument has been offered so far, and none is likely to be forthcoming, at least before we have a deeper understanding of several parameters and their effects, as pointed out in the previous section.

On the other hand, there is plenty of evidence that some highly proficient speakers have not been able to reset at least some parameters. To take an obvious example: Even highly knowledgeable and proficient speakers of Spanish fail on occasion to give phonetic form (to "spell out") agreement (as when they say "prohibido la entrada" for *prohibida la entrada* or "una situación autoritario" for *una situación autoritaria*), despite the fact that in this case the patchwork does not seem to present insurmountable difficulties.[68]

A more constrained variant of the "parameter resetting" view has been offered as an explanation of the following findings:

> Adults have difficulty moving from larger to smaller languages when a given principle is parameterized in a way that involves this distinction; that is, from this point of view, the usual acquisitional blindness to negative evidence. And further, adults encounter difficulty in moving from the unmarked setting of a parameter to a marked one when such a relationship does not involve the subset principle. There is also evidence that rule learning offers substantial difficulty for the adult learner.[69]

Since children encounter no such difficulties, it is natural to wonder about the root of the sharp difference between children and adults. Again, a plausible answer is suggested by the CPH, except perhaps for the special case of "rule learning," which brings to mind the distinction between "core" and "periphery." As is well known, the term "core grammar" was introduced to refer to the system determined "when the parameters of UG are fixed in one of the permitted ways," to be contrasted with an actual "language" incorporating "a periphery of borrowings, historical residues, inventions, and so on," that is, "a periphery of marked elements and constructions." But there appears to be no real basis for the contrast: "The only 'real' languages are core languages," in Chomsky's view.

> Given the fact that the things we call "languages" do not truly merit the name, we try to patch things up by talking about core and periphery. But it is patchwork. With more scientific sophistication, we'd give it all up.[70]

From this perspective, the fact that children do not have the difficulties adults have with "rule learning" in the course of language development might not tell us a great deal about the esssential nature of the language organ.

What arguably tells us a great deal about the esssential nature of the language organ is that "the most obvious differences between success in [native and nonnative language acquisition] is found in phonology" and in "the acquisition of inflectional morphology, where native-like language is notoriously hard to achieve" ("just those parts of the grammar for which the evidence available to the learner is so abundant").[71]

These differences are far from "irrelevant for the question of whether or not [LAD] operates in [nonnative language] acquisition."[72] They in fact provide the only evidence that is relevant for the parameterization of a language. It follows that a necessary consequence of the failure to internalize the morphological and phonological elements and principles properly is the failure of "parameter resetting."[73] In other words, there are two sides to acquisition, one of which is perhaps trivial (the invariant part provided by the initial state of the language organ, which is a part all languages have in common). The other side of acquisition, the nontrivial one, is the acquisition of the morphology in the broad sense of chapter 6 (including the basic and the derived elements of the vocabulary, with their morphological and phonological properties, and all the clues required for fixing the parameters at the right values).

The adult acquisition of phonology tended to dominate the discussion of adult acquisition until quite recently. A widely accepted result is that there is a critical period for the acquisition of accent-free speech. Generally, an accent-free pronunciation is said to be "virtually certain if acquisition begins before 6, fairly likely if acquisition begins before puberty, somewhat unlikely if acquisition begins in early adolescence, and highly unlikely if acquisition begins in late adolescence and adulthood."[74] It is easy to agree that "this in itself does not necessarily say anything about phonological knowledge as distinct from ability."[75]

It could be argued that the critical period for language development relates more to the peripherals of production and perception than to the central core of language (after all, what one notices most in nonnative language speakers is their accent), since there seems to be no critical period for at least one aspect of language acquisition, namely, the growth of the vocabulary, which is a lifelong process. Could it be that phonology is more impaired than syntax for the late learner, perhaps because of the nature of the physical mechanisms required for the production and perception of speech, that is, the particular modality involved in speaking and hearing?[76]

The study of sign language sheds a great deal of light on the matter. Since few deaf children have deaf parents and the accessibility of the language to which deaf children are exposed varies widely, late language acquisition in deaf people provides a natural laboratory for studying the age factor. Only a small proportion of deaf children whose parents and/or older siblings are deaf is likely to be exposed to fluent signing from birth. Many deaf children are exposed to signing only when they enter school, though some enter school as early as eighteen months of age. Perhaps the most typical cases are those of deaf children who are exposed only to spoken language through elementary school and permitted to learn to sign only after failing in the spoken/auditory channel, which means that these children begin their exposure to signing only after the age of twelve. A final group is those deaf people who are not exposed to sign language until adulthood.

Delayed sign language acquisition can therefore provide crucial evidence for the CPH, in particular about the period during which it is possible to fix the parameters of a language to its proper values. It is then of no small interest in this context that there seems to be "some evidence that the critical periods that have been hypothesized for spoken language hold true for signed languages, suggesting that these are critical periods for language and not just modality."[77]

We can now turn to the implications of the leading ideas and results reviewed in this chapter for the study of foreign languages, which is our next and final topic.

NOTES TO CHAPTER 7

1. Cf. Marler & Terrace (eds.) 1984, Mehler *et al.* 1984.

2. Siegel & Brainerd, eds., 1978, in particular the paper by Brainerd.

3. Needless to say, the ages of seven and twelve (roughly) had been identified as milestones by some religions long before Piaget. It is, incidentally, characteristic of humans to have evolved a strikingly longer period of infancy than other species, which has been taken to suggest that this period may have singular adaptive value (cf. Turkewitz & Kenney 1982).

4. Even if there is something to the stages, it certainly does not mean that every claim by Piaget and his colleagues is justified. For example, the claim that children are unable to form transitive inferences about quantity (for example, that they cannot infer $A > C$ from the information that $A > B$ and $B > C$) until they pass the stage of logical preoperations at about age seven is challenged in Bryant & Trabasso 1971, where two experiments are reported that demonstrate that "4 year old children can make transitive inferences about quantity provided that they can remember the items of information that they are asked to combine" (that is, "if precautions are taken to prevent deficits of memory from being confused with inferential deficits").

5. These remarks draw on Chomsky's answers over the years to questions raised after his lectures. Cf. Chomsky 1980, chapter 1.

6. Among these, there were some who made considerable efforts to quantify language aptitude in order to provide a reliable measure for predicting success in the

classroom (see Neufeld 1978 for a brief overview). Cf. Schneiderman & Desmarais 1988.

7. See, for example, Sperry 1951. We return to the topic.

8. Chomsky 1971, pp. 13–14. The quotes from Monod are given by Chomsky in his own translation from Monod's book, which was published in 1970 and was widely read at the time.

9. An early discussion of cerebral dominance is found in Penfield & Roberts 1959, a book with many virtues that recommend it to the nonprofessional reader, in particular case reports which "will interest many students, and stimulate them to ask new questions," and a useful historical survey (Lenneberg 1960b:111).

10. Lenneberg 1967, p. 176. Here is another expression of the same basic idea, taken virtually at random: "Young children in suitable environments pick up a second language with little trouble, whereas adults seem to struggle ineffectively with a new language and to impose the phonology of their mother tongue on the new language" (Macnamara 1973:63). We return to the question of foreign accents in the next section.

11. The question is raised in Penfield & Roberts 1959. It has been suggested that "it is at least conceivable that there is an element of Orwell's problem in the second language acquisition situation" (Hale 1988). If the view sketched in this chapter is on the right track, there is a fundamental difference between Lenneberg's Problem and what Chomsky calls Orwell's Problem, that is, the problem of explaining "why we know and understand so little, even though the evidence available to us is so rich," which for him is "an analogue in the domain of social and political life of what might be called 'Freud's problem'." The difference is that the root of Lenneberg's Problem is innate (thoroughly biological and entirely beyond the control of the individual, in contrast with Orwell's Problem, which is at least partially cultural and personal), hence completely independent of "the mechanisms used to induce passivity and conformism" and from "the institutional and other factors that block insight and understanding in crucial areas of our lives" (Chomsky 1986a:preface).

12. See Chomsky 1980, p. 185. Lenneberg based his hypothesis mainly on three types of evidence: (1) neurological studies indicating that various maturational growth curves plateau during the early teens; (2) findings in childhood aphasia that seem to show that the chances for recovery of impaired language functions are very different from children and adults; (3) language development in mentally retarded (Down's syndrome) children, which appears to follow a normal but slowed-down course until it is "frozen" at puberty (cf. below, in particular note 15). He did not seem to expect that the study of feral children could provide reliable evidence (1967:142; cf. Chomsky 1980:57f. and note 15 below).

13. Lenneberg 1967a (except for the phrase in brackets, which is from Lenneberg 1969, p. 114, as is the next quote in the text about maturation; the following one, about "species-specific capacities," is from Lenneberg 1964, p. 95). For a brief reassessment a few years later, see Lenneberg 1971. Cf. Johnson & Newport 1989, pp. 63–65. See also Seliger 1978, Colombo 1982, Newport & Supalla 1987, Westphal 1989, Flynn & Manuel 1991, Hurford 1991, Johnson & Newport 1991, Johnson 1992. For a recent overview, Scovel 1988; cf. Nippold (ed.) 1988, Singleton 1989.

14. It has been claimed that "the deterioration in some individuals begins as early as age 6—not at puberty as is often claimed" (Long 1990:251). Krashen (1975) suggests that the critical age is closer to about five years.

15. Chomsky 1988, p. 179. Another possible illustration, perhaps more widely known, would be the cat visual system as studied in a much-admired 1962 paper by Hubel & Wiesel (see also Hubel & Wiesel 1963, Wiesel & Hubel 1963, and subsequent papers). Cf. Chomsky 1965, chapter 1, note 27.

16. Recall the remark in Lenneberg's quote above about "the period during which the brain goes through its last stages of physical maturation." This is of course an educated guess, since apparently nobody knows much about the matter at present. It should be kept in mind, however, that we do not know less about language maturation than about sexual maturation, and everybody takes it for granted that children undergo puberty during the appropriate critical period, as part of the unfolding of the genetic program.

17. The quote is from Long 1989, p. 257. See Curtiss 1977, 1981, 1982, 1988, 1990 (and now Rymer 1993); cf. Chomsky 1980, p. 57. In contrast, mentally retarded children do quite well during the critical period (Yamada 1981, 1988, 1990), mongoloid children passing through the same general stages of language development as normal children, though at a much slower rate (Lenneberg, Nichols & Rosenberger 1964, Lackner 1976). It has also long been known that deaf children coo and babble at the same age as hearing children (Lenneberg 1966). Blindness, even compounded with deafness, also makes little difference (Landau & Gleitman 1985, C. Chomsky 1986), as already mentioned. Cf. Lenneberg 1967; Gleitman 1984, 1986; Singleton 1989:26f.

18. Lenneberg 1967, p. 176. It should perhaps be mentioned here that Lenneberg was born in Germany on September 19, 1921: in 1933 he emigrated with his parents to Brazil and attended high school in Rio de Janeiro, and after graduation spent seven years in business in that country. Seeking broader educational experience, he came to the United States in 1945. After one year's service in the United States Army, he entered the University of Chicago in 1947, receiving a B.A. in 1949 and an M.A. in linguistics in 1951 (the year he met Chomsky). He obtained a Ph.D. from Harvard University in 1955 in both psychology and linguistics. He then became a postdoctoral fellow in medical sciences at the Harvard Medical School with further specialization in neurology sciences and children's developmental disorders, completing those studies in 1958. From 1959 to 1967 he held faculty positions at Harvard and MIT while conducting basic research on language development in defective children at the Children's Hospital Medical Center in Boston. (In 1964 he was a visiting professor for psychology for a year at the University of Zurich). From 1967 to 1968 he was professor of psychology at the University of Michigan, and in 1968 he was appointed professor of psychology and neurobiology at Cornell University, a position he held until his sudden and untimely death in White Plains, N.Y., on May 31, 1975. See Roslansky, ed., 1969, p. 110; Lenneberg & Lenneberg 1975, pp. v–vi; Chomsky 1980, ch. 5.

19. Chomsky 1988a. It is interesting to compare the quoted remark with a similar one he made two years earlier: "When we ask what language a child of five, or a foreigner learning English, is speaking, . . . we say that the child and foreigner are 'on their way' to learning English, and the child will 'get there,' though the foreigner probably will not, except partially" (1986c:1). Cf. Chomsky 1986a, p. 16.

20. Lenneberg 1969, p. 114. This may not be a very startling conclusion, as Lenneberg notes, but it often goes unrecognized. Cf. McLaughlin 1981.

21. The quote is from Johnson & Newport 1989, p. 95. Cf., e.g., Walsh & Diller (1981), which assumes that there is "overwhelming behavioral evidence" that the views presented in Penfield (1953, 1964) and Lenneberg (1967) are not correct and purports "to explain biologically why children sometimes appear to be the better language learners when adults in fact are superior in most respects" (3–5). See now Gleitman 1986, Newport 1990.

What has not received support from subsequent work is the particular neurological mechanism Lenneberg proposed to explain the critical period (cf. Krashen 1973, 1975, 1978, 1981). Also, it has been suggested that the gradual decline in the capacity for language acquisition "begins well before puberty," but "it also appears that this early decline is small, and that another more major change occurs around puberty." In a particular study of first language growth distinguishing "native learners" (exposed to American Sign Language from birth by their deaf parents), "early learners" (first exposed to ASL between the ages of four and six), and "late learners" (first exposed to ASL at age twelve or later), the "4–6 age group scored consistently, although not always significantly, below native performance"; in a particular study of nonnative language acquisition, "the age 3–7 group scored at ceiling. . . . Further research is therefore necessary to determine with certainty the exact point at which a decline in learning begins for second language acquisition" (Johnson & Newport 1989:96). Interestingly, there appears to be "a consistent decline in performance over age for those exposed to the language before puberty, but no systematic relationship to age of exposure, and a leveling off of ultimate performance, among those exposed to the language after puberty" (Johnson & Newport 1989:79; cf. Harley 1986).

22. See Johnson & Newport 1989, p. 61–68. The failure of ultimate attainment characteristic of language acquisition after puberty (in most cases at least), and in particular the fact that "transitional grammars" or "interlanguage grammars" (Selinker 1972) often fossilize (Tollefson & Firn 1983) in a state that bears little resemblance to the ultimate target language, could perhaps be counted as additional evidence for the CPH. See below.

23. Patkowski 1980b, pp. 466–67; cf. Colombo 1982, Johnson & Newport 1989, p. 91. This is not to say that experiential and attitudinal variables play no role whatsoever, only that they cannot explain the disparity between child and adult at issue. The obvious question is: Why are such variables of no significance in first language maturation? Needless to say, the contrary view has never lacked advocates (see, for example, Salkie 1990:92–93). Cf. Gregg 1984:90ff.

It goes without saying that the CPH is not incompatible with the hypothesis that the differences between the special talents and attitudes of two particular individuals might help explain the disparity in their success as adult language acquirers. Nor is it inconsistent with a number of other ideas found in the literature, for example the idea that the "successful learners" employ a set of strategies that is quite different from the set employed by all others.

24. As mentioned in chapter 1, experimental evidence is still to come. There are few studies on "the competence ultimately achieved in the second language" and "none of these directly examined grammatical competence in the second language" (Newport 1990:18); for discussion, see Patkowski 1980a, b and 1982; Harley 1986, Scovel 1988, Singleton 1989, Johnson & Newport 1989, and Long 1990 (cf. Larsen-Freeman & Long 1990, chapter 6).

25. A version of T0 is defended in Clahsen & Muysken 1986, a paper DuPlessis, et al. 1987 argue against, offering a version of T1 as an alternative.

26. It is important to keep in mind that in this section "first language (L1)" and "second language (L2)" stand for native language and foreign language, respectively, as is common in the literature on nonnative language acquisition. As indicated in the preface, in this book "first" and "second" are understood in their literal senses, so a "second language" can be native or nonnative (even in the case of a child, if it is the result of classroom teaching only, for example).

27. DuPlessis et al. 1987, p. 57.

28. Cf. White 1985b; 1989, chapter 2.

29. Chomsky 1986a, p. 7 (the next quote by Chomsky below is from p. 8). Perhaps it should be mentioned in passing that the first empirical study of this question, with three- to five-year-old children (Crain & Nakayama 1987), was carried out almost thirty years after the completion of *The Logical Structure of Linguistic Theory*, which is somewhat surprising given the often-heard complaint that the results of early generative grammar had little to offer the experimental psychologist.

30. It may also refer to something else, but this has no bearing on our discussion.

31. Compare Koster 1993, on binding errors; cf. Hyams & Sigurjónsdóttir 1990, Sigurjónsdóttir 1992, Sigurjónsdóttir & Hyams 1992, McKee 1992.

32. See Flynn 1987, 2.2, for discussion; cf. Kellerman & Sharwood Smith, eds., 1986; Odlin 1989. On first language acquisition, see Wanner & Gleitman (eds.) 1982; Berwick 1985; Hyams 1986; Goodluck 1991; Atkinson 1992; Weissenborn, Goodluck, & Roeper (eds.) 1992 (see also Slobin, ed., 1985; for Romance, Clark 1986).

33. Although such interference (or "negative transfer") is all too evident in some cases (a speaker of Spanish who is fluent in English may pronounce *state* as *estate*, or say *they asked how did she do it*), there are known apparent mirror-image differences between two languages that are not equally easy to acquire (e.g., a speaker of English learning German "will have relatively little difficulty pronouncing *Tag* [tak] 'day' with a final [k], as native German speakers do"; however, a speaker of German learning English "will have relatively more difficulty pronouncing *bag* with a final [g], as native English speakers do" (Parker & Riley 1993, chapter 9). Another type of fact not explained by interference is so-called "differential substitution," which may be exemplified by the substitution of /t/ and /d/ for the first consonant of English *thin* and *then*, respectively, by native speakers of Russian or Serbo-Croatian, and the substitution of /s/ and /z/ for the same English segments by native speakers of Japanese or French, even though both Russian and Japanese have /t,d,s,z/ in their inventories (Weinberger 1988, chapter 4). (For a refurbished version of the contrastive analysis approach, see Eckman 1977 and other publications by him.)

34. Cf. Krashen 1981, p. 51ff.

35. From the perspective of the principles-and-parameters framework, the contrastive approach, properly understood, may be indispensable, aside from the fact that few have ever doubted that it can shed light on a range of difficulties encountered by acquirers that can be related to systematic differences between native language and target language.

36. Example (14b) below and the *garage* example discussed in chapter 2 provide good illustrations of subjacency effects (only the questions not barred by subjacency, that is, *¿Qué lamentas haber perdido?* and *In which garage did John keep the car?* are possible); an aspect of directionality (head first/last) is discussed in chapter 6, section 6.2.1. See the papers by Felix, Flynn, White, and others (some included in

Flynn & O'Neil 1988 and Gass & Schachter 1989). The earliest study on the availability of subjacency (as understood before Chomsky 1986b) in adult language acquisiton is Ritchie (1978), which suggests that Japanese subjects learning English do not violate the principle (cf. Rutherford 1984). (Gregg [1984 note 7] finds it "quite possible" that errors such as *The student of chemistry is older than the one of physics* "can be explained without having to claim that UG is being violated," a conjecture that is likely to have wide application). Results about the effects of subjacency interpreted as showing the opposite are reported in Johnson & Newport 1990.

37. See Plann 1981 for discussion.

38. Cf. White 1989, p. 61. The importance of phonological representations in the theory of foreign language phonology is stressed in a forceful and illuminating way in Ard 1989.

39. See below, in particular note 66.

40. The term "competence" is frequently used, but "unfortunately the distinction between ability and knowledge has all too often been blurred, with a concomitant loss of clarity and coherence" (Gregg 1989:20).

41. See Perdue (ed.) 1984. Child-adult differences in language acquisition have been widely discussed (cf. the 1982 collection by Krashen et al. and references therein). The case of immigrant children who have failed to acquire a native language (cf. Ioup 1989) may not constitute evidence to the contrary, for obvious reasons (including inadequate exposure).

Bley-Vroman (1985, 1989) identifies nine "fundamental characteristics of foreign language learning, among them lack of general guaranteed success, general failure (aside from rare exceptions), wide variation in success, course, strategy and goals, fossilization, need for instruction and negative evidence, and lack of clear grammaticality judgements." Cf. White 1990a.

42. See Obler 1987, Obler & Fein, eds., 1988. Not everyone agrees. For example, Gregg writes (1984:81): "Of course, some adults do attain native-speaker competence in a second language, and of course such competence is largely unconscious; no one has ever denied this." He stresses, however, the need "to explain just why it is that so few adults successfully acquire a second language" (1984:80). Selinker (1972:212; cf. 1992:24) assumes that "a small percentage of learners—perhaps a mere 5%— . . . achieve native-speaker competence," and that "may be safely ignored." Cf. Coppieters 1987.

43. See Stockwell, Bowen, & Martin 1965.

44. The first quote is from Phinney 1987 (p. 232), the second from Liceras 1989 (p. 126). Liceras goes on to conclude that her results "provide evidence for the unmarked status of the pro-drop option" (p. 129), but she does not elaborate. She is aware (note 3) that her conclusion is inconsistent with the subset principle (see note 67 below), since the Spanish system is the less constrained (cf. Dresher & Kaye 1990:166). Relevant recent discussion of the differences between children and adults in the use of overt subjects can be found in Hyams & Wexler 1993 (the explanation is to be found in the deficient linguistic knowledge of the children) and Valian 1990, 1991, Bloom 1993 (the differences are due to performance factors), and references therein (see also McKee 1992, McKee & Emiliani 1992). It is well known that "Italian [as well as Spanish and other Romance] speakers of quite fluent English routinely produce and find nothing wrong with" expressions such as "this allows to conclude that . . . " for *this allows one/us to conclude that* . . . (Hale 1988; cf. Flynn & O'Neil 1992).

45. See Larson & Luján 1990, from which the next three pairs of examples are taken. Perhaps it should be added that this insightful paper appears to overstate the case somewhat in that not all overt subject pronouns are necessarily focalized. Thus, both (i) and (ii) were presumably grammatical in Medieval Spanish (as they are in Modern Galegan, which retains properties of Medieval Galegan plausibly shared by Medieval Spanish):

(i) yo mesmo gelo dixe, 'I myself told it to him'

(ii) yo dixegelo, 'I told it to him'

If so, the position of the verb in (ii) would suggest that *yo* is not focalized. See Otero 1991a, 1991b.

46. Liceras 1989, pp. 114, 129. For exemplification of the *that-t* effects, see (25c) below.

47. See Chomsky 1981, 4.3, and Sportiche 1992 (a synthesis of the base-generation approach to clitic constructions, first proposed in Strozer 1976, and a version of the variant of the movement approach first proposed in Kayne 1989), respectively. See also Sportiche 1993a.

48. See Picallo 1990 (TP is substituted for Picallo's IP, to use the same notation that will be used in the next tree). More recently it has been argued that modals (including English modals) take clausal complements and that "the epistemic/deontic distinction can be straightforwardly reduced to the raising/control distinction" (Sportiche 1993b). The difference in interpretation between *John could not do that* and *John couldn't do that* is taken to provide support for this view (the second expression means, "It is not the case that John could do that," but the first may mean the same or it may mean something like, "It is possible for John not to do that.").

49. Cf., for example, the French data analyzed in Sportiche 1988 with the wider range of options available in Spanish.

50. See Pollock 1989 (a proposal based on the insights of Emonds 1978), refined and developed in Chomsky 1988b, 1992b (and criticized in Iatridou 1990).

51. The picture is of course more complicated, as is to be expected, but the present sketch is enough for our purposes.

52. E.g., place an adverb of class C after a finite main verb or after a finite form of *avoir*, and other rules of thumb that native speakers do not have to resort to. Cf. Gregg 1984, pp. 83–84.

53. Cf. Zagona 1988, chapter 1. See now Sportiche 1993b.

54. For discussion, see Plann 1982 (and 1985) and Suñer 1993 (from which the example in the text is taken), two papers that serious students of Spanish cannot afford to miss. Plann's generalization is that in Spanish at least only those verbs of communication that can be used to quote a direct question (e.g. *decir,* 'say', *tartamudear,* 'stutter', but not *saber,* 'know', *explicar,* 'explain') are amenable to reporting a question in indirect speech.

55. The reason is that in terms of that tree diagram, *que* would be under C and since 1985 the interrogative element is generally assumed to occupy the Spec position of CP, which is to the left of C. The solution suggested by Susan Plann in 1982 (and by other linguists since, Iatridou & Kroch 1992 being a recent example) hinges on the recursion of CP, that is, the generation of an additional CP under the one headed by *que*, a proposal that is not without problems. See Otero 1991a.

56. For discussion, see Suñer 1992; cf. Otero 1991a. It is standardly assumed that the interrogative phrase occupies the Spec of CP (as mentioned in the preceding note) and that the verb is under C in direct questions, presumably because of Spec-Head agreement.

The next two sets of examples are from Bosque & Brucart 1991 and Bosque & Moreno 1984.

57. On the last parenthetical remark, see the references of chapter 6, notes 17 and 5. Cf. Muysken 1984.

Many other examples could be given. Additional ones may be readily found in writings by many authors, including Bolinger, Bosque, Brucart, Campos, Contreras, Demonte, Goodall, Hernanz, Jaeggli, Kempchinsky, Laka, Liceras, Luján, Masullo, Montalbetti, Otero, Parodi, Piera, Plann, Rivero, Suñer, Torrego, Uriagereka, Varela, Zagona, and Zubizarreta, on Spanish, and those of Belletti, Burzio, Cinque, Cortés, Giorgi, Herschensohn, Kayne, Longobardi, Manzini, Picallo, Quicoli, Raposo, Rigau, Rizzi, Saltarelli, Sportiche, Valois, and Vergnaud on other Romance languages, in particular some of those listed in the bibliography at the end of this book.

58. See Koopman 1993a for a more detailed description, and Sportiche 1992, 1993a for some of the general assumptions.

59. If the DP includes one or more Adjective Phrases (APs), the structures are even more complex. In particular, they would have to account for the fact that a written phrase such as *the industrious Chinese* is ambiguous between roughly the sense of *the Chinese, who are industrious* (with a comma) and the sense of *the Chinese who are industrious* (without a comma), that is, between the sense of Spanish *los industriosos chinos* and the sense of *los chinos industriosos*, respectively. It should be added that the underlying structural difference between the last two DPs is still a problem in want of a solution, to the best of my knowledge (though Sportiche 1993b may point the way to one). A step in the right direction perhaps would be to assume that there is some parallelism with verb movement; in particular, that in the derivation of DPs such as *los chinos industriosos*, the noun (*chinos*), which presumably is generated to the right of the adjective (*industriosos*) in both Spanish phrases, has moved past the adjective in the overt syntax (syntactic movement is always to the left, for fundamental reasons), in contrast with the phrase in which the adjective precedes the noun.

60. Since the late 1980s there have been a number of interesting studies. See (in addition to those already cited, and other writings by Felix, Flynn, Liceras, and White), Jordens 1988, Schachter 1988, Schwartz & Tomaselli 1989, Thomas 1989, 1991, Broselow & Finer 1991, Hulk 1991, Schwartz & Gubala-Ryzak 1992, and in particular two recent dissertations, Klein 1990a and Archibald 1991 (cf. Flynn & O'Neil 1994), among other publications.

61. A recent study of advanced learners of English led to the conclusion that "an essential property of any adult L2 [foreign language] grammar" (Schachter 1990) is "incompleteness" (knowledge of the parameter studied was insufficient and distinguishable from native-speaker knowledge), "the corollary being that 'completeness' is *not* a possible property of L2 grammars" (Selinker 1992:251; cf. pp. 246, 254: "I have tried to learn many languages and have become fossilized in all of them"; "I'm a fossilized learner *par excellence* in several languages." (Selinker is the originator of the term "interlanguage" and one of the leading students of fossilization.) See also Jordens, ed. 1987.

If it is true of the language organ in general that at least some of its principles "remain active in adult acquisition, while parameter-changing raises difficulties," as the work of Suzanne Flynn on LAP suggests to Chomsky, "then the steady state would be the state where all parameters are fixed," in which case the distinction between perception and acquisition (a distinction the Cartesians did not make) "might be a matter of some subtlety," in Chomsky's view (1988c, note 6).

62. The tentativeness of the conclusions in this emerging field has sometimes been explicitly recognized. Thus, Flynn & O'Neil 1994, one of the most searching papers on the topic of this section, closes with a few "words of caution," including the following: "It is not yet clear how to read the evidence on these matters, for the principles and parameters of UG are only now beginning to be understood" (as they write earlier in the paper, "at this point in the history of acquisitional studies, it should be clear that much more is needed to make a theoretical point than observational data"). Compare Flynn & Manuel 1991:140: "It may, of course, be the case that some aspects of language learning have a critical period; much more refined work and precise empirical evidence is needed before such claims can be made [or denied, we might add], however."

63. See Chomsky 1975, p. 210; the quote is from Chomsky 1980, p. 28. Two recent papers by Antonella Sorace (1993a, 1993b) are suggestive. After examining the linguistic intuitions of French and English "near-native" speakers of Italian about some properties related to unaccusativity, she concludes that the knowledge French subjects have of Italian exhibits divergence (interlanguage representations of Italian properties that are consistently different from native representation), whereas the knowledge English subjects have of Italian exhibits incompleteness of their competence (lack of given properties of Italian), and argues that "these competence differences reflect differences in the overall representations of unaccusitivity in French and English."

64. See Chomsky 1988, p. 134. St. Augustine was apparently already aware of the nature of the general process: "Passing hence from infancy," he writes in his *Confessions* (1.13), "I came to boyhood, or rather it came to me, displacing infancy. . . . For I was no longer a speechless infant but a speaking boy."

65. It is still common to refer to Universal Grammar (UG) rather than to the Language Acquisition Device (LAD) or to the Language Organ. Since we are reserving the term "grammar" for the linguist's theory of a particular language or the general theory of language (as in Cook's *Chomsky's Universal Grammar*), the availability of UG is a different matter. Compare White 1989, 2.6, where references to publications defending variants of the positions outlined in this section may be found.

66. Chomsky 1988b (note 23), 1989a, respectively. Compare the following remark by Lenneberg (1967:167), which could perhaps be read as a still somewhat blurred anticipation of the position underlying Chomsky's comment: ". . . we may assume that the cerebral organization for language learning as such has taken place during childhood, and since natural languages tend to resemble one another in many fundamental aspects the matrix for language skills is present." In other words, there are invariant principles of language, and they are presumably represented in the "cerebral organization" that "has taken place during childhood." Cf. Chomsky's remark (note 59 above) that if it is true that at least some of the principles "remain active in adult acquisition, while parameter-changing raises difficulties, . . . then the steady state [usually assumed to be reached during childhood] would be the state where all parameters are fixed."

67. For some suggestive "evidence against direct transfer in word order acquisition," see Clahsen & Muysken 1989 (the quote is from p. 7).

68. Cf. Andersen 1984; see also Harris 1991a, b and Ritter 1993. The underlying grammatical processes do not seem to be as simple or transparent as their surface manifestations. See Chomsky 1992b, Cortés 1992, Sportiche 1992, 1993a, b, Koopman 1993a, Kayne 1993a, and references therein.

69. Flynn & O'Neil 1994. They go on to raise the question of whether there are "language-particular rules outside of phonology and morphology—if indeed they exist in these components of the grammar at all," thus giving expression to a widespread sentiment among generative grammarians. We return to the topic directly.

The "subset principle" is the hypothesis that, when constructing a grammar, a child starts out with the generative procedure (or grammar, the linguist's theory of the generative procedure) that allows the smallest number of possibilities. For example, since a language like English allows only, say, *they arrived early*, while a language like Spanish allows both *ellos/ellas llegaron temprano* and simply *llegaron temprano*, under the subset principle the child would start out with the English value of the relevant parameter, which generates only a subset of the expressions that are equivalent to the set of expressions generated by the Spanish system. This is of course just a first approximation to the problem. See Hyams & Wexler 1993 and references therein.

70. The last two (1989) quotes are taken from Otero 1991b; the others are from Chomsky 1981, p. 8.

71. Cf. Andersen 1989.

72. The quotes are from White 1989, p. 42 (except for the remark within parentheses, which is from Flynn & O'Neil 1994). White goes on to say that "failure to achieve native-speaker-like pronunciation . . . tells us nothing about whether abstract principles and constraints of UG [i.e., LAD] play a part in the learner's internalization of a grammar." Cf. Borer 1984, p. 29.

73. Significantly, in a recent study (Bardovi-Harlig & Bofman 1989) advanced foreign language learners from five different language groups (Arabic, Chinese, Korean, Malay, and Spanish), "who show similar patterns in error distribution, all show relative strength in syntax . . . , but relative weakness in morphology, which is always a language specific system."

74. Tahta, Wood, & Loewenthal 1981b. See also Scovel 1969; Asher & Garcia 1969; Seliger, Krashen & Ladefoged 1975; Oyama 1976; Scovel 1981; Tahta, Wood, & Loewenthal 1981a; Patkowski 1990; Bond & Fokes 1991; and several papers included in Ioup & Weinberger (eds.) 1987.

75. Flynn & O'Neil 1994. "In order to get at phonological knowledge," they continue, "we need to consider some better explained aspects of phonology, such as stress-accent, for example," where there is "the potential" for "a major contribution to our understanding of adult second language acquisition." It is also easy to agree on this point. As of now the investigation of the setting of stress parameters appears to offer more surmountable difficulties than other language subsystems (cf. Dresher & Kaye 1990). An interesting case to explore may be the acquisition of the English stress system by speakers of Spanish, or vice versa. For example, it has been argued that all of the stress patterns that occur in a set of data from Hispanophone speakers of English taken to be representative "can be generated by the target stress system" under the hypothesis that "second language learners fail to apply rules of rime extrametricality that are highly marked in their native language" (Mairs 1990:281; see Flynn & O'Neil 1994 for a detailed critique of Archibald 1991, a more extensive study than Mairs'). On the acquisition of Spanish stress, see Hochberg 1988 (cf. Otero 1986b, Roca 1990, Harris 1991, and references therein).

76. There is some evidence that nonnative speakers of a language are capable of making surprisingly accurate judgments about some aspects of that language (see, for example, Felix 1988 and White 1988 for syntax, Archibald 1991 for phonology). In the case of pronunciation, poor speakers of a language often appear to be able to distinguish native speakers of that language from nonnative speakers. But it is not clear what one can make of this anecdotal evidence. For example, a famous comedian from Madrid, Ernesto Vilches, was apparently able to pretend that he was speaking English or German, for example, which he did not know at all, and give the impression that he was speaking the language and could not be understood because of some shortcoming in the transmission (a poor loudspeaker system, for example).

77. Fischer 1994. See Lillo-Martin 1985, 1986, 1990, 1991, where the matter of parameter setting in normal sign language acquisition and sign aphasia is discussed; also Newport & Supalla 1987; Mayberry and Fischer, 1989; Newport, 1990. (For a recent collection of technical articles, see Fischer & Siple, eds., 1990, Siple & Fischer, eds., 1991; for a general introduction to the cultural life of deaf people in the United States, see Padden & Humphries 1988.)

8

Language research and language teaching: A renewed promise

What are the implications of the foregoing discussion for the acquisition of language after puberty? To begin with, a crucial, if not often clearly articulated, question in language teaching has always been the role of the genetic endowment (the language faculty or language organ) in child and adult language acquisition—in the terms used in the preceding chapter, the role of what is sometimes referred to as the language acquisition device (LAD), a particular version of universal grammar (UG) being simply the linguist's theory of this cognitive structure, which is common to all normal humans as far as we know. As Cook remarks, "If the students' minds were equipped with an ability to acquire language, a LAD, the best course of action for the teacher is the laissez-faire approach of supplying sufficient samples of language for LAD to make use of; students would acquire language much better without teacher interference."[1] In fact, the very limited, unsystematic, and impoverished primary linguistic data that are sufficient for the child should be sufficient for the adult speaker under the assumption of full availability of the LAD (a claim rarely made, if ever). One of the purposes of this chapter is to suggest that the hypothesis underlying the laissez-faire approach is no longer a very plausible one, if it ever was. True, there is still much to be learned, but we are already much better off than our predecessors of a generation ago.

To be sure, the question of the role of the LAD of the language user or the UG of the linguist in adult language acquisition continues to be a central one, as we have seen in chapter 7. As some prominent students of the matter have put it, "UG or not UG, that is the question."[2] We have already seen that there has recently been much debate over whether "UG" (read: the LAD) is available in nonnative language acquisition, and that such debate might contribute to a better understanding of what is at issue and might even lead to a deeper understanding of the nature and growth of language by opening a new window on the study of unconscious linguistic knowledge and on the process of acquisition. Could it also have a beneficial impact on the teaching of foreign languages and on the prospects of the students engaged in acquiring them? This is the topic of the present chapter.

8.1. Language theory and methods of instruction

Since a principled way of teaching a foreign language must be based on some understanding of the nature of language that is at least on the right track, language theory has obvious implications for the design of a language program, of which at least some are "perhaps of a rather negative sort": If the underlying view of language structure is irredeemably wrong, if the concept of language assumed is diametrically opposed to a reasonable one, the method of instruction can do more harm than good.

It is then natural to turn at this point to a major theorist who "used to be a language teacher for children and also for college students" and was later "able to develop a number of very strong claims about acquisition simply by stating the problem" in the way he did; in fact, his model of language, transformational generative grammar, "is really no more (or less!) than a description of the problem of language acquisition."[3]

Almost thirty years ago, in a very little-known introduction to one of the earliest attempts to take advantage of transformational generative grammar in the classroom, Noam Chomsky wrote that "one of the traditional motives for teaching grammar has been to extend the range of situations in which the body of skill and knowledge that the speaker has developed can be put to effective use." He went on to say, "Pursuit of these traditional goals of grammatical instruction" should be

> facilitated by the use of a system of grammar that expresses the underlying regularities of the language as fully and explicitly as possible. To the extent that this is correct, progress in the understanding of linguistic structure should naturally be reflected in the English curriculum. But quite apart from this, the intrinsic intellectual interest of the investigation of linguistic structure, with its many and varied implications for a broad range of questions, surely provides sufficient motivation for introducing the student to the systematic study of his native language and for doing so in a manner that is responsive to the issues that give substance and significance to current work.[4]

A case can be made that "the intrinsic intellectual interest of the investigation of linguistic structure" if anything increases (perhaps exponentially) when the systematic study of the structure of the student's native language is part of a larger study that includes at least one foreign language. Recall Goethe's well-known admonition (with *those* for *he*): "Those who know no foreign language know nothing of their own." A fact mentioned in the previous chapter provides a good illustration: The written expression *the industrious Chinese* may be equivalent to two Spanish expressions, *los industriosos chinos* or *los chinos industriosos*, which are very different in meaning (the first one implies that all Chinese are industrious, the second one refers only to those who are industrious, with no implication that all are). Many other examples could be given. Compare, for example, *the invited ones arrived* and "arrived the invited" (which is not English) with Spanish *llegaron los invitados* and *llegados los invitados*, which is enough to suspect that *to arrive* is not intransitive in the sense that, say, *to telephone* is, not exactly an insignificant observation without consequences—or, reversing direction, that the mental representation of the Spanish expressions may include a "silent noun" as a counterpart to *ones*. There are of course innumerable other examples, including far more intriguing ones that are less suitable in this context.[5] The point is that only by comparing two or more languages can students begin to see what is peculiar to their native language and what is shared by all humans, what is deep and what is superficial, even trivial. To the extent that this is correct, "progress in the understanding of linguistic structure should naturally be reflected in the [foreign language] curriculum," not just in the English curriculum.

It is highly significant that immediately after noting that a child is something like a pigeon that will never be able to fly if kept in a box beyond a certain age at which pigeons have to fly (beyond "maybe two weeks or so") and that "very probably" human language is not unlike bird flying in this respect (recall the discussion in Chapter 7), Chomsky went on to draw the conclusion that

> For the language teacher, that means that you simply cannot teach a language to an adult the way a child learns a language. That's why it's such a hard job.[6]

The quote makes it clear that Chomsky is not among the advocates of the "natural method." His view derives explicitly from the Critical Period Hypothesis (CPH): Under normal conditions, the human brain undergoes crucial changes between the early years of childhood and the onset of puberty that cannot be ignored.[7] It is also well known that he is strongly against the method called "pattern practice," in which a certain linguistic pattern is senselessly repeated over and over again. It is no secret that the "pattern practice" method was a direct outgrowth of the behavioristic psychology (including linguistics) of an earlier generation. A quote from Leonard Bloomfield's *Outline Guide for the Practical Study of Foreign Languages*, published in 1942, may serve as illustration:

It is helpful to know how language works, but this knowledge is of no avail until one has practiced the forms over and over again until he can rattle them off without effort. Copy the forms, read them out loud, get them by heart, and then practice them over and over again day after day, until they become entirely natural and familiar. Language learning is overlearning; anything less is of no use.

Bloomfield's treatise, which provided only a point of departure, was to guide the theory and practice of language teaching for decades. The following echo (to mention just one) appears in a treatise in its wake written by a professor of foreign language education at Yale almost a quarter of a century later:

The single paramount fact about language learning is that it concerns not problem-solving, but the formation and performance of habits. The learner who has been made to see only how language works has not learned any language; on the contrary, he has learned something he will have to forget before he can make any progress in that area of language.[8]

This approach, based on the conception of psychology of a generation ago, achieved a certain influence in educational circles in the 1960s, and it was the one most directly shaping the curriculum when Chomsky's ideas began to receive a sympathetic hearing. The contrast between the two perspectives could not have been sharper. Compare Chomsky's view, as expressed in *The Pedagogic Reporter* in 1969, with Bloomfield's:

It can be said with fair confidence that the worst possible conditions for language learning are those marked by rigidity and intellectual and emotional vacuity. There can be nothing more stultifying than language drill, whether it is mere memorization of paradigms or the mindless repetition of patterns divorced from any meaningful context.

As Chomsky pointed out at the time, for a behaviorist, language learning "is kind of like catching a ball or something like that." It was commonly assumed that language, "like other forms of behavior, is a system of habits developed through drill and training, reward and punishment," and the structure of language was assumed to be "a system of patterns that are acquired through constant repetition and 'overlearning' under proper conditions of reinforcement." This view led naturally to "pattern practice" as a method of instruction, a method that came to be regarded as an essential component of the language curriculum.

Not surprisingly, the method was not successful. The most obvious reason for the failure appears to have been that such "pattern practice" is extremely boring:

> Learning doesn't achieve lasting results when you don't see any point to it. Learning has to come from the inside; you have to want to learn. If you want to learn, you'll learn no matter how bad the methods are. . . . And if you use methods which are designed to ensure that no sensible person could possibly pay attention, then there's no hope.

A particularly illuminating assessment of this method of foreign-language instruction is to be found in a 1968 interview in which Chomsky stresses that it is "a very bad way—certainly an unprincipled way—to teach language" because the underlying view of language structure is "entirely erroneous." It is "based on the assumption that language really is a habit structure, that language is a system of skills and ought to be taught by drill and by the formation of stimulus-response associations," hence it is not "a method that is based on any understanding of the nature of language." In his view, this is a case in which psychologists and linguists "have caused a good deal of harm by pretending to have answers to [the relevant] questions and telling teachers . . . how they should behave."

Underlying this assessment is the belief that our understanding of the nature of language seems to show quite convincingly that, contrary to what is assumed in a behavioristic approach, "with its emphasis on habit and skill and pronunciation ability, . . . language is not a habit structure"; rather, "it has a kind of creative property and is based on abstract formal principles and operations of a complex kind." As Chomsky put it in the closing words of his celebrated address at the Northeast Conference on the Teaching of Foreign Languages in August 1966, "research in the coming years . . . will show that certain highly abstract and highly specific principles of organization are characteristic of all human languages, are intrinsic rather than acquired, play a central role in perception as well as in production of sentences, and provide the basis for the creative aspect of language use." (This is even less open to question now, as discussed in chapter 5.) It is ideas such as these that "may have some potential impact on the teaching of language." In the 1968 interview he went on to express the feeling that from our knowledge of the organization of language and of the principles that determine language structure one cannot *immediately* construct a teaching program. All we can suggest is that a teaching program be designed in such a way as to give free play to those creative principles that humans bring to the process of language-learning, and I presume to the learning of anything else. I think we should probably try to create *a rich linguistic environment* for the *intuitive heuristics* that the normal human automatically possesses. (Emphasis supplied.)

Summarizing and clarifying, we may say that what Chomsky was advocating a quarter of a century ago was a principled teaching program, based on some understanding of the nature of language, which relies and counts mostly on the student's mind and goes some way toward creating "a rich linguistic environment for the intuitive heuristics that the normal human automatically possesses." In the next section we consider one possible way of contributing to bringing about a particularly rich linguistic environment.

8.2. Scientific grammars and pedagogic grammars

As is well known, Chomsky has repeatedly emphasized that "the concerns of traditional and generative grammar are, in a certain sense, complementary." A representative recent characterization is the following:

A good traditional or pedagogical grammar provides a full list of exceptions (irregular verbs, etc.), paradigms and examples of regular constructions, and some general observations about the form and meaning of expressions. But it does not examine the question of how the reader of the grammar uses such information in attaining the capacity to form and interpret new expressions. . . . With not too much exaggeration, one could describe such a grammar as analogous to the *data* presented to a child learning a language. Generative grammar, in contrast, was concerned primarily with the intelligence of the reader, the *principles* and procedures brought to bear to attain full knowledge of a language. (Emphasis supplied.)[9]

The foregoing discussion suggests that from the perspective of the principles-and-parameters theory a good pedagogical grammar will differ from both a traditional and a generative grammar. It will differ from a generative grammar in assuming that at least some of the invariant principles of language need not be specified in detail, since they will be automatically provided by the LAD. But, crucially, it will differ from a nongenerative grammar in that it will provide a pedagogically appropriate but full account of the significant differences between the native language of the student and the target language. In particular, it will systematically present and draw the student's attention (in a way consistent with known pedagogical principles) to many simple facts illustrating differences between the two languages that are not found in even the most compendious traditional or teaching grammars, some of which may in fact not have been noticed by anyone, let alone by the typical student, for many years or centuries, perhaps not noticed until quite recently (as is the case with some of the ones discussed in chapter 7).

It seems fair to say that to this day perhaps the most detectable influence of transformational generative grammar on language teaching has been of a negative character. The evidence it provides in support of innate knowledge, and the related emphasis on freedom of choice and creativity, has been used as a helpful resource against behavioristic approaches to language acquisition—a resource that can still be used to good effect in some cases, we might add.[10]

The new principles-and-parameters theory makes possible refined or entirely new "applications." One of these is a far more sophisticated study of nonnative language acquisition than was conceivable before the 1980s.[11] It seems that, at long last, it has become possible to take a fresh look at the fundamental issues raised by nonnative language acquisition, in particular, language acquisition after puberty (LAP), and to examine from a new perspective problems of language study and language teaching that have resisted insightful treatment or have not been investigated at all.

The new work on the nature of LAP with a central interest in explanation has a very short history.[12] Among the earliest and most extensive contributions based on the principles-and-parameters framework are those of Suzanne Flynn (from 1980 on) and Juana M. Liceras and Lydia White (from 1983 on, in the wake of White's 1982 book on language acquisition). Some of the most interesting papers have appeared in a new journal, *Second Language Research*, founded, not exactly by sheer chance, in 1985 (rather than ten years earlier). Of special interest for many researchers and teachers is that perhaps the earliest book-length monograph is on "the Spanish non-native grammar of English speakers," and that Spanish is one of the languages more often studied and mentioned.[13] Perhaps the most representative collections of papers from the new perspective to date are the ones edited by Flynn and Wayne O'Neil in 1988, essentially a revised and expanded version of the proceedings of a conference held at MIT in October 1985, and by Gass and Schachter in 1989. A general introduction and overview by White also appeared in 1989.

In light of this work it is possible to envision a new kind of pedagogical grammar that will differ sharply from a nongenerative grammar, as discussed above. This will be particularly true of the facts that can be traced to the effects of the parameters. The so-called rules of traditional grammars are really only hints that presuppose that the reader already knows the basic structure of language, and they do not have much to say about the effects of the values of the parameters, which obviously cannot be taken for granted by an up-to-date pedagogic grammar. In the case of the study of a foreign language, an up-to-date pedagogic grammar will attend to the parametric differences between the target language and the native language of the acquirer, thus showing considerable factual overlap with the more technical and perhaps wider ranging comparative grammar of the theoretical linguist.[14] It would seem that only such a parameter-oriented grammar can provide a reliable basis for either successful textbooks or the design of informed and carefully planned language teaching programs of foreign languages. With not too much exaggeration, one could describe such a pedagogic grammar as analogous to the data used by the linguist studying the language rather than to the data (the so-called primary data) that suffices for the child. It is hard enough to gain a degree of mastery of a foreign language with all the resources available. Arbitrarily limited to the primary data, a grown-up would not go very far.

To illustrate briefly, a pedagogic grammar of Spanish has to somehow incorporate the information that would allow the student to derive only the nonstarred examples in the following paradigm:[15]

(1) a. Es obvio que necesita gafas.
  'It's obvious that he/she needs glasses.'
 b. Que necesita gafas es obvio (=1a).
  'That he/she needs glasses is obvious.'
(2) Question:
  ¿Pepe necesita gafas? 'Does Pepe need glasses?
 Answer:
 a. Es obvio que necesita. 'It is obvious that he needs.'
 b. * Que necesita es obvio. 'That he needs is obvious.'

It should also incorporate crucial facts about the *ser/estar* contrast, a hallmark of Spanish (and a few other Romance languages). For example, recent work suggests that there is a close interrelation between this contrast and the properties of individual-level/stage-level predicates (independently discovered).[16] As the late Dwight Bolinger observed twenty years ago, *be-*

ser (that is, the individual-level predicate) "is more independent of its complement than *be-estar*." Consider examples such as the following:

(3) (a) * Ana es orgullosa de su triunfo.
'Ana is (*ser*) proud of her triumph.'
(b) Ana está orgullosa de su triunfo.
'Ana is (*estar*) proud of her triumph.'
(c) Ana es/está orgullosa.
'Ana is (*ser/estar*) proud.'
(4) (a) Ana es merecedora de su triunfo.
'Ana is (*ser*) deserving of her triumph.'
(b) * Ana está merecedora de su triunfo.
'Ana is (*estar*) deserving of her triumph.'
(c) * Ana es/está merecedora.
'Ana is (*ser/estar*) deserving.'
(5) (a) Ana parece lista. 'Ana seems clever/ready.'
(b) Ana me parece lista. 'Ana seems clever/*ready to me.'

(Compare *Ana es lista*, where *lista*, an individual-level predicate, is understood as clever by nature, that is, 'ready-witted', with *Ana está lista*, where *lista*, a stage-level predicate, is understood as just ready, that is, 'all set' to do something; similarly, *Ana es bonita* means that Ana is a pretty girl, while *Ana está bonita* means that Ana is pretty in her new dress, with her new hairdo, etc.)

An even more subtle point is suggested by the observation that the Portuguese structural equivalent of (6) is ambiguous and can be disambiguated by pseudoclefting, as in (7):[17]

(6) Encontramos a Luis cansado.
'We found Louis tired.'

(7) (a) Lo que encontramos allí __ fue a [Luis cansado].
'What we found there __ was Louis tired.'
(b) A quien encontramos allí __ [cansado] fue a [Luis].
'Who we found there __ tired was Louis.'

In (a), where [*Luis cansado*] is a small clause and *cansado* is a stage-level predicate, we find a state of affairs: that of Luis being tired; in (b), where [*cansado*] is a secondary predicate, we find someone who is tired. One may suggest that there is still another (third) interpretation: In (b) (minus *allí*), *cansado* can be understood by some speakers as 'tiresome', perhaps a less readily shiftable instantiation of an individual-level predicate. Compare the following contrast (in Castilian Spanish):[18]

(8) (a) Juan parece cansado.
　　　　'John seems tired/tiresome.'
　　　(b) Me parece cansado hablar con tanta gente.
　　　　'It seems tiresome to talk to so many people.'
　　　(c) Es/*está cansado hablar con tanta gente.
　　　　'It is *(ser/*estar)* *tired/tiresome to talk with so many people.'

Not every teacher of Spanish will find it easy to discover manifestations of the contrast in English (however indirect), and mostly everyone (teacher, linguist, or student) will appreciate any help they can get with this and similar tasks. A contrast that might be helpful to any speaker of English considering the matter is the following:

(9) (a) I thought him (to be) clever.
　　　　'Lo creía (*ser/*estar) inteligente.'
　　　(b) *I thought him (to be) ready.
　　　　*'Lo creía (ser/estar) listo.'

Similarly, we say *I thought her to be pretty (to be a really pretty girl)*, but not *I thought her to be pretty in her new dress*. The reason is that *to think X (to be) Y* is an expression of "essence," that is, an expression involving an individual-level property. On the other hand, the use of *all* as an intensifier in English can only be an expression of "accident," that is, an expression involving a stage-level property, as in *My hands are all dirty* (but not *That joke is all dirty*, since a dirty joke is dirty by nature, and no amount of soap and water will be able to clean it up).[19]

A Spanish peculiarity of an entirely different order is the syntax of the unstressed pronouns usually called clitics, which sometimes are the key to the underlying structure. Consider the following quasi-minimal pair:

(10) (a) Pablo denunció a dos.
　　　　'Pablo denounced two.'
　　　(b) Pablo renunció a dos.
　　　　'Pablo renounced two.'

The only superficial difference (hence the only possible difference in the "input") between (a) and (b) is the difference between two closely related coronal sounds (*d* and *r*, respectively). The corresponding underlying structures, however, are crucially different, as becomes apparent when we replace *a dos* by a pronoun in each case:

(11) (a) Pablo los denunció.
     'Pablo denounced them.'
 (b) * Pablo los renunció.
     Pablo renunció a ellos.
     'Pablo renounced them.'

It is a fair guess that most students would rather not have to discover the contrast all by themselves, particularly those who take long to discover that oddities such as "vio a mí" are not Spanish. And it is even more likely that not every student or teacher would find it possible, let alone easy, to discover the following facts—even going beyond a "naturalistic" input, since speech does not come in conveniently arranged pairs:

(12) (a) El niño (le) dio la manzana a Pablo.
     'The child gave the apple to Pablo.'
 (b) El niño *(le) comió la manzana a Pablo.
     'The child ate the apple on/for Pablo.'
 (c) El niño (*le) comió la manzana de Pablo.
     'The child ate Pablo's apple.'

In (a) *le* may be left out without impairing the acceptability of the expression, as the parentheses indicate, but in (b), which is superficially parallel, *le* is required, hence the star before the parentheses (i.e., the parentheses of optionality are not allowed). On the other hand, in (c), with *de* instead of *a*, *le* is excluded, hence the star inside the parentheses.[20]

Consider now the following pair:

(13) (a) Ana dice que estudia todos los días.
     'Ana says that he/she studies every day.'
 (b) Ana dice que estudie todos los días.
     'Ana says for him/her to study every day.'

Again, the superficial difference between (a) and (b) is minimal (it reduces to the difference between *a* and *e*, a contrast signaling indicative and subjunctive, respectively), but the difference in underlying structure is considerable. To mention just the obvious: In (a) Ana could be the one doing the studying (though this is not the only possible interpretation), while in (b) she cannot be.[21] Another crucial difference between the two underlying structures is partially reflected in the following pair of examples, where the embedded subject follows the verb:

(14) (a) Ana dice que estudia el niño todos los días.
        'Ana says that the boy studies every day.'
     (b) Ana dice que estudie el niño todos los días.
        'Ana says for the boy to study every day.'

Of the two, only (b), the expression making use of the subjunctive mood, is perfectly natural with normal intonation.[22]

Many more examples could be given, including perhaps more representative ones that cannot be properly presented without a more developed background. But perhaps this small sample is enough for the purposes of this chapter, so we leave the discussion hanging at this point and turn to the next and final question.

8.3. A range of options for language programs

Few would fail to recognize that present-day "linguistics and psychology cannot support a 'technology' of instruction in the sense in which physics supports a technology of nuclear reactor design or space exploration."[23] And everyone would agree that a specific language teaching program cannot be directly derived from even the most illuminating results of the comparative study of the native language of the students and the target language. The question is whether such study could at least provide boundary conditions for the range of empirically based programs with a fair chance of achieving a considerable level of success. A positive answer does not seem unreasonable. It is hardly in doubt that, other things being equal, a teacher who is thoroughly familiar with what is known about the subject matter (what is relevant here is conscious knowledge, not just the unconscious knowledge of the native speaker) will be able to do a better job than one who is not, as a physician who knows medicine will be able to do a better job than one who does not.

No one would expect miracles from a physician who does not know anything about viruses and bacteria, even less from one who believes, as the ancient Egyptians did, that the seat of the higher mental functions (in particular "the basic emotional part of a person") is the gut (we still speak of people *with guts* or *gutless*, as the case may be), or the liver (as implied by the author of the Psalms), or the heart, as taught by Aristotle (who believed that the brain was just a thermoregulator that cooled the blood) and by many after him (*heartless* can still be understood as "lacking feeling"), a step back from Plato. And no one would expect miracles from a teacher who believes that everything one wants to know about language is to be found in the environment, even less from a teacher who wittingly or unwittingly assumes that everything known about language that is of any worth is contained in a few books published before 1980, perhaps even before 1950.

On the other hand, it is easy to show that students invariably benefit from the preparation and true understanding of their teachers (the deeper, the better), consistently reflected in the information they provide and the knowledge they unveil. Adult language acquisition is no exception. The little relevant information available suggests that the proper use of grammatical knowledge (not necessarily overt in the teaching) can make a contribution to successful teaching.[24] In particular, it can contribute to making the subject interesting. As Chomsky has stressed again and again, "at any level, from the nursery to graduate school, teaching is largely a matter of encouraging natural development," so "the best 'method' of teaching is to make it clear that the subject is worth learning, and to allow the child's—or adult's—natural curiosity and interest in truth and understanding to mature and develop."[25] Intriguing properties such as the ones exemplified above are likely to be of interest to at least some language students.

Against this background it seems clear that the laissez-faire approach to teaching referred to at the beginning of this chapter is not one full of promise. If it is true that the parameters for a new language cannot be fixed after the critical period, there is little similarity between the child and the adult acquirer with respect to the range of data needed to internalize the structure of the language. Rather, the similarity in range of data is between the adult language acquirer and the linguist, who is in need of far more evidence, and far more sophisticated information, than that provided by the primary linguistic data the child is limited to. No language program involving English and French, for example, will deserve high marks if it does not include an appropriate number of carefully selected and selectively contrasted "minimal pairs" such as those in (28) and (29) of chapter 7. More generally, the "differences between French and English" linguists have been writing about since the early 1980s, which are interesting in themselves, can only help the French textbook writer.[26] The same could be said of recent work on other Romance languages, some of which are among the most widely spoken and are also of special interest to a large number of students (two of the three languages most frequently taught in the United States are Spanish and French).[27] It would seem that the preparation of language materials that meet the standards that can now be envisioned—which are already much higher than what was barely conceivable in the late 1970s, a not insignificant fact—will require both far more solid linguistic knowledge and more considerable pedagogical sophistication than were required a mere generation ago.[28] The informed and responsible language teacher is likely to welcome these developments and to build on them.

In chapter 7 we saw that there are two classes of facts that need not be learned by the child. The first class, discussed in section 7.3.1, includes knowledge that is innate and completely independent of experience. The second class, discussed in section 7.3.2, is automatically derived once the value of each parameter has been fixed, but choosing the proper value for each parameter requires linguistic experience even in native language acquisition. To illustrate: Once the parametric values have been fixed, the facts exemplified in (8), for example, do not have to be learned by the native speakers of Spanish/Italian and French, respectively; they follow from the values of the parameters in each of the languages. The situation appears to be different, however, in LAP. This is a problem for both the student and the teacher. On the other hand, the facts derived from innate knowledge need not be taught in any case.[29]

What is it, then, that the postpubescent language student has to assimilate? It is clear that a necessary step for everyone is to learn the vocabulary items of the language and their properties, something inescapable even for the native speaker. This would be an impossible task for anyone not born with a conceptual system in place, as discussed in chapter 3. Fortunately for every human, to a large extent this task seems to reduce to "a problem of finding what labels are used for preexisting concepts, a conclusion that is so surprising as to seem outrageous but that appears to be essentially correct nevertheless."[30] The family resemblance between the labels of the native language of the student and the target language seems to facilitate the task, possibly giving an initial advantage to the adult.[31] However, the fact is that the postpubescent student will be no match for the child along other dimensions. We all know about foreign accents.[32] But this does not seem to be the only disadvantage of the adult. Just think that at age three or earlier a native speaker of English may exhibit a command of the verb-particle construction that will forever elude even highly proficient adult acquirers and may matter-of-factly correct, instantly and unhesitantly, the errors of the grown-ups.[33]

This first necessary step may be close to being a sufficient one for those interested just in "communication." It is no secret that "we can often make out what is said in a foreign language when we can identify some of the words, impose a thematic and aitiational structure and use contextual cues, even without much knowledge of the grammar," a feat that in some ways is not unlike "normal comprehension under noisy conditions in our own language."[34] But in the case of foreign-language acquirers this success would surely not lie in their possession of knowledge of the language they hear, apart from peripheral aspects, a fact some foreign-language teachers and researchers tend to forget.

Another aspect of the language that both the child and the adult must learn is the irregularities, although again child and adult may learn them in very different ways.[35] This is likely to be true also of the morphological regularities (a quite different type of task for the native speaker), some of which are the keys to the parameter settings for the child.

Even the logical problem of language acquisition the child and the adult face has much in common. Ideally, they both have to internalize a system that accounts for the distribution of * in cases such as those exemplified above and numerous other instances (in fact, an infinite number of them), well beyond the small sample the child is exposed to or the sample available to the adult (even if the distribution of * does not have the same basis or the same range for both the child and the adult). In other words, the paradigms of interrelated surface facts (or some of them, in the case of the adult) must be derivable from a finite, if not simple, set of principles that ideally should be internalized by language acquirers if they are to go beyond the utterances they memorize and those they appear to construct by analogy with those they are exposed to.[36] To carry out this task, they both have to rely heavily on the inborn invariant principles of language.

At this point the similarities appear to end. It is an indisputable fact that every normal child is perfectly capable of unconsciously determining the values of the languages of their communities, without training or instruction. In sharp contrast with this, most adults (if not all) and younger nonnative speakers appear to encounter insurmountable difficulties when they deliberately try to duplicate the effortless feat of the child.[37] The research now available does not offer much reason to suppose that it is possible to set the values of the parameters for another language after childhood, even with the help of negative evidence (correction) and other resources not available to the child. The well-known facts cited in chapter 7 suggest that linguistic parameter setting is possible only for a brain undergoing maturation at a particular (early) stage. Extremely accomplished language acquirers report that their mastery of a foreign language differs in nontrivial ways from their mastery of their native languages, and presumably there is much they are not aware of. To give just one example, for teachers or students interested in more than "communicating," it may not be a secret that, for example, the type of sentence exemplified in (15) is admissible in Spanish, or that it is not admissible in French,

(**15**) (a) Juan no sabe si ir al cine.
 (b) * Jean ne sait si aller au cinéma
  'John doesn't know whether to go to the movies.'

but their being error free on this score is a far cry from their being able to represent and compute the structure underlying (a) or the structure underlying (b) as a native speaker does.[38]

This is not to deny that the output of some of the highly accomplished foreign language acquirers may be difficult to distinguish from that of a native speaker and may even be superior to the output of the native speaker in some ways (richness of vocabulary, effectiveness of expression, and so on). Clearly, not all native speakers of English come close to matching the achievement of Joseph Conrad, for example. But, as noted in chapter 7, even in the best cases nonnative performance is likely to involve a great deal of conscious or half-conscious patchwork on the part of the speaker, who, for all we know, is using strategies and auxiliary routes that the native speaker does not have to resort to. This appears to be related to the fact that adults acquire languages in ways at great variance with the course of native language development, or so it seems, not to mention the well-known fact that when we learn a foreign language, we tend to concentrate on the respects in which it differs from our own.[39]

It is precisely at this point that a good pedagogic grammar, based on the best available linguistic research, can be most helpful. There is much that the student-teacher team can do to smooth what otherwise could turn out to be a very rough and not very rewarding ride. Since "it stands to reason that graded reading materials and oral practice should be central to the curriculum," the teacher may begin by providing a carefully selected and properly graded pool of reliable and revealing facts, as needed for further advancement, including "input either in the form of grammar teaching, or correction, or other forms of emphasis on particular structures," geared toward further goals. This may in fact be "a teacher's most important job."[40] At the very least, the adult's data base must contain revealing evidence for the conscious mind about the parametric properties that are unconsciously known by the native speaker. To be concrete, part of the challenge for the teacher of Spanish to speakers of English is to open the way to some generative system of knowledge (presumably not isomorphic with that of the native speaker) from which such facts as those exemplified in (2) and (4) of chapter 7 are derivable.

It would seem that linguistic research can make a contribution here. This expectation is not inconsistent with an awareness of the limits of well-established theory in fields like psychology and linguistics. Recall Chomsky's assessment of 1966, which cannot be lightly dismissed:

> The applications of physics to engineering may not be seriously affected by even the most deep-seated revolution in the foundation of physics, but the applications of psychology or linguistics to language teaching, such as they are, may be gravely affected by changing conceptions in these fields, since the body of theory that resists substantial modification is fairly small.

Still, much progress has been made in the last quarter of a century, particularly in the last decade, and the avenues recently opened appear to hold a great deal of promise.

There is nothing negative or pessimistic about the conclusions that a foreign language can be acquired only through persistent study and that a teaching program can only provide necessary but not sufficient help. A high level of success in this enterprise, after years of sustained effort, is in a way a far greater individual achievement than coming to master a language natively. As noted in chapters 6 and 7, a human language is a system of remarkable complexity, but coming to have native mastery of it is not something that the child does; rather, it is something that happens to the child, any normal child. In contrast, the challenge posed by a relative mastery of a foreign language, which involves will and deliberate choice, is met with a high degree of success only by some. Paraphrasing Chomsky we may say that to come to know a foreign language is an extraordinary intellectual achievement for a brain not especially designed for postpubescent language acquisition—even with the help of extended exposure, negative evidence (correction), and specific training.[41]

Relative mastery of a foreign language appears to go even a step further than relative mastery of, say, mathematics or physics through conscious and extended effort (there are students who are quite successful in mathematics or physics and total failures in the study of a foreign language, we may note in passing).[42] In the case of a foreign language, conscious knowledge is at most a first step, since "there is no reason to believe that a person could consciously master a grammar as a guide to behavior"; rather, "people learn language from pedagogic grammars by the use of their unconscious universal grammar (and for all we know this may be unavoidable in principle)." Thus every fluent speaker of Spanish unconsciously knows, without having to learn it from a teacher or a book, that (2a) of chapter 7 is not the question associated with (1) or that Spanish sentences such as (5)–(6) of chapter 7 have the properties determined by the binding theory. And if speakers were to be made conscious of the principles that lead to these results, "there is little doubt that these principles could not be consciously applied in real time, to 'guide' performance." Since this is also true of the parameterized principles for native speakers, which we are assuming cannot be determined after the critical period, postpubescent language students must find a way of applying, in real time, the alternative "approximative systems" they use, perhaps based in part on what they consciously know, which "will be a rather ill-defined and, perhaps, a scattered and chaotic subpart of the coherent and important systems and structures" that they unconsciously know.[43]

A possible bonus of the type of language study that takes advantage of some of the results of comparative language research now available is that it may shed considerable light on one's own language. As already mentioned, it is a common idea that those who know only their language do not "know" their language—or at least they are not consciously aware of many of the fascinating particular properties of the language they speak natively, of which the previous chapters offer only a sample. Comparative study of two languages at some level of sophistication provides an understanding of how language works, which might shed much light on one's native language, hence on whatever the student ends up doing in life (a careful reader of Cervantes will never miss the idea that "language is the gate to all sciences"). As Edwin Williams recently put it, "Leonardo da Vinci learned anatomy in order to paint better; when you understand the internal structure of something, you can do more with it."[44]

The already available results of research on the nature of language make it possible for the creative language teacher and more generally the educator to aim at a higher goal than was conceivable just a mere quarter of a century ago. Now it could, and perhaps should, be argued that the study of mathematical logic and the study of scientific grammar should be at the core of any well-designed curriculum. If a person unaware of the Copernican revolution is not considered "educated," why should a person who is unaware of the revolution in our understanding of language be considered "educated" in the 1990s?[45] Chomsky elaborates on this theme in a remarkable letter to a teacher written on March 4, 1984:

I don't see how any person can truly be called "educated" who doesn't know the elements of sentence structure, or who doesn't understand the nature of a relative clause, a passive construction, and so on. Furthermore, if one is going to discuss literature, including here what students write themselves, and to come to understand how it is written and why, these conceptual tools are indispensable.

For this purpose, I think traditional grammar so-called (say, the grammar of Jespersen) remains today a very impressive and useful basis for such teaching. I can't see any reason for teaching [behavioristic] structural grammars of English, or for teaching transformational grammar *in the manner of some instructional books that I have seen* (I really don't know the literature very well at all), which simply amount to *memorizing meaningless formulas*. (Emphasis supplied.)[46]

These observations may come as something of a surprise to those given to quoting out of context the following remark from his 1966 "famous and influential address" at a conference of foreign-language teachers: "I am, frankly, rather skeptical about the significance, for teaching languages, of such insights and understanding as have been attained [up to 1966] in linguistics and psychology."[47] But as has been occasionally pointed out, this is just one more instance in which Chomsky urges people to be cautious and skeptical of presumed expertise and to think, assess, evaluate, and decide for themselves.[48] "Teachers, in particular," he stresses in the same address, "have a responsibility to make sure that ideas and proposals are evaluated on their merits, and not passively accepted on grounds of authority, real or presumed." He continues,

> The field of language teaching is no exception. It is possible—even likely—that principles of psychology and linguistics, and research in these disciplines, may supply insights useful to the language teacher. But this must be demonstrated, and cannot be presumed. It is the language teacher himself who must validate or refute any specific proposal. There is very little in psychology or linguistics that can be accepted on faith.

In other words, teachers "must certainly draw what suggestions and hints they can from psychological research, but they will be well-advised to do so with the constant realization of how fragile and tentative are the principles of the underlying discipline." As he put it twenty years later,

People who are involved in some practical activity such as teaching languages, translation, or building bridges should probably keep an eye on what's happening in the sciences. . . .

I think it's a good idea to pay attention to what [linguistics] is doing and to see if it gives you some ideas that might enable a translator or teacher to do better, but that's really for the person involved in the practical activity to decide. . . .

The proper conclusion, I think, is this: Use your common sense and use your experience and don't listen too much to the scientists, unless you find that what they say is really of practical value and of assistance in understanding the problems you face, as sometimes it truly is."[49]

Beyond this goal, the contemporary study of language can provide students with a way to understand how science works that could also be used to advantage in the teaching of foreign languages. Every student has command of a huge mass of very puzzling facts about the language they speak, which they can compare or contrast with the facts of the target language. There are now explanatory theories of a rather nontrivial sort that explain some of these facts and do so "without resort to higher mathematics or other conceptual tools not available to the student (or teacher, generally)." Using this rarely exploited possibility, the student might be introduced into "the marvelous world of inquiry in which one learns to wonder about the nature of what seem, superficially, to be obvious phenomena, and to ask why they are the way they are, and to come up with answers, . . . an experience generally lacking in the study of the sciences unless the instruction is done really superlatively well." It is easy to see that these are all "reasons for studying contemporary grammar—as a branch of science, which deals with questions of central human concern and which happens to be fairly accessible, as compared, say, with quantum physics."[50]

A superb language teacher could aim at an even higher goal. Transformational grammar can be taken as a model for other cognitive sciences, thus offering a difficult-to-match point of entry into the study of the human mind.[51] This is an entirely new opportunity, undreamed of just a generation ago. It would be a great pity if today's students continue to leave the university as unaware of the groundbreaking discoveries of the second half of our century as their parents did. The challenge and the accomplishments of the study of language are both very real. If the study of language is to return gradually "to the full scope of its rich tradition," some way will have to be found "to introduce the students to the tantalizing problems that language has always posed for those who are puzzled and intrigued by the mysteries of human intelligence."[52]

NOTES TO CHAPTER 8

1. Cook 1988, p. 172.

2. The reference is to duPlessis et al. 1987, in their critique of Clahsen and Muysken 1986. Recall the discussion in the previous chapter.

3. Chomsky 1989, p.108, 1989, p. 274 (cf. 502); Gleitman & Wanner 1982, p. 7.

4. Chomsky 1964. It is interesting to compare this and other ideas of Noam Chomsky about language teaching (see Corson 1980:168–9/180–1), in particular Chomsky 1954 and Chomsky 1969, with the ideas presented in William Chomsky's books, in particular those published in 1956 and 1957, the year in which *Syntactic Structures* was published.

5. Recall (12) of chapter 7, just one of an intriguing family of examples involving (often puzzling) logical operators, in this case negation. Another is an expression such as *it was a near miss*, speaking of two planes, which is never interpreted literally, as Chomsky pointed out in a lecture last year to make the point that parsing is not easy and quick, as often assumed (if it had been a *near miss*, literally, that is, if the two planes did not quite miss each other, they would have hit; compare *the car missed hitting me* and Spanish *el coche por poco me atropella* or *faltó poco para que el coche me atropellara*). Recall that Spanish *perder* translates both *to miss* and *to lose* (a beginning Spanish student of English may say "I lost the train" for *I missed the train*).

6. Chomsky 1988, p. 179. The answer, which deserves to be read in full and with some care, was elicited from the floor after one of the Managua lectures, possibly by a language teacher.

7. See Diller 1981. Cf. Albert & Obler 1978; Whitaker 1978; Kinsbourne 1981; Whitaker, Bub, & Leventer 1981; Obler 1988.

8. Brooks 1964. For the following quotes, see Chomsky 1969c (the notion of overlearning was touched upon in chapter 5, section 5.1.1); 1988, p. 181–82; 1989, p. 108–109 (for the quotes from the 1968 interview); 1988, p. 180 (for remark about the harm caused by teachers). The 1966 address was repeatedly reprinted (see the Chomsky 1966a entry in the bibliography).

9. Chomsky 1986a, pp. 6–7; cf. 1980, p. 237.

10. As Cook reports (1988:171–72), "the negative use of Chomsky's creativity argument is widespread among language teachers up to the present day and is still cited in Stern 1983, Harmer 1983, Howatt 1984, and Richards and Rodgers 1986, to take a small sample of methodological texts, none of which cite any work by Chomsky later than 1968."

11. As repeatedly noted, the term "nonnative" (in some cases, foreign) is perhaps preferable to "second." The terms "second language acquisition"/"second language learning" can be quite misleading. From the perspective adopted in this book, the crucial distinction is between what Chomsky calls growth of language (first, second, third, or *n*th), that is, the process by which a child develops native or perfect mastery of a language, and acquisition of a foreign language (second, third, or *n*th) after the critical period. As noted in the preface, the term "acquisition" seems preferable to "learning" to refer to the process of developing an imperfect, but sometimes remarkably proficient, mastery of a foreign language, which the postulated availability of the language organ (arguably limited to the invariant principles after the speaker reaches a certain state of maturation) makes possible. This usage of the terms "acquisition" and "learning" is not to be identified with that of Krashen 1982 (see Gregg 1984:79–80 *et passim*). Cf. Salkie 1990, pp. 22–23.

12. Cf. Rutherford (1988:404–405): "L2 [second language] acquisition study would be difficult to trace back more than perhaps fifteen years. Moreover, this brief history is one that is characterized, until only two or three years ago, largely by exclusively data-driven descriptive work. . . . It is essentially a record of research *in need of*, if not implicitly *in search of*, theories of L2 acquisition within which to accommodate and account for the data being described. . . . There is a fundamental distinction to be drawn, however, between the kind of research just described and particular kinds of L2 acquisition study that have begun to emerge within the last two or three years." According to Lightbown 1985 (p. 173), "Most people in the field identify two significant papers which mark the beginning: Corder's (1967) paper *The Significance of Learners' Errors* and Selinker's 1972 paper, which, in its title, gave a name to the object of the investigation, 'Interlanguage'." Cf. Selinker 1992, in particular chapter 1; also Broselow 1988, Flynn 1988, the editors' introduction to Flynn & O'Neil 1988, Lightbown & White 1987, Newmeyer 1987, Newmeyer & Weinberger 1988, Eubank & Beck 1993, and references therein, among many other references. It is interesting to compare what was seen as new frontiers in LAP fifteen years ago (cf., e.g., Schumann & Stenson 1974) and now (cf., e.g., Gass & Schachter, eds., 1989).

13. See Liceras 1986; see also other studies by Liceras and by Flynn in particular (e.g., Flynn 1989), and Zagona 1988; also Hochberg 1988 (cf. Chela de Rodriguez 1979, Mairs 1989). Cf. Delattre 1965, Stockwell & Bowen 1965, Stockwell *et al.* 1965, Cohen 1974, Lococo 1975, Andersen (ed.) 1979 (in particular Plann 1979), Van Naerssen 1980, Luján *et al.* 1984, Muysken 1984, Hill & Bradford 1991, Whitley 1986, Hoover 1992.

14. For a very impressive early attempt at an up-to-date reference grammar for native speakers, see Renzi (ed.) 1988; the contributors to the first volume (of three planned) are P. Benincà, A. Calabrese, M. Castelli, G. Cinque, P. Cordin, L. Frisson, A. Giorgi, G. Longobardi, A. Marcantonio, M. Nespor, L. Rizzi, G. Salvi, and M. Scorretti, by any measure an impressive roster of distinguished linguists. An extensive descriptive grammar of Spanish (to be edited by Ignacio Bosque and Violeta Demonte) is in preparation.

15. What is involved is "indefinite object drop," that is, a silent indefinite pronoun. See Campos 1986, p. 356.

16. Torrego 1989, Strozer 1989, building on work by A. Kratzer and M. Diesing. The defining property of stage-level predicates is that they contain an event argument of the sort discussed by the philosopher Donald Davidson back in 1967. See Stowell 1991, p. 114f.

17. Raposo & Uriagereka 1990, p. 531. The classic paper on the theory of small clauses is Stowell 1983.

18. For extensive discussion, see Torrego 1989.

19. See Bolinger 1975, 151; 1991, 47f. (first published in 1944, 1947, and 1973). As his 1991 collection (in particular Part IV) shows, Bolinger had few rivals in finding diverse manifestations of the same underlying principle in English and Spanish.

20. Strozer 1976, p. 138–40. See now Demonte 1992b.

21. This is due to what has been called the subjunctive disjoint reference effect. See Strozer 1976:308f., Guéron 1978, Picallo 1985, Kempchinsky 1986, p. 37f., Laka 1990, p. 234f.

22. We attend to relevant interpretations only (not, for example, 'that he/she studies the boy'). It should be added that in an earlier stage of the language, the difference at issue would be easier to detect. Thus if we replace *estudiar* by, say, *divertirse* 'to amuse oneself'), *se* would appear before the verb in both (a) and (b), while in Medieval Spanish (or present day Galegan, we may add), *se* would appear after the verb in (a). See Rivero 1986, 1991, Otero 1991a, b.

23. Chomsky 1969c. The advances of the last quarter century have not made much difference in this respect.

24. This is explicitly recognized in the ACTFL [American Council on the Teaching of Foreign Languages] Provisional Guidelines for Foreign Language Teacher Education, which focus on three areas, one of them being the development as a "specialist in the language" (including "a basic understanding of the principles of linguistics"). See Guntermann (ed.) 1993, p. 213f.; see also several papers in the volume, in particular the chapters by Joiner (and Hudelson & Faltis) and Lafayette, which are interesting to compare with those in Waltz (ed.) 1992 and Magnan (ed.) 1991. Cf. Roca 1979, Celce-Murcia 1985, Chastain 1987, Rutherford 1987, Celce-Murcia & Hilles 1988, Celce-Murcia 1991b, Fotos & Ellis 1991, Gass 1991, Terrell 1991, Green & Hecht 1992, among others. Some scholars do not favor formal instruction of any kind (Felix 1981, Krashen 1982). In contrast, other scholars suggest that the eventual achievement of a high level of proficiency in a foreign language can be significantly aided by (or even depends on) focusing on specific aspects of the language in some orderly manner and error correction. A third position is "consciousness raising," that is, the deliberate attempt to draw the learner's attention specifically to the formal properties of the target language to help in speeding up the rate of development or in compensating for the low frequency or limited saliency of certain features of the target language. A fourth view is that some features of the target language may have to be taught because the relationship between the language of the students and the target language makes it virtually impossible for them to discover them. See Lightbown 1991 and references therein (also Rutherford & Sharwood Smith, eds., 1988, Part 1; Ellis 1989, 1990, 1991; Scott 1989, 1990; Shaffer 1989; Doughty 1991; Sharwood Smith 1991, among others). There are also those who think that "the notion that an individual can develop anything other than a rudimentary communication ability without an extensive mastery of the grammatical system is absurd" (Wilkins 1981:85, cited in Rivers 1990:51), perhaps a sign that the tide is turning (see Mitchell & Redmont 1993, where it is concluded that "since much of current research favors more explicit teaching of grammar . . . , it seems clear that grammar and communication must join together in order to produce more proficient language users").

25. Chomsky 1989, p. 502. "That is about 90% of the problem, if not more," he continues. "Methods of instruction may influence the residue."

26. See Kayne 1981, which in retrospect appears to have been a real trailblazer, and much work influenced by Kayne's research and teaching, in particular Belletti & Rizzi 1981 for Italian and subsequent work by them and others.

27. Among the book-length studies, Burzio 1986, for example, contains a wealth of data that a textbook writer may find helpful, and so does Zagona 1988.

28. Cf. Rutherford & Sharwood Smith (eds.) 1988, Parts 2 and 3.

29. For examples from Spanish, see Chomsky 1988, pp. 16, 24f., 45, 63f., 91, 99, 111f., 119 and *passim*.

30. Chomsky 1988, p. 134. See also Chomsky 1980, p. 54f.

31. For example, the difference in maximum lengths of intensive language courses (e.g., twenty weeks for German, Spanish, Italian, or French; twenty-four for Dutch, Swedish, or Portuguese; forty-four for Russian, Arabic, or Japanese) at the Foreign Service Institute of the U.S. State Department (Odlin 1989:39) seems to reflect in part the proportion of cognate vocabulary and the transparency of the relation. Cf. Carroll 1992.

32. See Penfield 1953, where they are related to changes in the brain. It has been repeatedly observed that although adults can often communicate in a foreign language, native or even native-like pronunciation is virtually unattainable after puberty, if not long before, as discussed in chapter 7 (cf. Seliger *et al.* 1975, Broselow 1987). A study of the topic (Scovel 1969) discusses the notable case of Joseph Conrad, who acquired English as a young adult well enough to become a major English fiction writer without ever overcoming his nonnative accent. "Speaking English he had so strong a French accent that few who did not know him well could understand him at first" (Ford Madox Ford, quoted in Lieberman 1984, p. 194).

33. For a review of some of the difficulties adult learners of this construction experience, see Fitzgibbon 1959. (When he was introduced to the author of this book in Madrid in 1986, Noam Chomsky is said to have commented that it should be recommended to a common friend of his and the introducer—a well-known linguist—remarking that his English was otherwise nearly flawless.)

34. Chomsky 1980, p. 56. Recall that some cases of "comprehension under noisy conditions in our own language" may correlate with nativeness, as mentioned in chapter 1.

35. As Chomsky writes (1980:238), "the irregularities, which alone concern us in normal life, **are** learned," as "we learn how to do the high jump and so forth."

36. "As with children, adults are not limited to what they hear alone"; rather, they "exhibit an infinite productivity of new sentences" (Flynn & Manuel 1991; see also Felix 1988, Flynn & O'Neil 1988, White 1988, 1989). Recall (7.3.1) that the appeal to "analogy" is quite misleading and that even identity (and nothing can be more "analogous" that complete identity) fails to give the right results in some of the paradigm examples above and innumerable other cases.

37. Even immersion students perform significantly worse on some tasks than native speakers (Swain 1985:244; cf. Cohen 1974, Sandra Plann 1979). Notice that if it turns out that some adults are exceptionally capable of fixing the whole collection of parameters of a new language at their proper values, the picture is essentially the same because any child can become, in principle, a native speaker of any language. (In answer to a question about exceptional language acquirers posed to him after one of his lectures at UCLA in January 1988, Chomsky suggested, possibly only semiseriously, that "perhaps some maturational process did not take place.") See Obler & Menn 1982, Obler & Fein 1988, Schneiderman & Desmarais 1988, Obler 1989, Skehan 1990. Cf. O'Malley & Chamot 1990, Harley *et al.*, eds. 1990.

38. See Kayne 1990. For the limits of just "communicating," see Gregg 1984, p. 83; 1989, p.35.

39. For some discussion of similarities and differences between native and nonnative performance, see Van Naerssen 1980.

40. The first quote is from Chomsky 1969, the second one from White 1987c, p. 108, and the last one from Gregg 1984, p. 94. For a study of the linguistic accuracy and clarity of presentation of a particular determiner system (the French one) in eleven representative college textbooks (none included an accurate account of the forms), see Herschensohn 1988. See also Herschensohn 1990 and in press for much relevant material.

41. Cf. Chomsky 1975, p. 4, where it is pointed out that language is "created anew in each individual by operations that lie far beyond the reach of will or consciousness," which is only partly true of foreign language acquisition, since it may involve a degree of hypothesis-forming of the type sometimes erroneously read into the technical discussions of early generative grammar. See also Chomsky 1988, p. 149–50, in particular the observation that "possibly a human could come to understand" a certain type of nonhuman language "by using other faculties of the mind, much in the manner in which humans come to understand many things about the nature of the physical world through an arduous process of controlled inquiry. . . ."

42. There is research (Gajar 1987) suggesting a method for identifying predictors of success in learning a foreign language at the university level, and some suggestions have been made (Ganschow *et al.* 1991) for diagnosing a foreign language disability (sometimes apparently related to underlying native language problems).

43. Chomsky 1975, 248 notes 24, 249, 165, respectively (the term "approximative system" is from Nemser 1971, which appeared just before the term "interlanguage" was proposed by Selinker). Cf. Gregg 1984, p. 81.

44. Quoted in *Princeton Weekly Bulletin* 80:6, Oct 22, 1990, p. 2.

45. Needless to say, the underlying presupposition is not commonly accepted. See, for example, the view expressed in McCrum *et al.* 1986, p. 353, immediately after the remark that "the subject of linguistics has produced one of the greatest literatures (measured in shelf-space) of any subject in our time," in particular their reference to "those who wish to venture further into the Chomskian interior."

46. For more on the discussion of literature and student writing, see the volumes of the Interface Series (in particular Durant and Fabb 1990, Toolan 1990), the aim of which is "to examine topics at the 'interface' of language studies and literary criticism and in so doing to build bridges between these traditionally divided disciplines." Many would be willing to endorse a statement by Roman Jakobson made over a quarter of a century ago ("but which is no less relevant today") that serves as an epigraph to the series:

A linguist deaf to the poetic function of language and a literary scholar indifferent to linguistic problems and unconversant with linguistic methods, are equally flagrant anachronisms.

And so are other scholars, teachers, and students who are unfamiliar with the advances in the study of language of the last quarter of a century, some might be willing to add. Cf. Kiparsky 1988; see also Kuroda 1973, Kiparsky 1983, Kiparsky & Youmans (eds.) 1989, and Piera 1980.

47. Chomsky 1966, p. 43. (The remark before the quote is from Stern 1983, p. 327.) Chomsky "neglected to explain," commented Dwight Bolinger a couple of years later (1968:34), "that the insights he was talking about are those having more to do with how one gets a linguistic system into a student's head, and less with offering some workable description of the system." Cf. Saporta 1966, Hanzeli 1968b.

48. Notably in his first "nonprofessional" paper, "The responsibility of intellectuals" (1966/1967), reprinted in Chomsky 1987. See Diller 1978, p. 139.

49. Chomsky 1966, p. 45–46, 1988, p. 179, 180, 182.

50. Chomsky 1984. See also Honda & O'Neil 1994 (a different version of essentially the same paper appears in Hale & Keyser 1993).

51. To mention just one of the most startling recent developments (see Neville *et al.* 1991): "Recent studies of electrical activity of the brain (event-related potentials, ERPs) show distinctive response to nondeviant and deviant expressions, and among the latter, to violations of (1) word meaning expectancies, (2) phrase structure rules, (3) the specificity-of-reference condition on extraction of operators; (4) locality conditions on movement" (Chomsky 1992a). See Corballis 1991, Otero (ed.) 1994, vol. 4, and references therein.

52. Chomsky 1966, p. 595. See Otero 1991, p. 19f., and vol. 4 of Otero (ed.) 1994, in particular the introduction.

9

Overview: New prospects for the study of language

In the preceding chapters we have been guided by three fundamental dichotomies, which have served as headlights as we moved along the sometimes poorly illuminated path we have followed. It seems a good idea to close the discussion by looking back, briefly, from the point we have now reached, at each of the three dichotomies that we used as beacons on our way, and to try to fix the contours of each of them for recapitulation and reconsideration. The three dichotomies are taken up in turn in the first three sections. This leads naturally to the "modest proposal" of the fourth section, which closes the chapter and the book.

9.1. Baby or beast: Human language and other semiotic systems

Our first dichotomy, baby or beast, follows from the assumption that the evolutionary leap between the ancestors we shared with the chimps (if current understanding is essentially right on this point) and our earliest fully human ancestors was a leap over a now unbridgeable chasm. Rousseau, who actually deviated from the Cartesian conception of human being in some important respects, appears to have surmised that the problem of the chicken and the egg cannot be resolved along empiricist lines when he came to realize that he was running up against a problem he would have to abandon: "Which was most necessary, previously formed society for the institution of languages, or previously invented languages for the establishment of society?"

As Chomsky rightly emphasizes in his still-unassimilated paper "Language and freedom" (January 1970), for the Cartesian there was "no need to explain the origin of language in the course of historical evolution." Rather, because of the evolutionary leap between our closest prehuman ape ancestors and the first humans, our nature "is qualitatively distinct." He continues:

> We might reinterpret this idea in more current terms by speculating that rather sudden and dramatic mutations might have led to qualities of

intelligence that are, so far as we know, unique to humans, possession of language in the human sense being the most distinctive index of these qualities.[1]

This is not to deny that evidence about the **evolutionary development** of language is slight. Nevertheless,

it seems reasonable to assume that evolution of the language faculty was a development specific to the human species long after it separated from other primates. It also seems reasonable to suppose that possession of the language faculty conferred extraordinary selectional advantages, and must be a primary factor in the remarkable biological success of the human species, that is, its proliferation. It would be something of a biological miracle if we were to discover that some other species had a similar capacity but had never thought to put it to use, despite the remarkable advantages it would confer, until instructed by humans to do so— rather as if we were to discover in some remote area a species of bird that had the capacity of flight but had never thought to fly. There seems little indication that this biological miracle has occurred. Upright posture has also no doubt been a factor in human biological success, and, as has often been remarked, though dogs and horses can be taught to walk, in a sense, we do not therefore conclude that this capacity is part of their biological endowment, as bipedal locomotion is part of the endowment of the human species.[2]

A reasonable and plausible conclusion then is that the neural structures involved in human language may not exist in the same form in other primates, and the evolutionary history appears to be quite separate.

Evolutionary development is only one of the basic dimensions any serious inquiry into the question under consideration would have to include. Another basic dimension is **structure**. As has long been recognized and was argued in chapter 1, the structure of human language has little in common with other semiotic systems, including the semiotic system of the higher apes. Along the dimension of structural principles, "the most elementary property of human language is that it involves a denumerable infinity of functionally distinct expressions, in contrast to systems that involve continuity (like the dance of bees) or strict finiteness (calls of apes)." There is little doubt that the language system must be a generative procedure that makes infinite use of finite means (in Humboldt's characterization, a century and a half ago), in particular use of a finite number of principles. In the case of human language, these principles crucially involve a hierarchy of phrases, abstractly represented, and structure-dependent principles operating on these phrases (as discussed in chapter 6). Recursive embedding of phrases within phrases, of several types, is the basic device for constructing new phrases, exploiting the possibility of making infinite use of finite means. Some of the principles involved are invariant across languages, others are parameterized (they can have one of several values, possibly only two).

No one has ever claimed that the systems that have been taught to apes have any of these properties. In fact, they differ from human language at the most primitive and elementary level, since they are

strictly finite systems (apart, perhaps, from trivial devices such as conjoining), with no significant notion of phrase and no recursive rules of embedding or structure-dependent operations. Thus they belong to a category of systems entirely unlike human language from the point of view of their essential formal structure. Similarly, elements basic to the semantics of human language, such as modality and propositional attitude, description and presupposition, aspect and anaphora and quantification, and so on, seem to be entirely lacking. As we turn to less elementary properties of human language, there seem to be no comparable features in the systems taught to other species. Similarities have been noted at a very general level: e.g., 'use of symbols' in reference or to evoke action, serial order, perhaps some kind of limited substitution in frames. While human language also manifests these properties, there is little reason to suppose that they are specific to human language, to humans, or even to primates.

Where interesting similarities may perhaps be found is between apes and those humans suffering language deficit (severely aphasic patients) who have the ability to learn certain conventional symbol systems, for example, a system of visual symbols, and to use it to act upon command, answer questions, and describe actions in their immediate situational environment, and possibly to express their own wants, even with some limited productivity.

A third basic dimension that would have to be considered is **ontogenetic development**, which involves the innate universal schematism that determines the essential nature of human language, that is, the basic framework within which growth of language in the individual proceeds. Actual language development (onset, character, relative order, etc.)

has been studied primarily at the very early stages, and this study has quite often been concerned with properties of language about which very little of substance is known even at the mature stage (e.g., naming, social conditions of language use). Given these limitations, results of any generality or explanatory force are meagre. While this work is of considerable potential importance, it is necessary to regard it with some caution. Crawling precedes walking, and there are incipient motions prior to bird flight, but one must be cautious in drawing conclusions about the character of some biological system from observation of its early manifestations.

Here again there are apparently vast and qualitative differences between human language, which is developed effortlessly and without training by the child (even without linguistic input in the case of deaf children), and the systems laboriously taught to apes.

A fourth basic dimension to be considered is **function** or manner of use. Although there is little in the way of explanatory theory regarding function, "human language is characteristically used for free expression of thought or feeling (say, to write a poem), for establishing social relations (to avoid an embarrasing silence, for example), for communication of information (or with the intent to deceive), for clarifying one's ideas, and in numerous other ways." As Chomsky notes, "crucially, there is no basis for the belief that human language is used 'essentially' for 'instrumental ends'—to obtain some benefit."

The difference along this dimension between human language and the systems taught to apes could not possibly be greater. In sharp contrast with human language (though perhaps not with the alternative systems taught to global aphasics), the functions of the ape systems appear to be strictly instrumental, and they are utterly unrelated to "such elementary and primitive uses of language as telling a story, requesting information merely to enhance understanding, expressing an opinion or a wish (as distinct from an instrumental request), monologue, casual conversation, and so on, all typical of very young children."

Finally, a fifth dimension that we might want to consider is the **interaction** of the mental language system with other cognitive systems of the mind, although this investigation appears to be premature at the present state of our understanding (there are no deep analyses of other related systems). The question of interaction arises in particular with regard to studies of word meaning, which appears to involve other systems of knowledge and belief in an intimate and perhaps inseparable way (contrary to what is sometimes assumed in literary studies, for example), a matter of much recent discussion. The proposal defended in chapter 2 is that

> the study of word meaning is not, properly speaking, part of the study of language at all, but rather concerns other cognitive systems which are connected in part to language through some sort of 'labelling.' To the extent that this assumption is valid, the study of semantics of human language will be concerned with compositional properties, that is, the ways in which the meaning of a phrase relates to the meaning of its parts.

Here we find a possible source of the confusion about the nature of the systems taught to apes that is still widespread (as readers of the popular press may attest), which seems to derive from the identification of the conceptual system (discussed in chapter 3) responsible for the meaning of words, and the language system, which is a computational system of quite a different character. What might plausibly be argued is that there is a similarity between the conceptual system of the ape and that of the human. This is, however, a far cry from finding a similarity between a mental system of the ape and the computational system of human language since there is no reason to accept the widely spread belief that the human conceptual system and the human language system are one and the same system.

So even if the chimp is our closest relative (and there is no denying that the genetic distance between humans and chimps is very small), at least one of the organismal differences between the two species is vast: There are no speakers or signers of human language among the chimps (with all due respect to Vickie, Lana, Washoe, Nim, Sarah, and many other less famous but perhaps no less enterprising apes). There is not then the slightest reason to doubt the traditional assumption that chimps lack the mental makeup underlying human language. This is not to say that they cannot think or solve some problems retarded humans are incapable of solving. It is also clear that they are in possession of a system of communication of their own. This semiotic system, however, has virtually nothing in common with human language. For one thing, it consists of a finite (in fact, fairly small) number of discrete and not very structured calls, whereas a human language, which is intricately structured, defines an infinite number of expressions. We conclude then that failure to distinguish between the "human language" and "language" in the loose sense of system of communication can easily lead one astray. A human language is far more than a vocabulary linked to a conceptual system. It is a generative procedure that, as far as we know, is way beyond the chimp's intellectual reach. This is part of the chasm between a baby and a beast.

These considerations lead directly to the two claims of chapter 1, the first of which expresses a long-held traditional belief:

Claim #1: **No** nonhuman animal is capable of mastering a human language.

Claim #2: **Any** normal human child has the capacity to become a native speaker of any human language (from Arabic, Berber, Cantonese, Danish, or English, to Spanish, Turkish, Urdu, Vietnamese, Xhosa, Yoruba, or Zulu). What is more, any child can attain any language without explicit instruction, with surprising ease, in a relatively short time, provided it is before puberty.

These claims, it appears, are hardly open to doubt.

9.2. Child or grown-up: Language universals and language particulars

Claim #2 leads directly to the second dichotomy, child or grown-up, which has to do with what we have called Lenneberg's Problem, in reference to the scientist who first formulated it in essentially the right way. In chapter 7 it was argued that the solution to this problem is to be sought in the nature of the physical mechanisms of the brain that underlie the development of language. This is another dimension, a sixth dimension, that any serious inquiry about human language will have to consider.

Although little is known about the physical mechanisms underlying language, "it seems clear that lateralization plays a crucial role and that there are special language centers, perhaps linked to the auditory and vocal systems." A particularly striking fact is that "very severe peripheral defects can be overcome in acquisition and use of language, a biological function of humans that matures even under serious conditions of deprivation."[3] If the language system is independent not only from the conceptual system but also from a system of pragmatic competence, we would expect to find that these interacting systems can be selectively impaired and developmentally dissociated, and that their properties are quite different. Interestingly enough, evidence has been accumulating that is beginning to fulfill such expectation.[4]

In the language module itself (the language organ), an innate universal schematism that determines the essential nature of human language, we have distinguished (in chapter 6) the invariant principles from the parameters of variation, which are fixed by experience. A particular language is just a full collection of parameter settings. Thus each particular language specifies a specific instance among those made possible by the universal schematism. From this perspective, attaining a native language is not unlike filling out a questionnaire in which the proper value of each parameter is to be checked. This seems to offer no problem to the normal child up to a certain stage of maturation that apparently does not extend beyond puberty (it may not extend even to puberty). It is not even something that the child does, but rather something that happens to the child.

In sharp contrast, the grown-up appears to be out of luck. This is seen most clearly in the case of immigrant children, who usually acquire the indigenous language easily, rapidly, and thoroughly, while their parents, who are not necessarily less intelligent or resourceful than their offspring, usually do not. More generally, although all normal children are totally successful at acquiring the language or languages of their communities, most adults who try do not succeed in developing a native mastery of a single foreign language no matter how hard they try or for how long, even with the help of instruction and other resources unavailable to children.

This sharp disparity along various lines, which at first may strike us as paradoxical (the greatest success is achieved by the least developed organisms, which are in fact less capable at most things than adult organisms), can be explained by the so-called Critical Period Hypothesis (CPH), if chapter 7 is on the right track. This seemingly unavoidable conclusion is still controversial, however, even though, under our assumptions, it is just the null hypothesis (the growth of language is not unlike the growth of other organs of the body) and no one has ever tried to show that an adult has succeeded in fixing the collection of parameters of a foreign language at their proper values. Claims that the value of a particular parameter has been fixed, even if not dubious, are obviously not sufficient to establish that parameter setting is available beyond the relevant period of biological maturation, and those claims that have been made so far, based at best on the limited theoretical understanding of the 1980s, are not very persuasive.

9.3. Design or randomness: A new kind of language program

Some of the best research in language acquisition after puberty (LAP), more precisely after the maturational stage associated with the development of a first language, has centered around the basic issue of whether children and adults are or are not capable of the same kind of achievement. It appears to be a fact that adults, as a rule, fail to achieve native-speaker competence in a new language, whereas children seem to be generally able to develop full command of either a first or a second language (actually, of a number of languages, under appropriate circumstances) as a concomitant by-product of maturation: The development of a "mother tongue" and, more generally, what may be called a "peer tongue," is just part of the whole maturational process of the child; on the other hand, acquisition of a foreign language often begins only after the maturational process is complete, or largely complete. It is clear then that the development of a "mother tongue" or "peer tongue" is inevitable, whereas there is no such inevitability about the acquisition of a foreign language: There is no guarantee that attempted acquisition will prove even relatively successful (by reaching a certain level of proficiency).

This inability of the postpubescent adult to attain the kind of achievement invariably attained by the child (unwittingly, in fact) comes as no surprise to those who take the Critical Period Hypothesis seriously, assuming essential differences in the capacity for language of child and adult because of genetically determined changes in the maturing organism. This book is mainly an attempt to show (in what is hopefully a disciplined, partly speculatory framework grounded on a well-supported theory of language) that there is no known reason to doubt the validity of this position, and the main motivation for the book is the belief that it is particularly in the direction it suggests that progress can be made from now on (there was no possibility for progress in this area a mere generation ago).

The biological fact of adulthood appears to be enough to establish an insurmountable obstacle to nativeness in a new language, which is assumed to have a physiological basis (it is presumably dependent on various yet unknown changes that take place in the brain as the process of maturation unfolds) and presumably concomitant cognitive correlates. This does not mean, of course, that no language acquisition is possible after a certain age or that other factors, such as methods of instruction or affective elements like attitude and motivation, cannot contribute to determine varying degrees of proficiency in one or more foreign languages. Nor does it mean that there is no point in taking what is known about the universal principles of grammar (invariant or parameterized) that constrain language development in the maturing child as a necessary framework for the investigation of foreign language acquisition.

Quite the contrary. Research on LAP has much to gain by not being light on general language theory. It might make sense for students of language to limit themselves to theoretical investigations, but trying to do "applied linguistics" (in particular, LAP research) without a theoretical foundation is like building castles in the sand (or in the air).[5] There is no serious medicine without a biological foundation. One of the papers that is often taken as one of the very first, if not the first, in the serious study of adult language acquisition already assumes that "it would be reasonable to see how far" the principles of first language acquisition "might also apply" to the acquisition of a foreign language. But it also notes that the assumption that the "same hypothesis applies in both circumstances" (native and foreign) was typical of behaviorist psychology a generation ago: If the burden of explanation is placed on the environment, there is every reason to expect adults to do no less well (or even better, given their greater cognitive development) than children.[6] In contrast, today it is widely understood that part of the explanation can only be provided by the language organ. A direct consequence of this conception is that a language exists only in the brain of an individual and should be studied in "an individual psychology setting."[7]

If parameter setting were available beyond the period of biological maturation, the best course of action for the teacher would be the laissez-faire approach. People would acquire language much better without teacher intervention. Since the hypothesis underlying the laissez-faire approach does not appear to be plausible (admittedly, there is still much to be learned, but it is highly unlikely that future research will make the hypothesis more plausible), two conclusions come immediately to mind. One is that exposure to a second, third, or *n*th language should come as early as possible in the life of the individual.[8] The other is that, since what happens to children when they unconsciously develop a language natively does not happen to most (perhaps all) adults, a well-designed and properly implemented language program has much to contribute to whatever degree of success is attainable by ordinary people in the acquisition of foreign languages. Even under the most favorable circumstances, attaining a nontrivial degree of competence in a foreign language is a hard job (a direct consequence of the CPH, if the discussion in chapter 7 is on the right track).

One of the possible advantages of such a program comes readily to mind. If it is true that there are compelling reasons to believe that the study of language is of great intrinsic intellectual interest, we would expect that this interest would be enhanced when the systematic study of the structure of the student's native language is part of a larger study that includes at least one foreign language. To begin with, the student will be made aware of covert features of one language that are overt in the other one, as exemplified in chapter 8 and earlier chapters. It is easy to see that only under exposure to a foreign language can students begin to see which properties are peculiar to their first language and which are universally shared, which are fundamental and which are superficial and without consequence, even trivial.

What is being advocated here is a principled teaching program, based on some understanding of the nature of language, which relies and counts mostly on the student's mind and goes some way toward creating a rich linguistic environment, rich enough to put the intuitive heuristics students are in possession of to work.

Such a program will not aim just at "communication." It is no secret that we can often make out what is said in a foreign language, even without much knowledge of the grammar, when we can identify some of the words and use contextual cues, as we can when we understand our native language under noisy conditions. But for foreign-language speakers, success in communicating is surely no indication that they have extensive or deep knowledge of the language that they hear and attempt to speak. Even Tarzan was a fairly successful communicator (if not exactly a great one).[9]

There is much that the student can do with the help of the teacher if the teaching program contributes to bring out the best in them. Most would agree that there is no substitute for graded reading materials and oral practice, some would even concede that communication should be a by-product, not the only or supreme aim.[10] Without a carefully selected and properly graded pool of reliable and revealing facts, including well-chosen structural paradigms with crucial contrasts skillfully presented so as to shed light on the hidden principles of the language, ultimate attainment will necessarily be less than perfect.[11] At the very least, the adult's data base must contain compelling evidence for the conscious mind about the parametric properties of the language that are unconsciously known by the native speaker.[12] For example, part of the challenge for the teacher of Spanish to English speakers is to open the way to some generative system of knowledge (which there is little reason to expect to be essentially the same as that of the native speaker) from which the facts of the language, including those exemplified in chapters 7 and 8, are derivable. It seems that linguistic research can already make a contribution here and will no doubt make a greater contribution in the (perhaps near) future. This expectation is not inconsistent with the full realization that well-established theory in fields like psychology and linguistics does not reach very far.

The conclusion that a foreign language can be acquired only through persistent study, and that a teaching program can only provide valuable but never sufficient help, is neither negative nor pessimistic. A high level of success on the part of the student, after a considerable amount of prolonged effort, is in a way a far greater individual achievement than becoming a native speaker in childhood (it is not a particular merit of children to allow this to happen to them). As noted in chapters 6 and 7, a human language is a system of remarkable complexity, far from easy to master. Legions of linguists working uninterruptedly for many years have yet to succeed in understanding (consciously) even one of the thousands of languages spoken throughout the world that many children know perfectly (unconsciously, of course).

In contrast with the giveaway that is the lot of the child, the challenge posed by a relative mastery of a foreign language, involving will and deliberate choice, is met with a high degree of success only by those with the determination to attain it. Moreover, to come to know a foreign language is an extraordinary intellectual achievement for a brain not especially designed to acquire a language after puberty—even with the help of extended exposure, negative evidence (correction), and specific training, all of which the child can do without. Relative mastery of a foreign language appears to go even a step further than relative mastery of, say, mathematics or physics through conscious and unmitigated effort. In the case of a foreign language, conscious knowledge is at most a first step, since there is little reason to believe that a person could consciously master a grammar as a guide to behavior (supposing that the linguists had already produced a full grammar ready to be mastered). As Chomsky noted almost a quarter of a century ago, "it must be recognized that one does not learn the grammatical structure of a second language through 'explanation and instruction,' beyond the most elementary rudiments, for the simple reason that no one has enough explicit knowledge about this structure to provide explanation and instruction."[13]

Presumably people come to develop some knowledge of a foreign tongue from instruction or pedagogic grammars by the unconscious joint use of their invariant principles of language and other faculties or organs of the mind (and for all we know this duality may be unavoidable in principle). Thus every fluent speaker of Spanish unconsciously knows some of the important facts exemplified in chapter 7, without having to learn them from a teacher or a book. Were speakers to be made conscious of the principles that lead to this unconscious knowledge, these principles could not be consciously applied in real time to guide performance. Since this is also true of the parameterized principles for native speakers, which we are assuming cannot be determined after the critical period, postpubescent language students must find a way of applying, in real time, the "approximative systems" they use, perhaps based in part on what they consciously know. It is a reasonable guess that the resulting "interlanguage," somewhere in the spectrum between no knowledge and perfect knowledge of the language, will not be well defined. Perhaps it is just a scattered and chaotic subpart of the systems and structures that native speakers know (unconsciously, as noted in chapters 6 and 7), which are presumably fairly coherent.

The type of language study that takes advantage of some of the results of comparative language research now available may shed considerable light on one's own language. The common idea that those who know only their language do not "know" their language is not without merit, since generally monolingual speakers are not consciously aware of many of the fascinating particular properties of their native language (recall the discussion in chapter 8). Comparative study of two languages at some level of sophistication provides an understanding of how language works, which might shed much light on one's native language, hence on whatever the student ends up doing in life.

Summing up: The thesis that at least some invariant principles of the language organ remain active after the critical period appears to be a highly plausible one. Recent work suggests that some form of this thesis (the null hypothesis) is true. It seems a fair guess that stronger evidence is obtainable and will perhaps be made available in the nondistant future.

On the other hand, the thesis that adults are capable of parameter fixing in the process of language acquisition after puberty (LAP) has not been demonstrated. Furthermore, it does not appear to be plausible. The failure of ultimate attainment characteristic of adults, and the fact that stages of "transitional competence" ("interlanguage") often fossilize in a state that bears little ressemblance to the ultimate target (something not unlike the mental language of a native speaker), suggests that a form of the Critical Period Hypothesis that places the burden of explanation on the unavailability of parameter fixing after a certain stage of maturation (perhaps after puberty) appears to be quite plausible in the light of the evidence now available.

If this assessment of current understanding is on the right track, we can derive some implications for language teaching design, even if such understanding is far from offering real insight into the best way of teaching a language. An area where research based on our understanding of the universal principles of language (in other words, based on our understanding of universal grammar) "does offer potential implications for language teaching is over the question of what kind of evidence can be used" to reconstruct the effects of the parametric values of the target language.[14] That is because on the basis of the foregoing discussion we would expect that (1) postpubescent students will not have difficulty with those aspects of a new language they encounter that derive from general unparameterized principles of human language, and (2) that they will experience considerable difficulty in the attempt to develop anything approaching native mastery of those aspects that derive from parameterized principles—the greatest difficulty perhaps being in those areas in which the parameterization leads to divergent outputs in the native and the target languages. This suggests that carefully selected and ordered input may play an especially important role in LAP and that recent advances in comparative grammar may have a contribution to make in the preparation of future textbooks and in the design of carefully planned language programs.

The sharp contrast between the child and the adult on this score also suggests that the data from LAP will provide a new kind of evidence for the study of language in general, a welcome source of data given the impossibility of direct experimentation on humans to answer the many questions that arise. More than ten years ago it was pointed out that adult language acquisition data provide important evidence to motivate phonological descriptions.[15] We are now beginning to see that the study of adult language acquisition may provide a new kind of evidence in the investigation of the theory of language. Work on LAP could very well shed light on the nature and structure of the language organ, which is only beginning to be understood; in particular, it may help in our attempts at uncovering possible parameterized principles of language. When adult language acquirers come to know more than the linguistic environment has to offer, this may be a hint that an invariant principle is at work. When, on the other hand, adults experience difficulty in acquiring a particular systematic property of a target language, it may be an indication that a parametric difference is at stake, all other things being equal.[16]

Needless to say, specific conclusions must be established on independent grounds, a tall order. Chomsky once remarked that "for the conscious mind, not especially designed for the purpose, it remains a distant goal to reconstruct and comprehend what the child has done intuitively and with minimal effort."[17] It is a vast understatement to say at this point (just after a few of the earliest strivings to overcome the new challenge) that it remains a distant goal to reconstruct and comprehend what the postpubsecent language-acquirer is capable of doing with enormous effort.

It has sometimes been pointed out that "applied linguistics" has tended to be more concerned with its "self-determination" as a discipline than with building bridges between the teaching of language and the scientific study of language (in particular the ideas that might enable a teacher or a translator to do better). If the foregoing remarks are on the right track, this is about to change, if it is not already changing.[18] It is no longer utterly unlikely that "the barriers that have impeded collaboration between theoretical linguists and those engaged in 'applied' research will break down in the near future."[19] Hopefully it will not be long before we witness progress in answering questions of great interest to both the researcher and the teacher—and of great benefit to both teacher and student.[20]

Needless to say, the preceding discussion and some of the ideas underlying it are even more tentative than other empirical proposals and discussions, the reason being that research in LAP is still in its infancy.[21] It will have to be validated (or rejected, as the case may be) in at least two ways: by teachers and students in the classroom, who may or may not find it helpful, and by knowledgeable LAP researchers, who will have to test the most reliable results obtained by putting into practice some of the most appealing alternatives, including some discussed above, in search of relevant predictable differences—if this book is on the right track and can be of use to the practitioner.

9.4. Conclusion: A modest proposal

We are finally back where we started. It is a well-known fact that major advances of understanding brought about by the modern natural sciences tend to become part of general education, often within the span of a generation. It is natural to wonder why the study of language continues to be an exception. It cannot be because our understanding of language continues to be what it was two generations ago. Nor can it be because the study of language is less central or less important than other intellectual pursuits, since language is a gateway to all the others. The explanation for the current state of affairs must lie elsewhere.

The main concern of this book has not been to search for an explanation for the oddity but to make a contribution, no matter how modest, to overcoming it by bridging the gap in one particular direction, the one the author is most familiar with. The book has examined what the recent advances in grammatical theory suggest with respect to an important and still poorly understood phenomenon, the acquisition of a language after childhood, which is here assumed to differ in important respects from the attainment of one or more languages natively by the child. In order to do this it was necessary to first present an overview of current issues as they relate to the fundamental questions involved and discuss them with a degree of sustained attention. The three main points proposed for serious consideration were the following:

(1) Language is a unique defining property of our humanity. It is not much of a hyperbole to say that language turns the not-so-remote descendant of a chimplike creature into a person.

(2) Full command of a language is only attainable in the course of brain maturation (roughly during childhood). Even partial bilingualism is a hard-to-come-by achievement of enormous value, to be pursued by the individual and the community both as part of their own development and as a gateway to understanding other peoples and cultures.[22]

(3) No program of studies is more basic or more central to the curriculum (at any level) than a language program. A well-designed and properly

executed language program should be expected to be the hallmark of a culturally advanced society.

As noted in chapter 8, one of the traditional motives for teaching grammar has been to extend the range of situations in which the knowledge that the speaker has developed can be put to effective use. Since it is reasonable to assume that the pursuit of the traditional goals of language instruction can only be facilitated by the use of a system of grammar that expresses the underlying regularities of the language as fully and explicitly as possible, it is only natural that any advances made in our understanding of the invariant and parameterizable principles of linguistic structure should be reflected in the curriculum at every level (in an appropriate way).

A further reason is that the investigation of linguistic structure, with its many and varied implications for a broad range of questions, has an intrinsic intellectual interest of its own and provides sufficient motivation for introducing the student to the systematic study of his native language and for doing so in an up-to-date manner (as in the case of other natural sciences, teaching should be responsive to the issues that give substance and significance to current work). The already available results of research on the nature of language make it possible for the creative language teacher, and more generally for the educator, to aim at very high goals.

It is difficult to argue against a proposal that the study of scientific grammar should be at the core of any well-designed curriculum. Unless we apply a double standard, if a person unaware of the Copernican revolution has not been considered "educated" since the Enlightenment, a person who is unaware of the revolution in our understanding of language (which touches more directly every human pursuit) cannot be considered "educated" in the 1990s. Furthermore, if there is to be any real understanding of how a range of writings (philosophical or literary, including essays by the students themselves) are written, and why, the conceptual tools provided by the scientific study of language are indispensable.

Moreover, the contemporary study of language can provide students with a way to understand how science works that could be used to advantage in language teaching. As is well known, every student has at his fingertips an inexhaustible treasure of very puzzling facts about the language they speak. Since now we have explanatory theories of a rather nontrivial sort that shed considerable light on some of these facts, the students might be introduced into the marvels of natural inquiry, which will lead them to wonder about the nature of phenomena that appear to be obvious, to ask why they are the way they are, even to come up with answers of their own, and do so without resort to conceptual tools not available to the student (or teacher, generally), in particular higher mathematics—a experience that is quite rare even in the study of the sciences unless the instruction is really out of the ordinary. In other words, the science of language, which deals with questions of central human concern, happens to be fairly accessible, as compared, say, with quantum physics; in fact, there is no more familiar or less steep way of introducing the student to the natural sciences, one of the needs most widely felt at the moment (and for many years). It is easy to see that these are all compelling reasons for studying contemporary grammar as a branch of natural science.

It is not unreasonable to expect that the intrinsic intellectual interest of the investigation of linguistic structure if anything increases when the systematic study of grammar is not limited to the structure of the student's native language but also encompasses the structure of at least one foreign language. Only by looking at other languages can students come to appreciate the linguistic facts they know and begin to see what is peculiar to their own. To the extent that this is correct, it is natural to expect that the foreign language part of the curriculum should reflect the present level of our understanding of linguistic structure. There is no more effective way of responding to those who argue, not always without cogency, that a college or university is not the place for Berlitz-type courses, preempted of any intellectual substance, which could very well be taught with less waste of resources at practically any other level, including exposure in grade school (not without advantages in this case, if the Critical Period Hypothesis is essentially correct). If university language classes do not compare with university-level classes in the natural and formal sciences, it is not because there is no more to offer today than there was when a gene was still called a "factor."

A superb language teacher could aim at an even higher goal. Transformational grammar can reasonably be taken as a model for other cognitive sciences. It is difficult to think of a more appealing point of entry into the serious study of the human mind. This is an entirely new opportunity, which would have been hard to imagine just a generation ago. Today's students do not have to leave the university as unaware of the groundbreaking discoveries of the second half of our century as their parents did. The accomplishments of the study of language are very real and worthy of attention, and so is the challenge. If the study of language is to be up to its rich tradition, some way will have to be found to bring to an end the current deprivation of the students, who have little chance of coming to know about the tantalizing problems that language has always posed for those who are intrigued by the challenging problems and inscrutable abysses of human intelligence. Recall that a knowledge of science, which provides all kinds of interesting questions, can only add to the excitement and mystery and awe of a natural phenomenon; it can never subtract.[23]

It is our good fortune to find ourselves on the threshold of a new age that invites us to participate in thoughtful reexamination of some of our ways and to take full advantage of the current opportunity for renovation. This is not a time to stunt professional growth or stifle individual initiative in teachers or students, but to promote self-development, to stress personal responsibility, to examine action in the light of both knowledge and experience. It is reasonable to imagine that the future will be unlike the present in crucial respects and will considerably expand our horizons. It is in this spirit that current programs of teacher and student development should be examined and promising alternatives considered. Needless to say, no model will be appropriate for all students, teachers, and institutions. Each may be different from the others, but each will have much to lose if the need to provide more meaningful language study fails to be addressed in present-day terms. To quote from the opening paragraph of a "flagship" volume in a series on teacher development just off the presses, which is meant "to serve as a catalyst for change":

> As long as teachers continue to teach as they were taught, the past is perpetuated into the future. Yet tomorrow's schools will not be the same as yesterday's, and the old knowledge and skills will not suffice. The current demands for change in American education can be seen as an opportunity as well as a challenge.[24]

The days in which there was no true alternative are long past.

NOTES TO CHAPTER 9

1. Chomsky 1973, p. 396; 1987, p. 147. In a footnote he remarks that he "need hardly add that this is not the prevailing view." For discussion, see Otero 1990a.

2. Chomsky 1978, p. 36. In what follows, Chomsky's discussion will be followed closely. The following unindentified quotes are from pages 33, 35–36, 37, 38, 39.

3. Perhaps the most serious known are the cases of three adult deaf-blind subjects (two since infancy, one after age seven) who developed extensive language abilities, "comparing favorably in many areas with hearing individuals," through touch (placing a hand on the face of the speaker and monitoring the speaker's articulatory motions, a method of speech reading known as Tadoma). See C. Chomsky 1986.

4. See Curtiss 1981, Yamada 1990, Smith and Tsimpli 1991.

5. Surprising as it may seem, not everyone assumes that successful application of linguistics is not likely for anyone without a degree of familiarity with the best that linguistics has to offer (some are even explicit about not being interested in linguistics, just in "applied linguistics"). It is true that engineers have occasionally managed to get ahead of physics, but they did not seem to have thought of it as "applied physics." Cf. Saporta 1966, Courchêne 1981, Els *et al.* 1984, Taylor 1988, Newmeyer 1990, Jacobs and Schumann 1992.

6. Corder 1967, p. 163.

7. See Chomsky 1987a. Here we find a fundamental difference between a current view of language and a view that prevailed over the centuries. See Otero 1988, where the point is made, and Mercier 1992 for extended discussion of "individualism and anti-individualism" in linguistics and philosophy.

From this perspective, it is to be expected that LAP research may benefit by not limiting itself to the study of groups. Statistical pooling of information may have its uses, but it is not without drawbacks. The case study method, with a focus on stages of development common to various cases, has been an alternative for over a century now, and it does not seem to have been sufficiently exploited in language studies, particular in LAP research.

8. See Penfield 1953 and Lenneberg 1960a.

9. To just hint at the gist of the problem: In one of the earliest studies of systematic errors it is claimed that a strategy of foreign-language communication seemed to dictate to the two elderly Russian speakers of English under study that a formal property such as the English plural "was not necessary for the kind of communication they used" (Coulter 1968:30, cited in Selinker 1972:220). For a serious study of communication and cognition, see Sperber & Wilson 1986.

10. But see Holt 1989, p. 159, *passim.*

11. To quote from one of the earliest serious studies of the topic, the realization that "response strength through rote memory and repetition" is not exactly what is involved "ought not to lead us to pessimism about the potential usefulness of language *teaching*" (understood as the facilitation of the student's task), since "there is strong evidence that the attainment of grammatical [principles] can be facilitated by proper presentation of speech materials" (Jakobovits 1970:15).

12. It is important to keep in mind that nondeaf native speakers receive the decisive information through their sense of hearing, not through their sense of sight (sight is apparently not an alternative channel for them, although touch appears to be—see note 3 above).

13. Chomsky 1969a, p. 68. The 'explanation and instruction' proposal Chomsky argues against had been suggested by one of his former teachers (the distinguished philosopher Nelson Goodman).

14. White 1989, p. 182. Perhaps something can be learned from the successes and failures of the MLA project, which was spearheaded by Dwight Bolinger (1907–92), one of the most gifted and productive students of foreign language acquisition to date (see Bolinger 1991 and references therein). Cf. Sacks 1992, Stockwell 1993.

15. Kenstowicz & Kisseberth 1979. Cf. Ioup & Weinberger (eds.) 1987, James & Leather (eds.) 1987, Ard 1989, Mairs 1989, Archibald 1991, Broselow & Finer 1991, and Leather & James 1991 and references therein.

16. See introduction to Flynn & O'Neil (eds.) and references therein.

17. Chomsky 1975, 4.

18. See Newmeyer 1983, Flynn 1990, 1991a, 1991b. For reviews of current approaches, see Richards & Rodgers 1986, Rutherford 1987, Yalden 1987, Carter & McCarthy 1988, Chaudron 1988, Rutherford & Sharwood Smith (eds.) 1988, Kramsch 1989, Shaffer 1989, Pennycook 1989, Alatis (ed.) 1990, Birckbichler (ed.) 1990, Richards 1990, Scott 1990, Celce-Murcia 1991a, Cook 1991, Ervin (ed.) 1991, Savignon 1991, Rivers 1992, VanPatten 1992, Hadley 1993, Hudelson & Faltis 1993. One of the things that would have to be recognized is that native-speaker knowledge of a language is far more complex than is usually assumed, a tendency that is a legacy or a resurgence of empiricism. A more sophisticated revival of empiricism is connectionism, which has attracted some attention among LAP scholars (cf., e.g., Terrell 1991). See Lachter & Bever 1988.

19. Newmeyer 1983, p. 148. Cf. Flynn & O'Neil (eds.) 1988, Flynn 1988, 1991, Fischer 1994; also Graunstein 1989. See note 5 above.

20. Corder 1967, one of the earliest and most celebrated papers in the field, already ventured to suggest that a consequence of the development of generative grammar for language teaching "is likely to be far reaching."

21. In at least some respects much of the actual classroom practice is still not very far from its renaissance and medieval antecedents. See, e.g., Breva-Claramonte 1987, Bischoff 1961. For an attempt at a general history, see Kelly 1969; for a history of English language teaching, Howatt 1984.

22. The important questions that arise in this connection in a multilingual society are beyond the scope of this book. Suffice it to say that the distinction between "dialect" and "language" is not a linguistic one (a well-known quip defines "language" as a dialect with an army and a navy). A moment's thought suffices to see that, since many languages, say Dutch and German, blend into each other, it makes as much sense to say that a particular language is better than a particular dialect as to say that Dutch is better than German, or German than Dutch or English or Spanish. It is often more accurate to refer to two varieties of a so-called language, English, for example, as different languages in their own right. In fact, the plural "Englishes" is sometimes used, and rightly so. (Cf. McCrum *et al.* 1986, Crystal 1988, Kachru 1990, O'Donnell & Todd 1991, Kachru [ed.], 1992.)

Recall that there are reasons to believe that, in a precise sense, a language exists only in the head of an individual (although presumably there is considerable overlap between the system of linguistic principles and sometimes even the vocabularies two carefully chosen lifelong neighbors carry in their heads). From this perspective, the questions raised by the choice of a language of instruction are not simple ones and, as Chomsky has noted, "There is no reason to believe that there is any uniform answer to them." The reason is that "too many factors vary." An obviously important one is that if children "were to be instructed in what amounts to a foreign language, their intellectual development might be inhibited; there is little doubt, for example, that it would be harder for them to learn to read if the language of instruction . . . is not the language that they acquired in their preschool environment."

Chomsky's "personal judgment" is that: "speakers of a language that is not that of the groups that dominate some society should probably be taught in their own languages at least at very early stages, until basic skills are acquired, and should be taught in the dominant language at later stages, so that they can enter the society without suffering disadvantages that are rooted in prevailing power, privilege and domination." "One might hope to modify these features of the dominant society," he continues,

> but that is another question. Children have to be helped to function in the world that exists, which does not mean, of course, that they—or others—should not try to change it to a better world.
>
> I am not presuming to express any firm judgments or to offer general proposals. There are a great many factors to consider, and the answers will surely not be the same for every person or every circumstance. We have to do here not with the problems of language, but of the society at large, and they have to be confronted in these terms. (Chomsky 1989:503).

23. See chapter 4, note 5.

24. Guntermann (ed.) 1993 (one in a series of projects of the ACTFL [American Council on the Teaching of Foreign Languages]), foreword and p. 1. The books attempts "to describe the current status of the national agenda and the place of language teaching within it; clarify standards for the content of language teacher development and suggest steps for meeting them; outline what we know and do not know about language teachers and teacher development and present the principal paradigms, constraints and avenues for research; and, pulling it all together, point to further direction for action, searching out emerging models that can provide guidance" (pp. 1–2). An appendix provides "provisional program guidelines" (to be used "with caution") under three headings: Personal Development, Professional Development, and Specialist Development. One of the three areas addressed under the Specialist Development heading is "knowledge of the target language itself as well as a basic understanding of the principles of linguistics" (p. 223). (For "an introduction to introductions to linguistics," see Aitchinson 1992.) The "language analysis" area includes "knowledge of theories of first and second language acquisition and learning" as well as "knowledge of the phonological, morphological, syntactical and lexical components of the target language" and "knowledge of how communication occurs in real life, to include: (a) the contribution of grammatical and lexical elements in expressing basic functions and notions of the target language within the context in which they occur; (b) analysis of discourse and communication strategies." It is further suggested that programs should be evaluated "in terms of how they are preparing future teachers to view and explain grammar as it contributes to real-life communication" (pp. 226–27). Cf. Birckbichler 1990, Ervin 1991.

Bibliography

Abbreviations

AL=*Applied Linguistics*
AP=*American Psychologist*
BBS=*The Behavioral and Brain Sciences*
CE=*College English*
FLS=*French Language Studies*
HER=*Harvard Educational Review*
JADD=*Journal of Autism and Developmental Disorders*
JPR=*Journal of Psycholinguistic Research*
JSHR=*Journal of Speech and Hearing Research*
JSHD=*Journal of Speech and Hearing Disorders*
IAL=*Issues in Applied Linguistics*
IJAL=*International Journal of Applied Linguistics*
IRAL=*International Review of Applied Linguistics*
L&S=*Language and Speech*
LA=*Linguistic Analysis*
LAJDL=*Language Acquisition: A Journal of Developmental Linguistics*
Lg.=*Language*
LI=*Linguistic Inquiry*
LL=*Language Learning*
MLJ=*The Modern Language Journal*
NLLT=*National Language and Linguistic Theory*
SA=*Scientific American*
SLR=*Second Language Research*
SSLA=*Studies in Second Language Acquisition*
TESOL=Teachers of English to Speakers of Other Languages
TLR=*The Linguistic Review*

Adjémian, C. 1982. La spécificité de l'interlangue et l'idéalisation des langues se-
condes. In Guéron & Sowley (eds.), 421–39. (Spanish translation in Liceras,
ed., 1992, 242–62.)

—— and Liceras, J. 1984. Accounting for adult acquisition of relative clauses:
Universal grammar, L1, and structuring the intake. In Eckman et al.

Aitchison, J. 1992. *Linguistics*. Lincolnwood, IL: NTC. (Part of the series "Teach
Yourself Books.") (Originally published in 1978.)

Alatis, J. E., ed. 1990. *Linguistics, language teaching, and language acquisition: The
interdependence of theory, practice, and research*. Washington, DC: Georgetown
University Press. (Georgetown University Round Table on Languages and Linguistics 1990.)

—— 1991. *Linguistics and language pedagogy: The state of the art*. Washington,
DC: Georgetown University Press. (Georgetown University Round Table on
Languages and Linguistics 1991.)

—— and de Marco, B. 1981. Issues of major concern in foreign-language learning
and foreign-language acquisition. In Winitz, ed., 1–8.

Albert, M., and L. Obler. 1978. *The bilingual brain: Neuropsychological and neurolinguistic aspects of bilingualism*. New York: Academic Press.

Alderson, J. and A. Beretta, eds. 1992. *Evaluating second language education*. Cambridge University Press.

Allen, H. B., ed. 1964. *Readings in applied English linguistics*. New York: Appleton-
Century-Crofts.

Altube, S. 1929. *Erderismos*. Bilbao: Euskaltzaindia.

Andersen, R. W. 1984. What's gender good for, anyway? In Andersen (ed.) 1984, 77–99.

—— 1989. La adquisición de la morfología verbal, *Lingüística* 1, 90–142.

——, ed. 1979. *The acquisition and use of Spanish and English as first and second
languages*. Washington, DC: TESOL.

——, ed. 1983. *Pidginization and creolization as language acquisition*. Rowley,
MA: Newbury House.

——, ed. 1984. *Second languages: A cross-linguistic perspective*. Rowley, MA:
Newbury House.

Anderson, S. R. 1992. *A-morphous morphology*. New York: Cambridge University
Press.

Anderson-Hsieh, J., R. Johnson, and K. Koehler. 1992. The relationship between
native speaker judgments of nonnative pronunciation and deviance in segmentals,
prosody, and syllable structure. *LL* 42, 529–55.

Archibald, J. 1991. *Language learnability and phonology: The acquisition of L2
metrical parameters*. Doctoral dissertation, University of Toronto. (Published
1993 as *Language learnability and L2 phonology: The acquisition of metrical
parameters*. Dordrecht, Holland: Kluwer Academic).

Ard, J. 1989. A constructivist perspective on nonnative phonology. In Gass and
Schachter, eds., 243–59.

Asher, J. J. and R. Garcia. 1969. The optimal age to learn a foreign language. *MLJ*
53, 334–42.

Atkinson, M. 1992. *Children's syntax*. Oxford: Blackwell.

Baker, C. L. 1978. *Introduction to generative-transformational grammar*. Englewood
Cliffs, NJ: Prentice Hall.

Baker, M. 1992. *In other words: A coursework on translation*. London: Routledge.

Bardovi-Harlig, K., and T. Bofman. 1989. Attainment of syntactic and morphological accuracy by advanced language learners. *SSLA* 11, 17–34.

Bartsch, R., and T. Vennemann, eds. 1975. *Linguistics and neighboring disciplines*, Amsterdam: North-Holland.

Bailey, M., M. Long, and S. Beck, eds. 1983. *Second language acquisition studies*. Rowley, MA: Newbury House.

Beebe, L. M. 1988. *Issues in second language acquisition: Multiple perspectives*. New York: Newbury House.

Bell, R. 1991. *Translation and translating: Theory and practice*. London: Longman.

Belletti, A. 1990. *Generalized verb movement: Aspects of verb syntax*. Torino: Rosenberg and Sellier.

———— and L. Rizzi. 1981. The syntax of *ne*: Some theoretical implications. *TLR* 1, 117–54.

Bellugi, U., and R. Brown, eds. 1964. *The acquisition of language*. Chicago: University of Chicago Press.

Beretta, A. 1991. Theory construction in SLA: Complementarity and opposition. *SSLA* 13, 493–511.

———— 1993. 'As God said, and I think, rightly . . . ': Perspectives on theory construction in SLA: An introduction. *AL* 14, 221–24. (Introduction to special issue on theory construction in SLA.)

———— and G. Crookes. 1993. Cognitive and social determinants of discovery in SLA. *AL* 14, 250–75.

Berwick, R. C. 1985. *The acquisition of syntactic knowledge*. Cambridge, MA: MIT Press.

———— 1991. Principle-based parsing. In Sells et al., 115–226.

———— and S. Fong. 1990. Principle-based parsing: Natural language processing for the 1990s. In Winston and Shellard, eds. Vol. 1.

———— and A. Weinberg. 1984. *The grammatical basis of linguistic performance*. MIT Press.

————, S. P. Abney, and C. Tenny, eds. 1991. *Principle-based parsing: Computation and psycholinguistics*. Dordrecht, Holland: Kluwer Academic.

Bialystok, E. 1978. A theoretical model of second language acquisition. *LL* 28, 69–83. (Spanish translation in Liceras, ed., 1992, 178–92.)

————, ed. 1991. *Language processing in bilingual children*. New York: Cambridge University Press.

———— and M. Sharwood-Smith. 1985. Interlanguage is not a state of mind: An evaluation of the construct for second-language acquisition. *AL* 6, 101–107.

Bickerton, D. 1990. *Language and species*. Chicago: University of Chicago Press.

Biguenet, J., and R. Schulte, eds. 1989. *The craft of translation*. Chicago: University of Chicago Press.

Bini, M., J. M. Liceras, and E. de Miguel. 1992. Operaciones sintácticas y estrategias de focalización. Paper presented at the VII Congreso de Lenguajes Naturales y Lenguajes Formales, Gerona, Spain.

Birckbichler, D. W., ed. 1990. *New perspectives and new directions in language teaching*. Lincolnwood, IL: National Textbook Co.

Birdsong, D. 1989. *Metalinguistic performance and interlinguistic competence*. Berlin: Springer-Verlag.

———— 1992. Ultimate attainment in second language acquisition. *Lg.* 68, 706–55.

———— and J.-P. Montreuil, eds. 1988. *Advances in Romance Linguistics*. Dordrecht, Holland: Foris.

Bischoff, B. 1961. The study of foreign languages in the Middle Ages, *Speculum* 36:2, 209–24.

Bley-Vroman, R. 1985. The logical problem of language acquisition (manuscript). Austin: University of Texas. Revised version in *LA* 20 (1990), 56–104.

———— 1989. What is the logical problem of foreign language learning? In Gass and Schachter, eds., 41–68.

———— and C. Chaudron. 1990. Second language processing of subordinate clauses and anaphora—first language and universal influences: A review of Flynn's research. *LL* 40, 245–85.

————, S. W. Felix, and G. Ioup. 1988. The accessibility of universal grammar in adult language learning. *SLR* 4, 1–32.

Bloom, P. 1993. Grammatical continuity in language development: The case of subjectless sentences. *LI* 24, 721–34.

Bloomfield, L. 1942. *Outline guide for the practical study of foreign languages*. Baltimore: Linguistic Society of America.

Bly, R. 1984. The eight stages of translation. In Frawley, ed., 67–91.

Bogen, J. E. 1975. The other side of the brain. VII: Some educational aspects of hemispheric specialization. *UCLA Educator* 17, 24–32.

Bolinger, D. 1968. The theorist and the language teacher. *Foreign Language Annals* 2:1, 30–41.

———— 1975. *Aspects of language*. 2d ed. New York: Harcourt Brace Jovanovich.

———— 1980. *Language, the loaded weapon: The use and abuse of language today*. London and New York: Longman.

———— 1989. First person, not singular. In Koerner, ed., 20–45.

———— 1991. *Essays on Spanish: Words and grammar*. Newark, DE: Juan de la Cuesta.

Bond, Z. S., and J. Fokes. 1991. Perception of English voicing by native and nonnative adults. *SSLA* 13, 471–92.

Bonet, E. 1991. *Morphology after syntax: Pronominal clitics in Romance*. MIT doctoral dissertation.

Bordelois, I., H. Contreras, and K. Zagona, eds. 1986. *Generative Studies in Spanish Syntax. Studies in Generative Grammar*. Vol. 27. Dordrecht, Holland: Foris.

Borer, H. 1984. *Parametric syntax: Case studies in Semitic and Romance languages*. Dordrecht, Holland: Foris.

————, ed. 1986. *The syntax of pronominal clitics. Syntax and Semantics*. Vol. 19. Orlando: Academic Press.

Bosque, I. 1980a. *Sobre la negación*. Madrid: Cátedra.

———— 1980b. *Problemas de morfosintaxis*. Madrid: Editorial de la Universidad Complutense.

———— 1984a. Sobre la sintaxis de las oraciones exclamativas. *Hispanic Linguistics* 1, 283–303.

—— 1984b. La selección de las palabras interrogativas. *Verba* 11, 245–73.

—— 1989. Anáforas distributivas: La gramática de *sendos* (manuscript). Universidad Complutense de Madrid.

—— 1990. *Las categorías gramaticales: Relaciones y diferencias.* Madrid: Editorial Síntesis.

—— 1990a. Sobre el aspecto en los adjetivos y en los participios. In Bosque et al., 177–214.

—— 1992. La negación y el principio de las categorías vacías (manuscript). Universidad Complutense de Madrid.

—— 1993. Éste es un ejemplo de predicación catafórica, *Cuadernos de Lingüística* 1, 27–57.

——, ed. 1990. *Indicativo y subjuntivo.* Madrid: Taurus.

—— and J. M. Brucart. 1991. QP raising in Spanish superlatives (manuscript). Universidad Complutense de Madrid, Universitat Autonoma de Barcelona.

—— and J.-C. Moreno. 1984. A condition on quantifiers in logical form. *LI* 15, 164–67.

—— and J.-C. Moreno. 1990. Las construcciones con *lo* y la denotación del neutro. *Lingüística* 2, 5–50.

—— et al. 1990. *Tiempo y aspecto en español.* Madrid: Cátedra.

Bot, K. de, R. B. Ginsberg, and C. Kramsch, eds. 1991. *Foreign language research in cross-cultural perspective.* Amsterdam/Philadelphia: John Benjamins.

Bowers, J. 1993. The syntax of predication. *LI* 24, 591–656.

Boyd, W., and E. J. King, 1964. *The History of Western education.* 7th enlarged ed. Totowa, NJ: Barnes and Noble. (First published in 1921.)

Brainerd, C. J. 1978. Learning research and Piagetian theory. In Siegel and Brainerd, eds., 69–109.

Brame, M., H. Contreras, and F. J. Newmeyer, eds. 1986. *A Festschrift for Sol Saporta.* Seattle: Noit Amrofer.

Branchadell, A. et al., eds. 1992. *Catalan Working Papers in Linguistics 1992.* Universitat Autònoma de Barcelona.

Braun, F. 1975. Linguistics and the teaching of foreign language. In Bartsch and Vennemann, eds., 227–47.

Breva-Claramonte, M. 1987. A reanalysis of Juan-Luis Vives' (1492–1540) '*Exercitatio Linguae Latinae*'. In Aarsleff et al., 167–77.

Brière, E. J. 1968. *A psycholinguistic study of phonological interference.* The Hague: Mouton.

Brinton, D. M., M. A. Snow, and M. B. Wesche. 1989. *Content-based second language instruction.* New York: Newbury House.

Brooks, N. H. 1964. *Language and language learning theory and practice.* New York: Harcourt.

Broselow, E. 1983. Nonobvious transfer: On predicting epenthesis errors. In Gass and Selinker, eds., 267–80.

—— 1984. An investigation of transfer in second language acquisition. *IRAL* 22, 253–69.

—— 1987. An investigation of transfer in second language phonology. In Ioup and Weinberger, eds., 261–78.

—— 1988. Second language acquisition. In Newmeyer, ed. Vol. 3, 194–209.

———— and D. Finer. 1991. Parameter setting in second language phonology and syntax. *SLR* 7, 35–59.

Brown, D. 1991. TESOL at twenty-five: What are the issues? *TESOL Quarterly* 25, 245–78.

Brucart, J. M. 1992. Some asymmetries in the functioning of relative pronouns in Spanish. In Branchadell et al., eds., 113–43.

Bryant, P. E., and T. Trabasso. 1971. Transitive inferences and memory in young children. *Nature* 232, 456–58.

Burzio, L. 1986. *Italian syntax: A government-binding approach*. Dordrecht, Holland: Reidel.

Burt, M. K., and H. C. Dulay, eds. 1975. *New directions in second language learning, teaching, and bilingual education*. Washington, DC: TESOL.

————, H. Dulay, and M. Finocchiaro, eds. 1977. *Viewpoints of English as a second language*. In honor of James E. Alatis. New York: Regents.

———— and C. Kiparsky. 1972. *The Gooficon: A repair manual for English*. Rowley, MA: Newbury House. (3rd printing, 1975.)

Campos, H. 1985. Un modelo lingüístico para la enseñanza de la secuencia de tiempos en español (manuscript). Scripps College.

———— 1986. Indefinite object drop. *LI* 17, 354–59.

———— 1989. Impersonal passive *se* in Spanish. *Lingvisticae Investigationes* 13, 1–21.

———— 1990. Pseudo-raising in Spanish (manuscript). Georgetown University.

———— 1991. Silent prepositional phrases and pro-PP in Spanish. *Probus* 3, 1–21.

———— 1992. Seudo-elevación y seudo-relativas en español. *Nueva Revista de Filología Hispánica* (to appear).

———— 1993. *De la oración simple a la oración compuesta: Curso superior de gramática española*. Washington, DC: Georgetown University Press.

———— and P. Kempchinsky. 1991. Case theory, theta role absorption, and pronominal verbs in Spanish. In Kibbee and Wanner, eds., 171–85.

———— and F. Martínez-Gil, eds. 1992. *Current studies in Spanish linguistics*. Washington, DC: Georgetown University Press.

Caplan, D. 1987. *Neurolinguistics and linguistic aphasiology: An introduction*. New York: Cambridge University Press.

———— ed. 1980. *Biological studies of mental processes*. Cambridge, MA: MIT Press.

Carey, S. 1979. A case study: Face recognition. In Walker, ed., 175–202.

———— 1985. *Conceptual change in childhood*. Cambridge, MA: MIT Press.

———— 1988. Conceptual differences between children and adults. *Mind and Language* 3, 167–81.

———— and R. Diamond. 1980. Maturational determination of the developmental course of face encoding. In Caplan, ed., 60–93.

Carroll, S. E. 1989. Second-language acquisition and the computational paradigm. *LL* 39:4, 535–94.

———— 1992. On cognates. *SLR* 8, 93–119.

———— and J. M. Meisel. 1990. Universals and second language acquisition: Some comments on the state of current theory. *SSLA* 12, 201–208.

Carstens, V. M. 1991. *The morphology and syntax of determiner phrases in Kiswahili*. UCLA doctoral dissertation.

———— 1993. On grammatical subjects and NP-internal subjects. *GLOW Newsletter* 30, 64–65.

Carter, R., and M. McCarthy. 1988. *Vocabulary and language teaching*. London and New York: Longman.

Cavalli-Sforza, L. 1991. Genes, people, and languages. *SA* (November), 104–110.

Celce-Murcia, M. 1985. Making informed decisions about the role of grammar in language teaching, *TESOL Newsletter* (February), 1, 4–5.

———— 1991a. Language teaching approaches: An overview. In Celce-Murcia, ed., 3–11.

———— 1991b. Grammar pedagogy in second and foreign language teaching. *TESOL Quarterly* 25, 459–79.

———— and S. Hilles. 1988. *Techniques and resources in teaching grammar*. New York: Oxford University Press.

————, ed. 1985. *Beyond basics: Issues and research in TESOL*. Rowley, MA: Newbury House.

————, ed. 1991. *Teaching English as a second or foreign language*. 2d ed. New York: Newbury House.

Chastain, K. 1971. *The development of modern language skills: Theory to practice*. Philadelphia: Center for Curriculum Development.

———— 1987. Examining the role of grammar explanation, drills, and exercises in the development of communication skills. *Hispania* 70, 160–66.

Chaudron, C. 1988. *Second language classrooms. Research on teaching and learning*. New York: Cambridge University Press.

Chela de Rodriguez, B. 1979. Teaching English suprasegmentals to Spanish speakers. In Eckman and Hastings, ed., 234–45.

Chien, Y.-C., and K. Wexler. 1990. Children's knowledge of locality conditions in binding as evidence for the modularity of syntax and pragmatics. *LAJDL* 1, 225–95.

Child, J. 1992. *Introduction to Spanish translation*. Lanham, MD: University Press of America.

Chomsky, C. 1969. *The acquisition of syntax in children from 5 to 10*. Cambridge, MA: MIT Press.

———— 1970. Reading, writing, and phonology. *HER* 40, 287–309. Reprinted in Otero, ed. 1994, Vol. 1, 200–220.

———— 1972. Stages in language development and reading exposure. *HER* 42, 1–35. Reprinted in Otero, ed., 1994, Vol. 4, 518–47.

———— 1979. Approaching reading through invented spelling. In Resnick and Weaver, eds. Vol. 4, 43–56. Reprinted in Otero, ed., 1994, Vol. 4, 620–42.

———— 1979a. Consciousness *is* relevant to linguistic awareness. Paper presented at the International Seminar on Linguistic Awareness and Learning to Read, University of Victoria, Canada.

———— 1986. Analytic study of the Tadoma method: Language abilities of three deaf-blind subjects. *JSHR* 29, 337–47. Reprinted in Otero, ed. 1994, Vol. 4, 548–81.

Chomsky, N. 1951. *Morphophonemics of modern Hebrew*. Master's thesis. University of Pennsylvania. (Published in 1979 by Garland Publications in its series "Outstanding Dissertations.")

———— 1954. Review of Rieger 1953. *Language 30,* 180–81.

———— 1955. *The Logical structure of linguistic theory.* Manuscript, MIT. (Published in 1975 by Chicago University Press.)

———— 1957. *Syntactic structures.* The Hague: Mouton.

———— 1961. Formal discussion [of Miller and Ervin]. In Bellugi and Brown, eds., 35–39.

———— 1964. Introduction to Roberts 1964.

———— 1965. *Aspects of the theory of syntax.* Cambridge, MA: MIT Press.

———— 1965a. The current scene in linguistics: Present directions. Paper read at the NCTE [Northeast Conference on the Teaching of Foreign Languages] convention in November 1965. It first appeared in *CE* 27:8, 587–95. Reprinted in Reibel and Schane, eds., 1969, 3–12.

———— 1966. *Cartesian linguistics: A chapter in the history of rationalist thought.* New York: Harper and Row. (Reprinted by University Press of America, Lanham/ New York/London in August 1983.)

———— 1966a. Linguistic theory [and language teaching]. In Robert G. Mead, Jr., ed. *Language teaching: Broader contexts. (Reports of the Working Committees, Northeast Conference on the Teaching of Foreign Languages, 1 August 1966.)* Menasha, Wisconsin: George Banta, 43–49. Reprinted in Chomsky 1971a, 152–59; also in Lester, ed., 1970, 51–60 and 1973, 36–45, and in Oller et al., eds., 1973 (and 1975), 29–35.

———— 1968. *Language and mind.* New York: Harcourt, Brace and World.

———— 1969a. Linguistic and philosophy. In Hook, ed., 51–94. Reprinted in Chomsky 1972a.

———— 1969b. Should traditional grammar be ended or mended? *Educational Review* 22, 5–17. (School of Education, Birmingham, Great Britain. Reprinted in Wade, ed., 1982, 10–22.)

———— 1969c. Some observations on the teaching of language, *The Pedagogic Reporter* 21:1, 5–6, 13.

———— 1970. Phonology and reading. In Levin and Williams, eds., 3–18.

———— 1971. *Problems of knowledge and freedom: The Russell lectures.* New York: Pantheon.

———— 1971a. *Chomsky: Selected readings.* Ed. by J. P. B. Allen and Paul van Buren. London and New York: Oxford University Press. (=*Language and Language Learning,* 31.)

———— 1972a. *Language and mind.* Enlarged ed. San Diego, New York, etc.: Harcourt Brace Jovanovich.

———— 1972b. *Studies on semantics in generative grammar.* The Hague: Mouton.

———— 1975. *Reflections on language.* New York: Pantheon.

———— 1976. Equality: Language development, human intelligence, and social organization. *Philosophy and Social Policy* 2, 1–20. Reprinted in Chomsky 1987.

———— 1977. *Essays on Form and interpretation.* New York: North-Holland.

———— 1978. A naturalistic approach to language and cognition. Talk delivered at the plenary address at the December 1978 meetings of the American Psychoanalytic Association. (Printed in *Cognition and Brain Theory* 4 (1981), 3–22.)

———— 1979. Human language and other semiotic systems, *Semiotica* 25, 31–44.

———— 1980. *Rules and representations.* New York: Columbia University Press.

—— 1981. *Lectures on government and binding*. Dordrecht, Holland: Foris.

—— 1982. *Some concepts and consequences of the theory of government and binding*. Cambridge, MA: MIT Press.

—— 1984. Noam Chomsky writes to Mrs. Davis about grammar and education. *English Education* 16:3 (October), 165–66.

—— 1986a. *Knowledge of language: Its nature, origin, and use*. New York: Praeger.

—— 1986b. *Barriers*. Cambridge, MA: MIT Press.

—— 1986c. Language and problems of knowledge. Paper delivered at the Madrid Chomsky Symposium, 28 April 1986.

—— 1987. *The Chomsky reader*. New York: Pantheon.

—— 1987a. *Language in a psychological setting*. Tokyo: The Graduate School of Languages and Linguistics, Sophia University (=*Sophia Linguistica* 22.)

—— 1988. *Language and problems of knowledge: The Managua lectures*. Cambridge, MA: MIT Press.

—— 1988a. Language and interpretation: Philosophical reflections and empirical inquiry. Paper delivered at UCLA on 28 January 1988. To appear in the University of Pittsburgh *Series on Philosophy of Science*. (Included in Earman 1992.)

—— 1988b. Some notes on economy of derivation and representation. Paper delivered at UCLA on 29 January 1988. Revised version in *MIT Working Papers in Linguistics* 10 (1989), 43–74; edited version in Freidin, ed., 1991, 417–54.

—— 1988c. Prospects for the study of language and mind. Paper delivered at "The Chomskyan Turn" symposium in Tel Aviv on 11 April 1988. In A. Kasher, ed., 26–53.

—— 1989. *Language and politics*. Ed. by C. P. Otero. Montréal: Black Rose.

—— 1989a. Language and mind. The "Darwin Lecture," delivered in Darwin College, Cambridge, in January 1989.

—— 1992a. Explaining language use. *Philosophical Topics* 20, 205–31.

—— 1992b. A minimalist program for linguistic theory (manuscript), MIT. (Reproduced by the *MIT Working Papers in Linguistics* as Occasional Paper 1.) Slightly corrected version in Hale and Keyser, eds., 1993, 1–52.

—— 1992c. Naturalism and dualism in the study of language and mind (manuscript), MIT. (Evans Lecture.)

—— and H. Lasnik. 1977. Filters and control. *LI* 8, 425–504. Reprinted in Lasnik 1990, 42–124.

—— and H. Lasnik. 1991. Principles and parameters theory (manuscript), MIT. Published in Jacobs et al., Vol. 1, 1993, 506–69.

Chomsky, W. 1956. *Teaching Hebrew*. New York: Jewish Ed Committee Press.

—— 1957. *Hebrew: The eternal language*. Philadelphia: The Jewish Publication Society of America.

Cinque, G. 1988. On *si* constructions and the theory of *arb*. *LI* 19, 521–81.

—— 1990. *Types of A-Dependencies*. Cambridge, MA: MIT Press.

Clahsen, H. 1990. The comparative study of first and second language development. *SSLA* 12, 135–53.

—— 1991. Constraints on parameter setting: A grammatical analysis of some acquisition stages in German child language. *LAJDL* 1:4, 361–91.

———— and P. Muysken. 1986. The accessibility of universal grammar to adult and child learners. A study of the acquisition of German word order. *SLR* 2, 93–119.

———— and ———— 1989. The UG paradox in L2 acquisition. *SLR* 5, 1–29.

Cohen, A. D. 1974. The Culver City Spanish immersion program: How does summer recess affect Spanish speaking ability? *LL* 24, 55–68.

———— 1975. Forgetting a second language. *LL* 25, 127–38.

Coleman, J., and R. Towell, eds. 1987. *The advanced language learner*. London: CILT.

Colombo, J. 1982. The critical period concept: Research, methodology, and theoretical issues. *Psychological Bulletin* 91, 260–64.

Contreras, H. 1963. La lingüística aplicada a la enseñanza de idiomas. *Revista de Lingüística Aplicada* 1:1, 1–13.

———— 1976. *A theory of word order with special reference to Spanish*. Amsterdam/New York/Oxford: North-Holland.

———— 1986. Spanish bare NPs and the ECP. In Bordelois et al., eds., 25–49.

———— 1989. Closed domains. *Probus* 1, 163–80.

———— 1990. Two kinds of minimality. *LI* 21, 467–70.

———— 1992. On the position of subjects. In Rothstein, ed., 63–79.

———— 1993a. On null operator structures. *NLLT* 11, 1–30.

———— 1993b. A Larsonian analysis of small clauses (manuscript), University of Washington.

Cook, V. J. 1985. Chomsky's Universal Grammar and second language learning. *AL* 6, 2–18.

———— 1988. *Chomsky's universal grammar: an introduction*. Oxford: Basil Blackwell.

———— 1990. Timed comprehension of Binding in advanced L2 learners of English. *LL* 40, 557–99.

———— 1991. The poverty-of-the-stimulus argument and multicompetence. *SLR* 7, 103–17.

———— 1991. *Second language learning and language teaching*. London: Edward Arnold.

———— 1992. Evidence for multicompetence. *LL* 42, 557–91.

————, ed. 1986. *Experimental approaches to second language acquisition*. Oxford: Pergamon.

Coppieters, R. 1987. Competence differences between native and near-native speakers. *Lg.* 3:3, 544–73.

Corballis, M. C. 1991. *The lopsided ape: Evolution of the generative mind*. Oxford University Press.

Corder, S. P. 1967. The significance of learners' errors. *IRAL* 5, 161–69. Reprinted in Richards, ed., 1974, 19–30. (Spanish translation in Liceras, ed., 1992, 31–40.)

———— 1971. Idiosyncratic dialects and error analysis. *IRAL* 9, 147–60. (Spanish translation in Liceras, ed., 1992, 63–77.)

———— 1973. *Introducing applied linguistics*. Harmondsworth: Penguin.

———— 1981. *Error analysis and interlanguage*. New York: Oxford University Press.

Corson, D. J. 1980. Chomsky on education. *The Australian Journal of Education* 24, 164–85. Reprinted in Otero, eds., 1994, Vol. 3, 176–98.

Cortés, C. 1992. *Issues in Catalan syntax.* UCLA doctoral dissertation.

Coulter, K. 1968. *Linguistic error-analysis of the spoken English of two native Russians.* University of Washington masters thesis.

Courchêne, R. 1981. The history of the term "applied" in applied linguistics. In Savard and Laforge, eds., 66–88.

Cowper, E. A. 1992. *A concise introduction to syntactic theory: The government-binding theory.* Chicago: University of Chicago Press.

Clark, E. V. 1986. *The acquisition of Romance with special reference to French.* Hillsdale, NJ: LEA.

Crain, S. 1992. Language acquisition in the absence of experience. *BBS* 14, 597–650.

———— and M. Nakayama. 1987. Structure dependence in grammar formation. *Lg.* 63, 522–43. Reprinted in Otero, ed., 1994, Vol. 4, 490–517.

Crick, F., and C. Koch. 1992. The problem of consciousness. *Scientific American,* September, 152–59.

Cromer, R. F. 1970. "Children are nice to understand": Surface structure clues for the recovery of a deep structure. *British Journal of Psychology* 61, 397–408.

———— 1987. Language growth with experience without feedback. *JPR* 16, 223–31.

Culicover, P. 1976. *Syntax.* New York: Academic Press.

Curtiss, S. 1977. *Genie: A psycholinguistic study of a modern day "wild child."* New York: Academic Press.

———— 1981. Dissociation between language and cognition: Cases and implications. *JADD* 15–30.

———— 1982. Developmental dissociation of language and cognition. In Obler and Menn, eds., 285–312.

———— 1988. Abnormal language acquisition and the modularity of language. In Newmeyer, ed., Vol. 2, 96–116.

———— 1990. Language as a cognitive system: Its independence and selective vulnerability. Unedited version in Otero, ed., 1994, Vol. 4, 211–54.

Damasio, A. R., and H. Damasio. 1992. Brain and language. *SA,* September, 88–95.

Damen, L. 1987. *Culture learning: The fifth dimension in the language classroom.* Reading, MA: Addison-Wesley.

Dato, D., ed. 1975. *Developmental psycholinguistics: Theory and applications.* Georgetown Round Table on Language and Linguistics. Washington, DC: Georgetown University Press.

Davies, A., C. Criper, and A. P. R. Howatt, eds. 1984. *Interlanguage.* Edinburgh: Edinburgh University Press.

Delattre, P. 1965. *Comparing the phonetic features of English, French, German, and Spanish: An interim report.* Philadelphia/New York: Chilton Books.

Demonte, V. 1987. C-Command, prepositions, and predication. *LI* 18, 147–57.

———— 1988. Remarks on secondary predicates: C-Command, extraction, and reanalysis. *TLR* 6, 1–39.

———— 1991. *Detrás de la palabra: Estudios de gramática del español*. Madrid: Alianza Editorial.

———— 1992a. Linking and case: The case of prepositional verbs. In Laeufer and Morgan, eds., 415–56.

———— 1992b. Ditransitivity in Spanish: Syntax and semantics (manuscript). Universidad Autonoma de Madrid.

———— and M. Fernández Lagunilla, eds. 1987. *Sintaxis de las lenguas románicas*. Madrid: El Arquero.

———— and B. Garza Cuarón. 1990. *Estudios de lingüística de España y México*. México: UNAM/El Colegio de México.

Demopoulos, W. and A. Marras, eds. 1986. *Language learning and concept acquisition: Foundational issues*. Norwood, NJ: Ablex.

Deprez, V., and A. Pierce. 1993. Negation and functional projections in early grammar. *LI* 24, 25–67.

Diamond, J. 1992. *The third chimpanzee: The evolution and future of the human animal*. New York: HarperCollins.

Diamond, S., ed. 1960. *Culture in history: Essays in honor of Paul Radin*. New York: Columbia University Press.

Díaz Rodríguez, L., and J. M. Liceras. 1990. Formulación de parámetros y adquisición de lenguas extranjeras. In Martín Vide, ed., 1990, 465–80.

Dikken, M. den. 1993. Auxiliaries and participles: Minimalist explorations in the syntax of multiverbal constructions (manuscript). University of Groningen and University of Amsterdam.

Diller, K. C. 1971. *Generative grammar, structural linguistics, and language teaching*. Rowley, MA: Newbury House.

———— 1978. *The language teaching controversy*. Rowley, MA: Newbury House. (Revised edition of Diller 1971.)

———— 1981. "Natural methods" of foreign-language teaching: Can they exist? What criteria must they meet? In Winitz, ed., 75–86.

———— ed. 1981. *Individual differences and universals in language learning aptitude*. Rowley, MA: Newbury House.

———— and T. M. Walsh. 1981. "Living" and "dead" languages—a neurolinguistic distinction. In Savard and Laforge, eds., 99–114.

Dinnen, F. P., ed. 1990. *Studies in the history of linguistics: North American contributions to the history of linguistics*. Amsterdam: John Benjamins.

Di Pietro, R. J. 1971. *Language structures in contrast*. Rowley, MA: Newbury House.

Dittmar, N. 1992. Grammaticalization in second language acquisition. *SSLA* 14, 249–57.

Dixon, R. M. W. 1970. The semantics of giving. In Gross et al., eds., 205–23.

Doughty, C. 1991. Second language instruction does make a difference: Evidence from an empirical study of SL relativization. *SSLA* 13, 431–70.

Dresher, B. E. and J. D. Kaye. 1990. A computational learning model for metrical phonology. *Cognition* 34, 137–95.

Dulay, H. C., M. K. Burt. 1972. Goofing: An indicator of children's second language learning strategies. *LL* 22, 235–52.

———— 1973. Should we teach children syntax? *LL* 23, 245–58.

———— 1974a. Natural sequences in child second language acquisition. *LL* 24, 37–53. (Spanish translation in Liceras, ed., 1992, 105–22.)

———— 1974b. A new perspective on the creative construction process in child second language acquisition. *LL* 24, 253–78.

———— 1974c. Error and strategies in child second language acquisition. *TESOL Quarterly* 8, 129–36.

———— 1974d. You can't learn without goofing. In Richards, ed., 95–123.

———— 1975a. A new approach to discovering universal strategies of child second language acquisition. In Dato, ed., 209–33.

———— 1975b. Creative construction in second language learning and teaching. In Burt and Dulay, eds., 21–32.

———— 1977. Remarks on creativity in second language acquisition. In Burt, Dulay, and Finocchiaro, eds., 95–126. Reprinted in Ritchie, ed., 1978, 65–89.

————, Burt, M. K., and S. D. Krashen. 1982. *Language two*. New York: Oxford University Press.

duPlessis, J., D. Solin et al. 1987. UG or not UG, that is the question: A reply to Clahsen and Muysken. *Second Language Research* 3, 56–75.

Durant, A., and N. Fabb. 1990. *Literary studies in action*. London and New York: Routledge.

Earman, J., ed. 1992. *Inference, explanation, and other philosophical frustrations*. Berkeley: UC Press.

Eckman, F. R. 1977. Markedness and the contrastive analysis hypothesis. *LL* 27, 37–53. (Spanish translation in Liceras, ed., 1992, 208–24.)

———— 1981. Markedness and degree of difficulty in second language learning. In Savard and Laforge, eds., 115–26.

————, and A. J. Hastings, eds. 1979. *Studies in first and second language acquisition*. Rowley, MA: Newbury House.

————, Bell, L., D. Nelson, eds. 1984. *Universals of second language acquisition*. Rowley, MA: Newbury House.

————, Moravscik, E. and J. Wirth, eds. 1986. *Markedness*. New York: Plenum Press.

Eilfort, W. H., P. D. Kroeber, K. L. Peterson, eds. 1985. *Papers from the parasession on causatives and agentivity*. Chicago: Chicago Linguistic Society. (CLS 21, Part 2.)

Eliasson, S. 1982. Transfer as evidence for phonological solutions. *Studia Anglica Posnaniensia* 14, 185–96.

Ellis, R. 1985. Sources of variability in interlanguage. *AL* 6, 118–238.

———— 1989. Are classroom and naturalistic acquisition the same? A study of the classroom acquisition of German word order rules. *SSLA* 11, 305–28.

———— 1990. *Instructed second language acquisition*. Oxford: Basil Blackwell.

———— 1991. Grammaticality judgments and second language acquisition. *SSLA* 13, 161–86.

Els, T. van, et al., 1984. *Applied linguistics and the learning and teaching of foreign languages*. London: Edward Arnold.

Emonds, J. 1976. *A transformational approach to English syntax: Root, structure-preserving, and local transformations*. New York: Academic Press.

———— 1978. The verbal complex V'-V in French. *LI* 9, 151–75.

Ehrman, M., and R. Oxford. 1989. Effects of sex differences, career choice, and psychological type on adult language learning strategies. *MLJ* 73, 1–13.

Ervin, G. L., ed. 1991. *International perspectives on foreign language teaching*. Lincolnwood, IL: National Textbook Co.

Ervin-Trip, S. 1974. Is second language learning like the first? *TESOL Quarterly* 8, 111–27.

Eubank, L. 1993. Sentence matching and processing in L2 development. *SLR* 9, 253–80.

——— and M. Beck. 1993. Generative research on second-language acquisition. In Hadley (ed.), 24–45.

———, ed. 1991. *Point counterpoint: Universal grammar in the second language*. Amsterdam/Philadelphia: John Benjamins.

Fabb, N., et al., eds. 1988. *The linguistics of writing: Arguments between language and literature*. New York: Methuen.

Faerch, C., and G. Kasper. 1986. The role of comprehension in second-language learning. *AL* 7, 257–74.

Falk, J. S. 1992. Otto Jespersen, Leonard Bloomfield, and American structural linguistics. *Lg.* 68, 465–91.

Fanselow, G., ed. 1993. *The parametrization of universal grammar*. Amsterdam/Philadelphia: John Benjamins.

Feldman, H., S. Goldin-Meadow, and L. Gleitman. 1977. Beyond Herodotus: The creation of language by linguistically deprived children. In Lock, ed.

Felix, S. W. 1981. The effect of formal instruction on second language acquisition. *LL* 31, 87–112.

——— 1984. Maturational aspects of universal grammar. In Davies et al., 133–61.

——— 1985. More evidence on competing cognitive systems. *SLR* 1, 47–72.

——— 1987. *Cognition and language growth*. Dordrecht, Holland: Foris.

——— 1988. UG-generated knowledge in adult second language acquisition. In Flynn and O'Neil, eds., 277–94.

——— 1988a. The effects of principles of universal grammar in adult second language acquisition. In the proceedings of the II Euskal Mundu-Biltzarra/II Congreso Mundial Vasco, 263–75.

——— and W. Weigl. 1991. Universal grammar in the classroom: The effects of formal instruction on second language acquisition. *SLR* 7, 162–81.

Fente, Gómez, R., A. Martínez González, and J. A. de Molina Redondo, eds. 1988. *Actas de las Primeras Jornadas Pedagógicas de ASELE (Asociación para la enseñanza del español como lengua extranjera)*. Madrid: ASELE.

Feynman, R. P. (as told to Ralph Leighton). 1988. *"What do you care what other people think?": Further adventures of a curious character*. New York/London: W. W. Norton & Co.

Ferguson, C. A. 1975. Towards a characterization of English foreigner talk. *Anthropological Linguistics* 17, 1–14.

Finer, D. 1991. Binding parameters in second language acquisition. In Eubank, ed.

Fischer, S. 1974. Sign language and linguistic universals. In Rohrer and Ruwet, eds., 187–204.

——— 1994. The study of sign languages and linguistic theory. In Otero, ed., Vol. 4, 582–601.

———— and P. Siple. eds. 1990. *Theoretical issues in sign language research: Linguistics.* Chicago: University of Chicago Press.

Fitzgibbon, J. P. 1959. *Escollos del inglés.* Madrid: E.P.E.S.A.

Fletcher, P., and M. Garman, eds. 1986. *Language acquisition.* New York: Cambridge University Press.

Flynn, S. 1980. The effects of first language branching direction on the acquisition of second language. Paper presented at the Winter LSA Meeting, San Antonio, Texas.

———— 1981. The effects of first language branching direction on the acquisition of second language. In *Cornell Working Papers in Linguistics,* ed. by W. Herbert and J. Herschensohn, 5–63. Ithaca, NY: Cornell University.

———— 1983. A study of the effects of principal branching direction in second language acquisition: The generalization of a parameter of universal grammar from first to second language acquisition. Ph.D. dissertation, Cornell University.

———— 1985. Similarities and differences between first and second language acquisition: Setting the parameters of universal grammar. In Rogers and Sloboda, eds.

———— 1986. Production versus comprehension: Differences in underlying competences. *SSLA* 8, 135–64.

———— 1987. *A parameter-setting model of L2 acquisition: Experimental studies in anaphora.* Dordrecht, Holland: Reidel.

———— 1988. Second language acquisition and grammatical theory. In Newmeyer, ed., Vol. 2, 53–73.

———— 1989. The role of the head-initial/head-final parameter in the acquisition of English relative clauses by adult Spanish and Japanese speakers. In Gass and Schachter, eds., 89–108.

———— 1990. Theory, practice, and research: Strange or blissful bedfellows? In Alatis, ed., 1990, 112–22.

———— 1991a. Linguistic theory and foreign language learning environments. In Bot et al., eds., 197–215.

———— 1991b. The relevance of linguistic theory to language pedagogy: Debunking the myths. In Alatis, ed., 1991, 547–54.

———— and I. Espinal. 1985. Head-initial/head-final parameter in adult Chinese L2 acquisition of English. *SLR* 1, 93–117.

———— and B. Lust. 1990. In defense of parameter-setting in L2 acquisition: A reply to Bley-Vroman and Chaudron. *LL* 40, 419–49.

———— and S. Manuel. 1991. Age-dependent effects in language acquisition: An evaluation of "critical period" hypotheses. In Eubank, ed., 117–45.

———— and W. O'Neil. 1994. Adult next-language acquisition and the theory of grammar. In Otero, ed., Vol. 4, 657–79.

———— and W. O'Neil, eds. 1988. *Linguistic theory in second language acquisition.* Dordrecht, Holland: Kluwer.

Fries, C. C. 1947. *Teaching and learning English as a foreign language.* Ann Arbor, MI: University of Michigan Press.

Fodor, J. A. and J. J. Katz. eds. 1964. *The structure of language: Readings in the philosophy of language.* Englewood Cliffs, NJ: Prentice-Hall.

Fodor, J. A., T. G. Bever, and M. F. Garrett. 1974. *The psychology of language: An introduction to psycholinguistics and generative grammar.* New York: McGraw-Hill.

Fontana, J. M., and J. Moore. 1992. VP-internal subjects and *se*-reflexivization in Spanish. *Linguistic Inquiry* 23, 501–10.

Fotos, S., and R. Ellis. 1991. Communicating about grammar: A task-based approach. *TESOL Quarterly* 25, 605–27.

Fowler, C. A. 1986. An event approach to the study of perception from a direct-realist perspective. *Journal of Phonetics* 14, 3–28.

Frawley, W. ed. 1984. *Translation: Literary, linguistic, and philosophical perspectives*. Newark, DE: University of Delaware Press.

Freed, B., ed., 1991. *Foreign language acquisition research and the classroom*. Lexington, MA: D. C. Heath.

Freidin, R. 1992. *Foundations of generative syntax*. Cambridge, MA: MIT Press.

——— ed. 1991. *Principles and parameters in comparative grammar*. Cambridge, MA: MIT Press.

——— ed. (to appear). *Current issues in comparative grammar*. Dordrecht, Holland: Kluwer Academic Publishers.

Friedman, S., K. Klivington, and R. Peterson, eds. 1986. *The Brain, Cognition, and Education*. New York: Academic Press.

Fukui, N. 1988. Deriving the differences between English and Japanese: A case study in parametric syntax. *English Linguistics* 5, 249–70.

Gair, J. W. 1988. Kinds of markedness. In Flynn and O'Neil, eds., 225–50.

Gajar, A. H. 1987. Foreign language learning disabilities: The identification of predictive and diagnostic variables. *Journal of Learning Disabilities* 20, 327–30.

Ganschow, L. et al., 1991. Identifying native language difficulties among foreign language learners in college: A "foreign" language learning disability? *Journal of Learning Disabilities* 24, 530–41.

Gardner, B. and R. A. Gardner. 1969. Teaching sign language to a chimpanzee. *Science*. 165: 664:72.

——— 1975. Evidence for sentence constituents in the early utterances of child and chimpanzee. *Journal of Experimental Psychology: General* 104, 244–67.

——— 1978. Comparative psychology and language acquisition. In Salzinger and Denmark, eds., 37–76.

Gardner, R. A., B. T. Gardner, and T. E. Van Cantford, eds. 1989. *Teaching sign language to chimpanzees*. Albany: State University of New York Press.

Gardner, H. 1991. *The unschooled mind: How children think and how schools should teach*. New York: Basic Books.

Gass, S. M. 1988. Integrating research areas: A framework for second language studies. *AL* 9:2, 198–217.

——— 1989. Language universals and second-language acquisition. *LL* 39:4, 497–534.

——— 1991. Grammar instruction, selective attention, and learning process. In Phillipson et al., eds., 134–41.

——— 1993. Second language acquisition: past, present, and future. *SLR* 9, 99–117.

——— and U. Lakshmanan. 1991. Accounting for interlanguage subject pronouns. *SLR* 7:3, 181–203.

——— and L. Selinker. 1993. *Second language acquisition: An introductory course*. Hillsdale, NJ: Lawrence Erlbaum Associates.

—— and C. G. Madden eds. 1985. *Input in second language acquisition*. New York: Newbury House.

—— et al., eds. 1989. *Variation in second language acquisition volume 2: Psycholinguistic issues*. Clevedon/Philadelphia: Multilingual Matters LTD.

—— and J. Schachter, eds. 1989. *Linguistic perspectives on second language acquisition*. New York: Cambridge University Press.

—— and L. Selinker, eds. 1983. *Language transfer in language learning*. Rowley, MA: Newbury House. (Revised ed., Philadelphia: John Benjamins, 1992.)

Genesee, F. 1988. Neuropsychology and second language acquisition. In Beebe, ed., 81–112.

George, A. 1990. Whose language is it anyway? Some notes on idiolects. *The Philosophical Quarterly* 40:160, 275–98.

Giacalone Ramat, A. 1992. Grammaticalization processes in the area of temporal and modal relations. *SSLA* 14, 297–322.

Giacobbe, J. 1992. A cognitive view of the role of L1 in the L2 acquisition process. *SSLA* 14, 232–50.

Gibson, R. F. 1982. *The philosophy of W. V. Quine: An expository essay*. Tampa, FL: University Presses of Florida.

Gingras, R., ed. 1978. *Second language acquisition and foreign language teaching*. Washington, DC: Center for Applied Linguistics.

Giorgi, A., and G. Longobardi. 1991. *The syntax of noun phrases*. New York: Cambridge University Press.

Gleitman, L. R. 1984. Biological predispositions to learn language. In Marler and Terrace, 553–84.

—— 1986. Biological preprogramming for language acquisition? In Friedman et al., eds.

—— 1990. The structural sources for verb meanings. *LAJDL* 1:1, 3–55.

—— and E. Wanner. 1982. Language acquisition: The state of the art. In Wanner and Gleitman, eds., 3–48.

Goldin-Meadow, S. 1982. The resilience of recursion: A study of a communication system developed without a conventional language model. In Wanner and Gleitman, eds., 51–77.

—— and H. Feldman. 1977. The development of language-like communication without a language model. *Science* 197, 401–403.

—— and C. Mylander. 1990. Beyond the input given: The child's role in the acquisition of language. *Lg.* 66, 323–55.

—— and C. Mylander. 1991. Home sign systems in deaf children: The development of morphology without a conventional language model. In Siple and Fischer, eds.

González-Bueno, M. 1993. Variaciones en el tratamiento de las sibilantes—inconsistencia en el seseo sevillano: Un enfoque sociolingüístico, *Hispania* 76, 392–98.

Goodall, G. 1993. On case and the passive morpheme. *NLLT* 11, 31–44.

Goodluck, H. 1991. *Language acquisition: A linguistic introduction*. Oxford: Basil Blackwell.

—— and B. Birch. 1988. Late-learned rules in first and second language acquisition. In Pankhurst et al., 94–115.

———— and M. Rochemont, eds. 1993. *Island constraints: Theory, acquisition, and processing*. Dordrecht, Holland: Kluwer Academic.

Goody, J. 1986. *The logic of writing and the organization of society*. New York: Cambridge University Press.

Gopnik, A. 1988. Conceptual and semantic development as theory change: The case of object permanence. *Mind and Language* 3, 197–216.

Gould, J. L., and P. Marler. 1987. Learning by instinct. *Scientific American* (January), 74–85.

Gràcia, L. 1992. *-ble* adjectives and middle-constructions: A problem for inheritance. In Branchadell et al., eds., 163–82.

Graunstein, G., and G. Leitner, eds. 1989. *Reference grammars and modern linguistic theory*. Tübingen: Max Niemeyer Verlag.

Gregg, K. R. 1984. Krashen's monitor and Occam's razor. *AL* 5, 79–100.

———— 1988. Epistemology without knowledge; Schwartz on Chomsky, Fodor, and Krashen. *SLR* 4, 66–80.

———— 1989. Second language acquisition theory: The case for a generative perspective. In Gass and Schachter, eds., 15–40.

———— 1990. The variable competence model of second language acquisition and why it isn't. *AL* 11, 364–83.

———— 1993. Taking explanation seriously; or, let a couple of flowers bloom. *AL* 14, 276–94.

Green, P. S., and K. Hecht. 1992. Implicit and explicit grammar: An empirical study. *AL* 13, 168–84.

Greene, J. 1972. *Psycholinguistics: Chomsky and psychology*. Baltimore, MD: Penguin.

Grimshaw, J. 1990. *Argument structure*. Cambridge, MA: MIT Press.

———— 1991. Extended projection, manuscript, Brandeis University.

———— and S. T. Rosen. 1990. Knowledge and obedience: The developing status of the binding theory. *LI* 21, 187–222.

Grodzinsky, Y. 1990. *Theoretical perspectives on language deficits*. Cambridge, MA: MIT Press.

Gross, M., M. Halle, and M. P. Schützenberger, eds. 1970. *The formal analysis of natural languages*. The Hague: Mouton.

Guéron, J., and S. Sowley, eds. 1982. *Grammaire transformationelle: Théorie et methodologies*. Vincennes: Université de Paris VIII.

Gunnarson, K. 1993. Expression of distance and theory of theta-roles. *Nordic Journal of Linguistics* 16, 3–32.

Guntermann, G., ed. 1993. *Developing language teachers for a changing world*. Lincolnwood, IL: National Textbook Co.

Hadley, A. O. 1993. *Teaching language in context*. 2d. ed. Boston: Heinle and Heinle. (Cf. Omaggio 1986.)

———— ed. 1993. *Research in language learning: Principles, processes, and prospects*. Lincolnwood, IL: National Textbook Co.

Haegeman, L. 1988. The categorical status of modals in L2 acquisition. In Flynn and O'Neil, eds., 252–76.

———— 1991. *Introduction to government and binding theory*. Oxford: Basil Blackwell. (Revised ed., 1994.)

——— 1992. *Generative syntax: Theory and description: A case study from West Flemish*. New York: Cambridge University Press.

Hakuta, K. 1986. *Mirror of language: The debate on bilingualism*. New York: Basic Books.

Hale, K. 1988. Linguistic theory: Generative grammar. In Flynn and O'Neil, eds., 26–33.

——— and J. Keyser. 1991. On the syntax of argument structure. Center for Cognitive Science, MIT. Revised version in Hale and Keyser, eds., 53–109.

——— and Keyser, J., eds. 1993. *The view from Building 20: Essays in linguistics in honor of Sylvain Bromberger*. Cambridge, MA: MIT Press.

Halle, M., and A. Marantz. 1993. Distributed morphology and the pieces of inflection. In Hale and Keyser, eds., 111–76.

Hammerly, H. 1992. The need for directed language learning in the FL classroom. *SSLA* 14, 215–16.

Hammond, M., and M. Noonan, eds. 1988. *Theoretical morphology*. San Diego: Academic Press.

Hanzeli, V. E. 1968a. Internship training for teaching assistants. *Improving College and University Teaching* 16, 110–112.

——— 1968b. Linguistics and the language teacher. *Foreign Language Annals* 2, 42–50.

Harley, B. 1986. *Age in second language acquisition*. San Diego: College Hill Press.

——— et al., eds. 1990. *The development of second language proficiency*. New York: Cambridge University Press.

Hanard, S. R., H. D. Steklis, and J. Lancaster, eds. 1976. *Origins and evolution of language and speech*. (=*Annals of the New York Academy of Sciences* 280.)

Harmer, J. 1983. *The practice of English language teaching*. London: Longman.

Harris, J. W. 1991a. The exponence of gender in Spanish. *LI* 22, 27–62.

——— 1991b. The form classes of Spanish substantives. *Morphology Yearbook*, 65–88.

——— 1991c. With respect to metrical constituents in Spanish. In Campos and Martínez-Gil, eds., 447–73.

——— 1993a. The morphology of Spanish clitics, manuscript, MIT.

——— 1993b. How "prosodic" are Mexican Spanish diminutives? A reply to Crowhurst 1993, manuscript, MIT.

Hatch, E., ed., 1977. *Second language acquisition: A book of readings*. Rowley, MA: Newbury House.

——— ed. 1983. *Psycholinguistics: A second language perspective*. Rowley, MA: Newbury House.

Hawkins, J. A. 1987. Implicational universals as predictors of language acquisition. *Linguistics* 25, 453–73.

Hawkins, R., and R. Towell. 1992. Second language acquisition research and the second language acquisition of French. *FLS* 2, 97–121.

Hayakawa, S. I. 1978. *Language in thought and action*. 4th ed. San Diego: Harcourt Brace Jovanovich.

Hayes, B. 1984. Review of Derek Attridge, *The rhythms of English poetry*. In *Language* 60, 914–23. Reprinted in Otero, ed. 1994, Vol. 4, 824–36.

Hedgcock, J. 1993. Well-formed vs. ill-formed strings in L2 metalingual tasks: Specifying features of grammaticality judgments. *SLR* 9, 1–21.

Hentoff, N. 1992. *Free speech for me—but not for thee: How the American left and right relentlessly censor each other*. New York: HarperCollins.

Hernanz, M. L., and J. M. Brucart. 1987. *La sintaxis: 1. Principios técnicos. La oración simple*. Barcelona: Crítica.

Herschensohn, J. 1981. French causatives: Restructuring, opacity, filters, and construal. *LA* 8, 217–80.

——— 1988. Linguistic accuracy of textbook grammar: The determiner system of French. *MLJ* 72, 409–14.

——— 1990. Toward a theoretical basis for language pedagogy. *MLJ* 74, 451–58.

——— 1992. Teaching assistant development: A case study. In Walz, ed., 25–45.

——— 1993. Applying linguistics to teach morphology: Verb and adjective inflection in French. *IJAL* 31:2, 97–112.

——— (forthcoming). *Binary case and argument structure: A study of French nonthematic subject constructions*. Manuscript, University of Washington.

Herslund, M., and F. Sorensen., eds. 1993. *The Nordlex project: Lexical studies in the Scandinavian languages*. Special issue of *Lambda*, Copenhagen Business School.

Hervey, S., and I. Higgins. 1992. *Thinking translation: A course translation method: French to English*. London and New York; Routledge.

Higgs, T. V., ed. 1982. *Curriculum, competence, and the foreign language teacher*. Lincolnwood, IL: National Textbook Co.

Hill, S. 1985. *Contrastive English-Spanish grammatical structures: A manual with exercises*. Lanham, MD: University Press of America.

——— and W. Bradford. 1991. *Bilingual grammar of English-Spanish syntax: A manual with exercises*. Lanham, MD: University Press of America. (Fully revised and expanded version of Hill 1985.)

Hilles, S. 1989. *Adult access to universal grammar*. UCLA doctoral dissertation.

Hirschbuhler, P., and K. Koerner, eds. 1992. *Romance languages and modern linguistic theory*. Amsterdam: John Benjamins.

Hochberg, J. G. 1988. Learning Spanish stress. *Lg*. 64, 683–706.

Holt, J. 1989. *Learning all the time*. Reading, MA: Addison-Wesley.

Honda, M., and W. O'Neil. 1994. Constructing and evaluating theories using linguistics in the science curriculum. In Otero, ed., Vol. 4, 643–56.

Hook, S., ed. 1969. *Linguistics and philosophy*. New York: New York University Press.

Hooper, J. B. 1975. On assertive predicates. *Syntax and Semantics* 4, 91–124.

Hoover, M. L. 1992. Sentence processing strategies in Spanish and English. *JPR* 21, 275–99.

Horgan, J. 1991. Word games: Another attempt to create a universal parsing machine. *SA*, October, 34.

Horning, B. 1991. Language busters. *Technology Review*, October, 51–57.

Howatt, A. 1984. *A history of English language teaching*. Oxford: Oxford University Press.

Hubel, D., and T. Weisel. 1962. Receptive fields, binocular interaction, and functional architecture in the cat's visual cortex. *Journal of Physiology* 160, 106–54.

——— 1963. Receptive fields of cells in striate cortex of very young, visually inexperienced kittens. *Journal of Neurophysiology* 26, 994–1002.

——— 1979. Brain mechanisms of vision. *SA*, September, 130–44.

Hudelson, S., and C. Faltis. 1993. Redefining basic teacher education: Preparing teachers to transform teaching. In Guntermann, ed., 23–42.

Hulk, A. 1991. Parameter setting and the acquisition of word order in L2 French. *SLR* 7:1, 1–34.

Hurford, J. R. 1991. The evolution of the critical period for language acquisition. *Cognition* 40, 159–201.

———— and B. Heasley. 1983. *Semantics: A coursebook*. New York: Cambridge University Press.

Hyltenstam, K., and L. K. Obler, eds. 1989. *Bilingualism across the lifespan: Aspects of acquisition, maturity, and loss*. New York: Cambridge University Press.

———— and M. Pienemann, eds. 1985. *Modelling and assessing second language acquisition*. San Diego, CA: College-Hill Press.

Hyams, N. 1986. *Language acquisition and the theory of parameters*. Dordrecht, Holland: Reidel.

———— and S. Sigurjónsdóttir. 1990. The development of "long distance anaphora": A cross-linguistic comparison with special reference to Icelandic. *LAJDL* 1:1, 57–93.

———— and K. Wexler. 1993. On the grammatical basis of null subjects in child language. *LI* 24, 421–59.

Hyman, L. M., C. N. Li, eds. 1988. *Language, speech, and mind: Studies in honour of Victoria Fromkin*. London and New York: Routledge, 1988.

Iatridou, S. 1990. About Agr(P). *LI* 21, 551–77.

———— and A. Kroch. 1992. The licensing and distribution of CP recursion. *GLOW Newsletter* 28, 26–27.

Ingram, D. 1989. *First language acquisition: Method, description, and explanation*. New York: Cambridge University Press.

Ioup, G. 1989. Immigrant children who have failed to acquire native English. In Gass et al., eds., Vol. 2, 160–175.

———— and S. H. Weinberger, eds. 1987. *Interlanguage phonology: The acquisition of a second sound system*. New York: Newbury House.

Jackendoff. R. 1987. *Consciousness and the computational mind*. Cambridge, MA: MIT Press.

———— 1990. *Semantic structures*. Cambridge, MA: MIT Press.

———— 1991. Is there a faculty of social cognition? Presidential Address to the Society for Philosophy and Psychology. Included in Jackendoff 1992, 69–81, and in Otero, ed., 1994, Vol. 3, 629–43.

———— 1992. *Languages of the mind*. Cambridge, MA: MIT Press.

———— 1993. *Patterns in the mind: Language and human nature*. Hemel Hempstead: Harvester Wheatsheaf. (American edition: New York: Basic Books, 1994.)

———— and D. Aaron. 1991. Review of Lakoff and Turner 1989. *Lg.* 67, 320–38.

Jacobs, B. 1988. Neurobiological differentiation of primary and secondary language acquisition. *SSLA* 10, 303–37.

———— and J. Schumann. 1992. Applied linguistics, language acquisition, and neuroscience: Towards a more integrative perspective. *AL* 13, 282–301.

Jacobs, J., et al., eds. 1993. *Syntax: An international handbook of contemporary research*. Berlin: Walter de Gruyter.

Jaeggli, O. 1981. *Topics in Romance syntax*. Dordrecht, Holland: Foris.

————— 1986. Three issues in the theory of clitics: Case, doubled NPs, and extraction. In Borer, ed., 15–42.

————— and K. Safir, eds. 1989. *The null subject parameter*. Dordrecht, Holland: Kluwer.

Jakobovits, L. A. 1968. Implications of recent psycholinguistic developments for the teaching of a second language. *LL* 18, 89–109.

————— 1970. *Foreign language learning: A psycholinguistic analysis of the issues*. Rowley, MA: Newbury House.

Jakobs, B. 1988. Neurobiological differentiation of primary and secondary language acquisition. *SSLA* 10, 303–37.

James, A., and J. Leather, eds. 1987. *Sound patterns in second language acquisition*. Dordrecht, Holland: Foris.

James, C. 1971. The exculpation of contrastive linguistics. In Nickel, ed., 53–68.

————— 1980. *Contrastive analysis*. London: Longman.

Jenkins, L. 1988. Second language acquisition: A biolinguistic perspective. In Flynn and O'Neil, eds., 109–116.

Jespersen, O. 1905. *Growth and Structure of the English language*. Chicago: The University of Chicago Press.

Johnson, D. M. 1992. *Approaches to research in second language learning*. New York and London: Longman.

Johnson, J. S. 1992. Critical period effects in second language acquisition: The effect of written versus auditory materials on the assessment of grammatical competence. *LL* 42, 217–48.

————— and E. Newport. 1989. Critical period effects on second language learning: The influence of maturational state on the acquisition of English as a second language. *Cognitive Psychology* 21, 60–99.

————— and E. Newport. 1991. Critical period effects on universal properties of language: The status of subjacency in the acquisition of a second language. *Cognition* 39, 215–58.

Johnson, R., and P. Smith, eds. 1982. *Studies in honor of José Rubia Barcia*. Lincoln, NE: Society of Spanish and Spanish-American Studies.

Johnston, M., and M. Pienemann. 1985. *Second language acquisition: A classroom perspective*. Sidney, Australia: New South Wales Adult Migrant Education Service.

Joiner, E. C. 1993. Reflecting on teacher development. In Guntermann, ed., 187–212.

Jonas, D., and J. D. Bobaljik, 1993. Specs for subjects: The role of TP in Icelandic. Manuscript, Harvard University and MIT.

Jones, M. L., and S. P. Quigley, 1979. The acquisition of question formation in spoken English and American Sign Language by two hearing children of deaf parents. *JSHD* 44, 196–208.

Jordens, P. 1980. Interlanguage research: Interpretation or explanation? *LL* 30, 195–207. (Spanish translation in Liceras, ed., 1992, 226–39.)

————— 1988. The acquisition of word order in Dutch and German as L1 and L2. *SLR* 4, 41–65.

—————, ed. 1987. *Interlanguage development*. Dordrecht, Holland: Foris.

Juffs, A. 1992. Review of Larsen-Freeman and Long 1991. *SLR* 8, 161–66.

Juul, A., and H. F. Nielsen, eds. 1989. *Otto Jespersen: Facets of his life and work.* Amsterdam and Philadelphia: John Benjamins.

Kachru, B. B. 1990. *The alchemy of English: The spread, functions, and models of non-native Englishes.* Urbana, IL: University of Illinois Press.

———, ed. 1992. *The other tongue: English across cultures.* 2d ed. Urbana, IL: University of Illinois Press.

Kamimoto, T., A. Shimura, and E. Kellerman. 1992. A second language classic reconsidered: The case of Schachter's avoidance. *SLR* 8, 251–77.

Kandel, E. R., and J. H. Schwartz, eds. 1985. *Principles of neural science.* 2d., enlarged, ed. New York: Elsevier.

Karmiloff-Smith, A. 1985. Language and cognitive processes from a developmental perspective. *Language and Cognitive Processes* 1:1, 60–85.

——— 1988. The child is a theoretician, not an inductivist. *Mind and Language* 3, 183–95.

Kasher, A., ed. 1991. *The Chomskyan turn.* Oxford: Blackwell.

Katz, N., E. Baker, and J. Macnamara. 1974. What's in a name? A study of how children learn common and proper names. *Child Development* 45, 469–73.

Kaufman, D., and M. Aronoff. 1989. Morphological interaction between L1 and L2 in language attrition. In Gass et al., eds., Vol. 2, 202–15.

Kaye, J. 1989. *Phonology: A cognitive view.* Hillsdale, NJ: Lawrence Erlbaum Associates.

Kayne, R. 1975. *French syntax: The transformational cycle.* Cambridge, MA: MIT Press.

——— 1981. On certain differences between French and English. *LI* 12, 349–71. Reprinted in Kayne 1984.

——— 1984. *Connectedness and binary branching.* Dordrecht, Holland: Foris.

——— 1989. Null subjects and clitic climbing. In Jaeggli and Safir, eds.

——— 1991. Romance clitics and PRO. *LI* 22, 647–86.

——— 1993a. Toward a modular theory of auxiliary selection. *Studia Linguistica* 47, 3–31.

——— 1993b. The antisymmetry of syntax. Manuscript, City University of New York.

Kean, M.-L. 1986. Core issues in transfer. In Kellerman and Sharwood Smith, eds., 80–90.

——— 1988a. The relation between linguistic theory and second language acquisition: A biological perspective. In Pankhurst et al., 61–70.

——— 1988b. Brain structures and linguistic capacity. In Newmeyer, ed., Vol. 2, 74–95.

Kellerman, E. 1984. The empirical evidence for the influence of the L1 in interlanguage. In Davies et al., eds., 98–122.

——— and M. Sharwood Smith, eds. 1986. *Crosslinguistic influence in second language acquisition.* Oxford/New York: Pergamon Institute of English.

Kelly, L. G. 1969. *Twenty-five centuries of language teaching: 500 BC–1969.* Rowley, MA: Newbury House.

Kempchinsky, P. 1986. *Romance subjective clauses and logical form.* UCLA doctoral dissertation.

—— 1991. On the characterization of a class of ditransitive verbs in Spanish. In Campos and Martínez-Gil, eds., 201–40.

—— 1992a. Clausal complements and case theory in Romance. *Probus* 4, 17–51.

—— 1992b. The Spanish possessive dative construction: Theta role assignment and proper government. In Hirschbuhler and Koerner, eds., 135–50.

—— 1992c. Syntactic constraints on the expression of possession in Spanish. *Hispania* 75, 697–704.

Kenstowicz, M., and C. Kisseberth. 1979. *Generative phonology*. New York: Academic Press.

Kessler, C., ed. 1992. *Cooperative language learning. A teacher's resource book*. Englewood Cliffs, NJ: Prentice Hall.

Keyser, S. J., and T. Roeper. 1992. Re: The abstract clitic hypothesis. *LI* 23, 89–125.

Kibbee, D., and D. Wanner, eds. 1991. *New analyses in Romance linguistics*. Philadelphia: John Benjamins.

Kim, Y., and R. Larson. 1989. Scope interpretation and the syntax of psych-verbs. *LI* 20, 681–88.

Kimball, J. P. 1973. *The formal theory of grammar*. Englewood Cliffs, NJ: Prentice Hall.

Kimura, D. 1992. Sex differences in the brain. *SA*, September, 118–25.

King, L. D., and A. Maley, eds. 1985. *Selected papers from the 13th Linguistic Symposium on Romance Languages, Chapel Hill, NC, 24–26 March 1983*. Amsterdam/Philadelphia: J. Benjamins.

King, M-C., and A. C. Wilson. 1975. Evolution at two levels in humans and chimpanzees. *Science* 188 (11 April), 107–116.

Kinsbourne, M. 1981. Neuropsychological aspects of bilingualism. In Winitz, ed., 50–58.

Kiparsky, P. 1983. Roman Jakobson and the grammar of poetry. In Halle, ed., 27–38.

—— 1988. On theory and interpretation. In Fabb et al., eds., 185–98. Reprinted in Otero, ed., 1994, Vol. 4, 808–23.

—— and Youmans, G., eds. 1989. *Rhythm and meter*. San Diego: Academic Press.

Kitcher, P. 1988. The child as parent of the scientist. *Mind and Language* 3, 217–27.

Klein, E. C. 1990a. *The null-prep phenomenon in second language acquisition*. City University of New York doctoral dissertation. (Published as *Toward second language acquisition: A study of null-prep*. 1993. Dordrecht, Holland: Kluwer Academic.)

—— 1990b. What UG does not explain. In Burmeister and Rounds, eds., 417–28.

Klein, W. 1986. *Second language acquisition*. New York: Cambridge University Press.

Kobayashi, H., and C. Rinnert. 1991. Effects of first language on second language writing: Translation versus direct composition. *LL* 41, 183–215.

Klima, E., and U. Bellugi; with Battison, R., et al., 1979. *The signs of language*. Cambridge, MA: Harvard University Press.

Koerner, K., ed. 1991. *First person singular II: Autobiographies by North American scholars in the language sciences*. Amsterdam/Philadelphia: John Benjamins.

Koopman, H. 1986. The genesis of Haitian: Implications of a comparison of some features of the syntax of Haitian, French, and West African languages. In Muysken and Smith, eds., 231–58.

——— 1993a. The internal structure and distribution of DPs. Manuscript, UCLA.

——— 1993b. On verbs that fail to undergo V-second. Manuscript, UCLA.

Koster, C. 1993. *Errors in anaphora acquisition*. University of Utrecht doctoral dissertation.

Koster, C. J., and T. Koet. 1993. The evaluation of accent in the English of Dutchmen. *LL* 43, 69–92.

Koster, J. 1993a. Towards a new theory of anaphoric binding. Manuscript, University of Groningen.

——— 1993b. Predicate incorporation and the word order of Dutch. Manuscript, University of Groningen.

——— and E. Reuland, eds. 1991. *Long-distance anaphora*. New York: Cambridge University Press.

Kramsch, C. 1989. New directions in the teaching of language and culture. National Foreign Language Center of the Johns Hopkins University. Occasional Papers, 4.

——— and S. McConnell-Ginet, eds. 1992. *Text and context: Cross-disciplinary perspectives on language study*. New York: D. H. Heath.

Krashen, S. D. 1973. Lateralization, language learning, and the critical period. *LL* 23, 63–74.

——— 1975. The development of cerebral dominance and language learning: More new evidence. In Dato, ed.

——— 1977. The monitor model for adult second language performance. In Burt et al., eds., 152–61. (Spanish translation in Liceras, ed., 1992, 144–51.)

——— 1981. *Second language acquisition and second language learning*. Oxford: Pergamon Press.

——— 1982. *Principles and practice in second language acquisition*. Oxford: Pergamon Press.

——— and L. Galloway. 1978. The neurological correlates of language acquisition. *SPEAQ Journal* 21, 21–35.

———, R. Scarcella, and M. H. Long, eds. 1982. *Child-adult differences in second language acquisition*. Rowley, MA: Newbury House.

Kroll, B. 1990. *Second language writing: Research insights for the classroom*. New York: Cambridge University Press.

Kuroda, S.-Y. 1973. Reflections on the foundations of narrative theory from a linguistic point of view. Included in Kuroda 1979, 205–31. Reprinted in Otero, ed., 1994, Vol. 4, 779–807.

——— 1979. *The (w)hole of the doughnut: Syntax and its boundaries*. Ghent: E. Story-Scientia.

——— 1986. Whether we agree or not: Rough ideas about comparative syntax of English and Japanese. Manuscript, University of California, San Diego. Revised version in *Linguisticae Investigationes* 12 (1988), 1–47, and in Posser, ed., 1988, 103–44.

Lackner, J. R. 1968. A developmental study of language behavior in retarded children. *Neuropsychologia* 6, 301–20. Reprinted in Morehead and Morehead, eds., 1976, 181–208.

Lachter, J., and T. G. Bever. 1988. The relation between linguistic structure and associative theories of language learning: A constructive critique of some connectionist learning models. In Pinker and Mehler, eds., 195–247.

Lafayette, R. C. 1993. Subject-matter content: What every foreign language teacher needs to know. In Guntermann, ed., 124–58.

Laka Mugarza, M. I. 1990. *Negation in syntax: On the nature of functional categories and projections*. MIT doctoral dissertation.

Lakoff, G., and M. Turner. 1989. *More than cool reason: A field guide to poetic metaphor*. Chicago: University of Chicago Press.

Landau, B., and L. R. Gleitman. 1985. *Language and experience: Evidence from the blind child*. Cambridge, MA: Harvard University Press.

Larsen-Freeman, D. 1975. The acquisition of grammatical morphemes by adult ESL students. *TESOL Quarterly* 9, 409–30.

——— 1976. An explanation for the morpheme acquisition order of second language learners. *LL* 26, 125–34.

——— 1991. Second language acquisition research. Staking out the territory. *TESOL Quarterly* 25, 315–20.

——— and M. H. Long. 1990. *An introduction to second language acquisition research*. London and New York: Longman.

Larson, R. K. 1988. On the double object construction. *LI* 19, 335–91.

——— 1990. Double objects revisited: Reply to Jackendoff. *LI* 21, 589–632.

——— 1991. *Promise* and the theory of control. *LI* 22, 103–39.

——— and M. Luján. 1990. Focused pronouns. Manuscript, MIT/University of Texas. (Revised in May 1992.)

Lasnik, H. 1990. *Essays on restrictiveness and learnability*. Dordrecht/Boston/London: Kluwer Academic Publishers.

———, and M. Saito. 1992. *Move α*. Cambridge, MA: MIT Press.

Leather, J., and A. James. 1991. The acquisition of second language speech. *SSLA* 13, 305–41.

Lee, J. F. and B. Van Patten. 1991. The question of language program direction is *academic*. In Magnan, ed., 113–27.

Lees, R. B. 1959. Linguistically oriented grammars and the substitution-in-frames technique. Manuscript, IBM.

——— 1960. Optical illusions and grammatical blindness. *Syntax and Semantics* 7 (1976), 21–26.

——— 1962. Transformational grammars and the Fries framework. In Allen, ed., 137–46.

——— 1965. Two views of linguistic research. *Linguistics* 11, 21–29.

Lefkowitz, N. 1984. *A maximization of favorable conditions for oral fluency: An application of SLA theory and approach to FL instruction*. University of Washington masters thesis.

Legutke, M., and H. Thomas. 1991. *Process and experience in the language classroom*. London and New York: Longman.

Lenneberg, E. H. 1953. Cognition in ethnolinguistics. *Lg.* 29, 463–71.

—— 1954. A note on Cassirer's *Philosophy of language*. *Phil. Phenomenol. Res.* 15, 512–22.

—— 1960a. Language, evolution, and purposive behavior. In Diamond, ed.

—— 1960b. Review of Penfield and Roberts 1959. *Lg.* 36, 97–112.

—— 1962. Understanding language without the ability to speak. *Journal of Abnormal Social Psychology* 65, 419–25.

—— 1964a. Speech as a motor skill with special reference to nonaphasic disorders. In Bellugi and Brown, eds., 115–27.

—— 1964b. Speech development: Its anatomical and physiological concommitants. In Hall, ed.

—— 1964c. The capacity for language acquisition. In Fodor and Katz, eds. (A revised and extended version of Lenneberg 1960a.)

—— 1964d. A biological perspective of language. In Lenneberg, ed. Reprinted in Oldfield and Marshall, eds., 32–47.

—— 1966. The natural history of language. In Smith and Miller, eds.

—— 1967. *Biological foundations of language*. New York: John Wiley.

—— 1967a. The biological foundations of language. *Hospital Practice*. December, 59–67. Reprinted in Lester, ed. 1970.

—— 1969. A word between us. In Roslansky, ed., 111–31.

—— 1971. Of language knowledge, apes, and brains. *JPR* 1, 1–29. Reprinted in Otero, ed. 1994, Vol. 4, 145–73.

——, ed. 1964. *New directions in the study of language*. Cambridge, MA: MIT Press.

—— and E. Lenneberg, eds. 1975. *Foundations of language development: A multidisciplinary approach*. 2 vols. New York: Academic Press/Paris: UNESCO Press.

——, I. Nichols, and E. Rosenberger. 1964. Primitive stages in language development in mongolism. *Disorders of Communication* 42, 119–37.

Lennon, P. 1989. Introspection and intentionality in advanced second-language acquisition. *LL* 39:3, 375–96.

Leonard, L. et al., 1992. Morphological deficits in children with specific language impairment: The status of features in the underlying grammar. *LAJDL* 2:2, 151–79.

Lester, M. 1970. *Readings in applied transformational grammar*. New York: Holt. (Revised edition, 1973.)

Levin, H., and J. P. Williams. 1970. *Basic studies in reading*. New York: Basic Books.

Lieberman, P. 1984. *The biology and evolution of language*. Cambridge, MA: Harvard University Press.

—— 1991. *Uniquely human: The evolution of speech, thought, and selfless behavior*. Cambridge, MA: Harvard University Press.

Liceras, J. M. 1981. Markedness and permeability in interlanguage systems. *Working Papers in Linguistics* 2, 123–50.

—— 1983. *Markedness, contrastive analysis, and the acquisition of Spanish syntax by English speakers*. Doctoral dissertation, University of Toronto.

—— 1985a. The value of clitics in nonnative Spanish. *Second Language Research* 1, 151–68.

—— 1985b. The role of intake in the determination of learners' competence. In Gass and Madden, eds., 354–73.

———— 1985c. A pedagogical grammar of Spanish reflexive passive. *Bulletin of the CAAL* [Canadian Association of Applied Linguistics] 2, 137–45.

———— 1986. *Linguistic theory and second language acquisition: The Spanish nonnative grammar of English speakers.* Tübingen: Guntar Narr Verlag.

———— 1986a. La teoría lingüística y la adquisición del español como lengua segunda. In Meisel, ed., 156–81.

———— 1986b. Sobre el concepto de permeabilidad. *Revista Española de Lingüística Aplicada* 2, 49–61.

———— 1988a. Syntax and stylistics: more on the pro-drop parameter. In Pankhurst et al., eds., 71–93.

———— 1988b. La idiosincrasia de los sistemas no nativos. In Martín Vide, ed., 1988, 583–93.

———— 1988c. La adquisición de las relativas especificativas del español por adultos de habla inglesa: ¿Dificultad o dificultades? *Boletín del I.C.E. de la Universidad Autónoma de Madrid* 12, 4–36.

———— 1988d. L2 learnability: delimiting the domain of core grammar as distinct from the marked periphery. In Flynn and O'Neil, eds., 199–224.

———— 1988e. Adquirir, aprender y enseñar: El español como lengua extranjera. In Fente Gómez et al., 47–59.

———— 1989a. On linguistic theory and Spanish grammars. In Graunstein and Leitner, eds., 184–204.

———— 1989b. On some properties of the "pro-drop" parameter: Looking for missing subjects in nonnative Spanish. In Gass and Schachter, eds., 109–33.

———— 1991. La adquisición de L2: La perspectiva lingüística. In Martín Vide, ed., 1991, 51–83.

————, ed. 1992. *La adquisición de lenguas extranjeras: Hacia un modelo de análisis de la interlengua.* Madrid: Visor.

————, B. Soloaga, and A. Carballo. 1992. Los conceptos de tema y rema: Problemas sintácticos y estilísticos de la adquisición del español. *Hispanic Linguistics* 5, 43–85.

Lier, L. van. 1988. *The classroom and the language learner: Ethnography and second-language classroom research.* London and New York: Longman.

Lightbown, P. M. 1983. Exploring relationships between developmental and instructional sequences in L2 acquisition. In Seliger and Long, 217–43.

———— 1985. Great expectations: Second-language acquisition research and classroom teaching. *AL* 6, 173–89.

————, N. Spada, and L. White, eds. 1993. *The role of instruction in second language acquisition.* (=*SSLA* 15:2.)

———— and L. White. 1987. The influence of linguistic theories on language acquisition research: Description and explanation. *Language Learning* 37:4, 483–510.

Lightfoot, D. 1991. *How to set parameters: Arguments from language change.* Cambridge, MA: MIT Press.

Lillo-Martin, D. C. 1985. *Parameter setting: Evidence from use, acquisition, and breakdown in American Sign Language.* Doctoral dissertation, UCSD. (See Lillo-Martin 1991.)

———— 1986. Two kinds of null arguments in American Sign Language, *NLLT* 4, 415–44.

———— 1990. Parameters for questions: Evidence from WH-movement in American Sign Language. In Lucas, ed., 211–22.

———— 1991. *Universal grammar and American Sign Language: Setting the null argument parameters*. Dordrecht, Holland: Kluwer.

Limber, J. 1977. Language in child and chimp? *AP* 32, 280–94.

Linden, E. 1976. *Apes, men, and language*. New York: Penguin Books.

Lock, A., ed. 1977. *Action, gesture, and symbol: The emergence of language*. New York: Academic Press.

Lococo, V. 1975. An analysis of Spanish and German learner's errors. *Working Papers on Bilingualism* 7, 96–124.

———— 1976. A comparison of three methods from the collection of second language data. *Working Papers on Bilingualism* 8, 59–86.

Long, M. H. 1983. Does second language instruction make a difference? A review of research. *TESOL Quarterly* 17, 359–82.

———— 1988. Instructed interlanguage development. In Beebe, ed., 115–41.

———— 1990. Maturational constraints on language development. *SSLA* 12, 251–85.

———— 1990a. The least a second language acquisition theory needs to explain. *TESOL Quarterly* 24, 649–65.

Lucas, C., ed. 1990. *Sign language research: Theoretical issues*. Washington, DC: Gallaudet University Press.

Lugton, R., and C. Heinle, eds. 1971. *Toward a cognitive approach to second-language acquisition*. Philadelphia: Center for Curriculum Development.

Luján, M., L. Minaya, and D. Sankoff. 1984. The universal consistency hypothesis and the prediction of word order acquisition stages in the speech of bilingual children. *Lg.* 60, 343–71.

McCrum, R., W. Cran, and R. MacNeil. 1986. *The story of English*. New York: Elisabeth Sifton Books/Viking.

McDonough, S. H. 1986. 2d. ed. *Psychology in foreign language teaching*. London: Allen and Unwin.

McKee, C. 1992. A comparison of pronouns and anaphors in Italian and English acquisition. *LAJDL* 2:1, 21–54.

———— and M. Emiliani. 1992. Il clitico: c'è ma non si vede. *NNLT* 10, 415–37.

McLaughlin, B. 1978. *Second Language acquisition in childhood*. Hillsdale, NJ: Lawrence Erlbaum Associates.

———— 1978a. The monitor model: Some methodological considerations. *LL* 28, 309–32. (Spanish translation in Liceras, ed., 1992, 154–76.)

———— 1981. Differences and similarities between first- and second-language learning. In Winitz, ed., 23–32.

———— 1987. *Theories of second-language learning*. London: Edward Arnold.

———— 1990. "Conscious" versus "unconscious" knowledge. *TESOL Quarterly* 24, 617–34.

Macnamara, J. 1973. The cognitive strategies of language learning. In Oller and Richards, eds., 57–65.

———— 1982. *Names for things: A study of human learning*. Cambridge, MA: MIT Press.

McNeill, D. 1966. Developmental psycholinguistics. In Smith and Miller, eds.
———— 1970. *The acquisition of language: The study of developmental psycholinguistics*. New York: Harper and Row.
———— 1987. *Psycholinguistics: A new approach*. New York: Harper and Row.
MacWhiney, B., ed. 1987. *Mechanisms of language acquisition*. Hillsdale, NJ: Lawrence Erlbaum Associates.
Mager, R. F. 1961. On the sequencing of instructional content. *Psychological Reports*, 405–12.
Mairs, J. L. 1989. Stress assignment in interlanguage phonology: An analysis of the stress system of Spanish speakers learning English. In Gass and Schachter, eds., 260–83.
Magnan, S. S., ed. 1991. *Challenges in the 1990s for college foreign language programs*. Boston: Heinle and Heinle. (AAUSC [American Association of Supervisors, Coordinators, and Directors of Foreign Language Programs]: Issues in Language Program Direction. A series of annual volumes.)
Magni, F. and S. Vaccaro, eds. 1987. *Oltre la pace: Saggi di critica al complesso politico-militare*, Milano, Italy: Franco Angelli.
Mallén, E. 1990. Spanish partitive constructions. *Revue Roumaine de Linguistique* 35, 33–52.
Marcus, G. E. et al., 1992. *Overregularization in language acquisition*. With commentary by Harold Clahsen. Chicago: University of Chicago Press. (=*Monographs of the Society for Research in Child Development*, serial no. 228, Vol. 57, No. 4.)
Marler, P., and H. S. Terrace, eds. 1984. *The biology of learning*. Berlin: Springer-Verlag.
Marshall, J. C. 1980. The new organology. *BBS* 3, 23–25.
Martín Vide, C., ed. 1988. *Lenguajes naturales y lenguajes formales: Actas del III Congreso de Lenguajes Naturales y Lenguajes Formales*. Barcelona: Universidad de Barcelona.
————, ed. 1990. *Lenguajes naturales y lenguajes formales: Actas del V Congreso de Lenguajes Naturales y Lenguajes Formales*. Barcelona: Universidad de Barcelona.
————, ed. 1991. *Lenguajes naturales y lenguajes formales: Actas del VI Congreso de Lenguajes Naturales y Lenguajes Formales*. Barcelona: Universidad de Barcelona.
Martohardjono, G. 1993. *Wh-movement in the acquisition of a second language: A crosslinguistic study of three languages with and without movement*. Cornell University doctoral dissertation.
Masullo, P. J. 1992. *Incorporation and case theory in Spanish: A crosslinguistic perspective*. University of Washington doctoral dissertation.
Mayberry, R. I., and S. Fischer. 1989. Looking through lexical form to sentence meaning: The effect of experience on sign language processing. *Memory and Cognition* 17: 740–54.
Mehler, J., J. Morton, and P. W. Jusczyk. 1984. On reducing language to biology. *Cognitive Neuropsychology* 1, 83–116.
Meisel, J. M., ed. 1992. *The acquisition of verb placement: Functional categories and V2 phenomena in language acquisition*. Dordrecht, Holland: Kluwer.

Mendikoetzea, A., and A. Battye. 1990. Arb *se/si* in transitive contexts: A comparative study. *Rivista di Grammatica Generativa* 15, 161–98.

Menyuk, P. 1977. *Language and maturation*. Cambridge, MA: MIT Press.

Mercier, A. 1992. *Linguistic competence, convention, and authority: Individualism and anti-individualism in linguistics and philosophy*. UCLA doctoral dissertation.

Miguel, E. de. 1986. Sulla regola di formazione degli aggettivi in *-ble* in spagnuolo. *Rivista di Grammatica Generativa* 11, 127–65.

Miller, G. A. 1967. *The psychology of communication*. New York: Basic Books. (Reprinted, with a new forword, in 1975.)

——— 1981. *Language and speech*. San Francisco: W. H. Freeman.

——— 1990. The place of language in a scientific psychology. *Psychological Science* 1:1, 7–14. Reprinted in Otero, ed., 1994, Vol. 4, 343–57.

———, ed. 1973. *Communication, language, and meaning: Psychological perspectives*. New York: Basic Books.

Miller, W., and S. Ervin. 1964. The development of grammar in child language. In Bellugi and Brown, eds., 9–34.

Mitchell, J. T., and M. L. Redmond. 1993. Rethinking grammar and communication. *Foreign Language Annals* 26, 13–19.

Miyagawa, S. 1993. Case, agr, and *ga-no* conversion in Japanese. *Proceedings of the Third Conference on Japanese/Korean Linguistics*. Stanford: CSLI.

Monleón, J., ed. (In press). *De la dictadura a la democracia*. Madrid: Akal.

Moorecroft, R., and R. Gardner. 1987. Linguistic factors in second language loss. *LL* 37, 327–40.

Morehead, D. M., and A. E. Morehead, eds. 1976. *Normal and deficient child language*. Baltimore, MD: University Park Press.

Moreno, J. 1985. Anticausatives: A typological sketch. In Eilfort et al., ed., 172–81.

Morley, J. 1991. The pronunciation component of teaching English to speakers of other languages. *TESOL Quarterly* 25, 481–520.

Muysken, P. 1983. Parametrizing the notion head. *The Journal of Linguistic Research* 2, 57–76.

——— 1984. The Spanish that Quechua speakers learn: L2 learning as norm-governed behavior. In Andersen, ed., 101–119.

——— and H. van Riemsdijk, eds. 1986. *Features and projections*. Dordrecht, Holland: Foris.

——— and N. Smith, eds. 1986. *Substrata versus universals in Creole languages*. Amsterdam/Philadelphia: John Benjamins.

Napoli, D. J. 1993. *Syntax: Theory and problems*. New York: Oxford University Press.

Nelson, B. E. 1988. *Good schools: The Seattle public school system, 1901–1930*. Seattle: University of Washington Press.

Nemser, W. J. 1971. Approximative systems of foreign language learners. *IRAL* 9, 115–23. Reprinted in Richards, ed., 1974, 55–63. (Spanish translation in Liceras, ed., 1992, 51–61.)

Neufeld, G. 1978. On the acquisition of prosodic and articulatory features in adult language acquisition. *The Canadian Modern Language Review* 34, 163–74. Reprinted in Ioup and Weinberger, eds., 1987, 321–32.

Neville, H. et al., 1991. Syntactically based sentence processing classes: Evidence from event-related brain potentials. *Journal of Cognitive Neuroscience* 3, 151–65.

Newmeyer, F. J. 1983. *Grammatical theory: Its limits and possibilities*. Chicago: University of Chicago Press.

———— 1987. The current convergence in linguistic theory: Some implications for second language acquisition research. *SLR* 3, 1–19.

————, ed. 1988. *Linguistics: The Cambridge survey*. 4 vols. New York: Cambridge University Press.

———— 1990. Competence vs. performance; theoretical vs. applied: The development and interplay of two dichotomies in modern linguistics. In Dinnen, ed.

———— and S. Weinberger. 1988. The ontogenesis of the field of second language learning research. In Flynn and O'Neil, eds., 34–45.

Newport, E. L. 1984. Constraints on learning: Studies in the acquisition of American Sign Language. *Papers and Reports on Second Language Development* 23, 1–22.

———— 1990. Maturational constraints on language learning. *Cognitive Science* 14, 11–28.

———— and T. Supalla. 1987. *Critical period effects in the acquisition of a primary language*. Manuscript, University of Rochester.

Nickel, G., ed. 1971. *Papers in contrasting linguistics*. New York: Cambridge University Press.

Nippold, M. A., ed. 1988. *Later language development: Ages nine through nineteen*. Boston: College-Hill Press.

Norrish, J. 1983. *Language learners and their errors*. London: Macmillan Press.

Nunan, D. 1989. Toward a collaborative approach to curriculum development: A case study. *TESOL Quarterly* 23, 9–26.

———— 1991a. Communicative tasks and the language curriculum. *TESOL Quarterly* 25, 279–98.

———— 1991b. Methods in second language classroom-oriented research: A critical review. *SSLA* 13, 249–74.

Obler, L. K. 1982. The parsimonious bilingual. In Obler and Menn, (eds.), 339–46.

———— 1988. Neurolinguistics and parameter setting. In Flynn and O'Neil, eds., 117–25.

———— 1989. Exceptional second language learners. In Gass et al., eds., 141–59.

———— and D. Fein, eds. 1988. *The exceptional brain: Neuropsychology of talent and special abilities*. New York: Gilford Press.

———— and L. Menn, eds. 1982. *Exceptional language and linguistics*. New York: Academic Press.

Odlin, T. 1989. *Language transfer: Cross-linguistic influence in language learning*. New York: Cambridge University Press.

———— 1992. Transferability and linguistic substrates. *SLR* 8, 171–202.

O'Donnell, W. R., and L. Todd. 1991. *Variety in contemporary English*. 2d ed. London: HarperCollins.

Oldfield, R. C., and J. C. Marshall, eds. 1968. *Language: Selected readings*. Harmondsworth: Penguin.

Oller, J. W., and J. C. Richards, eds. 1973. *Focus on the learner: Pragmatic perspectives for the language teacher*. Rowley, MA: Newbury House.

——— and P. A. Richard-Amato, eds. 1983. *Methods that work: A smorgasbord of ideas for language teachers.* Boston: Heinle and Heinle.

Olson, G. A., and L. Faigley. 1991. Language, politics, and composition: A conversation with Noam Chomsky. *Journal of Advanced Composition* 11, 1–35.

O'Malley, J. M. 1990. The cognitive basis of second language acquisition. In Alatis, ed., 478–95.

——— and A. U. Chamot. 1990. *Learning strategies in second language acquisition.* Cambridge: Cambridge University Press.

Omaggio, A. C. 1986. *Teaching language in context: Proficiency-oriented instruction.* Boston: Heinle and Heinle.

Oster, J. 1989. Seeing with different eyes: Another view of literature in the ESL class. *TESOL Quarterly* 23, 85–104.

Otero, C. P. 1972. *Letras I.* Barcelona: Seix Barral.

——— 1980a. Lenguaje e imaginación: La nueva novela en castellano. Paper read at the International Symposium on "La novela española, hoy," Indiana University, September 18–20, 1980. Published in part in *Quimera: Revista de Literatura* 2 (December 1980), 9–21.

——— 1980b. Typology and dialectology: A modular view. *Yearbook of Romanian Studies,* 22–33.

——— 1981a. [Contribution to the international round table on] The conception of human nature in Chomsky. *Quaderni di Semantica* 2, 241–47; 3, 263–73. Reprinted in Otero 1994, Vol. 3, 283–90, 294–307.

——— 1981b. Una métrica de nueva planta. *Verba* 8, 307–20.

——— 1982. Cernuda y los románticos ingleses. *Quimera: Revista de Literatura* 15 (Enero), 33–38. (Edited version in Johnson and Smith, eds. 1982, 125–40.)

——— 1983. Towards a model of paradigmatic grammar. *Quaderni di Semantica* 4, 134–44, 311–26.

——— 1984. *La revolución de Chomsky: Ciencia y sociedad.* Madrid: Tecnos.

——— 1986a. Arbitrary subjects in finite clauses. In Bordelois, Contreras, and Zagona, eds., 81–109.

——— 1986b. A unified metrical account of Spanish stress. In Brame, Contreras, and Newmeyer, eds., 299–332.

——— 1987a. Chomsky's view of semantics and Orwell's problem. In Sijs et al., eds., Vol. 2 (Theoretical and Applied Semantics), 357–71.

——— 1987b. Il nostro ritardo culturale e la sopravvivenza dell'umanità. In Magni and Vaccaro, eds., 75–101.

——— 1988a. Review article on Fred D'Agostino's *Chomsky's system of ideas* (1986). *Mind and Language* 3:3, 229–42, and, with correct pagination, in 3:4, 306–19. Reprinted in Otero, ed., 1994, Vol. 2, 472–85.

——— 1988b. The third emancipatory phase of history. Introduction to Chomsky 1989.

——— 1990a. The emergence of *homo loquens* and the laws of physics. *BBS* 13:4 (December 1990), 747–50. Reprinted, slightly adapted, in Otero, ed., 1994. Vol. 2, 707–19.

——— 1990b. La libertad de expresión como piedra de toque: Historia y cultura. Paper read at the "From dictatorship to democracy symposium" (UCLA, November 8–10, 1990). To appear in Monleón, ed.

———— 1991. The cognitive revolution and the study of language: Looking back to see ahead. In Campos and Martínez-Gil, ed., 3–69.

———— 1991a. Galegan and Romance word order. Manuscript, UCLA.

———— 1991b. Head movement, cliticization, precompilation, and word insertion. In Freidin, ed. (To appear).

———— 1992. From Lebrixa's grammar (1492) to Cartesian language theory. Keynote address, 22d Linguistic Symposium on Romance Languages, El Paso, Texas, 21 February 1992 (to appear in the proceedings, to be published by Benjamins).

———— Forthcoming. *Chomsky's revolution*. Oxford: Blackwell.

————, ed. 1994. *Noam Chomsky: Critical assessments*. 4 vols. London: Routledge.

Ouhalla, J. 1991. *Functional categories and parametric variation*. London and New York: Routledge.

———— Functional categories, agrammatism, and language acquisition. *Linguistische Berichte* 143, 3–36.

Oxford, R. L. 1990. *Language learning strategies: What every teacher should know*. Boston: Heinle and Heinle.

Oyama, S. C. 1976. A sensitive period for the acquisition of a nonnative phonological system. *Journal of Psycholinguistic Research* 5, 261–83.

———— 1978. The sensitive period and comprehension of speech. *Working Papers in Bilinguialism* 16, 1–17.

———— 1979. The concept of sensitive period in developmental studies. *Merrill-Palmer Quarterly* 25, 83–103.

Padden, C. A. 1983. *Interaction of morphology and syntax in American Sign Language*. University of California at San Diego doctoral dissertation. (Published in 1988 by Garland Press, New York, in the series "Outstanding Dissertations in Linguistics.")

———— 1988. Grammatical theory and signed languages. In Newmeyer, ed., Vol. 2, 250–66.

———— and T. Humphries. 1988. *Deaf in America: Voices from a culture*. Cambridge, MA: Harvard University Press.

Pankhurst, J., M. Sharwood Smith, and P. Van Buren, eds. 1988. *Learnability and second languages: A book of readings*. Dordrecht, Holland: Foris.

Parker, F. 1986. *Linguistics for nonlinguists*. Boston: Little, Brown and Co.

———— and K. Riley. 1993. *Linguistics for nonlinguists: A primer with exercises*. 2d ed. Needham Heights, MA: Allyn and Bacon.

Parodi-Lewin, C. 1991. *Aspect in the syntax of Spanish psych-verbs*. UCLA doctoral dissertation.

———— 1993. Agreement and the structure of DP: Adjectives. Manuscript, UCLA.

Parry, K. 1991. Building a vocabulary through academic reading. *TESOL Quarterly* 25, 629–54.

Patkowski, M. 1980a. *The sensitive period for the acquisition of syntax in a second language*. Doctoral dissertation, New York University.

———— 1980b. The sensitive period for the acquisition of syntax in a second language. *LL* 30, 449–72.

———— 1982. The sensitive period for the acquisition of syntax in a second language. In Krashen et al., 52–63.

———— 1990. Age and accent in a second language: A reply to James Emil Flege. *AL* 11, 73–89.

Patterson, F. (1979). The gestures of a gorilla: Sign language acquisition in another pongid species. *Brain and Language* 5, 72–97.

Pavesi, M. 1986. Markedness, discoursal modes, and relative clause formation in a formal and informal context. *SSLA* 8, 38–55.

Pearce, R. H. 1988. *Savagism and civilization: A study of the Indian and the American mind.* Berkeley, CA: University of California Press. (Reprint of the 1965 text.)

Penfield, W. 1953. A consideration of the neurophysiological mechanism of speech and some educational consequences. *Proceedings of the American Academy of Arts and Sciences* 82, 201–14.

——— 1964. The uncommitted cortex: The child's changing brain. *The Atlantic Monthly* 214:1, 77–91.

——— and L. Roberts. 1959. *Speech and brain mechanisms.* Princeton, NJ: Princeton University Press.

Pennycook, A. 1989. The concept of method, interested knowledge, and the politics of language teaching. *TESOL Quarterly* 23:4, 589–618.

Perdue, C., and W. Klein. 1992. Why does the production of some learners not grammaticalize? *SSLA* 14, 259–72.

Perdue, C. ed. 1984. *Second language acquisition by adult immigrants: A field manual.* Rowley, MA: Newbury House.

Perlmutter, D. M. 1988. The split morphology hypothesis: Evidence from Yiddish. In Hammond and Noonan, eds.

——— 1992. Sonority and syllable structure in American Sign Language. *LI* 23, 407–42.

Petitto, L. A., and M. S. Seidenberg. 1979. On the evidence for linguistic abilities in signing apes. *Brain and Language* 8, 162–83.

Pfaff, C., ed. 1987. *First and second language acquisition processes.* Cambridge, MA: Newbury House.

Phillipson, R. et al., eds. 1991. *Foreign/second language pedagogy research. A commemorative volume for Claus Faerch.* Clevedon/Philadelphia: Multilingual Matters LTD.

Phinney, M. 1987. The pro-drop parameter in second language acquisition. In Roeper and Williams, eds., 221–38. (Paper presented at University of Massachusetts at Amherst Conference on Parameter Setting in May 1985.)

Piattelli-Palmarini, M. 1986. The rise of selective theories: A case study and some lessons from immunology. In Demopoulos and Marras, eds.

——— 1988. Evolution, selection, and cognition: From "learning" to parameter setting in biology and in the study of language. Manuscript, Center for Cognitive Science, MIT, September (Edited version; cf. *Cognition* 31 (1989), 1–44. Reprinted in Otero, ed., 1994, Vol. 4, 98–144.)

Picallo, C. 1985. *Opaque domains.* CUNY doctoral dissertation.

——— 1990. Modal verbs in Catalan. *Natural Language and Linguistic Theory* 8, 285–312.

Pierce, A. E. 1992. *Language acquisition and linguistic theory: A comparative analysis of French and English child grammars.* Dordrecht, Holland: Kluwer.

Piera, C. 1980. *Spanish verse and the theory of meter.* UCLA doctoral dissertation.

——— 1983. On the representation of higher order complex words. In King and Maley, eds., 287–313.

—— 1989. Sobre la estructura de las cláusulas de infinitivo. In Demonte and Fernández Lagunilla, eds., 148–66.

Pinker, S. 1991. *Learnability and cognition.* Cambridge, MA: MIT Press.

—— and J. Mehler, eds. 1988. *Connections and symbols.* Cambridge, MA: MIT Press. (A *Cognition* special issue.)

Plann, S. 1979. The Spanish immersion program: Towards native-like proficiency or a classroom dialect. In Andersen, ed., 1979, 119–32.

Plann, S. 1980. *Relative clauses in Spanish without overt antecedents and related constructions.* Berkeley, CA: University of California Press.

—— 1981. The two *el*+infinitive constructions in Spanish. *LA* 7, 203–40.

—— 1982. Indirect questions in Spanish. *LI* 13, 297–312.

—— 1984a. To translate the English gerund into Spanish, don't use the infinitive. *Hispania* 67, 232–39.

—— 1984b. The syntax and semantics of *más/menos . . . que* versus *más/menos . . . de* in comparatives of inequality. *Hispanic Linguistics* 1, 191–213.

—— 1984c. Cláusulas cuantificadas. *Verba* 11, 101–28.

—— 1985. Questions in indirect discourse in Spanish. *Hispania* 68, 267–72.

—— 1986a. On case-marking in Spanish: Evidence against the case resistance principle. *LI* 17, 336–44.

—— 1986b. Substantive: A neutralized syntactic category in Spanish. In Bordelois et al., eds., 121–42.

—— 1988. Prepositions, postpositions, and substantives. *Hispania* 71, 920–26.

—— (In preparation). *A history of the deaf in Spain.* Manuscript, UCLA.

Platzack, C. 1993a. A triune lexicon: An approach to a lexical description within the minimalist program. In Herslund and Sorensen, eds., 305–18.

—— 1993b. Small *pro*, weak Agr, and syntactic differences in Scandinavian. Manuscript, University of Lund.

Pollock, J.-I. 1989. Verb movement, universal grammar, and the structure of IP. *LI* 20, 365–424.

Popkin, R. H. 1979. *The history of scepticism from Erasmus to Spinoza.* Berkeley, CA: University of California Press.

Posser, W., ed. *Papers from the Second International Workshop on Japanese Syntax.* Stanford: CSLI. (Distributed by the University of Chicago Press.)

Prator, C. H. 1969. Adding a second language. *TESOL Quarterly* 3, 95–104.

Premack, D. 1971. Language in chimpanzee? *Science* 172, 802–22.

—— 1976. *Intelligence in ape and man.* Hillsdale, NJ: Lawrence Erlbaum Associates.

—— 1986. *Gavagai! or the future history of the animal language controversy.* Cambridge, MA: MIT Press.

—— and A. J. Premack. 1983. *The mind of an ape.* New York: Norton.

—— and G. Woodruff. 1978. Does the chimpanzee have a theory of mind? *BBS* 1, 515–26.

Preston, D. R. 1989. *Sociolinguistics and second language acquisition.* Oxford: Basil Blackwell.

Progovac, L. 1993a. Subjunctive: The (mis)behavior of anaphora and negative polarity. *The Linguistic Review* 10, 37–59.

—— 1993b. Long-distance reflexives: Movement-to-infl versus relativized SUB-JECT. *LI* 24, 755–72.

Quicoli, C. 1989. Inflection and parametric variation: Portuguese vs. Spanish. In Freidin, ed. (To appear).

Quine, W. V. 1987. *Quiddities: An intermittently philosophical dictionary*. Cambridge, MA: Harvard University Press.

Radford, A. 1990. *Syntactic theory and the acquisition of English syntax: The nature of early child grammars in English*. Oxford: Basil Blackwell.

Raposo, E., and J. Uriagereka. 1990. Long-distance case assignment. *LI* 21, 505–37.

Ravin, Y. 1992. Review of Jackendoff 1990. *Lg.* 68, 399–402.

Reibel, D. A., and S. A. Schane, eds. 1969. *Modern studies in English: Readings in transformational grammar*. Englewood Cliffs, NJ: Prentice-Hall.

Reinhart, T., and E. Reuland, 1993. Reflexivity. *LI* 24, 657–720.

Renfrew, C. 1994. World linguistic diversity. *SA*, January, 116–23.

Renzi, L., ed. 1988. *Grande grammatica italiana di consultazione*, a cura di Lorenzo Renzi. Vol. 1 Bologna: Il Mulino.

Resnick, L. B., and P. A. Weaver, eds. 1979. *Theory and practice of early reading*. Hillsdale, NJ: Lawrence Erlbaum Associates.

Restak, R. M. 1988. *The mind*. Toronto: Bantam Books.

Rice, M. L. and S. Kemper. 1984. *Child language and cognition*. Baltimore: University Park Press.

Richard-Amato, P. A. 1988. *Making it happen: Interaction in the second language classroom*. New York and London: Longman.

Richards, J. C. 1971. A noncontrastive approach to error analysis. *English Language Teacher* 25. Reprinted in Richards, ed., 1974, 172–88.

———— 1990. *The language teaching matrix*. New York: Cambridge University Press.

————, ed. 1974. *Error analysis: Perspectives in second language acquisition*. London: Longman.

————, ed. 1978. *Understanding second and foreign language learning: Issues and approaches*. Rowley, MA: Newbury House.

———— and D. Nunan, eds. 1990. *Second language teacher education*. New York: Cambridge University Press.

————, and T. S. Rodgers. 1986. *Approaches and methods in language teaching: A description and analysis*. Cambridge: Cambridge University Press.

Richards, W., and S. Ullman, eds. 1987. *Image understanding, 1985–1986*. Norwood, NJ: Ablex.

Rieger, E. 1953. *Modern Hebrew*. New York: Philosophical Library.

Ringbom, H. 1987. *The role of the first language in foreign language learning*. Clevedon/Philadelphia: Multilingual Matters LTD.

Ristau, C. A., and D. Robbins. 1982. Language in the great apes: A critical review. In Rosenblatt, ed., 142–255.

Ritchie, W. C. 1967. Some implications of generative grammar for the construction of courses in English as a foreign language. *LL* 17, 11–131.

———— 1968. On the explanation of phonetic interference. *LL* 18, 183–97.

———— 1978. The right roof constraint in an adult-acquired language. In Ritchie, ed., 1978, 33–63.

———— 1991. Linguistic theory: Contribution to second language acquisition. *SSLA* 13, 77–85.

——, ed. 1978. *Second language research: Issues and implications*. New York: Academic Press.

Ritter, E. 1993. Where's gender? *LI* 24, 795–803.

Rivero, M.-L. 1986. Parameters in the typology of clitics in Romance and Old Spanish. *Lg.* 62, 774–807.

—— 1991. Clitic and NP climbing in Old Spanish. In Campos and Martínez-Gil, eds., 241–82.

Rivers, W. M. 1964. *The psychologist and the foreign language teacher*. Chicago, IL: University of Chicago Press.

—— 1968. *Teaching foreign language skills*. Chicago, IL: University of Chicago Press.

—— 1990. Mental representations and language in action. In Alatis, ed., 49–64. (Also, Mental representations and language in action, *The Canadian Modern Language Review/La Revue canadienne des langues vivantes* 47 (1991), 249–65.)

—— 1992. *Teaching languages in college: Curriculum and content*. Lincolnwood, IL: National Textbook Co.

——, ed. 1987. *Interactive language teaching*. London: Cambridge University Press.

Rizzi, L. 1982. *Issues in Italian Syntax*. Dordrecht, Holland: Foris.

—— 1989. Une théorie de la syntaxe comparative. Preface to Roberge and Vinet, 8–10.

Roberge, Y., and M.-T. Vinet. 1989. *La variation dialectale en grammaire universelle*. Montréal: Les Presses de l'Université de Montréal/Sherbrooke: Les Éditions de l'Université de Sherbrooke.

Roberts, P. 1964. *English syntax: A programmed introduction to transformational grammar*. Alternate edition. New York: Harcourt, Brace and World.

Roca, I. M. 1979. Language acquisition and the Chomskyan revolution. *Studia Anglica Posnaniensia* 10, 141–209.

—— 1990. Morphology and verbal stress in Spanish. *Probus* 2, 321–50.

——, ed. 1990. *Logical issues in language acquisition*. Dordrecht, Holland: Foris.

Rochemont, M.S., and P. Culicover. 1990. *English focus constructions and the theory of grammar*. New York: Cambridge University Press.

Roeper, T., and E. Williams, eds. 1987. *Parameter setting*. Dordrecht, Holland: Reidel.

Rogers, D. R., and J. A. Sloboda, eds. 1985. *Acquisition of symbolic skills*. New York: Plenum.

Rohrer, C. and N. Ruwet, eds. 1974. *Actes du Colloque Franco-Allemand de Grammaire Transformationelle*. Band 2: Etudes de Sémantique et Autres. Tübingen: Max Niemeyer Verlag.

Ronat, M., ed. 1977. *Langue: Théorie générative étendue*. Paris: Hermann.

—— and D. Couquaux, eds. 1986. *La grammaire modulaire*. Paris: Les Editions de Minuit.

Ronjat, J. 1913. *Le developpement du langage observé chez en enfant bilingue*. Paris: Champion.

Rosenbaum, P. S. 1965. On the role of linguistics in the teaching of English. *HER* 35, 332–48. Reprinted in Otero, ed., 1994, Vol. 4, 603–19.

Rosenberg, S. 1993. Chomsky's theory of language: Some recent observations. *Psychological Science* 4, 15–19.

Rosenblatt, J. S., ed. 1982. *Advances in the study of behavior*, Vol. 12. New York: Academic Press.

Roslansky, J. D., ed. 1969. *Communication*. Amsterdam/London: North-Holland.

Rothstein, S., ed. 1992. *Perspectives on phrase structure: Heads and licensing*. San Diego: Academic Press. (=*Syntax and Semantics* 25.)

Rothweiler, M., ed. 1990. *Spracherwerb und Grammatik*. Opladen, Germany: Westdeutscher Verlag.

Rubin, J., and I. Thompson. 1982. *How to be a more successful language learner*. Boston: Heinle and Heinle.

Rubin, J. M., and W. A. Richards. 1987. Spectral categorization of materials. In Richards and Ullman, eds., 20–44.

Rumbaugh, D., and S. S. Rumbaugh. 1977. *Language learning by a chimpanzee: The Lana project*. New York: Academic Press.

Rutherford, W., ed. 1984. *Language universals and second language acquisition*. Amsterdam: Benjamins.

———— 1987. *Second language grammar: Learning and teaching*. London: Longman.

———— 1988. Grammatical theory and L2 acquisition: A brief overview. In Flynn and O'Neil, eds., 404–16.

———— 1989. Preemption and the learning of L2 grammars. *SSLA* 11, 441–57.

———— and M. Sharwood Smith, eds. 1988. *Grammar and second language teaching: A book of readings*. New York: Newbury House.

Rymer, R. 1993. *Genie*. New York: HarperCollins.

Sacks, N. 1992. In memoriam: Dwight Bolinger [1907–1992]. *Hispanic Review* 5, 485–93.

Sacks, O. 1985. *The man that mistook his wife for a hat*. New York: Summit Books.

Salkie, R. 1990. *The Chomsky update: Linguistics and politics*. London: Unwin Hyman.

Saltarelli, M. 1992. The subject of psych-verbs and case theory. In Hirschbuhler and Koerner, eds., 251–68.

Salzinger, K. and F. Denmark, eds. 1978. *Psychology: The state of the art*. Annals of the New York Academy of Sciences 309.

Saporta, S. 1966. Applied linguistic and generative grammar. In Valdman (ed.), 81–92.

————, ed. *Psycholinguistics*. New York: Holt, Rinehart and Winston.

Savard, J.-G., and L. Laforge, eds. 1981. *Actes du 5e. Congrès de l'association internationale de linguistique appliquée*. Québec: Les Presses de l'Université Laval.

Savignon, S. J. 1991. Communicative language teaching: State of the art. *TESOL Quarterly* 25, 261–78.

Scarcella, R. C., and S. D. Krashen, eds. 1980. *Research in second language acquisition*. Rowley, MA: Newbury House.

Schachter, J. 1974. An error in error analysis. *LL* 24, 205–14. (Spanish translation in Liceras, ed., 1992, 196–205.)

———— 1988. Second language acquisition and its relationship to UG. *AL* 9, 219–35.

———— 1991. Corrective feedback in historical perspective. *SLR* 7:2, 89–102.

———— and M. Celce-Murcia. 1977. Some reservations concerning error analysis. *TESOL Quarterly* 11, 441–51.

————, A. Tyson, and F. Diffley. 1976. Learner intuitions of grammaticality. *LL* 30, 67–76.

———— and V. Yip. 1990. Grammaticality judgments: Why does anyone object to subject extraction? *SSLA* 12, 379–92.

Schmidt, R. 1990. The role of consciousness in second language learning. *AL* 11, 129–58.

Schneiderman, E. I., and C. Desmarais. 1988. The talented language learner: Some preliminary findings. *SLR* 4:2, 91–109.

Schreuder, R., and B. Weltens, eds. 1993. *The bilingual lexicon.* Philadelphia: John Benjamins.

Schumann, J. 1976. Second language acquisition: The pidginization hypothesis. *LL* 26, 391–408. Reprinted in Hatch, ed., 1977, 256–71. (Spanish translation in Liceras, ed., 1992, 123–41.)

———— 1990. Extending the scope of the acculturation/pidginization model to include cognition. *TESOL Quarterly* 24, 667–84.

———— and N. Stenson, eds. 1974. *New frontiers in second language acquisition.* Rowley, MA: Newbury House.

Schwartz, B. D. 1986. The epistemological status of second language acquisition. *SLR* 2:2, 120–59.

———— 1987. *The modular basis of second language acquisition.* University of Southern California doctoral dissertation.

———— 1988. A reply to Gregg: In defence of theory building. *SLR* 4, 157–73.

———— 1991. Conceptual and empirical evidence: A response to Meisel. In Eubank, ed., 277–304.

———— and M. Gubala-Ryzak. 1992. Learnability and grammar reorganization in L2: Against negative evidence causing the unlearning of verb movement. *SLR* 8:1, 1–38.

———— and A. Tomaselli. 1989. Analyzing the acquisition stages of negation in L2 German: Support for UG in adult SLA. *SLR* 6, 1–38.

Scott, V. M. 1989. An empirical study of explicit and implicit teaching strategies in French. *MLJ* 73:1, 14–22.

———— 1990. Explicit and implicit grammar teaching strategies: New empirical data. *The French Review* 63:5, 779–89.

Scovel, T. 1969. Foreign accents, language acquisition, and cerebral dominance. *LL* 19, 245–53.

———— 1981. The recognition of foreign accents in English and its implications for psycholinguistic theories of language acquisition. In Savard and Laforge, eds., 389–401.

———— 1988. *A time to speak: A psycholinguistic inquiry into the critical period for human speech.* Cambridge, MA: Newbury House.

———— 1988a. Multiple perspectives make singular teaching. In Beebe, ed., 169–90.

Seelye, H. N. 1974. *Teaching culture: Strategies for foreign language educators*. Skokie, IL: National Textbook Co.

Seidenberg, M., and L. Petitto. 1979. Signing behavior in apes: A critical review. *Cognition* 7, 177–215.

––––––– and L. Petitto. 1981. Ape signing: Problems of method and interpretation. *Annals of the New York Academy of Sciences* 364, 115–19.

Seliger, H. W. 1978. Implications of a multiple critical periods hypothesis for second language learning. In Ritchie, ed., 11–19.

––––––– 1982. On the possible role of the right hemisphere in second language acquisition. *TESOL Quarterly* 16, 307–14.

–––––––, S. Krashen, and P. Ladefoged. 1975. Maturational constraints in the acquisition of a native-like accent in second language learning. *Language Sciences* 36, 20–22.

––––––– and E. Shohamy. 1989. *Second language research methods*. New York: Oxford University Press.

––––––– and M. H. Long, eds. 1983. *Classroom-oriented research in second language acquisition*. Rowley, MA: Newbury House.

Selinker, L. 1969. Language transfer. *General Linguistics* 9, 67–92.

––––––– 1972. Interlanguage. *IRAL* 10, 209–31. Reprinted in Richards, ed., 1974, 31–54, and in Schumann and Stenson, eds., 1974. (Spanish translation in Liceras, ed., 1992, 79–101.)

––––––– 1992. *Rediscovering interlanguage*. London: Longman.

––––––– and J. Lamendella. 1978. Two perspectives on fossilization in interlanguage. *Interlanguage Studies Bulletin* 3, 143–91.

Sells, P., S. M. Shieber, and T. Wasow, eds. 1991. *Foundational issues in natural language processing*. Cambridge, MA: MIT Press.

Shaffer, C. 1989. A comparison of inductive and deductive approaches to teaching foreign languages. *MLJ* 73, 395–403.

Sharwood Smith, M. 1990. Second language learnability. In Roca, ed., 259–76.

––––––– 1991. Speaking to many minds: On the relevance of different types of language information for the L2 learner. *SLR* 7, 118–32.

Shulman, L. S. 1987. Knowledge and teaching: Foundations of a new reform. *HER* 57, 1–22.

Siegel, L. S., and C. J. Brainerd. eds. 1978. *Alternatives to Piaget: Critical essays on the theory*. New York: Academic Press.

Sigurjónsdóttir, S. 1992. *Binding in Icelandic: Evidence from language acquisition*. UCLA doctoral dissertation.

––––––– and N. Hyams. 1992. Reflexivization and logophoricity: Evidence from the acquisition of Icelandic. *LAJDL* 2, 359–413.

Sijs, N. van der et al., eds. 1987. *Aspects of language: Studies in honour of Mario Alinei*. Amsterdam: Rodopi.

Singh, R. 1991. Interference and contemporary phonological theory. *LL* 41, 157–75.

Singleton, D. 1987. The fall and rise of language transfer. In Coleman and Towell, eds.

––––––– 1989. *Language acquisition: The age factor*. Clevedon/Philadelphia: Multilingual Matters LTD.

———— and D. Little. 1991. The second language lexicon: Some evidence from university-level learners of French and German. *SLR* 7:1, 61–81.

Siple, P., and S. Fischer, eds. 1991. *Theoretical issues in sign language research: Psychology*. Chicago: University of Chicago Press.

Skehan, P. 1991. Individual differences in second language learning. *SSLA* 13, 275–98.

Slobin, D. I., ed. 1985. *The crosslinguistic study of language acquisition*. Hillsdale, NJ: Lawrence Erlbaum Associates.

Smith, F., and G. Miller, eds. 1966. *The genesis of language: A psycholinguistic approach*. Cambridge, MA: MIT Press.

Smith, N. 1989. *The twitter machine: Reflections on language*. Oxford: Blackwell.

———— and I. M. Tsimpli. 1991. Linguistic modularity? A case study of a "savant" linguist. *Lingua* 84, 315–51.

Smith, P., Jr. 1970. *A comparison of the cognitive and audiolingual approaches to foreign language instruction: The Pennsylvania Foreign Language Project*. Philadelphia: Center for Curriculum Development.

Smolla, R. A. 1992. *Free speech in an open society*. New York: Alfred A. Knopf.

Sorace, A. 1993a. Incomplete vs. divergent representations of unaccusativity in nonnative grammars of Italian. *SLR* 9, 22–47.

———— 1993b. Unaccusativity and auxiliary choice in nonnative grammars of Italian and French: Asymmetries and predictable indeterminacy. *FLS* 3, 71–93.

Speas, M. J. 1990. *Phrase structures in natural language*. Dordrecht, Holland: Kluwer Academic.

Sperber, D., and D. Wilson. 1986. *Relevance: Communication and cognition*. Oxford: Blackwell. (Reprinted in 1988 by Harvard University Press.)

Sperry, R. W. 1951. Mechanisms of neural maturation. In Stevens, ed., 236–79.

Spolsky, B. 1966. A psycholinguistic critique of programmed foreign language instruction. *IRAL* 4, 119–29.

———— 1977. The comparative study of first and second language acquisition. In Eckman and Hastings, eds., 167–84.

———— 1985. Formulating a theory of second language learning. *SSLA* 7, 269–88.

———— 1989. *Conditions for second language learning*. Oxford: Oxford University Press.

———— 1990. Introduction to a colloquium: The scope and form of a theory of second language learning. *TESOL Quarterly* 24, 609–16.

Sportiche, D. 1988. A theory of floating quantifiers and its corollaries for constituent structure. *LI* 19, 425–49.

———— 1992. Clitic constructions. Manuscript, UCLA.

———— 1993a. Subject clitics in French and Romance: Complex inversion and clitic doubling. Manuscript, UCLA.

———— 1993b. Adjuncts and adjunction. Manuscript, UCLA.

Springer, S. P., and G. Deutsch. 1989. *Left brain, right brain*. 3rd ed. New York: W. H. Freeman and Co.

Starkey, P., E. S. Spelke, and R. Gelman. 1990. Numerical abstraction by human infants. *Cognition* 36, 97–127.

Steele, C. 1985. *Narrativa indigenista en los Estados Unidos y México*. México: Instituto Nacional Indigenista.

Stern, H. H. 1983. *Fundamental concepts of language teaching*. New York: Oxford University Press.

Stevens, S. S., ed. 1951. *Handbook of experimental psychology*. New York: John Wiley and Sons.

Stockwell, R. P. 1993. Obituary: Dwight L. Bolinger [1907–1992]. *Lg.* 69, 99–112.

―――― and J. D. Bowen. 1965. *The sounds of English and Spanish*. Chicago: University of Chicago Press.

――――, J. D. Bowen, and J. W. Martin. 1965. *The grammatical structures of English and Spanish*. Chicago: University of Chicago Press.

Stowell, T. 1983. Subjects across categories. *TLR* 2, 285–312.

―――― 1992. The alignment of arguments in adjective phrases. In Rothstein, ed., 105–34.

―――― and E. Wehrli, eds. 1992. *Syntax and the lexicon*. San Diego, CA: Academic Press. (=*Syntax and Semantics* 26)

Strozer, J. 1976. *Clitics in Spanish*. UCLA doctoral dissertation.

―――― 1978. On the so-called dative of interest. *Hispania* 61, 117–23.

―――― 1987. Nonnative language learning from a principles-and-parameters perspective. Manuscript, University of Washington.

―――― 1989. *Ser/estar* and individual-level/stage-level predicates. Paper presented at the South Central MLA, Linguistics Session, New Orleans, 26–28 October 1989.

―――― 1991. Nonnative language acquisition from a principles and parameters perspective. In Campos and Martínez-Gil, eds., 71–113. Reprinted in Otero, ed., 1994, Vol. 4, 680–721.

Studdert-Kennedy, M. 1983. *Psychobiology of language*. Cambridge, MA: MIT Press.

Swaffar, J. K., K. M. Arens, and H. Byrnes. 1991. *Reading for meaning: An integrated approach to language learning*. Englewood Cliffs, NJ: Prentice-Hall.

Swain, M. 1985. Communicative competence: Some roles of comprehensible input and comprehensible output in its development. In Gass and Madden, eds., 235–253.

Suñer, M. 1982. *Syntax and semantics of presentational sentence-types*. Washington, DC: Georgetown University Press.

―――― 1988. The role of agreement in clitic-doubled constructions. *Natural Language and Linguistic Theory* 6, 391–434.

―――― 1990. Impersonal *se* passives and the licensing of empty categories. *Probus* 2:2, 209–31.

―――― 1992. V-movement and the licensing of argumental wh-phrases in Spanish. Manuscript, Cornell University.

―――― 1993. About indirect questions and semi-questions. *Linguistics and Philosophy* 16, 45–77.

Tahta, S., M. Wood, and K. Loewenthal. 1981a. Foreign accents: Factors relating to transfer of accent from the first language to a second language. *L&S* 24, 265–72.

―――― 1981b. Age changes in the ability to replicate foreign pronunciation and intonation. *L&S* 24, 363–72.

Talmy, L. 1975. Semantics and syntax of motion. *Syntax and Semantics* 4, 181–238.

———— 1985. Force dynamics in language and thought. In Eilfort et al., ed., 293–337.

Tarone, E. 1983. On the variability of interlanguage systems. *AL* 4, 142–64. (Spanish translation in Liceras, ed., 1992, 264–92.)

Taylor, D. 1988. The meaning and use of the term "competence" in linguistics and applied linguistics. *AL* 9, 148–68.

Terrace, H. 1979. *Nim: A chimpanzee who learned sign language*. New York: Alfred A. Knopf.

Terrell, T. D. 1991. The role of grammar instruction in a communicative approach. *MLJ* 75, 52–63.

Teschner, R. V. 1988. *Spanish orthography, morphology, and syntax for bilingual educators*. Revised ed. Lanham, MD: University Press of America.

Thomas, M. 1989. The interpretation of English reflexive pronouns by nonnative speakers. *SSLA* 11, 281–303.

———— 1991. *Universal grammar and knowledge of reflexives in a second language*. Harvard University doctoral dissertation. (See Thomas 1993.)

———— 1991a. Universal grammar and the interpretation of reflexives in a second language. *Lg.* 67, 211–39.

———— 1993. *Knowledge of reflexives in a second language*. Philadelphia: John Benjamins.

Thompson, I. 1991. Foreign accents revisited: The English pronunciation of Russian immigrants. *LL* 41, 177–204.

Tollefson, J. W., and J. T. Firn, 1983. Fossilization in second language acquisition: An intermodel view. *RELC Journal* 14, 19–34.

Toolan, M. J. 1988. *Narrative: A critical linguistic introduction*. London and New York: Routledge.

Torrego, E. 1989. Experiencers and raising verbs in Spanish. Paper presented at the Second Princeton Workshop on Comparative Grammar, 27–29 April. (Revised version in Freidin, ed., to appear.)

Tropf, H. 1987. Sonority as a variability factor in second language phonology. In James and Leather, eds., 173–91.

Turkewitz, G., and P. Kenny. 1982. Limitations on input as a basis for neural organization and perceptual development: A preliminary theoretical statement. *Development Psychobiology* 15, 357–68.

Uziel, S. 1993. Resetting universal grammar parameters: Evidence from second language acquisition of subjacency and the empty category principle. *SLR* 9, 49–83.

Valdman, A., ed. 1966. *Trends in language teaching*. New York: McGraw-Hill.

Valian, V. 1990. Null subjects: A problem for parameter-setting models of language acquisition. *Cognition* 35, 105–22.

———— 1991. Syntactic subjects in the early speech of American and Italian children. *Cognition* 40, 21–81.

Valois, D. 1991. *The internal syntax of DP*. UCLA doctoral dissertation.

Van Naerssen, M. 1980. How similar are Spanish as a first language and Spanish as a second language? In Scarcella and Krashen eds., 146–54.

VanPatten, B., T. R. Dvorak, and J. F. Lee, eds. 1987. *Foreign language learning: A research perspective*. Cambridge, MA: Newbury House.

——— 1992. Second-language-acquisition research and foreign language teaching. *ADFL Bulletin* 23:2, 52–56; 23:3, 23–27.

——— and J. F. Lee, eds. 1990. *Second language acquisition/foreign language learning*. Clevelon, England: Multilingual Matters.

Varela Ortega, S. 1990. *Fundamentos de morfología*. Madrid: Editorial Síntesis.

Vázquez-Ayora, G. 1977. *Introducción a la traductología: Curso básico de traducción*. Washington, DC: Georgetown University Press.

Velletri-Glass, A., M. Gazzaniga, and D. Premack. 1973. Artificial language training in global aphasics. *Neuropsychologia* 11, 95–104.

Vergnaud, J.-R. 1985. *Dépendences et niveaux de représentation on syntaxe*. Amsterdam: John Benjamins.

——— and M. L. Zubizarreta. 1992. The definite determiner and inalienable constructions in French and English. *LI* 23, 595–652.

Verhoeven, L. T. 1991. Predicting minority children's bilingual proficiency: Child, family, and institutional factors. *LL* 41, 205–33.

Villalba, X. 1992. Case, incorporation, and economy: An approach to causative constructions. In Branchadell et al., eds., 345–89.

Wade, B., ed., 1982. *Language perspectives*. London: Heinemann Educational Books Ltd.

Walker, E. ed. 1979. *Explorations in the biology of language*. Cambridge, MA: MIT Press.

Wallace, M. J. 1991. *Training foreign language teachers: A reflective approach*. New York: Cambridge University Press.

Walls, G. 1942. *The vertebrate eye and its adaptive radiation*. New York: Hafner Publishing Co.

Walsh, T. M., and K. C. Diller. 1981. Neurolinguistic considerations on the optimal age for second language learning. In Diller, ed., 3–21.

Waltz, J. C., ed. 1992. *Development and supervision of teaching assistants in foreign languages*. Boston, MA: Heinle and Heinle.

Wanner, E., and L. R. Gleitman, eds. 1982. *Language acquisition: The state of the art*. New York: Cambridge University Press.

Wardhaugh, R. 1970. The contrastive analysis hypothesis. *TESOL Quarterly* 4, 123–30. (Spanish translation in Liceras, ed., 1992, 41–49.)

——— 1971. Teaching English to speakers of other languages: The state of the art. In Lugton and Heinle, eds.

——— 1974. *Topics in applied linguistics*. Rowley, MA: Newbury House.

Watanabe, A. 1993. Unlearnable parameter setting. *GLOW Newsletter* 30, 82–83.

Webelhuth, G. 1992. *Principles and parameters of syntactic saturation*. New York: Oxford University Press.

Wheatley, B. et al., eds. 1985. *Current approaches to second language acquisition: Proceedings of the 1984 University of Wisconsin-Milwaukee linguistics symposium*. Bloomington, IN: Indiana University Linguistics Club.

Weerman, F. 1993. Reconsidering the role of parameter setting in language change. *GLOW Newsletter* 30, 84–85.

Weinberger, S. H. 1988. *Theoretical foundations of second language phonology.* University of Washington doctoral dissertation.

Weissenborn, J. 1990. Functional categories and verb movement: The acquisition of German syntax reconsidered. In Rothweiler, ed., 190–224.

———, H. Goodluck, and T. Roeper, eds. 1992. *Theoretical issues in language acquisition: Continuity and change in development.* Hillsdale, NJ: Lawrence Erlbaum Associates.

Weist, R. M., et al., 1984. The defective tense hypothesis: On the emergence of tense and aspect in child Polish. *Journal of Child Language* 11, 347–74.

Westphal, G. F. 1989. The critical age, individual differences, and grammar rules in adult language acquisition. *The Canadian Modern Language Review/La Revue canadienne des langues vivantes* 46:1, 83–102.

Wilkins, D. 1974. *Second-language learning and teaching.* London: Edward Arnold.

William, E. 1980. Predication. *LI* 11, 208–38.

——— 1981. Argument structure and morphology. *The Linguistic Review* 1, 81–114.

Whitaker, H. A. 1978. Bilingualism: A neurolinguistic perspective. In Ritchie, ed., 21–32.

———, D. Bub, and S. Leventer. 1981. Neurolinguistic aspects of language acquisition and bilingualism. In Winitz, ed., 59–74.

White, L. 1982. *Grammatical theory and language acquisition.* Dordrecht, Holland: Foris.

——— 1985a. The acquisition of parameterized grammars: Subjacency in second language acquisition. *SLR* 1, 1–17.

——— 1985b. Is there a logical problem of second language acquisition? *TESL Canada* 2:2, 29–41.

——— 1985c. The pro-drop parameter in adult second language acquisition. *LL* 35, 47–72.

——— 1985d. Universal grammar as a source of explanation in second language acquisition. In Wheatley et al., eds.

——— 1986a. Implications of parametric variation for adult second language acquisition: An investigation of the "pro-drop" parameter. In Cook, ed.

——— 1986b. Markedness and parameter setting: Some implications for a theory of adult language acquisition. In Eckman et al. (Paper presented in 1983.)

——— 1987a. A note on parameters and second language acquisition. In Roeper and Williams, eds., 239–46. (Paper presented at University of Massachusetts at Amherst Conference on Parameter Setting in May 1985.)

——— 1987b. Markedness and second language acquisition: The question of transfer. *SSLA* 9:3, 261–86.

——— 1987c. Against comprehensible input: the input hypothesis and the development of L2 competence. *AL* 8, 95–110.

——— 1988a. Island effects in second language acquisition. In Flynn and O'Neil, eds., 144–72.

——— 1988b. Universal grammar and language transfer. In Pankhurst et al., 36–60.

—————— 1989. *Universal grammar and second language acquisition.* Amsterdam/ Philadelphia: John Benjamins.

—————— 1990a. Another look at the logical problem of foreign language learning: A reply to Bley-Vroman. *LA* 20, 50–63.

—————— 1990b. Second language acquisition and universal grammar. *SSLA* 12, 121– 33.

—————— 1991a. The verb-movement parameter in second language acquisition. *LAJDL* 1:4, 337–60.

—————— 1991b. Adverb placement in second language acquisition: Some effects of positive and negative evidence in the classroom. *SLR* 7:2, 133–61.

—————— 1991c. Argument structure in second language acquisition. *FLS* 1, 189–207.

—————— 1991d. Second language competence versus language performance: UG or processing strategies? In Eubank, ed.

—————— 1992. On triggering data in L2 acquisition: A reply to Schwartz and Gubala-Ryzak. *SLR* 8, 120–37.

—————— Spada, N., P. M. Lightbown, and L. Ranta. 1991. Input enhancement and L2 question formation. *AL* 12, 417–32.

Whitley, M. S. 1986. *Spanish/English contrasts: A course in Spanish linguistics.* Washington, DC: Georgetown University Press.

Wilkins, D. A. 1972. *Linguistics in language teaching.* Cambridge, MA: MIT Press.

Winitz, H., ed. 1981. *Native language and foreign language acquisition.* New York: The New York Academy of Sciences.

Winston, P., and S. A. Shellard, eds. 1990. *Artificial intelligence at MIT: Expanding frontiers.* Cambridge, MA: MIT Press.

Wiesel, T. N., and D. H. Hubel. 1963. Single cell responses in striate cortex of kittens deprived of vision in one eye. *Journal of Neurophysiology* 26, 1003–17.

Wode, H. 1989. Maturational changes of language acquisitional abilities. In Gass et al., eds., 176–86.

—————— et al., 1978. Developmental sequence: An alternative approach to morpheme order. *LL* 28, 175–85.

Wood, D. 1988. *How children think and learn.* Oxford: Basil Blackwell.

—————— 1989. *Universal grammar and second language acquisition.* Amsterdam/ Philadelphia: John Benjamins.

Wu, A. 1993a. The S-parameter. *GLOW Newsletter* 30, 60–61. (Abstract.)

—————— 1993b. The spell-out of movement and features. Manuscript, UCLA.

—————— 1994. The spell-out parameters: A minimalist approach to syntax. UCLA doctoral dissertation.

Yalden, J. 1987. *Principles of course design for language teaching.* New York: Cambridge University Press.

Yamada, J. 1981. *Evidence for the independence of language from cognition: A case study of a mentally retarded adolescent.* UCLA doctoral dissertation.

—————— 1988. The independence of language: Evidence from a hyperlinguistic retarded individual. In Hyman and Li, eds., 175–206. Reprinted in Otero, ed., 1994, Vol. 4, 256–87.

—————— 1990. *Laura: A case study for the modularity of language.* Cambridge, MA: MIT Press.

Yoshitomi, A. 1992. Towards a model of language attrition: Neurobiological and psychological contributions. *Issues in Applied Linguistics* 3, 293–318.

Young-Scholten, M. 1991. *Acquisition at the interface: The L2 acquisition of pronominal cliticization in German*. University of Washington doctoral dissertation.

Zagona, K. 1986. Las perífrasis de gerundio y la restructuración. *Revista Argentina de Lingüística* 2, 232–44.

——— 1988. *Verb phrase syntax: A parametric study of Spanish and English*. Dordrecht, Holland: Kluwer.

——— 1990. *mente* adverbs, compound interpretation, and the projection principle. *Probus* 2, 1–30.

——— 1991. Perfective *haber* and the theory of tenses. In Campos and Martínez-Gil, eds., 379–403.

——— 1993. Spanish adjectival secondary predicates, time adverbs, and subevent structure. *Cuadernos de Lingüística* 1, 317–54.

Zeki, S. 1992. The visual image in mind and brain. *SA*, September, 68–76.

Zobl, H. 1983a. Contact-induced language change, learner language, and the potentials of a modified contrastive analysis. In Bailey et al., 104–114.

——— 1983b. Markedness and the projection problem. *LL* 33, 293–313.

——— 1989. Modularity in adult L2 acquisition. *LL* 39:1, 49–79.

——— 1992. Sources of linguistic knowledge and uniformity of nonnative performance. *SSLA* 14, 387–402.

Zribi-Hertz, A. 1989. Anaphor binding and narrative point of view: English reflexive pronouns in sentence and discourse. *Lg.* 65, 695–727.

Zubizarreta, M. L. 1986. Le statut morpho-syntaxique des verbes causatifs dans les langues romanes. In Ronat and Couquaux, eds., 279–311.

——— 1987. *Levels of representation in the lexicon and in the syntax*. Dordrecht, Holland: Foris.

Zwart, J.-W. 1992a. Verb movement and complementizer agreement. *GLOW Newsletter* 28, 58–59.

——— 1992b. SOV languages are head-initial. Manuscript, University of Groningen.

——— 1993. *Dutch syntax: A minimalist approach*. University of Groningen doctoral dissertation.

Index

A, A′, AP (*see* adjective)
Aaron, 80
ability, 34, 35, 56, 57, 82f., 147, 148, 160, 172, 176, 200
  vs. possibility, 148
  to use language, 11, 57
absolutive, 121f.
acceptability, 105, 189 (*see* also grammaticality)
accent
  foreign accent, 12
  accent-free speech, 160
accusative, 121f.
acquisition, ix, xii, 1, 15, 45, 82, 86, 89, 97, 106, 119, 124, 133f., 169, 171, 172, 173, 178, 184f., 193, 203, 204, 205, 206, 209, 210, 211 (*see* also learning)
  of morphology, 160
  age in language acquisition, 164
  language acquisition device (LAD), 89–90, 135, 137, 157, 158, 160, 169, 172, 178
  language acquisition after puberty (LAP), 215
  logical problem of knowledge acquisition, 86f.
  logical problem of language acquisition, x, xi, 186
  adult language acquisition, 137, 139, 166, 169, 170
  native language acquisition, 15, 165
  nonnative language acquisition, 137, 143, 178
    logical problem of nonnative language acquisition, 139
ACTFL (*see* American Council)
adequacy
  explanatory, 93
adjective, 75, 101, 107, 108, 114, 119
  A, A′, AP, 105, 107, 168

adults, 11, 13f., 26, 130f., 186f., 204, 206, 209, 210
affect α, 119, 128
affix hopping, 128
age, 13, 26, 38, 42, 131, 135, 136, 137, 144, 160, 161, 174, 185, 205, 214
  in language acquisition, 160
  of reason, 131
agent, 24, 36, 48, 76, 77, 116
agreement, 1, 24, 110f., 122, 147, 155, 159
  person-number, 111
  specifier-head, 168
Aitchinson, 217
Alatis, 216
Albert, 192
alphabet, 79
American Council on the Teaching of Foreign Languages (ACTFL), 194, 217
analogy, 98
analysis,
  contrastive, 141, 142, 145, 165
  analytic, analyticity, 61f., 134
  analytic-synthetic distinction, 62
anaphora, 200
Andersen, 170, 193
Anderson, 129
animal language controversy, 3f., 17
apes, 4, 10, 17, 34, 35, 37, 199, 200, 201, 202
  ape system of communication, 199
aphasia, 162
  global aphasics, 37, 201
  sign language, 52
application, 114, 117
approach
  behavioristic, 176
  derivational, 127
  representational, 127
Archibald, 168, 170, 215

Ard, 166, 215
argument, 118
    event argument, 193
Ariessohn, xiii
Aristophanes, 70
Aristotle, 38, 55, 78, 184
art, 56, 60, 61, 65, 82
    fine art, 56
    liberal art, 56
articulatory-perceptual, 116
artificial intelligence, 57
Asher, 170
ASL (*see* sign language)
association, 124
assonance, 19
Atkinson, 17, 165

Baker, C. L., 126
Baker, M., 78, 80
Bar-Hillel, 79
Bardovi-Harlig, 170
BASIC, 14
basic claims, 2f.
basic skills, 216
Beck, 193
behavior
    behavioral sciences, 92
    behaviorism, 79, 133
Bell, 80
Bellamy, 97
Belletti, 168, 195
Benincà, 193
Berlin, 53
Berlitz, 213
Bever, 216
Berwick, 99, 165
Biguenet, 80
bind
    bindable, 118
    binding, 117, 123, 140, 189
    binding theory, 118, 126, 139
biology, 40, 47, 67, 72, 131, 135
    biology and language, 130f.
bipedal locomotion, 198
Birckbichler, 216, 217
Bischoff, 216
Bley-Vroman, 166
blindness, 26, 41, 52, 159, 163
    and deafness, 26
    color-blind, 43
Bloom, 166
Bloomfield, 98, 174–5

Bly, 80
Bobaljik, 127
Bofman, 170
Bogen, 33, 39
Bolinger, 68, 168, 179, 194, 197, 215
Bond, 170
Bonet, 129
bound
    unboundedness, 98
    bounding theory, 119
Bosque, 168, 193
Borer, 170
Borreguero, xiii
Bowen, 166, 193
Bradford, 193
brain, x, 52, 89, 90, 196
    changes, 195
    lesions, 52
Brainerd, 161
braketting, 104, 108
    branching, 127
        binary, 100, 107
Breva-Claramonte, 216
Broca, 30
    Broca's area, 30
Brooks, 192
Broselow, 168, 193, 195, 215
Brucart, 168
Bryant, 161
Bub, 192
Burzio, 168, 195

C, C', CP (*see* complementizer)
Calabrese, 193
Calder mobile, 65
Campos, xiii, 168, 193
Caplan, 52
Carey, 53, 54, 79
Carroll, 195
Carstens, 127
Carter, 216
Cartesians, 84, 169
case, 118, 123
    case theory, 118, 126
Castelli, 193
cat visual system, 163
category, 34
    conceptual, 44, 49f., 75
    conceptual-intentional, 116
    functional, 112
    lexical, 108, 112, 127
causation, 35, 50, 62f., 68, 76f.

CAUSE, 45, 50, 63f., 76f.
Celce-Murcia, 194, 216
cerebral dominance, 135, 162
cerebral organization, 169
Cervantes, 82, 189
Chamot, 196
chain, 118
    form chain, 128, 129
Chastain, 194
Chaudron, 216
Chela de Rodriguez, 193
Chien, 128
Child, 80
children, 1, 5, 6, 8, 10f., 26, 64, 96,
    118f., 130f., 173, 201, 204, 206f.
    blind, 52
    deaf, 5, 163
    feral, 162
    immigrant, 143, 166
    mongoloid, 163
    retarded, 6, 162, 163
    child-adult differences, 166
    childhood, 120, 169
chimps, 1, 3f., 9, 25, 55, 198, 202
choice
    parametric, 120, 122
Chomsky, Carol, 32, 163, 214
Chomsky, Noam, xi, 15f., 30f., 38, 41f.,
    51f., 58f., 64f., 78f., 82f., 96f.,
    114, 116, 127f., 133f., 144, 156,
    158, 159, 161f., 173f., 184, 188f.,
    192f., 198, 201, 208, 210, 214f.
Chomsky, William, 192
Cinque, 168, 193
Clahsen, 164, 170, 192
Clark, 165
clause
    relative clause, 190
    small clause, 180, 193
climb, 66
clitic
    climbing, 147
    constructions, 167
cognition, 93
    cognitive sciences, 93
    cognitive structures, x
Cohen, 193, 195
Colombo, 162, 164
colors, 40f.
    primary, 42
    color-blindness, 41, 43
communication, 202, 185f., 194f., 207,
    215, 217 (see also system)

and cognition, 215
animal communication, 4
compare, 66
competence, 15, 56, 73, 128, 143, 166,
    203, 204, 206, 209
    transitional, 209
complement, 101f., 127, 179
complementizer
    C, C′ CP, 109f., 149f., 167–8
    Complementizer Phrase, 109
computation, 35, 55, 56, 86, 88 (see also
    system)
    teory of computation, 1, 86
concepts, 6, 8, 35, 38f., 52, 62f., 73f.,
    80, 122, 185
    conceptual scheme, 64
    inborn concepts, 45f. (see also system)
conditioning, 124
connectionism, 216
Conrad, 187, 195
constituent
    conceptual, 78
    immediate, 127
    syntactic, 78
constructive skepticism, 15
context
    -free, 127
    -sensitive, 127
continuity, 36
Contreras, 168
Cook, 169, 172, 192, 216
Coppieters, 166
copy, 119
Corballis, 197
Corder, 193, 215, 216
Cordin, 193
core, 68, 74, 135, 159, 160, 189, 212
    (see also grammar)
Corson, 192
Cortés, 168, 170
Coulter, 215
Courchêne, 215
Cowper, 126
CPH (see critical period hypothesis)
Crain, 128, 165
creation, 131, 134
    artistic or scientific, 134
creativity, 92
    argument, 192
    creative imagination, 82
Crick, 53
criterion, 61, 83
    θ-Criterion, 80

critical age, 162
critical period hypothesis (CPH), x, 126,
    130f., 163, 164, 169, 174, 185,
    204f., 209, 213
Cro-Magnon, 29, 43
Crystal, 216
Culicover, 99
culture, 34f., 55, 59, 69, 70, 73, 132
    cultural wealth, 68f.
    culturally deprived, 72
current approaches to language teaching,
    216
Curtiss, 52, 163, 214

D, D', DP, 128, 154f., 168
Damasio, and Damasio, 52f., 80
Damen, 80
dar vs. *donar*, 24
Darío, 39
Davidson, 193
deafness, 3, 5, 12, 16, 160f., 201
    and blindness, 26, 214
dejar, 19
Delattre, 193
Demonte, 168, 193, 194
derivation, 118 (*see also* approach)
Descartes, 37, 58, 83f., 134
    Descartes's problem, 82, 88, 98
Desmarais, 162, 196
determiner, 196
Deutch, 33
development
    cognitive, 78
    cultural, 1, 40
    evolutionary, 199
    intellectual, 216
    language, 163
    ontogenetic, 200
deviant, 196
Dewey, 60
Diamond, J., 32
Diamond, R., 54
dichotic listening, 31, 78
dichotomies, 198f.
die, 66
Diesing, 193
Diller, 163, 192, 197
disciplines
    applied, 58, 215 (*see also* linguistics)
discontinuity, 34
Dixon, 31

Doughty, 194
Down syndrome, 162
Dresher, 166, 170
DuPlessis, 164f.
Durant, 196

Eckman, 165
economy, 93, 126, 129
education, ix
electrical activity, 197
electrical stimulation, 30
Eliot, 71
Ellis, 194
Els, 215
embryology, 95, 99, 136, 137
Emiliani, 166
Emonds, 128, 167
empiricism, 61f., 216
enlightenment, 212
environment, x, 15, 18f., 59, 80, 132,
    157, 177, 184, 200, 206, 207, 210
epistemology, 79
ergative, 123
error, 87, 142, 187, 193
    correction, 194
Ervin, 216, 217
estar, 19
Eubank, 193
Euclid, 96
evaluation metric, 93, 95
event-related potential (ERP), 196
evidence, 8, 12, 15, 22f., 63, 64 86, 92,
    133f., 178, 184f., 199, 203, 207f.
    negative, 15, 159, 166, 186, 188, 208
expect, 66
extension, 91
extrametricality, 171
extraposition, 122, 128

Fabb, 196
fact,
    linguistic, 116
faculties
    language faculty, 89, 199
    rational faculty, 109
Faltis, 194, 216
Fein, 166, 196
Feldman, 32
Felix, 165, 168, 171, 194, 195
Feynman, 58

Finer, 168, 215
Firn, 164
Fischer, 16, 171, 216
Fitzgibbon, 195
Flynn, 162, 165f., 178, 193, 195, 216
focalization, 167
Fokes, 170
force-dynamics, 72, 79
Ford, 195
form
    logical form (LF), 116f., 125
    phonetic form (PF), 116f.
formula, 102
fossilization, 164, 166, 168, 169
Fotos, 194
Fox, 51
Frawley, 80
free will, 84
freedom of speech, 67
Freidin, 126
Freud, 56
    Freud's Problem, 162
Frisson, 193
function, 199

Gajar, 196
Galileo, 57
    Galilean style, 82
Gall, 30, 135
GAME, 60, 65, 70
Ganschow, 196
Garcia, 170
Gardner, Beatrice, and Gardner, Allan, 4f., 16, 17
Gardner, Martin, 67
Gass, 166, 193, 194
general learning strategies, 156
generative procedure, 8f., 88, 91f., 99, 112, 144, 199, 202
genetic endowment, 27f., 87, 89, 96, 100f., 172
genetic program, 163
Genie, 38, 136, 141, 158
genotype, 22, 28, 132
Gibson, 78–79
Giorgi, 168, 193
Gleitman, 32, 52, 163f., 192
goal, 75, 116, 189, 191, 210, 213
Goethe, 82, 173
Goldin-Meadow, 32

Goodall, 168
Goodluck, 17, 165
Goodman, 215
Goya, 30
grammar, 22, 82, 87f., 100f., 205, 207, 208, 209, 210, 212, 213 (see also system)
    core grammar, 159
    paradigmatic grammar, 120f.
    syntagmatic grammar, 125f.
        phrase structure, 95, 103, 120, 127, 128, 196
        transformations, 93, 114f.
    generative grammar, 87, 89, 91f., 100f.
        and language teaching, 216
    pedagogic grammar, 140, 177f., 187
    scientific grammar, 189, 212
    teaching of, 173, 194, 196, 217
    traditional grammar, 107f., 177
    transformational generative grammar, xi, xii, 1, 87, 165, 173, 178
        development of, 87f.
        principles-and-parameters framework, x, 94f., 165, 169, 177, 178
    universal grammar (UG), x, 63, 89, 90, 93, 137, 138, 159, 169, 209
    and communication, 194
grammaticality, 166 (see also acceptability)
Graunstein, 216
Green, 194
Gregg, 164, 166, 167, 193, 196
Grimshaw, 127, 128
growth
    biological, 119
    maturational, 162
    of language, 95, 99, 192, 120
    of mind, 81f.
    of the vocabulary, 160
Gubala-Ryzak, 168
Guéron, 194
Gunnarson, 31
Guntermann, 194, 216

Hadley, 216
Haegeman, 126
Hale, 128, 167, 197
Halle, 128
Hampshire, Stuart, 78
Harmer, 192

Harley, 164, 196
Harris, 128, 170
Hayes, Keith, and Hayes, Virginia, 15
Hanzeli, 197
head, 74, 90, 91, 103f., 154 (*see also* parameter)
    functional, 109, 127
    lexical, 109, 127
    head movement
Hecht, 194
Hentoff, 79
Hernanz, 168
Herschensohn, xiii, 168, 196
Hervey, 80
Hetch
Higginbotham, 99
Higgins, 80
Hill, 193
Hilles, 194
history
    intellectual history, xii
    of language teaching, 216
Hochberg, 171, 193
Hockett, 98
Holt, 215
homo sapiens, 32
homology, 34, 36
Honda, 197
Hoover, 193
Horgan, 99
Horning, 99
house, 6f., 38f.
Howatt, 192, 216
Huarte, 82, 83, 97
Hubel, 163
Hudelson, 194, 216
Hulk, 168
human language, 6, 83, 100f. (*see also* language)
human nature, 22, 28f., 34, 66, 82, 83, 95
humanities, 55f.
Humboldt, 80, 91, 103, 199
    Humboldt's problem, 82, 85, 86, 88
Humphries, 16, 31, 171
Hurford, 162
Hyams, 128, 165f., 170

I, I′, IP (*see* inflection)
Iatridou, 167
imagery, visual, 134
immersion, 196

immigrants, 143, 166
immunology (*see* system)
indefinite object drop, 193
indeterminacy, 59f.
individual, 15
individualism, 215
inflection, 110
    I, I′, IP, 110f., 150, 155
input, 26, 87, 89, 138, 158, 182, 187, 201, 209
    zero input, 32
instruction, 91, 139, 156, 157, 173, 175, 176, 183, 186, 191, 203f., 208, 212f., 215
    formal instruction, 194
    method of instruction, xi, 173f., 194, 205
instrument, 36
INTEND, 45, 63f.
intension, 90–91
intention, 63, 68
    attribution, 35
interaction, 199
interface, 116, 125f.
interlanguage, 156, 164, 169, 196, 208f.
interpretation, 24f., 48, 51, 59f., 70f., 93, 134, 141, 180, 183
intertranslatability, 68f.
Ioup, 166, 170, 215
irregularity, 196

Jackendoff, 53–54, 78f., 98
Jacobs, 215
Jaeggli, 168
Jakobovits, 215
Jakobson, 196
James, 215
Jerne, 47, 53
Jespersen, 98, 190
John, 80
Johnson, 162f.
Joiner, 194
Jonas, 127
Jones, 16
Jordens, 168, 169
judgement, 166, 171
    failure, 142, 143
    symbolic, 35

Kachru, 216
Kalven, 79

Kant, 61, 134
Kandel, 52, 53
Kaye, 17, 166, 170
Kayne, 99, 127, 128, 167, 168, 170, 195, 196
Kellerman, 165
Kelly, 216
Kempchinsky, 168, 194
Kenney, 161
Kenstowicz, 215
Keyser, 128, 197
Kimball, 127
Kimura, Doreen, 33, 78
Kinsbourne, 192
Kiparsky, 78, 197
King, 16
Kisseberth, 215
Klein, 168
Klima, 16
knowledge, 2, 10f., 18f., 55f., 65, 66, 82, 84f., 92, 95, 183f., 201,
    conscious, 183, 208
    grammatical, 184, 207
    innate, 178
    of a foreign tongue, 208
    of language, 36, 65, 73, 81f., 100f., 134, 137, 139, 143, 146, 157, 158, 172f., 208, 212
    unconscious knowledge, 109f., 144, 151, 172
    use of, 2, 55f.
Koch, 53
Koehler, 16, 51
Koko, 16
Koopman, 127, 128, 168, 170
Koster, C., 165
Koster, J., 99, 128
Kramsch, 80, 216
Krashen, 162f., 170, 193, 194
Kratzer, 193
Kroch, 167
Kuroda, 197

L1, L2, . . . (see language)
La Mettrie, 16
Lachter, 216
Lackner, 163
LAD (see acquisition)
Ladefoged, 170
Lafayette, 194
Laka, 168, 194
Lakoff, 54

Lana, 3, 202
Landau, 32, 52, 163
landing site, 127
language, x, 1f., 18f., 81f., 69, 100f., 198f.
    (see also development)
    analysis, 217
    aptitude, 161
    curriculum, 176
    experience, 164
    instruction, 176, 208
    of instruction, 216
    universals and particulars, 203f.
    attitude for, 164
    study of, ix, xi, 1, 81, 83, 86, 89, 97, 135, 198, 202, 206, 210f.
    talent for, 164
    uniqueness of, 8f., 34
    use of, 37, 83, 84, 98, 134, 176, 201
        creative aspect of language use, 82f., 98, 176
    childhood language, 11f.
    dominant language, 217
    first language (L1), xii, 14, 15, 97, 136f., 157, 165, 204, 206
    foreign language, xii, 13, 144, 158, 165, 188f., 192f., 196, 207
        ability, 195
        acquisition, 215
        disability, 196
        research, x, xii, 172f., 193
        teacher   education/development, 194, 217
        teaching, 172f., 194, 216, 217
    mental language, 88, 91
    native language, xii, 11f., 99, 165, 195, 196
    nonnative language, xii, 137, 160, 192–93, 196
    primitive language, 40
    real language, 116, 216
    second language (L2), xii, 138, 162, 164, 165, 178, 192–93, 204, 208
    language and dialect, 216
    language and puberty, 195
    language and thought, 34f.
    language as a defining human attribute, 3f.
    language as instrument of thought and self-expression, 84
    language centers, 203
    language explanation, 81f., 215
    language faculty, x, 88–89, 199

language (*cont.*)
  language invariance, x, xi
  language maturation, 64, 78
  language program, xi, 15, 173f., 183f.
  language research, x, 1, 188
  language teaching, 12, 15, 165, 172f.,
    187f., 192, 215, 217
    place of, 217
  language theory, xi
  language variation, x
languages, 18f., 89, 93f., 101f., 198,
    200, 204, 205, 206, 208, 209, 211,
    213
  most frequently taught in the U.S.,
    184–85
  Indo-European
    Celtic, 127
      Irish, 127
      Welsh, 127, 155
    Germanic, 31, 71, 127
      Danish, 2, 203
      Dutch, 120, 195, 216
      English 2, 8f., 13, 18f., 38f., 85,
        89f., 97f., 101f., 127, 134f.,
        166, 167, 169, 173, 174, 178,
        181, 184, 185, 187, 190, 203,
        207, 216 ("Englishes,", 216)
        English vs Spanish, 71–73,
          127, 165, 194
      German, 30, 109, 165, 195, 216
      Norwegian, 155
      Swedish, 195
      Scandinavian, 127
    Indic
      Urdu, 2, 18, 203
    Romance, 2, 31, 70–72, 127, 149,
      166, 179, 184
      Catalan, 124, 148
      French, 30, 38, 39, 45, 109, 111,
        124, 127, 134, 145f., 165, 167,
        169, 184f., 195, 196
      Galegan, 167, 194
      Italian, 39, 109f., 145, 147, 166,
        169, 185, 195
      Portuguese, 109, 195, 180
      Spanish, 2, 8, 13, 18f., 31, 38f.,
        54, 57, 59, 63, 69f., 80, 82, 89,
        97, 98, 127, 166f., 195, 203,
        207, 208, 216
        Medieval, 167
    Slavic
      Russian, 165, 195, 215
      Serbo-Croatian, 165
  Other
    Arabic, 2, 18, 195, 203
    Berber, 2, 18, 119, 203
    Basque, 99, 119f.
    Cantonese, 2, 18, 203
    Chinese, 119
    Dani, 42
    Eskimo, 18
    Japanese, 13, 20, 39, 99, 119f., 165,
      195
    Ki-swahili (Bantu), 127
    Korean, 119
    Turkish (Altaic), 2, 18, 203
    Tzotzil (Mayan), 31
    Vietnamese, 2, 18, 203
    Walbiri, 41
    Xhosa, 2, 18, 203
    Yoruba, 2, 18, 203
    Zulu (Bantu), 2, 18, 203
langue, 56, 99, 128
LAP (*see* language acquisition after pu-
    berty)
Larson, 167
Larson-Freeman, 164
Lasnik, 129
lateralization, , 203
learning, xii, 6, 25, 34f., 50, 51, 66, 122,
    130, 134, 141, 142, 145, 156, 159,
    174f., 184, 193
  foreign language learning, 166
  label learning, 38f.
  successful learners, 164, 196
  learning vs acquisition, xii
Leather, 215
Lees, 126–27
Leibniz, 59, 61, 64, 87
Lenneberg, Eric, 33, 134f., 162f., 169,
    203, 215
  Lenneberg's Problem, 162
Lenneberg, Elizabeth, 163
Leopardi, 72
Leonardo, 189
level, 21
  level of understanding, 1, 68f.
  individual-level, 179
  stage-level, 179, 193
Leventer, 192
Levy, 79
lexicon, 78
LF (*see* form, logical)
licensing, 126
Liceras, xiii, 166f., 178, 193
Lieberman, 15, 195

Lightbown, 193, 194
Lightfoot, 128
Lillo-Martin, 16, 171
Limber, 17, 51
Linden, 16
linguistics, 1f., 43, 57, 114, 122,, 134,
    174, 183, 188, 190, 191, 194, 205,
    207, 210, 217
  applied, 205, 210, 215
  Romance, 2, 172f.
  structural, 93, 115f., 134
  and literature, 196
literature, 58
  literary critics, 64, 90
  literary use of language, 57
  literary study, 57
locality, 119, 196
localization, 31, 135
Lococo, 193
Loewenthal, 170
logic, 1, 161
  universal, 116
  logical operator, 192
  logical particle, 61
Long, 162f.
Longobardi, 168, 193
Lucas, 16
Luján, 167f., 193

Macnamara, 53, 162
Magnan, 194
Mairs, 171, 193, 215
Manuel, 162, 169, 195
Manzini, 168
Marantz, 128
Marcantonio, 193
markedness, 166
Marler, 161
Martin, 166
Marshall, 32
Masullo, 168
mathematics and language, 1
maturation, ix, 89, 162
  of language, 78, 132, 163
  of a physical organ, 132
  physical, 163
  sexual, 132, 163
maturity
  linguistic maturity, 130
  sexual maturity, 130
Mayberry, 16, 171
McCarthy, 216

McConnell-Ginet, 80
McCrum, 196, 216
McKee, 165f.
McLaughlin, 163
McNeil, 17
Mehler, 161
Menn, 196
mentalism, 79
  mental organ, 35, 90
  mental representation, 93, 139
  mental process, 132
Mercier, 215
metaphor, 70, 80
Miller, 32, 98
Mitchell, 194
mind
  study of the human mind, 191
minimal pair, 184
minimalist, 126, 127
modal, 167
modality, 4, 50, 160, 161, 200
  gestural/visual, 4
  spoken/auditory, 4
model, 93, 102, 173, 191, 213, 214
  model for the cognitive sciences, 191
  model of language maturation, 89
  model of the grammatical system, 106
modernism
  crisis of, 59
modifier, 118
modularity, 74
  module, 74, 107, 118, 126, 203
Monod, 134, 162
Montalbetti, 168
Moreno, 168
morphology, 120f., 170
  inflectional, 129, 160
  morphological regularity, 186
movement, 115, 150, 196
  Move α, 119, 129
Mozart, 30
music, tonal, 78
Muysken, 127, 164, 168, 170, 192, 193
Mylander, 32

Nakayama, 128, 165
NAP thesis (see Never after Puberty
    thesis)
natural sciences, ix, 7
  cognitive, 58
  volitive, 58

nature, 18, 21f., 28f., 55, 61, 63, 66f.,
    75, 89f., 124, 135f., 148, 158f.,
    172, 173, 176f., 189f., 198f., 206,
    210, 212
    human nature, 22, 28–29, 83
    nature's experiments, 37
negation, 192
Nemser, 196
Nespor, 193
Neufeld, 162
neural,
    neural structure, 52
    neurology, 134, 164
Never after Puberty (NAP) thesis, 11f.
Neville, 197
newborn's questionnaire, 119f.
Newmeyer, 193, 215, 216
Newport, 16, 162f., 171
Newspeak, 67f.
Newton, 23, 96, 115
Nichols, 163
Nim, 5, 202
Nippold, 162
nominalism, 67
nominative, 123
noun, 21, 26–27, 74, 75, 101f., 143, 154,
    174
    N, N', NP, 26–27, 104f., 147, 155
    Noun Phrase, 26–27, 85–86, 127
null subject, 166, 170 (see also parameter)
Num, Num', NumP, 155
number, 18, 22, 40f., 91, 92, 173, 184,
    186, 199, 202, 204
    grammatical, 107
nurture, 18f., 61

Obler, 166, 192, 196
Odlin, 165, 195
O'Donnell, 216
Omaggio, 80
O'Malley, 196
O'Neil, 166f., 193, 195, 197, 216
ontogenesis, 28
optical imaging, 32, 67
optimality, 126
oratio, 37
organ, 29, 30, 35, 89f., 94f., 132f., 172,
    203f.
    language organ, x, 88f., 99, 109, 114,
    169 (see also mental)

Orwell, 67
    Orwell's Problem, 162
overlearning, 84, 175, 192
Otero, xiii, 15, 53f., 78f., 98f., 128, 129,
    167f., 194, 197, 214, 215
output, 84–89, 144, 146, 147, 148, 149,
    151, 187
Oyama, 170

P, P', PP (see preposition)
Padden, 16, 31, 171
parameter, 97, 122, 138, 144, 145, 147,
    148, 149, 151, 154, 156, 158, 159,
    160, 179, 185, 186, 203, 204, 206,
    209 (see also choice)
    head direction, 120f.
    nominative-absolutive, 124
    null subject, 145, 166, 170
    stress, 170
    parameter fixing, 147, 149, 151, 156,
    159
    parameter setting, xi, 46f., 97, 133,
    144f., 170, 195, 204, 206
    parameter resetting, 144, 145, 149,
    158f.
    parameterization, x, 160, 119f., 171
Parker, 98, 165
Parodi, 127, 168
parole, 56, 128
particulars, 100f., 170, 203 (see also
    grammar)
parser, 99
passive, 94, 95, 115, 190
patient, 76
pathological
    cases, 6
    contexts, 37
Patkowski, 164, 170
pattern practice, 174f.
Patterson, 16
Paul, 98
Pearce, 79
Penfield, 33, 162, 164, 195, 215
Pennycook, 216
perception, 176 (see also problem)
    ape perception, 5
Perdue, 166
performance, 2, 55f., 73, 128, 156, 175,
    187, 189, 208
    factors, 166
    linguistic performance, 56

periphery, 159
Perlmutter, 16, 128
PERSON, 46, 53
person-number, 111
Petitto, 16
PF (*see* phonetic form)
phenotype, 22, 28
Phinney, 166
phonology, 72, 78, 160, 162, 169f., 210
    foreign language, 166
    phonological knowledge, 160, 170
    phonological representation, 78
phonetics, 36, 72, 159
    universal, 116
Piaget, 80, 130, 131, 161
Piattelli-Palmarini, 53
Picallo, 167, 168, 194
Piera, 78, 129, 168, 197
Plann, Susan, 16, 31, 166f.
Plann, Sandra, 193, 195
Plato, 82, 86, 87, 89, 90, 94, 132, 139, 184
    Plato's problem, 82, 86f., 132, 139
plural, 75, 154
Pollock, 127, 167
Popkin, 15
Port-Royal gramar and logic, 128
Post, 127
postmodernism, 59
poverty of the stimulus, 18, 45, 89
phrase, 103
phrase structure (*see* grammar)
Premack, 5, 10, 16, 17, 35, 51, 52
preposition, 103
    P, P′, PP, 103f., 151
    Prepositional Phrase, 103
pro-drop, 166 (*see also* null subject)
principle of language, 78
    invariant,
    parameterized, 119
problem (*see* Descartes, Freud, Humboldt, Lenneberg, Orwell, Plato)
    perception problem, 98, 169
    production problem, 98–99
    problem-solving, 175
    of language, 217
    of society, 217
processing, 17, 42
production, 176 (*see also* problem)
program (*see* language)
    genetic, 40
projection

functional, 127
lexical, 127
PROMISE, 65
pronunciation, 170, 171, 195
    ability, 176
Proust, 71
psychic distance, 23
psychology, 175
puberty, 11f., 29, 38, 40, 66, 90, 96, 130f. 143, 156, 157, 160f., 172, 174, 178, 195, 203, 204, 208, 209

Quicoli, 168
Quigley, 16
Quine, 59f., 78f.
Quirk, 80

raising, 48, 128
Raposo, 168, 193
ratio, 37
rational animal, 34f.
Ravin, 53, 80
Reagan, 60
reason, 37
recursive, 34, 85f., 200 (*see also* system)
    recursivity, 92
    recursive function theory, 1, 86, 127
    (*see also* computation, theory of)
Redmont, 194
Reinhart, 128
Renzi, 193
representation (*see* approach; mental)
    phonological, 78, 166
    semantic, 78
responsibility of intellectuals, 196
Restak, 17
Reuland, 128
rhyme, 19, 72
Richards, J., 192, 216
Richards, W., 52
Rigau, 168
Riley, 165
Ristau, 16
Ritchie, 166
Ritter, 170
Rivero, 168, 194
Rivers, 194, 216
Rizzi, 168, 193, 195
Robbins, 16
Roberts, 33, 162

Robbins, 16
Roca, 171, 194
Rodgers, 192, 216
Roeper, 165
role
    thematic role, 74, 75, 78
    theta role, 78
    θ-role, 75
Romantics, 83
Rosen, 128
Rosenberger, 163
Rousseau, 82, 198
Rosch, 53
Roslansky, 163
Rubin, 52
rules, 127, 196
    language particular, 170
    lowering, 128
    (*see also* grammar)
Rumbaugh, 16
Russell, 10, 41, 65, 87
Rutherford, 166, 193f., 216
Rymer, 163

Sacks, N., 215
Sacks, O., 54
Salinger, 69
Salkie, 164, 193
Saltarelli, 168
Salvi, 193
Sándor, 80
Saporta, 197, 215
Sarah, 5, 16, 51, 202
Saussure, 20, 57, 70, 98, 115, 128
    Saussurean arbitrariness, 20, 38f., 125
Savignon, 216
Schachter, 166, 168, 178, 193
schema
    innate, 90
    universal, 96–97
Schneiderman, 162, 196
Schopenhauer, 37
Schulte, 80
Schumann, 193, 215
Schwartz, B., 168
Schwartz, J., 52
science, 1, 40, 45, 47, 58, 60, 66, 67,
    191, 134, 212f.
Scorreti, 193
Scott, Sir Walter, 70
Scott, V., 194, 216

Scovel, 162, 164, 170, 195
Seelye, 80
segment, 71
Seidenberg, 16
selection vs. instruction, 46f.
Seliger, 162, 170, 195
Selinker, 164, 166, 168, 193, 196, 215
semantics, 55, 60, 63f., 200, 202
    universal, 78, 116
    semantic field, 41, 47f., 77
    semantic connections, 60f.
    semantic roles, 74f. (*see also* role)
semiotics, 3f. (*see also* system)
ser, 19, 54
Shaffer, 194, 216
Shakespeare, 38, 70f.
Sharwood Smith, 165, 194, 195, 216
Shaw, 143
Siegel, 161
sign language, 26, 80, 171
    American Sign Language, 3, 12, 137
    ASL, 3f., 12, 16, 31, 164
signal, 12
    signal-meaning pair, 5
Sigurjónsdóttir, 128, 165
symbol, 5f. (*see also* system)
Singleton, 162f.
Siple, 16, 171
sister, 106
    sisterhood, 106f.
Skehan, 196
Skinner, 133, 134
Slobin, 165
smells, 40f.
Smith, 85, 90, 91, 214
Smolla, 79
Sorace, 169
source, 75
speaker,
    native, xii, 215
    nonnative, xii, 137
speciation, 28
species-specific, 162
specifier, 110f., 127
spell-out, 115, 159
Sperber, 215
Sperry, 162
Spinoza, 29
split-brain patients, 31
Sportiche, 127f., 167, 168, 170
Springer, 33
St. Augustine, 169

steady state, 40, 170
Stenson, 193
Stern, 192, 197
Steel, 79
stimulus-response, 176
Stockwell, 166, 193, 215
Stowell, 193
stress, 170–1.
Strozer, 31, 79, 167, 193, 194
structure, 199f.
    aitiational, 186
    conceptual, 80
    syllable structure, 71
    underlying, 118
    language structure, 115
    operator-variable structure, 118
    structure dependence, 114f., 140
    structure preservation, 118
subjacency, 142, 165–6
subjunctive disjoint reference effect, 194
subset principle, 159, 166, 170
substantive, 107, 125
substitution,
    differential, 165
    -in-frames, 127
Suñer, 167f.
Supalla, 162, 171
supplementary motor cortex, 30, 31
Swahili (see Ki-swahili s.v. languages)
Swain, 195
switch box, 99
system, 116
    analytic, 134
    ape, 201
    approximative, 189, 196, 208
    articulatory-perceptual, 118
    computational, 10, 35f., 66, 90, 83,
        136, 202
    cognitive, 35, 134, 201
    conceptual, x, 6, 35f., 52, 78, 185,
        202f.
    conceptual-intentional, 118
    determiner system, 196
    belief system, 70, 201
    grammatical
        mastery of, 194
    immune, 46f.
    language system, 78
    of knowledge, 201
    of communication, 7, 199, 202
    olfactory, 44
    performance system, 116

    recursive, 91
    semiotic, 7, 199, 202
    symbolic, 3, 7
    transitional, 209
    visual,
    cat, 163

T, T', TP (see tense)
Tadoma method, 26, 32, 214
table, 66
Tahta, 170
Talmy, 54
Taylor, 215
tense, 74, 147f.
    T, T', TP, 71, 111f., 147f.
    Tense Phrase, 111
terms
    misapplied, 46
    technical, 66
Terrace, 16, 161
Terrell, 194, 216
textbooks, 196
that-trace, 147, 167
theme, 24, 73f., 189
    thematic, 74
    thematic hierarchy, 77
    thematic relations, 78
    thematic role (see role, semantics)
    thematic structure, 75
Thomas, 168
Thorpe, 16
thought, 58, 64, 71, 72, 82, 83, 84, 86,
        96, 141, 181, 199, 201
    imaginative, 134
tier, 77
    action tier, 76
    location tier, 76
Todd, 216
Tollefson, 164
Tomaselli, 168
tongue, 56, 83, 201, 208
    mother tongue, 162, 205
    peer tongue, 205
Toolan, 196
Torrego, 168, 193, 194
Trabasso, 161
trace, 114, 119, 150, 151
transformation, transformational, 93,
        114f., 127 (see also grammar)
transfer, 77, 138, 158, 170
    negative, 165

translatability, 68f.
translation, 25, 59f., 68f., 76, 80, 141, 144, 145, 191
   automatic, 79
   radical, 78
trigger, 124
try, 66
truths of fact, 61
truths of meaning, 48, 60f.
truths of reason, 61
Tsimpli, 214
Turkewitz, 161

UG (*see* universal grammar s.v. grammar)
unaccusative, 169
Unamuno, 71
uncommon sense, 22, 47
underdetermination, 86f.
universals, 100f., 203 (*see also* grammar)
University of California, 2, 5
University of Washington, 2, 4
Uriagereka, 168, 193

Valian, 166
Valois, 127, 168
VanPatten, 216
Van Naerssen, 193, 196
Varela, 168
variability, 119
Vázquez-Ayora, 80
verb, 74, 101f.
   V, V′, VP
   Verb Phrase, 147
   verb movement, 151f.
Vergnaud, 168
Vickie, 3–4, 202
Vilches, 171
vocabulary, x, 8–10, 19–20, 40f., 66f., 90, 160, 185, 187, 202
   cognate, 194
   development, 38
   primitive, 40
   substantive part of, 125

Walls, 41
Walsh, 163
Waltz, 194
Wanner, 165, 192
Washoe, 4–5, 7–8, 202

Watanabe, 128
Weerman, 128
Weinberger, 165, 170, 193, 215
Weissenborn, 165
Wernicke, 30
   Wernicke's area, 30
Westphal, 162
Wexler, 128, 166, 170
wh-movement, 147
Whitaker, 192
White, 165f., 178, 193, 195, 196, 215
Whitley, 193
Wiesel, 163
Wilkins, 194
Wilson, A., 16
Wilson, D., 215
Williams, 189
Wittgenstein, 57f.
Wood, 170
Woodruff, 52
word, x, 18–21, 23–24, 26–28, 30, 81f., 90f., 186
   categories, 128
   classes, 102
   meaning, 196, 202
   one/two-word stage, 131
   order, 120f., 152
   sequence of words, 128, 139
   container words, 23f.
   group of words, 103
   possible, 18
   word-form, 52
Wu, 99

X-bar schematism, 110
X-bar theory, 118, 127

Yalden, 216
Yamada, 163, 214
Youmans, 78, 197

Zagona, xiii, 167, 168, 193, 195
Zeki, 52
zero, 79
Zribi-Hertz, 128
Zubizarreta, 168
Zwart, 99, 128